NICOLAS POUSSIN

ALAIN MÉROT

NICOLAS POUSSIN

ABBEVILLE PRESS PUBLISHERS NEW YORK

This volume has
been prepared with the
cooperation and assistance of
the French Ministry of Culture
and Communications

Design and art direction: Sylvie Raulet

Text and documentary appendices translated from
the original French by Fabia Claris; other documents
translated from the Italian by Bridget Mason.

Library of Congress Cataloging-in-Publication Data
   Mérot, Alain.
      [Nicolas Poussin, English]
      Nicolas Poussin / Alain Mérot [text and documentary
   appendices translated from the original French by
   Fabia Claris; other documents translated from the
   Italian by Bridget Mason].
            p.   cm.
         Translation of Nicolas Poussin.
         Includes bibliographical references and index.
         ISBN 1–55858–120–6
         1. Poussin, Nicolas, 1594?–1665. 2. Painters—France—
   Biography. 3. Classicism in art—France. I. Poussin,
   Nicolas, 1594?–1665. II. Title.
   ND553.P8M4413   1990
   759.4—dc20
   [B]   90–39823
                                             CIP

CONTENTS

Introduction

Marginal references on text pages indicate
page numbers of works illustrated or relevant
catalogue numbers (see pp. 251–96).

'Things which partake of perfection should not be looked at in haste, but call for time, judgment and intelligence. The means employed in their appraisal must be the same as those used in their making.'
(Poussin to Chantelou, 20 March 1642)

The first of Poussin's paintings to make an impression on me was the often reproduced *Et in Arcadia Ego* which is still prominently displayed in the Louvre. It no longer ranks among my favourite pictures, but there is something undeniably evocative about this strangely still and melancholy debate around a tomb – it has the same quality as Millet's *The Angelus*, which comes to mind when I look at it. It is not an immediately striking picture: the setting and the figures are conventionally classical, there is no movement or obvious action, the brushwork is sound, the colour restrained, even banal. Many seventeenth-century paintings, including works by Poussin, possess far greater strength and brilliance than this. There was something enigmatic about it, however, which aroused my curiosity. There was the title, for a start, captivating in its obscurity.

Much later, I was to discover the key to this picture in Erwin Panofsky's famous article and realize that what it conjured up was the presence of death in the midst of bliss, and that it did so in the mournful voice of one who had himself been happy in Arcadia. Panofsky's analysis did nothing to alter the insidious charm of the picture, which remained as provoking as ever. My first encounter with Poussin made me aware, dimly but powerfully, of one essential feature of his art. The almost oracular quality of the inscription and the absorption of the figures force the viewer to dwell at length on the picture. Quietly and calmly the painting makes it disarmingly clear that it will not yield its meaning in a hurry, that it deserves more than that. It has nothing calculated to appeal to a young, still untrained mind. Other painters' works are more obviously accessible and stirring, and give us an immediate thrill of pleasure or fear. Like many others, I imagine, at sixteen, I preferred Caravaggio, Rembrandt, Delacroix and even Lebrun. Deep though they undoubtedly are, there is a heady quality to these pictures which makes them immediately accessible to even the most youthful viewer. Poussin himself was no stranger to such excitement, but once he reached the age of thirty, his art entered a new mature, experienced phase. Like Montaigne in his *Essays*, Poussin slowly built up an intellectual perspective, a way of thinking and a culture – the sort of culture, based in equal measure on the Classics and on Judaeo-Christianity, which is becoming more and more a thing of the past. Laborious though it may seem to us in an age of largely ephemeral images, we have to study Poussin, devoting time and patience to looking at his works, just as he believed them to be essential to his art. Whatever else it may have to offer us in the way of a philosophical message or

93

moral, *Et in Arcadia Ego* shows us that if we want to understand and savour this painting, we have to approach it by a roundabout route – through words. Only by reading the inscription, reading the picture in effect, can we hope to understand it. Although much has already been written on the subject, it is never difficult to find a reason for bringing out another book on the painter of the *Sacraments*: Poussin and his work have always had an extraordinary and deep affiliation with the written word and seem set to continue generating commentaries.

Not only did Poussin express his thoughts directly in his letters, roughly two hundred of which have survived, but he also had the rather rare advantage that his work immediately inspired others to write about it. In an age when illustrated 'art books' did not exist, the best way of getting a picture across and conjuring up its full beauty was to give a detailed description of it. Poussin's first annotators, Félibien and Bellori, followed the example which he himself set in his account, in a letter to his fellow painter Jacques Stella, of his great *Landscape with Pyramus and* 164 *Thisbe*, and attempted to give their readers as true and precise an account as possible of the most complex imagery. It is but a short step from this basic sort of *ekphrasis* to a full-blown historical and critical analysis of art. Félibien and Bellori were able to record Poussin's opinions and statements directly, and so provide first-hand information about the man and his work, following the tradition begun a century earlier by Vasari in his *Lives of the Artists*, blending biographical details with a catalogue of his works. They were also involved in the great aesthetic debates of their day, however, and used their hero to expound their theories on art. Félibien presents Poussin, as Vasari does Michelangelo, as the culmination – and the pinnacle – of an entire movement whose history he retraces. Poussin became the archetype of the 'perfect painter', setting the seal between 1660 and 1680 on the concept of the 'classical ideal' which had slowly been taking shape over the century. Poussin's art was itself influenced by this trend and as a result criticized and often misunderstood. The Paris academicians gave lectures in which they analyzed paintings like *The Israelites Gathering Manna* and *Eliezer and Rebecca at the Well* in minute detail as models for their students. They stressed only those aspects of a painting which conformed with their teaching – reliance on drawing rather than colour, the need to look to the antique rather than to contemporary taste – in an impoverished and reactionary interpretation of his work which reached its peak with the Neo-Classicists and did Poussin untold harm, particularly in France. In Italy, meanwhile, the foreigner who had settled in Rome in 1624 was all but forgotten, and in England he was viewed with a far more open mind by critics from Reynolds to Hazlitt and therefore with a fresher eye.

Poussin later came to be seen as the 'head' of the family, the 'father' of French painting, as Philippe de Chennevières put it in 1894. It is an image which fits with the severe *Self-Portrait* in the Louvre, but which is fundamentally ambivalent. With his uncompromising nature, Poussin comes across as a figure of absolute, compelling authority, and also as a symbol of strength and independence of character. For Ingres and Delacroix in the mid-nineteenth century he represented everything they valued: on the one hand he set an admirable example in terms of composition and expression, and on the other, he was one of the boldest innovators in the history of painting, who had dared to break with a mannered and bloodless tradition. For Cézanne, too, he was a 'classic' to hold on to: 'By looking at the work of a master, I hope to get a better sense of myself; every time I come away from Poussin I know better who I am.' Degas, Pissarro, Gauguin and Seurat all looked to him in turn, followed by the Cubists. Whenever it is a question of getting back to the basic tenets of art, the 'essential lines' and 'sculptural constants', as André Lhote was to call them, Poussin is cited. On a broader level, he was the founder of the 'French tradition', an antidote to the noxious charms of the Romantic and Decadent movements, intellectually on a par with Leonardo da Vinci whose 'method' Valéry sought to recapture in his work. The reappearance of *The Inspiration of the Poet* in 1911 and its entry into the Louvre were symbolic. While in Germany Otto Grautoff was celebrating the universality of Goethe in his basic monograph of 1914, writers in France were stressing the need for a perfect balance between inspiration and discipline, sensuousness and strictness. For a whole range of writers, from Paul Desjardins, whose *Méthode des Classiques* was published in 1904, to André Gide who wrote an essay on Poussin, by way of historians like Emile Magne and writers sympathetic to the *Nouvelle Revue Française*, Poussin stood for lucidity and a 'return to order'. If we ignore the purely nationalist slant – and, after all, controversy still rages over whether as a painter the man born in Normandy at Les Andelys is really French or Roman – this is still a widely held view.

54

Poussin gives us 'the *Latin* of painting': the term, first used by Sir John Summerson to describe the classic language of architecture, seems just as applicable to the creator of *The Judgment of Solomon*. Slowly during the turbulent first half of the twentieth century, doubtless as a reaction to the great upheavals of the period, the concept of a supremely coherent art began to develop – an art based on proportion, with its own specific language, one of whose main aims would be to 'achieve a demonstrable harmony of the parts'. We like to think of Poussin as embodying a set of essential values constantly re-formulated since Antiquity and founded on the simple and abiding features of human experience. Poussin's painting fascinates intellectuals because it has both the precision and the analytic and expressive potential of a fully developed language. It has been endlessly reconstructed, not least at the hands of the structuralists, the results tending to be somewhat extreme and absurd. A body of work as rich as Poussin's, with its steady evolution, cannot be reduced to an arid system, a single basic model that *functions* in this way or that. Poussin's painting is not just dissected in amazing detail by scientific minds, it is also embraced by poets. In Balzac's *Chef-d'œuvre inconnu* of 1832, Poussin becomes the symbol of a bold, exacting sort of art seen as a pursuit of the absolute. More recently Yves Bonnefoy and Claude Simon have both represented him as an instinctive, altogether unconventional painter. They are less atuned to the highly rational, meticulously constructed language of Poussin's later work than to the poetic freedom of the early *Bacchanals* and his late masterpieces like *Landscape with Diana and Orion*, and remind us that logic is not everything and that the expressive force, the emotive stillness of these images defies time and eludes explanation. All interpretations have their limits: no account, however full, can hope to define the largely indescribable aspect of the experience which, for want of a better term, Poussin called 'delight'.

Introduction

Delight, with its emphasis on contemplation, in no way precludes scholarship. Although it is commonly accepted that a work of art both can and should
stand or fall on its merits, and speak for itself without the support of a commentary
or the need for an introduction, in Poussin's case the opposite has been true. In
the last thirty years, both the man and his work have been painstakingly and lov-
ingly examined in all sorts of ways. The effect has been to add to the view that
Gide, say, had of Poussin and to transform it to such an extent that a single, simple
image of him is no longer possible. The monolithic Poussin of the past, the symbol
or 'gold standard' of painting, has been replaced by a complex personality closely
bound to a particular artistic background and to a particular cultural environment.
All of which makes the task of trying to present an impartial overview, while giving
a convincing portrait of the man, a distinctly daunting one.

The recent upsurge in research and literature on Poussin began with a painstaking survey of his œuvre, hand in hand with a more and more detailed chronology. The publication of the drawings was begun by Walter Friedländer in 1939,
and continued by Anthony Blunt. The real turning point, however, came after the
symposium which brought the world's experts together in Paris in 1958 and the
major exhibition held at the Louvre two years later. A new era of scholarship
began. There was a general desire to *place* Poussin precisely in his time while at
the same time adopting a firm critical – *filologica*, as the Italians would say –
approach. By relying first and foremost on documentary evidence wherever it
existed, and by making a careful study of the works themselves, Anthony Blunt and
Charles Sterling were able to establish a very tight chronology and to correct the
existing catalogues, by Magne and Grautoff respectively, both published in 1914.
The exhibition embraced the largest number of drawings and paintings by Poussin ever assembled, and set two Englishmen working along sometimes contradictory but complementary lines. In 1966 Blunt brought out his erudite thematic
catalogue raisonné, which is still regarded as authoritative. Taking the 1960 exhibition and the hypotheses of his arch-rival as his starting points, Denis Mahon produced a chronology which departed radically from those of his predecessors. He
brought forward the dates of many paintings, and regarded 1630–1 as a pivotal
point in Poussin's career, when a new, more severe concept of art began to inform
his work. Mahon's is a very logical approach, too much so perhaps. It has to be
admitted, however, that this incomparable connoisseur has often been proved
right by later developments, not least by the appearance of irrefutable documents.
The field was now opened up for debate. The chronology was still far from satisfactory, particularly where the very rarely documented early works, so vital to our
understanding of Poussin's development, were concerned. The attribution of
many paintings, not to mention drawings, was, and continues to be, fraught with
difficulty. There seems to be no objective way of deciding which works are definitely by Poussin and which are by other artists, more or less closely associated
with him, notably his rival, Charles Mellin. Hypothetical 'masters' have proliferated to cope with the problem: The Hovingham Master, the 'Master of the Clumsy
Children', the Master of the Bacchanals, and even the 'Silver Birch Master', who
turned out to be the young Gaspard Dughet, Poussin's brother-in-law. Two authors have recently attempted to answer some of the problems. Jacques Thuillier's

extremely cautious and flawlessly rigorous catalogue (first published in 1974) is a solid reference work in the Mahon tradition. Doris Wild, on the other hand, is far too radical in her rejection of established dates, and the catalogue, published in 1980, often seems lacking in coherence and throws little new light on the subject.

In recent years exhibitions have taken the place of purely scholarly publications. The one organized by Pierre Rosenberg and seen first in Rome, then in Düsseldorf in 1977–8, focused on 'difficult', little-known paintings and helped to clear up a few points. The one put on by Hugh Brigstocke and Hugh Macandrew in Edinburgh in 1981, entitled *Sacraments and Bacchanals*, looked at complementary areas in Poussin's work and thinking. In 1988 a combined exhibition and symposium were held in Fort Worth, Texas, devoted to Poussin's early years in Rome. Konrad Oberhuber's catalogue illustrates both the advances that can be made through *attributionism* and its inherent limitations, especially when based on daring hypotheses. He links paintings and drawings, many of them of dubious attribution, in an attempt to present an apparently meticulous chronology, which is in fact based on a belief that the creative process is geared to biological and psychic cycles which control, among other things, the way an artist sees and represents space. In reality, however, in the absence of any documentary evidence, Poussin's early years are likely to remain as much of a mystery as ever, and to imagine that one can date his early works not just to the year, but to the season and even the month, is pie in the sky. It seems unlikely that any new discoveries will be made which might disturb our ordering of Poussin's work from 1640 to his death, but anything is possible. The field of the drawings remains relatively unexplored. A new *catalogue raisonné* is due to replace the now outdated one by Friedländer and Blunt. Another large exhibition is planned (possibly to be held in 1994, to celebrate the quatercentenary of Poussin's birth), which should clarify certain issues currently dividing the experts, while giving the public a chance to explore the development of a unique artistic talent.

Poussin studies have also benefited from a whole range of books and articles that have shed new light on the environment in which his works were produced and on their meaning. The need to look at *Poussin in context* had already been propounded by Emile Magne in 1914 and by Werner Weisbach in his book on seventeenth-century French painting, published in 1932. The work of more recent art historians, however, like Francis Haskell, whose book on patronage in Italy was published in 1963, and Jacques Thuillier, who made a study of Poussin's 'early French companions' in Rome, published in 1960, has really pointed the way. A wave of ambitious and very precise studies on the background to Poussin's works followed, taking account not just of the artistic environment but also of the political, religious and literary climates of his day. Yves Bonnefoy's *Rome 1630* and Marc Fumaroli's 'dossier' on *The Inspiration of the Poet*, to mention just two 'literary' works, have gone a long way towards providing an understanding of Rome in the time of Pope Urban VIII, when Poussin was just starting out. Increasingly, studies are being made of Poussin's individual patrons, like Cassiano Dal Pozzo. Equally usefully, we are now seeing the publication of the inventories of their collections. There has also been a determined effort to define Poussin's personal cultural perspective more clearly and to illuminate both the sources and the meaning of his pictures. Panofsky and Gombrich, as well as a whole school of largely Anglo-Saxon writers following in their wake, have focused on paintings as enigmatic as *Bacchus/Apollo (Bacchus and Erigone)*, *Diana and Endymion* and the four *Seasons*. These highly academic studies tend to credit Poussin with a bookish culture and an encyclopaedic knowledge which he was far from possessing, and sometimes tend towards 'over-interpretation'. Even the most recent offerings, like Oskar Bätschmann's on *Landscape with Pyramus and Thisbe* and Matthias Winner's on the two *Self-Portraits* in oils, fall into this trap. The books which deal with art theory and practice are more solidly based, as many recent contributions, from Jan Bialostocki's to Elizabeth Cropper's, have shown. All the writers have stressed the extent to which Poussin referred to a wide range of sources, often known to him only at second or even third hand. As a result, the concept of Poussin as the founder of a doctrine no longer has any validity. Even though his stock-in-trade may have been of a somewhat superior kind to that of most of his fellow painters, stock-in-trade it was nevertheless – a collection of quotations from here, there and everywhere, which he would use in developing his ideas. This does not stop him from being portrayed firmly in the history of Western art as a leading exponent of seventeenth-century 'classicism' – a term which is being gradually re-assessed, particularly in the light of the exhibition of ideal landscapes held in Bologna in 1962 – in the wake of Caravaggism and the Baroque.

As research developed, it became increasingly apparent that Poussin would not fit conveniently into tidy categories or neat little schemes. It is significant that even Wölfflin, writing as early as the end of the nineteenth century, normally so quick to pigeonhole, could not do so in the case of Poussin. Clearly he could not force him into one of his customary slots without doing him a terrible injustice: Poussin simply will not be labelled – the painter of the four *Seasons* is neither a truly Baroque nor an entirely classical artist. Weisbach and Emile Magne were similarly cautious about presenting Poussin as an out-and-out supporter of the Counter-Reformation, whose ideals he was far from sharing unequivocally. Here again, the Paris exhibition and symposium played a key role in bringing together and laying out all the facts. In 1967, a year after his catalogue appeared, Anthony Blunt brought out a major monograph on Poussin, the fruits of twenty years' research and a large number of periodic publications. His book replaced Friedländer's earlier works of 1914 and 1965, and succeeded in placing Poussin firmly in his historical context – the France of Cardinal Richelieu and Louis XIII, and the Rome of Urban VIII and Innocent X. As a historical survey, Blunt's work is impeccable. It also attempts to put forward a particular thesis, however. Its avowed aim is to renew and develop the idea of Poussin as an artist-philosopher, as resolutely non-religious, as a free-thinker even, in contact with the most advanced thinkers of his day, from Marino to Campanella, and from Galileo to the 'Libertines' in France, and involved in his own way in the most progressive movements of his time. Blunt was reacting to the traditional aesthetics-based Anglo-Saxon approach, and his highly intellectual view had a great appeal: Kurt Badt's German monograph of 1969, for instance, is still clearly influenced by it. Blunt made a major contribution to Poussin studies. In recent years, however, people have begun to react against him and suggest changes. In his recent biography, for instance, Jacques

*cat. 126; 45
238–9, 246–7*

148, 149

Thuillier used documentary evidence to take Poussin firmly off his pedestal. Thuillier is due to bring out a new critical edition of Poussin's letters. Clovis Whitfield, Hugh Brigstocke and Konrad Oberhuber have all stressed the sensuousness and hedonism of Poussin's early years. Inevitably, this means that the catalogue needs to be revised: Blunt rejected many so-called 'free' works, attributing them to other hands. Paola Santucci, for her part, has concentrated on the religious works. For her, Poussin was more or less actively engaged in the service of the Jesuits striving to reconquer the Christian world. With Avigdor Arikha we once again have an artist's view of Poussin. Unlike André Lhote, whose interest was primarily in theory, Arikha concentrates on the technical problems now facing any artist who wants to produce paintings which are both learned and zesty. Scientific analysis, finally, can play its part, sometimes revealing unexpected sides to an art deemed to be incapable of surprise.

Certainly Poussin will never be a 'popular' artist. The commentaries which his highly demanding art have always generated, and the critical detour which his work requires us to make, have ensured that, from one generation to the next, his devotees have been confined to a relatively narrow circle. We can, of course, try to increase their numbers by making converts, and that is the aim of this book. This is not a *catalogue raisonné*: I mention the problems of attribution and dating, and am all too aware of their magnitude; but I have deliberately tried to present what amounts to a plausible consensus of opinion, rather than to put forward any new hypotheses of my own. It is not strictly an essay, either: there are already plenty of others far more learned, more involved and more brilliant than any I could hope to produce. It is more of a précis, aimed at the non-specialist, and designed to put the vast, and very uneven, range of literature that has been written on the subject into some kind of perspective. With the help of original documents included in an appendix, it aims above all to trace the unique course of one artist's development. Its structure is therefore essentially chronological except in a few cases, for the sake of coherence. Thus, the two sets of *Sacraments*, for instance, though separated by several years, are discussed in the same chapter. The book also aims to give a sense of what Poussin's work really has to offer us, which means inevitably that the author has to stand back somewhat and let Poussin speak. I have often found Poussin's own accounts or those of his contemporaries a good deal more enlightening than many recent interpretations of his work. Some of his contemporaries were well-informed. People often forget that Félibien was 'always free to watch him paint' during his stay in Rome. 'And it was then', he wrote, that 'the teachings and the practice would come together and he would point out, by giving me a palpable demonstration of it as he worked, the truth of the things he taught me in conversation.' We probably no longer look to painting to demonstrate a truth. What we must recover, however, and what this book seeks to re-establish between the reader and the pictures reproduced, is that contemplative rapport which Poussin intended there to be between the viewer and his paintings, and which was designed to yield varying degrees of knowledge and pleasure, depending on the individual. It takes time to absorb these paintings, to see into the depths of these slightly tarnished mirrors of ancient culture reflected in all its elements, the ages blended together beneath the shimmering, textured surface.

CHAPTER ONE

The Formative Years

FAMILY BACKGROUND.

QUENTIN VARIN AND FIRST EXPERIENCES OF PAINTING.

ROUEN, PARIS, FONTAINEBLEAU: STUDIO WORK AND FRESH ENCOUNTERS.

WANDERINGS AND STUDIES: THE POITOU EXPEDITION, THE APPEAL OF ITALY.

THE FIRST WORKS IN PARIS: THE JESUITS, MEETING

MARINO, 'THE DEATH OF THE VIRGIN'.

EARLY UNCERTAINTIES

Little is known of Poussin before he reached the age of thirty. Of the period from his birth in Normandy until his arrival in Rome in 1624 only a handful of accounts survives, and no painting that can be attributed to him with any certainty. By following up every available reference, we can glean something about his early career, but no amount of scholarship will help shed any real light on Poussin the man in those early days. And yet, by the time he settled in Italy he was more or less fully fledged as a painter, and one who had had his share of problems in the course of some reasonably adventurous forays into the world. He spent periods working under different artists, went off on abortive travels, and came into contact with all manner of people and places. His cultural perspective was, however, as much the product of a first-class education as of chance encounters. His was an education of the old school, and it was primarily the years he spent studying in places which were then somewhat old-fashioned that were to render him so distinct in seventeenth-century Rome. At that time Rouen, Paris, and Fontainebleau under Henri IV were still dominated by the northern painters who had migrated there and by the Mannerist approach and technique they had brought. Poussin's art and thinking of course continued to develop in Italy, but along lines already set in France. To understand the driving forces in Poussin's work, we have to look behind the image we now have of him as a wise elder in a toga, and examine his youth and the passions and struggles which were to produce the patriarch of painting we imagine taking his evening stroll in Rome.

Jean Poussin, father of Nicolas, belonged to a family of notaries from Soissons and served in Henri de Navarre's army during the Wars of Religion. When peace was restored, he married Marie Delaisement, daughter of a magistrate from Vernon and widow of an attorney, and retired to a small estate near the large market town of Les Andelys in the Seine valley. It was there, in the hamlet of Villers, in June 1594, that their son was born – just at the moment when France was beginning to emerge from the devastations of war. The Poussin family may not have been members of the gentility as has been claimed, but they did have connections with leading members of the legal profession and with people of good social standing. Theirs was a provincial, even rural, world, and in this environment Nicolas spent his childhood and adolescence. For Poussin, even more perhaps than for the Le Nain brothers (whose early life was comparable), the surroundings in which he grew up were to remain vitally important, and he maintained close ties with his Normandy relatives throughout his life, despite having settled in Italy. When he was well over fifty, he went out of his way to refer to his roots by including the word ANDELYENSIS in the inscriptions on his self-portraits of 1649 and 1650. In his mature works, like *Landscape with Diogenes* and *Landscape with Orpheus and Eurydice*, the lush greenery of rainy climates is worked harmoniously in with the strong light of Italy and the massive form of the Château Gaillard used as a backdrop to Roman ruins. It is surely not surprising that as an artist Poussin should have been obsessed with the idea of the inexhaustible richness of nature, when from so early an age he had such an eye for the earth and the sky, and taken such delight in the serenity of still waters, the vitality of young trees and the beauty of

Landscape with Orpheus and Eurydice (detail). Louvre, Paris. See also p. 161.

meadows. Poussin later invested the banks of the Tiber and the countryside around Rome with the same qualities as those of the beautiful Seine valley of his youth.

Although he was in many ways very like the country people with whom he came into contact, Poussin differed from them in that he received a good education. Intended no doubt for a career in the legal profession, he learned Latin, first at the parish school, and then at a college, perhaps the one run by the Jesuits in Rouen. It is not known how far Poussin pursued this initial course of study; but as early as 1662 Fréart de Chambray noted 'what a singular advantage it was to him to have had a literary education before he took up painting'. As he moved among the humanist circles of Paris and Rome, Poussin's initiation into the classics was complete. Though this training did not lead to a life of scholarship, it was fundamental to his art, giving rise to ambitious works which can be difficult to grasp without a high level of reading and thought. Poussin was an exception: unlike most of his fellow painters, whose parents were artisans or artists and who were apprenticed to a guild at a very early age, this most 'learned' of artists had as a child never been regarded as a future painter.

Quentin Varin, *The Martyrdom of St Clare*, Church of Notre Dame, Les Andelys.

There is perhaps an element of romantic wishful thinking in the accounts that Poussin's earliest biographers, Bellori (1672) and Félibien (1685), give of his artistic beginnings: the impression created by them is of a reluctant scholar who longs to draw and cannot wait to put his studies behind him. The boy's saviour is an itinerant artist he meets at the age of seventeen: the man opens his eyes to the world of great art and his future is set. His anxious parents intervene, and for a while he is prevented from following his high calling, until at last he manages to escape in what is just the start of a long series of adventures. Whatever the real facts, there is no doubt that Poussin's artistic career first developed in a way that was far from typical for the time. The norm in France in the early seventeenth century was for a career as a painter to pass from father to son, yet here was a complete outsider, encouraged to consider a career in art neither through the world in which he grew up nor through professional training. It was a chance contact which perhaps most spurred him on. In 1611 or 1612 a painter called Quentin Varin visited Les Andelys and there executed three pictures for the church of Notre Dame: *The Martyrdom of St Clare*, *The Martyrdom of St Vincent* and *The Virgin Surrounded by Angels*.

Varin was born *c.* 1570 in Beauvais. He belonged to that generation of artists who grew up during the civil upheavals and found themselves reaching adulthood when times were hard and fewer and fewer commissions were to be had – Paris was not yet the artistic centre it later became, and the blaze of activity at Fontainebleau under François I had come to a stop and would not start again until Henri IV embarked on a new building programme. Painters had to travel abroad and find work along the way. By 1597 Varin had completed his initial apprenticeship and was known to be working as a journeyman in Avignon. From there he may have gone to northern Italy – his work certainly reveals a familiarity with the Mannerist thinking prevalent in Parma and Venice and espoused by Correggio and the Bassano family. He may, however, have derived his knowledge from examples found closer to hand which would also have a powerful effect on the young Poussin and others – notably the work of Rosso Fiorentino and Primaticcio at Fontainebleau, and the engravings then flooding into France from the north, particularly from Antwerp. Varin's first base was in Amiens, from where he went on to Normandy before settling in Paris; there he produced his best work, such as *The Presentation in the Temple* (1624) for the Carmelite friary. The bulk of Varin's work is now lost, but we do know that his talent was wide-ranging and that he could work to any scale according to demand. His style was ambitious: his pictures, which were vividly narrative and contrived to incorporate a vast number of figures in taxing poses, generally with their heads thrown back, were by no means always successful in sustaining a polished and convincing effect. A young man from the provinces like Poussin, however, would have been quite bowled over by the three paintings for the church at Les Andelys. Only later when he was in Paris and saw the stronger, calmer pictures of Varin's mature work would Poussin begin to appreciate the subtleties of composition: Varin had moderated his sensationalist style and his figures were now an integral part of their monumental setting.

In 1612, however, Poussin was a long way from all this, and we have no way of knowing if Varin even had the chance to teach his young admirer the rudiments of his craft. According to Bellori and Félibien, who might have heard it from Poussin himself, Varin encouraged him and tried to persuade his parents to allow their son to pursue a career in art. In the face of his father's marked lack of enthusiasm, Nicolas ran away from home at the age of eighteen, in circumstances which are far from clear. For the next ten years or so he was constantly on the move: the only available evidence comes from second-hand accounts of doubtful reliability. Poussin was quickly drawn, of course, to Paris, perhaps after a brief spell in Rouen, which was, after all, not far from Les Andelys. One school of thought maintains that he studied 'the first principles of drawing' there under Noël Jouvenet, a forebear of the great Jean Jouvenet, but only a second-rate artist himself. Rouen had been a centre of artistic activity since the Renaissance, and more particularly as a result of the works initiated by Cardinal d'Amboise at the Château de Gaillon. Large numbers of painters had moved there from the north and were now competing with local artists for commissions for churches and convents. Studios proliferated, generating a wide range of work, and an enormous sense of creative freedom prevailed. It was an environment which someone like the young Poussin would certainly have found stimulating, especially because of the direct contact it afforded with the Italian and Italianate schools. Whether or not he went first to Rouen is of only incidental importance, however, for it was in Paris that Poussin's real ambitions lay: nowhere else could rival the attraction of the hustle and bustle and rich contrast of Marie de Médicis' Paris. There Poussin was adopted by a young (unidentified) nobleman from Poitou then in service at court, who provided him with board and lodging and recommended him to two well-known artists.

The first was the Calvinist Ferdinand Elle, a fashionable portrait painter Flemish by birth, who had lived in Paris since at least 1609. Poussin spent scarcely three months with him. Portraiture was not to his taste: having to work so closely from the model cramped his creative style, and he disliked hob-nobbing with society. He went on to work under a rather better-known master, the Nancy painter Georges Lallemant. Since 1601 Lallemant had run the most influential studio in Paris, and counted Philippe de Champaigne and Laurent de La Hyre among his successful pupils. Remembered today chiefly for his engravings, Lallemant had a range far more extensive than these Mannerist genre pieces in the style of the Lorraine painters (and Bellange in particular) might suggest. Although only a fraction of his œuvre survives, he was an accomplished portraitist, as his painting of a group of magistrates of 1611 proves, a decorative artist of some standing, as evidenced by his work in 1620 on the Vic family chapel at Saint-Nicolas-des-Champs, and a brilliant and prolific history painter. He and Varin together dominated the Paris art scene unchallenged for a quarter of a century until 1627, when Simon Vouet returned from Italy and a

Georges Lallemant,
St Martin Sharing his Cloak,
oil on canvas,
279 x 206 cm (109⁵⁄₄ x 81 in.).
Musée Carnavalet, Paris

21

new era began. It is quite likely that Poussin was set to work with a paintbrush during his time in Lallemant's studio, and that it was here that he began to learn his craft. He quickly grew tired of this, too, and left after a month. He was filled with an instinctive loathing for all that studio production entailed. Poussin could not come to terms with the mentality required of an apprentice when art was still regarded as a craft industry, and when paintings and frescoes dreamt up by a master were executed either wholly or in part by a team of assistants who were expected to imitate his manner and technique.

Brief though it was, Poussin's time with Lallemant convinced him that he was right to want to devote himself to history painting. In the seventeenth century 'history painting' covered all forms of painting depicting human events, regardless of whether or not they were what we would now term 'historical'. Truly narrative in the fullest sense, it is the most demanding and complex form of painting of all, requiring the artist to conjure up the workings of the minds and hearts of real or imaginary characters whom he sets up in a dynamic relationship. Unlike portrait, landscape, genre or still-life painting, all of which depend for their success on an artist's ability to capture something real, history painting calls for imagination and erudition. Paris gave Poussin the opportunity he needed to broaden his knowledge and to escape the grind of studio life. Bellori and Passeri (*c.* 1673), both of whom had direct contact with Poussin, maintain that he got to know Alexandre Courtois, who was valet to Marie de Médicis and later became keeper of the collections of the king and queen. Courtois collected prints and introduced the young painter to the great names in Italian Renaissance art – Raphael, Giulio Romano and Caldara – all of whose major works had been engraved in the sixteenth century. Through him, too, Poussin had access to the royal collections and the chance to study classical sculpture and Italian painting at first hand. For him this was a revelation, the second such in his artistic career, but of far greater impact than the introduction to painting which he had received from Varin: here were the very roots of modern art, from which all the Mannerist works he had seen hitherto were derived. It was almost certainly at this point that Poussin formulated his desire to go to Italy to see 'that light he had always craved'.

Meanwhile, Poussin embarked on a somewhat perilous undertaking which could have had disastrous consequences. When the time came for his young patron to return to Poitou, he asked Poussin to accompany him and decorate a gallery in his château, the precise location of which is uncertain – 'a hundred leagues' from Paris. One suggestion is Mornay en Saintonge: the gallery there, burnt down in 1947, is known to have been decorated with scenes from mythology and to have borne the inscription, '*Nicolas Poussin pinxit anno 1614*'. The *Diana and Actaeon* (now in a private collection) salvaged from the series is clearly based on a composition by Heintz later engraved by Saedeler; an awkward, plagiaristic piece, heavily Mannerist in style, this has been regarded by some as Poussin's earliest surviving work. It seems, however, that the young men's plans were thwarted by the patron's mother, a thrifty woman who firmly opposed them on grounds of cost, and that their scheme for transforming the château was never realized. Poussin had to return to Paris on foot, 'suffering extreme hardship and exhaustion'. He stopped at various points to earn money, and is supposed to have painted two pictures for the Capuchin monastery at Blois, in addition to several *Bacchanals* for a small pavilion in the grounds of the Château de Cheverny. All these works are now lost. It was not at all uncommon for expeditions like this to come to nothing – many artists worked in this way, travelling up and down the country at the behest of others, ever vulnerable to the twists and turns of fate. The episode exposed Poussin to poverty and illness – contrary to belief, these conditions were not peculiar to the so-called 'accursed' artists of the nineteenth and early twentieth centuries. Poussin found himself in such dire straits more than once. His first venture into the world left him penniless and in poor health. The prodigal son returned to Les Andelys to recuperate. After about a year, he was once again ready to set off for Paris, all parental objections to his chosen career apparently now dropped.

Poussin returned to Paris with ample funds at his disposal, and could pursue his studies as he chose, without involving himself in the studio system. Tentative experimentation gave way to a solid theoretical grounding as he studied perspective and anatomy, taking lessons in the latter at a local hospital. These were disciplines which all the great Italian painters from Leonardo to Michelangelo considered central to their art, but which were largely disregarded by the leading Parisian artists of Poussin's day. Bellori and Passeri saw Poussin very much as an artist-scholar in the fifteenth-century Florentine tradition, throwing himself into academic studies with enormous energy. This again represented a marked departure from contemporary practice, for only with the establishment of the Académie Royale did it become routine *c.* 1650 for painters working in the capital to receive a formal training. This brought about a clear distinction between artists and craftsmen, and painters were elevated into a social and intellectual class apart.

The call of Italy became increasingly urgent. Poussin's visits to Fontainebleau no longer satisfied him. However much he might admire Primaticcio's contributions to the Ulysses Gallery, he needed to go to the fountainhead from which this polished and decorative art, with its evocations of scenes from Ovid's *Metamorphoses* and the tales of Homer and other Greek and Roman authors, had sprung. Poussin's plans to reach Rome were dogged by all sorts of problems, not least ill-health and lack of money, and only at the third attempt was he successful. Of his first expedition to Italy *c.* 1617, little is known except that it was cut short at Florence and that his rather hasty departure from there was prompted by 'an accident'. He may in fact have been on a secret mission for the queen mother, who had been exiled to Blois by her son. Whatever the truth, the trip gave Poussin a chance to see something of Italy. Although Tuscany in its grand duchy days had not yet acquired anything like the reputation Rome then enjoyed among French artists, it had been renowned for its artistic excellence and had much to offer new generations of painters by way of example. Court art at the time was of considerable distinction, and its influence can be clearly detected not just in the work of the Lorraine artist Jacques Callot and of Jacques Stella, who lived and worked there, but in Poussin's earliest pictures.

On his return to Paris, Poussin went to live with the Jesuits in the Collège de Navarre. It seems probable that this is when he started painting for churches and convents. There are a number of surviving pictures which could have been painted by Poussin between 1618 and 1620. Jacques Thuillier has maintained that these include *St Denis Terrifying his Executioners* (Abbaye de La Meilleraye) and *St Denis Crowned by an Angel* (Musée des Beaux-Arts, Rouen), both having a Parisian church provenance. Other critics, however, dispute his attribution. Although there is in the Louvre a rapidly executed sketch for the first of these two paintings inscribed 'Poussin', the picture has hints not only of Varin and the Florentine school, but also of Saraceni and Leclerc, which implies some familiarity with the art then emanating from Venice. The second seems to be much more of an amalgam of different ideas culled from a wide range of sources: the figures in the middle distance, for instance, are similar in feeling to those in the first picture, whereas the

Attributed to Poussin,
St Denis Terrifying his Executioners,
oil on canvas, 68 x 82 cm (26³/₄ x 32¹/₂ in.).
Abbaye de la Meilleraye.

Frans Pourbus the Younger, *The Last Supper*, oil on canvas, 287 x 370 cm (113 x 145¹/₂ in.). Louvre, Paris.

stern-looking figure in the centre owes much more to the work of the Flemish painter Frans Pourbus the Younger, then active in Paris and developing a distinctive new style which the young Champaigne was to take further still. If these works are indeed by Poussin, they reflect a radical change of direction on his part – a move away from the kind of composition favoured by Varin and towards a far greater tautness of design. In 1618 Pourbus produced *The Last Supper* (now in the Louvre) as an altarpiece for the church of Saint-Leu-Saint-Gilles. Powerful in its simplicity, the painting soon became one of the most highly regarded in Paris and, according to Sauval, Poussin is reputed to have affirmed some time later that it was one of the finest he had seen. Pourbus was essentially a realist painter, and the sense of order and symmetry which his work displayed, the clear, almost abstract light he introduced into it, and the individual quality and depth of expression he brought to every face, could not have been more different from the studied elegance of Fontainebleau. This *Last Supper* made a lasting impression on the young Poussin: thirty years later, he incorporated two elements from it in *The Eucharist* of the second set of *Sacraments* – the curtain used to limit the focal area of the picture, and the paved floor which pulls the composition together.

106

Poussin made a fresh attempt to reach Rome in 1621 or 1622, again to no avail. This time he got no further than Lyons, then something of a halfway house on the road to Italy and an important meeting place for artists. A debt incurred with a merchant there forced him to curtail his journey and return to Paris. There he was commissioned by the Jesuits to paint a set of six large decorative pictures for the celebrations due to take place at the end of July 1622 in honour of the canonization of St Ignatius and St Francis Xavier. Now all lost, these occasional pieces were executed in tempera at great speed – it is said in as little as six days – and depicted scenes from the lives of the founder of the Society of Jesus, St Ignatius Loyola, and one of his original followers. Four of them were still in evidence in the Jesuit Collège Louis-le-Grand in the middle of the eighteenth century: *The Ecstasy of St Ignatius*, *St Ignatius Composing his Meditations*, *Christ and the Virgin Appearing to St Ignatius and St Francis Xavier* and *St Francis Xavier Persecuted by Demons*. The Jesuits are renowned for exploiting any occasion worthy of celebration and for making extensive use of visual imagery in propagating their ideas and in education. In choosing Poussin, they were clearly confident that he was both imaginatively and technically capable of producing at short notice the somewhat ambitious compositions they wanted.

The pictures evinced a refreshing new talent, and caught the eye of the Italian poet Giovanni-Battista Marino, generally known in France as the Cavalier Marin, who had been at court since 1615. In 1621 Marino bemoans, in a letter to one of his compatriots, the dearth of French painters able to tackle precisely this sort of 'narrative' with any success. For his part, Poussin had by then almost certainly moved away from the kind of art practised by Varin and Lallemant. Marino was taken as much with the artist as with the man, and became Poussin's first important patron. He took a keen interest in painting. His own scholarly yet sensuous verse, while displaying a high regard for the visual arts, also seeks to emulate them. As early as 1614 he asserted in his *Dicerie sacre* that 'poetry can be described as painting given the power of speech, painting as poetry rendered mute'. The year 1619 saw the publication in Venice of his *Galleria*, a kind of picture gallery where epigrams, not paint, were the medium. It was intended not just as a set of descriptions of real and imaginary pictures, but as a trenchant piece of criticism, very much in the tradition of Philostratus. Taking as its main subject pictures depicting tales from classical mythology, Marino's treatise dwells on allegorical details and questions of technique, and has a great deal to offer in the way of moral precepts, making skilful use of quotation wherever necessary. This poetry is no more content than the painting it describes simply to hold up a mirror to obvious perfection – it seeks constantly to get to the root of it, to discover in it the creative principle underlying all harmony. Marino is at once scholarly and imaginative, not only offering a learned commentary on the pictures, but endeavouring quite as much as the artists who painted them to give an insight into the emotions or '*affetti*' of the characters depicted; he talks of a 'reading' of *The Massacre of the Innocents* by Guido Reni, Titian's *Mary Magdalene* or *Meleager and Atalanta* by Rubens.

Poussin was exposed, and consequently won over, to Marino's extraordinarily erudite poetry at a time when he had already begun to reject the models on which he had hitherto based his thinking. Marino's reputation was at its height. His masterpiece, *L'Adone*, a very long poem based on the myth of Adonis and centred on the theme of the five senses, was written in France. In the humanist outlook and fine appreciation of the plastic arts displayed in his poem Marino more than anyone else prefigured the 'precious' school. Marino asked Poussin to follow him to Rome, arriving back there himself in April 1623. Poussin was still bound by various commitments, however, and left Paris only later in the year; as a result, the two men did not meet again until the spring of 1624.

Before he left, Marino had had time to commission from Poussin a series of drawings. After the poet's death in 1625, these passed into the hands first of Cassiano Dal Pozzo and then of Cardinal Massimi (both of whom were to be important patrons of Poussin's) before going to England in the eighteenth century when they entered the Royal Collec-

tion. Irrespective of whether they are the originals by Poussin or – as Konrad Oberhuber maintains – simply copies, the drawings provide us with our first benchmark when studying Poussin's early career. There are fifteen drawings in all, none of which illustrates Marino's *L'Adone* as Bellori believed. In fact, eleven are illustrations to Ovid's *Metamorphoses*, the remaining four being based on accounts of Roman battles described in Livy and Virgil. The poet was almost certainly responsible for the choice of episodes to be illustrated, and he may also have provided Poussin with a fairly free translation of Ovid's poem. The drawings are in pen and brown wash, an essentially northern technique popular with artists of the second School of Fontainebleau like Ambroise Dubois and Toussaint Dubreuil. The compositions are generally in landscape format, but in terms of style fall into two distinct groups. In the first, carefully balanced figures throng the page with all the economy and harmony of a bas-relief. The second eliminates symmetry and features great contrasts in scale, very much in the tradition of Mannerist illustrators like Goltzius and Martin de Vos. The strength of the drawings, however, lies chiefly in the clarity of the narrative: it limits the action to a single time and place, removes all trace of the supernatural, and conveys all the circumstances through the gestures of the protagonists. Poussin was slowly beginning to turn his back on Fontainebleau and look to the great works of classical art he had once studied via engravings. In terms of their subject matter (*Acis and Galatea Surprised by Polyphemus*, *The Birth of Adonis*, *Chion Killed by Diana*, the four *Battles* and so on), the drawings seem to alternate between cruelty and a hymn to happiness, the harsh blows of fate and all-conquering love. The technical range is fairly limited, and the actual drawing pretty elementary, even clumsy. Aware, however, that even the paper has a contribution to make, Poussin used the contrast between the dark wash and the white paper to create dramatic lighting effects. The earliest pictures testify to the multi-faceted nature of Poussin's character and talent. The variety of themes he painted between the *Battles* of 1624 and *The Triumph of Flora* of 1627 offer further proof of it, demonstrating his ability to bring a poetic vision to bear on the world and human experience as they appeared in even the most inauspicious of circumstances.

The year 1623, was, then, a crucial one. Poussin was exceptionally busy during the run-up to his departure for Italy. He still enjoyed the patronage of Marie de Médicis to some extent, and was taken on at her behest to work on the decoration of the Palais du Luxembourg under Nicolas Duchesne and alongside Philippe de Champaigne, with whom he struck up a lasting friendship. Poussin was probably responsible for some of the small paintings of figures surrounded by grotesques which adorn the panelling. This was mere bread-and-butter work, hardly the stuff of a great history painter in the making. A more creditable commission followed, clear evidence of Poussin's growing reputation: Archbishop Jean-François de Gondi asked him to paint *The Death of the Virgin* for his family's chapel in the Cathedral of Notre Dame. The picture itself, which disappeared in Brussels in 1815, was well documented in the seventeenth and eighteenth centuries, and a good number of references to and descriptions of it survive. In 1771 Gabriel de Saint-Aubin made a sketch of it in the margin of his copy of the guidebook to Notre Dame. A watercolour in the Worsley Collection (Hovingham Hall), was for long thought to be the original *modello* or finished sketch for the painting, which was over 2 m (6 ft 6 in.) high. Inspired perhaps by Saraceni's *Death of the Virgin* engraved by Jean Leclerc in 1619, its compostion was ambitious. The deathbed lay diagonally across the picture, with masses of figures pressing in around it from above and below. There was great dramatic strength

Opposite
(Above) *The Birth of Adonis*,
pen and brown ink with grey wash,
18.3 x 32.5 cm (7¼ x 12¾ in.).
Royal Library, Windsor.

(Below) *Acis and Galatea Surprised by Polyphemus*,
pen and grey-brown wash,
18.6 x 32.5 cm (7½ x 12¾ in.).
Royal Library, Windsor.

The Death of the Virgin,
pen and watercolour
heightened with white and black chalk,
39.5 x 31 cm (15½ x 12¼ in.).
Worsley Collection, Hovingham Hall.

both in the bold, largely horizontal gestures given to the figures and in the intensity of their expressions. The drapery was generous and finely executed, very much in the manner of Pourbus, whose influence was also clear in the prominence accorded to the archbishop depicted in the middle ground. The distraught individual in the centre foreground, on the other hand, was more reminiscent of Michelangelo and of the *Zachariah* in the Sistine Chapel. In its basic construction the painting was as much an amalgam of different influences as were the pictures Poussin executed for the Jesuits, although on a rather larger scale. As an evocation of lamentation, however, it was original enough to excite considerable attention, and in its sustained tragic tone this picture anticipates *The Death of Germanicus* of 1627: he had established a new way of expressing emotion. 43

Poussin's drawings for Marino and his *Death of the Virgin* alike reveal a talent which has yet to find independent expression. They reveal the influences to which he was most regularly exposed: the rather tame and stodgy Mannerism exemplified by the second School of Fontainebleau, the narrative style epitomized by Dubois and even more by Dubreuil in the sets of paintings they produced for Fontainebleau and Saint-Germain-en-Laye, and the vivid use of colour combined with sturdiness of form typical of Pourbus. Poussin's art pretty much reflects the taste for Flemish painting which dominated Paris from 1610 to 1630. In 1623 Poussin had an opportunity to see the first nine of Rubens's paintings illustrating *The Life of Marie de Médicis*, when Rubens himself brought them to the Palais du Luxembourg at the end of May, and in his *Death of Germanicus* Poussin later recalled one of the episodes portrayed by Rubens in his designs for the *Constantine* 39 *Cycle* of tapestries. At the same time Poussin's work was beginning to show traces of the influence of Italian art of the High Renaissance, which he might have encountered at first hand several years earlier in Florence or have known simply through engravings.

Poussin could certainly have made a successful career in Paris. His early essays in high religious painting were more than creditable, but the lure of Rome was irresistible: its charms were if anything increased by the taste Marino had given him of the poetry and independence of spirit to be found there, and Poussin had, as Marino told Sacchetti, 'the fury of the devil' in him and was not, by all accounts, easily deflected from a chosen course. Having honoured all his commitments, Poussin set off – perhaps as early as the autumn of 1623. He is first spoken of as being in Rome in March 1624, having visited Venice en route and quite probably spent the winter there. This detour was important for Poussin – several paintings dating from shortly after his arrival in Rome betray the influence of Bellini and Titian, examples of whose works he would have seen in Venice. He was then thirty, in seventeenth-century terms an age by which it was by no means uncommon for an artist to have at least one major work to his name. In Poussin's case, however, the 'great fire' of his creative genius was only just starting to flicker into life. Although his maturity effectively dates from the time when he went to live in Italy, Poussin had previously begun to emerge as a painter radically different from his peers.

What distinguished Poussin from his contemporaries was first and foremost his cultural outlook. His education was at once exceptionally advanced and broad for an artist of his day. Every aspect of it was to have to profound bearing on his work. Two distinct schools of thought, seemingly poles apart, informed Poussin's vision: classical literature, and up-to-the-minute contemporary Catholicism. This was a time of fusion of ideas, when Paris simultaneously abounded with free-thinkers and libertinism in all its manifestations and witnessed what Abbé Bremond so appositely termed a great 'spiritual surge'. For the devout humanists of the day who believed God's grace to be infinite and whose faith in man was therefore boundless, the struggles of individuals and the strength of character they displayed in their endeavour to fulfil their potential were of central concern. Both St Francis de Sales and the Jesuits who had recently established themselves in Paris shared this outlook and were committed advocates of 'magnanimity' towards men. Whatever Poussin's particular beliefs may have been, Jacques Thuillier is right in maintaining that in order to understand the way in which his art and thought developed, one must consider them in the context of the changes taking place in the Church's thinking. Following the Counter-Reformation, a new mood of optimism was evident in the Catholic Church, its aim now being a general reconquest of minds. The principles it was now putting forward were fundamentally at one with those of classical philosophy.

What also set Poussin clearly apart in those early years was his strength of character and independence of spirit. He was naturally proud, bold and determined. He did not serve an apprenticeship, as most artists did, with the comfortable prospect of an easy but limited career with the guild. It was not a way which could ever really have been open to him, given that he was not born into the trade. When eventually he did start work, it was in 'privileged' environments – in colleges, at court, for the Church – well away from the petty world of master craftsmen and their niggling rules and regulations. Then as later, Poussin would associate himself only with patrons he felt were kindred spirits. His output was limited, before long he confined himself to working for his own circle of admirers. From what we know of his early career, it is clear that Poussin was prone to changes of heart, sudden impulses and fits of impatience, but also that he could show extraordinary determination in striving to reach the goal which had long eluded him – Rome.

At a technical level, Poussin was largely self-taught. His work displays intelligence and strength of character rather than sophisticated ease or innate skill. Poussin was certainly no infant prodigy and – compared with his exact contemporary Simon Vouet, who was to return to Paris in 1627 at the behest of Louis XIII to one of the most brilliant careers of the century – lacked fluency. What seems to have impressed his earliest friends and patrons was not so much his pictorial skill, but the poetic imagination, the liveliness of mind, and the profundity of thought which informed his work. Bernini summed up the gulf between Poussin's ideas and his execution of them, when, looking at Chantelou's set of *Sacraments* in Paris much later, he tapped his forehead and declared that Poussin was an artist 'who works from up here'. Although Poussin was hampered by the inherent unevenness of his talent and, when an old man, tragically thwarted by it, unable to get his hand to express what was in his mind, it lent an extraordinary tension to his work. Cézanne alone seems to offer any kind of parallel to Poussin. Both took a long time to find their own style, and both refused equally firmly to get involved in slavishly following the manner of a master. Poussin's youth, or what we know of it, was a period of experimentation and reflection. The young protégé of the Jesuits and of Marino had yet to commit himself to any one of the many styles confronting him or choose between Fontainebleau, the example of the Flemish painters in Paris, and the work of Raphael and Caldara as he had seen it in engravings. On one side he was faced with the demise of the Mannerist movement which had become increasingly rigid and had only occasional flashes of brilliance to offer. Just discernible on the other were indications of a reawakening of interest in classical art. Poussin had yet to make sense of all these disparate elements and produce a coherent style of his own. Rome was to provide the catalyst he needed.

A French Artist in Rome

Piranesi, *The Piazza di Spagna, Rome*
engraving.

One day in March 1624, shortly before Easter, the clerk responsible for preparing a register of 'souls' in the parish of San Lorenzo in Lucina came upon a group of artists assembled, at what may well have been a life-drawing session, in the house of Simon Vouet, the leading name among French painters then living in Rome. Among the twenty or so artists recorded, some of their names in a pretty garbled form, was 'Nicolo Pusin'. This is the sole surviving documentary evidence for the period immediately before and after Poussin's arrival in Rome. Nothing is known today about either his journey there or the stop he made in Venice during the winter of 1623–4, nor is there any record of his arrival in the Eternal City or of his moving in there. From such isolated references as are to be found it is clear that Poussin's first home was in an area frequented largely by foreigners, close to the Spanish Steps. It was an area he would subsequently leave only rarely; he moved from one street to another – Strada Paolina, Via del Babuino, Via Paolina – in this Roman equivalent of Montparnasse in Paris, with its motley population of artists of all nationalities. Poussin had found his chosen goal, a place where he would live, paint and think, and which would provide the stimulus for his work. His initial circumstances were humble, and life in the city proved difficult and sometimes even dangerous, but the beauty and majesty of his environment amply made up for any hardship. He was surrounded by palaces, gardens and ruins, and by strong colours and forms, all steeped in a magnificent and compelling light.

Rome was unique in the scope it was able to offer artists, and especially painters, at this period. Patrons were rich, powerful and plentiful. Besides the Pope himself, there were the cardinals, always trying to outdo each other in the decoration of their palaces and chapels, who generated almost as much work, and the various religious orders, with the endless churches and foundations they spawned, were not far behind. The most prestigious commissions came from such lofty quarters, but they were not necessarily the most remunerative – those tended to come from another, broader group of patrons. Rome attracted a floating population of pilgrims, diplomats and wealthy travellers. Money flowed – and art was very much a business, with dealers and brokers peddling their wares to an ever-increasing circle of antiquarians and connoisseurs of painting. Exhibitions were held in the Pantheon and in churches. As well as being commercial ventures, these events brought the work of young painters to wider public attention, in much the same way that commissions executed for religious institutions did, and provided artists with opportunities to get to know each other. The city also boasted private art collections of outstanding quality and extraordinary range, remarkable too for being accessible to the public. The resource they provided was exceptional: in no other city (apart, perhaps, from Venice) was it possible to look at, compare and study examples of classical, Renaissance and contemporary art. Rome constituted a vast and glorious centre of learning. The Academy of St Luke, for instance, which was made up of painters and sculptors, organized formal lectures and fostered debate, while a number of establishments provided opportunities for life drawing, so vital as a basis for history painting.

A French artist in Rome

When he first arrived in Rome, Poussin was neither without friends nor entirely unknown. Marino recommended him to Marcello Sacchetti, a rich art-lover, who dabbled in landscape painting himself and was art adviser to the new Pope, Urban VIII. This connection brought him into contact with other members of the highly influential Barberini family. Poussin found particular favour with Cardinal Francesco Barberini, the Supreme Pontiff's nephew and a notable art collector, and with the Cardinal's secretary, Cassiano Dal Pozzo. Difficulties soon arose, however: Marino disappeared to Naples, where he died suddenly in March 1625; and the Cardinal was sent off to France on a diplomatic mission. Poussin found himself without any important patrons and was forced to sell his first paintings for next to nothing in order to survive: he was paid a niggardly 7 Roman crowns for each of the *Battles* (1625), and 8 crowns for a painting of *A Prophet*, a copy of which is reputed to have sold for half that amount. Slowly he began to get more lucrative commissions. In 1627 Francesco Barberini paid him 60 crowns for *The Death of Germanicus* and in 1631 another easel-painting, *The Plague of Ashdod*, was sold for 110 crowns. In the interim, the large altarpiece depicting *The Martyrdom of St Erasmus*, painted for St Peter's, brought in 400 crowns. It was hardly a fortune, but it was a comfortable enough beginning for a painter like Poussin who had been forced, as much by his own desire for independence as by circumstances, to eschew a life of ease in the service of some important individual. The turning point in his financial situation came in the early 1630s. Until then, however, uncertainties about the future had been complicated by a number of accidents. In 1625 Poussin narrowly escaped losing his right hand in a brawl with some Spaniards. In 1628–9 he became seriously ill following a venereal infection (an attack of 'the French disease', as one of his biographers puts it), and might have died but for the good offices of a neighbour, the cook Jean Dughet, whose daughter Anne-Marie he married the following year. Dughet's son Gaspard, who was Poussin's pupil for a while, later became one of the greatest landscape painters of the century.

Throughout this difficult period Poussin was able to count on the support of the rest of the French community in Rome. He struck up friendships with several other painters of his generation. His association with Vouet seems to have been the least important, for the two men did not see eye to eye, least of all where art was concerned. By contrast, Jacques Stella was unreserved in his admiration for Poussin, and the two soon became close friends. Claude Mellan, meanwhile, showed his respect for Poussin's drawings by engraving them. Of Poussin's early companions and sometime associates, three are particularly worthy of note: Jean Mosnier, Jean Lemaire, who specialized in painting architectural backgrounds and ruins, and the Flemish sculptor François Duquesnoy, with whom Poussin shared lodgings in 1626. Together they drew classical statues, which they would measure in detail, as well as from life. After 1630 Poussin's circle began to widen and included an increasing number of friends of other nationalities, like the Dutch genre painter Pieter van Laer, known for his 'bambocciata'; the German scientist Joachim von Sandrart, in whose memoirs Poussin was to feature quite prominently; and natives of Lorraine like Claude Gellée, who went off on trips with him to explore the countryside in the vicinity of Rome.

For Poussin finding buyers in Rome proved an uphill struggle at first, not least because he had to deal with a milieu which was completely unfamiliar to him, full of people quite unlike any he had encountered in Paris. Though Poussin was well grounded as an artist by the time he left for Rome, the process of looking and learning continued

43
59
47

unabated in Italy. The range of artistic options in the 1620s was extraordinarily wide, and reflected several major different schools of thought.

Mannerism had reached its zenith in Rome in the middle of the sixteenth century. At its height it combined a scholarly and decorative approach leading to some powerful and disquieting images. Its chief exponent in later years was Giuseppe Cesari, called the Cavaliere d'Arpino, one of the best-known painters of the day. He enjoyed considerable success with his toned-down version of Mannerism – his painting was accessible and generally pleasing, if repetitive, and quite unaffected by Caravaggio's battering down of convention. Caravaggio's revolutionary pictures of *The Calling of St Matthew* and *The Martyrdom of St Matthew* in the church of S. Luigi dei Francesi date from *c*. 1600. They were notorious for their brutal and disturbing realism and were the first in a series of similarly powerful renderings of religious subjects Caravaggio produced before he had to leave Rome in 1606. Caravaggio's followers were numerous, both in Italy and abroad, but most tended to ape his style in superficial fashion. Valentin de Boulogne, a French painter was the most renowned and inspired of his imitators. His particular brand of verism concentrated on the low life of Rome, conjuring up a dark, desperate side of humanity, and his half-length, close-up pictures of rowdy, drunken characters earned him enormous success. Even the young Vouet was swept up by Valentin's somewhat commercial style, but it was going out of fashion by the time Poussin arrived, and ended with Le Valentin's sudden death in 1632.

Caravaggio's reaction to Mannerism in its decline was to bring painting down to earth. His was not the only response, however. As early as the end of the sixteenth century, a group of Bolognese artists had come up with a less radical alternative which sought to combine the quality of draughtsmanship found in Roman and Florentine painting and the use of colour typical of Venetian art. It was a vigorous style which eschewed extravagant artifice and excessive realism alike, and strove to achieve a more realistic and convincing approach. Annibale Carracci, who had been summoned to Rome in 1595 to help decorate the Palazzo Farnese, was the inspiration behind this group of painters, who were to be a dominant force in Rome during the first half of the seventeenth century – Guido Reni, Albani, Lanfranco and Domenichino. Each responded differently to what Rome had to offer, and two distinct schools of thought began to crystallize within the 'happy medium' approach, exemplified by the purist painting of Domenichino on one side, and by Lanfranco's great decorative works on the other. The seeds of both were clearly present in the work of the Carracci, and the two trends were to continue to develop side by side, though with varying degrees of success. Domenichino's restrained and somewhat cold classicist art harked back to Raphael, and reached its peak during the brief reign of the Bolognese Pope, Gregory XV (1621–3). By the time Poussin settled in Rome, it had given way to a monumental style in which movement and colour played a far more important part, and whose chief exponents were a group of artists working for the Barberini family, the most famous being Bernini and Pietro da Cortona, two names associated with the beginnings of the Baroque. The paintings and sculptures they produced were often colossal since, as Annibale Carracci's fresco cycle for the Farnese Gallery had shown, such works needed to match the scale of the churches and palaces for which they were intended. This was an art which conjured up triumph and jubilation, but called for a careful balance of different elements in order to create its effects. Its impact was overwhelming, and even the champions of classicism and of a more intellectual approach had

Attributed to Poussin,
View of Rome from Monte Mario,
pen and ink, grey wash
and black chalk,
18.1 x 24.7 cm (7 x 9⅗ in.).
Albertina, Vienna.

The Ponte Molle
brown wash over black chalk,
19.7 x 37.1 cm (7⅗ x 14½ in.).
Ecole des Beaux-Arts, Paris.

to concede defeat, at least for a time: Domenichino, for instance, revealed a leaning towards the Baroque when painting the pendentives of the dome in S. Andrea della Valle (1624–8), and Poussin, too, was to show similar signs, as we shall see.

Never before, perhaps, had there been such a burgeoning of different ideas about art. Poussin spent his first two years in Rome, 1624 and 1625, furthering his studies, observing and working from the great examples of art of all kinds which he now had the opportunity to see at first hand. He did drawings of classical bas-reliefs and made notes of the proportions of the statues in the major art collections. He drew from life in various studios. He tried his hand at sculpture, and made a 'few reliefs of little figures' in wax. He set about copying the paintings by Raphael and Giulio Romano in the Vatican with the same zest as he did Titian's three paintings for Alfonso d'Este: *Offering to Venus, Baccha-* 38 *nal of the Andrians* and *Bacchus and Ariadne* (1518–19). These had been brought from Ferrara, and had been on show in their new home, the Villa Aldobrandini, since 1621. Poussin worked assiduously at every aspect of his craft, concentrating equally on drawing and colour, but perhaps showing a preference at this stage for the warm tones found in Titian's painting, from Bellini to Veronese, and that of contemporary successors to that tradition like Johann Liss and Domenico Feti. He had a keen awareness of light and shade and of their effect on colour and form, and made studies wherever he could – in the middle of the city and in the countryside around it, in houses and in the streets, on terraces and among trees. He avidly read everything he could find on anatomy, geometry, optics and perspective, helped by his having access to the remarkably fine libraries, first of the Barberini family and later of Cassiano Dal Pozzo, and so was able to read, frequently in rare manuscripts, both classical and contemporary treatises on art. Initially, this helped him to think constructively about his own work, and later to express in his letters his own ideas about art. Apparent in all this is the energy with which Poussin applied himself to learning.

It is almost impossible to establish which of Poussin's pictures were the first to be painted in Rome. Those who have tried have encountered problems of chronology arising from an almost complete lack of documentary evidence for the period. Loménie de Brienne referred *c.* 1695 to the 'dryness' of his early manner. What does that mean? Art historians have variously seen *Dido and Aeneas* (Toledo) and *Echo and Narcissus* (Dresden) as combining for the first time in a coherent – albeit clumsy – whole all the different styles to which Poussin had been exposed in 1624 and 1625: a bit of Mannerism, a touch of Raphael, a general Venetian flavour, echoes of classical sculpture. However, there are good grounds for contesting the attribution of these two pictures to Poussin. The first incontrovertible examples of his work in Rome must be the three bread-and-butter battle pictures said to have been sold for only 7 crowns apiece: *The Battle of Joshua against the* cat. 25 *Amalechites* (Leningrad), *The Battle of Joshua against the Amorites* (Moscow) and *The* cat. 26 *Battle of Gideon against the Midianites* (Vatican). These pictures hark back to several of 37 Poussin's drawings for Marino, and so to his early career in Paris, and are part of a long, but by then finally declining, tradition of Roman art – from the reliefs on Trajan's Column to the paintings of the Cavaliere d'Arpino, and evident in the work of Raphael's two disciples, Giulio Romano and Caldara. In these pictures the treatment of the mass of straining figures is almost sculptural, and the stark horror of the scenes is emphasized by a dramatic use of light and shade, particularly in the Vatican picture with its night-time setting – probably a little later in date than the other two. Poussin's first commission from

The Battle of Gideon against the Midianites,
oil on canvas,
98 x 137 cm (38$^{1}/_{2}$ x 54 in.).
Vatican Museums.

Titian, *Bacchanal of the Andrians*,
oil on canvas,
175 x 193 cm (69 x 76 in.).
Prado, Madrid.

The Nurture of Bacchus (detail);
see p. 41.

Cardinal Barberini late in 1625, *The Capture of Jerusalem by Titus* (now lost), for which he was paid 61 crowns, probably belonged stylistically with this group of battle pictures. It has been associated with an engraving teeming with figures in front of a huge temple, but its ambitious composition suggests a date considerably later than that of the painting.

Poussin's obsession with the most extreme forms of movement went hand in hand with a taste for rich colour, which his stay in Venice and his familiarity with the Aldobrandini *Bacchanals* had done much to heighten. Poussin would first have made copies of Titian's paintings and made small clay figures of playful putti after them, rather like those produced by his friend Duquesnoy, representing Eros and Anteros. Poussin would use these impish cupids again and again. They first appear in *The Triumph of Ovid* (Galleria Corsini, Rome), an allegorical work painted in Marino's honour and stylistically very close to Poussin's early work in Paris. The general delight of the scene, the butterfly, the suspended heart and the arrows are all allusions to the poet's lines; 'Love was my master, by loving I learned to write poetry and sing of love.' Close in feel are the two lively, if somewhat pedantic, little tempera paintings of putti (formerly in the Chigi collection), examples of works incorporating elements derived both from classical art and from Titian. Poussin was experimenting, using the full depth of the picture or limiting himself to the flat foreground, introducing movement or retaining a static composition. *Cephalus and Aurora* (Hovingham Hall, Worsley Collection) shows all the signs of such uncertainty. Here, as in the drawings for Marino, Poussin demonstrates his sound knowledge of mythology, but is also slightly clinical in his approach. Against the backdrop of a landscape still shrouded in darkness, the various characters cluster together in two distinct groups – the two lovers on one side, and the Horae (Seasons) who have come to fetch Aurora on the other – with a large empty space in between. In this picture Poussin harks back to Ovid and Marino's reworking of his ideas. The themes which he explores here – the impossibility of love between gods and mortals, sleep, death and metamorphosis – also provided the inspiration for *Apollo and Daphne* (Munich), *Venus and Adonis* (Fort Worth, Texas) and *Venus and Adonis* (Caen). As before, there is a warm glow to these paintings emphasized by Poussin's use of highlights, but already there is a sense of the tragedy inherent in all separation. Poussin has been described as something of a romantic in his youth. Certainly he is moved by the contrast between the beauty of youth and cruel death, but he is already attempting to convey more than the agony of a particular moment. The river-gods who look on seem to meditate on the inevitable outcome.

There are times when the sheer joy of being wipes away all trace of melancholy in Poussin's work. This is particularly true of a group of pictures, highly reminiscent of Titian's profane 'poems' and probably all painted in 1626 or 1627, on the theme, taken from Ovid, of Bacchus's childhood on Mount Nysa. This was first and foremost an excuse for Poussin to paint groups of beautiful naked figures in a rustic setting. He produced at least three variations on the theme, the version in the National Gallery, London, with its little goat, being the simplest and most innocent. The two satyrs who lean over the infant god as he drinks and the pensive nymph behind them all reappear in the Louvre picture, with the addition of a bacchante lying naked on the ground with her head thrown back. This drunken abandon is absent in the Chantilly version, the most balanced and controlled of the three. Here the two nymphs seem to be musing on their charge's future, and the seriousness of their expression introduces a new element into the scene. By comparison, many of Poussin's paintings of similar mythological subjects seem to follow up

40

cat. 117; 40
cat. 161

cat. 123

38

successful ideas, now reworked with the primary aim of making money (the various pictures of nymphs and satyrs, for instance, in Kassel, Madrid and Moscow), or to be slightly
cat. 163 laboured attempts at allegory, like *Venus and Mercury* (now two fragments, in Dulwich Picture Gallery, and the Louvre) which conjures up an image of the arts as the focus of celestial love, an idea Poussin later developed in *The Inspiration of the Poet* (Louvre).

Although deeply influenced by Marino's *L'Adone* and Titian's *Bacchanals*, Poussin did not confine his attentions solely to painting mythological subjects and *c.* 1625 tried his hand at religious subjects. In 1625 the Flemish painter Daniel Seghers arrived in Rome from Antwerp and remained until 1627. Seghers was a member of the Society of Jesus, and had become famous for the posies and garlands of flowers he added to oval
42 pictures of religious subjects, often the work of other, major artists. The *Pietà* (Cherbourg) and *The Virgin and Child* (Brighton), both originally in Cassiano Dal Pozzo's collection, can be fairly accurately dated and so provide a much-needed point of reference during Poussin's early years in Rome. They are small, intimate pictures, light and fluid in their execution, in marked contrast to the studied precision of Seghers's flowers. Warm and cold tones are skilfully combined, and in the *Pietà* the Virgin's red dress stands out like a splash of blood amid pale muted colours. Poussin tackled the same subject in
cat. 79 another picture of similar date, *The Deposition from the Cross* (Leningrad), and again a lit-
42 tle later (?1628) in the moving *Lamentation over the Dead Christ* (Munich), in which the figure of Christ harks back to that of Adonis in the Caen version of the Venus and Adonis myth. Beyond the lamenting women sits St John, his hands between his knees, quite alone in the grief which he seems to shout out to the heavens.

43 Poussin's first great work, *The Death of Germanicus* (Minneapolis), dates from 1627. Commissioned by Cardinal Francesco Barberini in the autumn of 1626 on his return to Rome from his diplomatic missions in France and Spain, it represents Poussin's first foray into Roman history since *The Capture of Jerusalem by Titus*. Its subject matter, however, has nothing to do with battles or military victories. In Book II of his *Annals* Tacitus describes how the Emperor Tiberius's jealousy towards his adopted son Germanicus – so-called because of his victories on the Rhine – leads him to have him poisoned by Piso, then governor of Syria. Poussin depicts the dying Germanicus commending his family to his comrades-in-arms and asking them to avenge his death. Poussin's treatment of this moving story has an extraordinary intensity, for he was able to derive inspiration from examples of both classical and contemporary art when working on this picture, and could refer as readily to the so-called Meleager sarcophagus and Timanthes's *Sacrifice of Iphigenia* as he could to the tapestry designed by Rubens depicting *The Death of Constantine* presented to Cardinal Barberini by the King of France. Two studies (London, British Museum, and Chantilly, Musée Condé) reveal Poussin working towards as simple and as striking a composition as possible. The result is suggestive of a bas-relief: closely packed figures are grouped around the bed; their movements are all carefully orchestrated to lead the eye back to Germanicus, seen against dark drapery

The novelty of the composition lies no doubt in the calculated contrast between the two groups – Germanicus's comrades-in-arms on the left, and the women and children at the head of the bed. On one side a series of soldiers are seen striking a complex sequence of heroic attitudes designed to articulate, in a single image, feelings ranging from despair to a resolve for revenge, as well as more or less generalized grief. The seated figures on the other side convey a sense of calm, almost of abstraction. Linking the two is the dying

page 48 ▷

Rubens, *The Death of Constantine*,
tapestry.
Mobilier National, Paris.

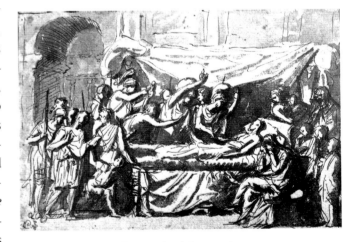

The Death of Germanicus,
pen and brown wash,
17.5 x 24 cm (7 x 9½ in.).
Musée Condé, Chantilly.

Cephalus and Aurora,
oil on canvas,
79 x 152 cm (31 x 60 in.).
Worsley Collection,
Hovingham Hall,
Yorkshire.

Venus and Adonis,
oil on canvas,
98.5 x 134.6 cm (38³/₄ x 53 in.).
Kimbell Art Museum,
Fort Worth, Texas.

The Nurture of Bacchus,
oil on canvas,
97 x 136 cm (38¹/₄ x 53¹/₂ in.).
Louvre, Paris.

(Far left) *Virgin and Child*,
oil on canvas,
58.5 x 49.5 cm (23 x 19$\frac{1}{2}$ in.).
Preston Manor, Brighton.

(Left) *Pietà*,
oil on canvas,
49 x 40 cm (19$\frac{1}{2}$ x 15$\frac{3}{4}$ in.).
Musée Thomas Henry,
Cherbourg.

Lamentation over the Dead Christ,
oil on canvas,
102.7 x 146 cm (40$\frac{1}{2}$ x 57$\frac{1}{2}$ in.).
Alte Pinakothek, Munich.

The Death of Germanicus,
oil on canvas,
148 x 198 cm (58¼ x 78 in.).
Minneapolis Institute of Arts.

The Triumph of Flora,
oil on canvas,
165 x 241 cm (65 x 95 in.).
Louvre, Paris.

Pietro da Cortona,
The Triumph of Bacchus,
oil on canvas,
144 x 207 cm (56³/₄ x 81¹/₂ in.).
Museo Capitolino, Rome.

Diana and Endymion,
oil on canvas,
122 x 169 cm (48 x 66½ in.).
Detroit Institute of Arts.

*The Virgin Appearing to
St James*,
oil on canvas,
301 x 242 cm (118¹/₂ x 95¹/₄ in.).
Louvre, Paris.

The Martyrdom of St Erasmus,
oil on canvas,
320 x 186 cm (126 x 73¼ in.).
Vatican Museums.

general, his last words scarcely spoken, his hand, pointing towards his family, already sinking onto the sheet. A century and a half later, David clearly had this picture in mind when painting *The Oath of the Horatii*, which has a comparable tension. The severe lines of the background architecture and the strength of the colour add to the overall vigour of Poussin's pithy, measured style which is so very appropriate to the subject. *The Death of Germanicus*, like Rubens's *Life of Marie de Médicis*, but in a different way and using different means, contrived to inject a heroic quality into history painting – the hero being cast as the victim of unjust persecution rather than as a champion showered with glory. It was a significant inversion. *The Death of Germanicus* was the quintessential modern *exemplum virtutis* of the kind later so beloved of Neo-Classicists. In looking to ancient history to provide the material for a morally edifying situation, and in successfully using a very formal structure to convey the most basic of human emotions, Poussin was opening up a whole new world in painting. For over three centuries the picture has been copied, imitated and trumpeted, it is not surprising if today it has lost something of its original impact. Hence we have to rediscover its extraordinary expressive power.

Poussin's success with *The Death of Germanicus* immediately brought him new and often prestigious commissions. In the pictures which can be assigned to 1627–8, Poussin is clearly developing existing ideas. The essential structure of *The Sacrifice of Noah* (Tatton Park), for instance, is in the manner of Raphael, but the style is Roman Baroque. Familiar elements creep into pictures of mythological and lyrical subjects like *Mars and Venus* (Boston) and more particularly *Diana and Endymion* (Detroit): the great dark curtain which Night draws towards Diana as Aurora comes into view is reminiscent of the one in *The Death of Germanicus*. There are still doubts about the precise subject matter of *Diana and Endymion*, but it was perhaps inspired by a poem by Gombaud published in 1624, in which the goddess appears before her bedazzled admirer one last time and grants him his wish to take his place among the stars. The light intensifies the rich colours of this meditation on the immortality which love brings. This ethereal glow is in contrast with *The Triumph of Flora* (Louvre), with its skilfully orchestrated procession of legendary figures, all turned into flowers according to Ovid; this work is closer to the tradition of the Carracci frescoes in the Farnese Gallery. A stormy light lends the figures a strongly sculptural quality. The composition is essentially horizontal, like a relief. Yet again, Poussin is attempting a marriage of classical art and Titian's *Bacchanals*, but he also seems to be adapting to a new and emergent convention. The profusion of figures, the balance achieved between the static and the dynamic elements and the luxuriant feel of the whole composition all betray a new approach. The picture, possibly painted for Cardinal Sacchetti, was perhaps intended to be hung in his collection next to the *The Triumph of Bacchus* by Pietro da Cortona (now Rome, Museo Capitolino), a fine example of Venetian-inspired painting of the 1620s. Pietro da Cortona and Bernini were to dominate the group of artists working for the Barberini family, and were to be the greatest exponents of the new vigorous, triumphal style of decoration.

Our image of Poussin has long been one of an artist with firmly entrenched ideas. It is difficult, therefore, to imagine him being uncertain, or flexible, enough to respond to new developments in art taking place in Rome under Urban VIII. The two altarpieces which he painted between 1628 and 1630, *The Martyrdom of St Erasmus* and *The Virgin Appearing to St James*, however, both show him to be completely in tune, temporarily at least, with the latest ideas. Even the normally restrained Domenichino adopted this mon-

cat. 3

cat. 148
45

44

47, 46

umental style when he painted the pendentives of the dome of S. Andrea della Valle (1624–8). He was competing with Lanfranco, who filled the dome itself with a 'glory' in the best Correggio tradition. Artists found themselves called upon, at this remarkable stage in the history of Roman painting, to tackle large surface areas – churches and palaces, ceilings and domes, frescoes and altarpieces – and to develop a correspondingly monumental style for subject matter worthy of the capital of the Christian world.

47 In February 1628, at the instigation of Cassiano Dal Pozzo and perhaps even of Bernini himself, Cardinal Barberini commissioned Poussin to paint an altarpiece for St Peter's, as part of the interior scheme. *The Martyrdom of St Erasmus* (Vatican) provided Poussin with a chance to square up to his better-known contemporaries. Poussin responded to the constraints imposed on him by the required size and shape – well over 3 m (10 ft) high, but relatively narrow – by producing a composition in which serried ranks of figures create a strong vertical emphasis. The subject matter, one of those gory martyr-dom scenes the Counter-Reformation was so fond of, presented another constraint. St Erasmus had become confused with St Elmo, patron saint of sailors, and as a result was commonly believed to have been eviscerated for refusing to sacrifice to idols, and to have had his entrails wound on to a windlass. In Poussin's painting, however, the figure flung down in the foreground has the indestructible beauty of an antique marble statue, and an expression of pain, certainly, but also of great nobility. Poussin is interested not only in the victim, but in the reactions of all the other people involved: the high priest in charge of proceedings, the actual perpetrators of the torture who appear either completely unconcerned or awe-struck, the mounted soldier pointing out the scene, and of course the inevitable cherubs bearing the martyr's crown. In the sweeping diagonals underlying its composition, the powerful, sculptural handling of form, and the use of broad brush-strokes, this picture calls to mind Pietro da Cortona or Bernini. There is no unnecessary commotion, however: the impact of the picture derives not from the horror or the drama of the scene, but from the steadfastness, the *constantia*, displayed by the martyred bishop. Poussin's work clearly found favour, for he was paid 300 crowns, and another 100 crowns as a bonus in September 1629. Despite the criticism it provoked from Guido Reni's supporters, the picture was an unequivocal success. For a long time it was the only work by Poussin on public display in Rome.

46 *The Martyrdom of St Erasmus* was followed immediately by *The Appearance of the Virgin to St James*, another altarpiece, but less strikingly vertical in format. It was painted as a result of a commission from Flanders or Spain for the church dedicated to the saint in Valenciennes, then in the Spanish Netherlands. The subject of the picture was not one to which Poussin's talents were obviously suited. The Virgin of Saragossa – the *Madona del Pilar* as she is known in Spanish – appears, seated on a column, to St James the Great and his companions, who display their amazement and awe in a variety of gestures. Although less taut in construction than the altarpiece for St Peter's, this is nevertheless a picture of considerable power and eloquence. The composition is compressed, and little short of chaotic, there are no real indications of depth, and the different levels are poorly differentiated. By contrast, the modelling of the figures is strong, and the colours are well judged: the Madonna's imperious gesture, the rough, slightly swollen faces, and the shafts of light are all perfectly set off by the blend of warm browns and reds interspersed with dashes of blue drapery. There is even a hint of Caravaggio in the soles of the feet of the otherwise firmly Raphaelesque figure prostrate in the foreground.

Rinaldo and Armida,
oil on canvas,
80 x 107 cm (31½ x 42 in.).
Dulwich Picture Gallery, London.

The Mystic Marriage of St Catherine,
oil on wood,
127 x 167.5 cm (50 x 66 in.).
National Gallery of Scotland, Edinburgh.

These two paintings are, in a sense, Poussin's most brutal works. Here he was exploring an avenue which he did not pursue further. A number of other, smaller pictures also show him experimenting with a monumental style, filling his canvases with large-scale figures, and these should be considered in this context: *Rinaldo and Armida* (Dulwich Picture Gallery), *The Holy Family with St John the Baptist* (Karlsruhe), the first version of *The Arcadian Shepherds: 'Et in Arcadia Ego'* (Chatsworth) and *The Return from Egypt* (Dulwich Picture Gallery). Attributed to Poussin but less certainly by his hand are *Moses Sweetening the Bitter Waters of Marah* (Baltimore) and especially *The Assumption of the Virgin* (Washington), a delightful but nevertheless disciplined picture which, with its blues, pinks and pale greys, betrays a lightness of tone and delicacy of subject matter hardly consistent, it must be said, with the severity and drama we expect of Poussin. There have been doubts, too, over the attribution of *The Mystic Marriage of St Catherine* (Edinburgh), a large composition remarkable not only for being painted on wood, but also for its intense yet subtle colours, and for the tender, sprightly mood it conveys. Some art historians have preferred to attribute this work to Charles Mellin, a painter from Lorraine who had arrived in Rome in 1622 and was thus a direct rival to Poussin.

Mellin was involved in an affair in June or July 1630 which was to have a direct bearing on Poussin's career. The members of the Confrérie de Saint Louis had decided to commission decorations for the chapel of the Virgin in the French church in Rome, S. Luigi dei Francesi. Three painters were short-listed: Lanfranco, Poussin, and one 'Carolus Lotharingus', i.e. Mellin. Domenichino and the Cavaliere d'Arpino were asked to make the final choice, and they opted for the painter from Lorraine, who subsequently executed three frescoes in 1631–3 depicting *The Visitation*, *The Annunciation* and *The Coronation of the Virgin*. This setback gave Poussin pause for thought. From then on he steered clear both of official commissions and of decoration on a grand scale, and it required all the authority and insistence of Louis XIII and Richelieu to persuade him to undertake the decoration of the Grande Galerie in the Louvre. He chose to concentrate instead on easel-paintings for private individuals, people who appreciated the precision and poetry he strove to achieve. Henceforward, Poussin's private life was to conform more closely to his rigorous concept of art and his slow but steady rhythm of working, and he became more regular and rather more retiring in his habits. His marriage in 1630 to Anne-Marie Dughet doubtless had something to do with these changes in his lifestyle. Poussin was by then nearly forty, and the next few years, from 1630 to 1632, brought him considerable stability on all fronts: the family settled, along with Poussin's brother-in-law Gaspard Dughet, in the Via del Babuino; Poussin was elected to the Academy of St Luke in 1631; Cassiano Dal Pozzo became his chief patron and sponsor; and his clientèle broadened to embrace a more cosmopolitan mixture of merchants and adventurers, Spaniards and Italians. Poussin was by then an established figure in Rome and could see his way forward. It was time for him to get a new grip on his art and to revert to the models he had temporarily abandoned.

The most important of these was undoubtedly Domenichino. In outlook and character, this well-read artist and sometime architect and musician had much in common with Poussin: touchy and private by nature, slow-working, a thinker and a loner by inclination. He was part of the Bolognese circle in Rome headed by the humanist prelate Giovanni-Battista Agucchi (1570–1632), who held the office of Segretario dei Brevi under Gregory XV and was the author of a treatise on painting inspired by Leonardo da Vinci,

Charles Mellin, *The Annunciation*, fresco.
S. Luigi dei Francesi, Rome.

Charles Mellin, *The Annunciation*, pen and black ink and brown wash, 20 x 23.5 cm (8 x 9¼ in.). Albertina, Vienna.

(Above left) Domenichino,
The Scourging of St Andrew,
fresco.
S. Gregorio Magno, Rome.

(Above right) Guido Reni,
St Andrew being led to Martyrdom,
fresco.
S. Gregorio Magno, Rome.

which remained largely unpublished. While his friend Annibale Carracci wanted to combine the precision and truth of drawing with the sensuous quality of colour, Agucchi held that the *disegno* was all-important and laid stress on the expression of emotions or *affetti*. Domenichino took the second course, and the lucidity of expression and clarity of composition he achieved encapsulate the classical ideals propounded by Agucchi and subsequently promulgated by Bellori. Poussin was influenced chiefly by the calm, measured quality of Domenichino's first great Roman pictures: *The Last Communion of St Jerome* for St Peter's (1614), the frescoes depicting *Scenes from the Life of St Cecilia* in S. Luigi dei Francesi (1615), and especially *The Scourging of St Andrew* in S. Gregorio Magno (1609). According to Bellori, Poussin was almost alone in preferring Domenichino's picture to Guido Reni's *St Andrew being led to Martyrdom* on the opposite wall, and in recommending it as an object of study. Domenichino's rigorous simplicity of style was a far cry from the exuberance and *dolcezza* of Reni. It was the result of long thought, and cogency and exactness were its keynotes: Domenichino used architecture to establish a definite perspective and lend clarity to the whole composition, making the different planes within it quite distinct, and treated human figures with similar precision. Domenichino's influence is visible in much of Poussin's mature work: in his expressive use of gesture, in the way he conveys emotion through facial detail, in his fondness for painting heroic subjects in tightly structured landscapes.

Poussin was as yet still absorbing the basic tenets of Domenichino's art: trying new figure groupings, creating a sense of several distinct planes, conveying the meaning of a subject by means of different expressions and gestures. His early efforts culminated in a work of extraordinary intensity, *The Massacre of the Innocents* (Chantilly), an unusual and violent picture intended in all probability for Vincenzo Giustiniani. The date of the picture is a matter of dispute. Jacques Thuillier maintains that it was 'Poussin's first major bid to make a name for himself in Rome with a large-scale canvas', and suggests *c*. 1625–6. A date *c*. 1630 seems far more likely, however. In this picture there are echoes not only of

55

the famous engraving after Raphael by Marcantonio (d. 1534), also of Guido Reni's painting of the same subject dating from *c*. 1611 (Bologna) and praised by Marino in his *Galleria*. Poussin's painting is less complex in terms of its composition, but the economy with
which he conveys his subject is almost obsessive. He makes use of great contrasts in scale,
not part of his normal stock-in-trade. A group of figures brilliantly lit against an austere
architectural background is presented in close-up as if seen from below, *da sotto in sù*,
giving them a sculptural quality. In counterpoint to them, and seen in profile, is the distraught figure of a woman running, her dead child under her arm. Just discernible in the
distance, and at a lower level than the tragic scene on the podium on which attention is focused, are the partial outlines of yet more women. Here, rather than portraying an entire
episode, Poussin leaves us to guess at the whole by choosing one small incident; as the
soldier crushes the child with his foot, a tiny spurt of blood issues from its mouth, while
the mother, held by her hair, screams, her face resembling a gaping tragic mask. The picture combines Giulio Romano's version of classical form, Guido Reni's sense of pathos
and a bluntness almost worthy of Caravaggio. Poussin was still feeling his way: planes, volumes and light were his raw material, and he was manipulating them in an attempt to establish a basic and harmonious structure for his thoughts.

The Massacre of the Innocents,
pen and brown ink with touches of wash,
14.6 x 16.9 cm (5³/₄ x 6¹/₂ in.).
Musée des Beaux-Arts, Lille.
For the painting, see p. 55.

The Inspiration of the Poet,
oil on canvas,
184 x 214 cm (72$\frac{1}{2}$ x 84$\frac{1}{4}$ in.).
Louvre, Paris.

The Massacre of the Innocents,
oil on canvas,
147 x 171 cm (58 x 67½ in.).
Musée Condé, Chantilly.

Andrea Sacchi, *Divine Wisdom*,
ceiling painting.
Palazzo Barberini, Rome.

A year before Agucchi died, Domenichino had set off for Naples, where he had been asked to decorate the Treasury chapel in the Cathedral – a commission which brought him nothing but trouble. His departure coincided with Poussin's first forays into classicism. Artistic thinking was changing fast in Rome. A number of artists were beginning to reject the ornate whirls of the Baroque in favour of what Denis Mahon has called a 'purified' form with simpler compositions and calmer, more generous lines. The principal advocates of this reform were members of Poussin's own immediate circle, the sculptor François Duquesnoy and the painter Andrea Sacchi. Duquesnoy's *St Susanna* (Sta Maria di Loreto) and Sacchi's *Divine Wisdom*, painted on a ceiling in the Palazzo Barberini, both of which date from the period 1630–3, each represent something of a manifesto. So too does *The Inspiration of the Poet* (Louvre), also painted in the early 1630s. Poussin had very recently treated the same subject in a lyrical and sensual vein in a smaller picture (Hanover), in which the scene is one of glorious poetic intoxication, as Apollo leans over to the young poet kneeling before him, awaiting initiation, and proffers a golden cup filled with water from the spring of Hippocrene. The painting, upright in format, was one

57

54

of the first in a series of *Bacchanals* in the Venetian tradition. A sense of calm prevails in the large painting in the Louvre, with its strictly balanced composition achieved only after a great deal of reworking. The picture, in landscape format, is dominated by the vertical lines of the three imposing figures: the Muse, Apollo and the poet. From his stately seated position, his arm resting on his lyre, the god dictates to the poet, now seen standing and portrayed as his servant. The picture combines two episodes: the poet is being crowned as he calls for inspiration. Poussin is looking to classical art and to Raphael: Euterpe has given way to Calliope, lyric poetry to epic, and almost, one might say, Dionysus to Apollo. By looking at this painting in the context of the intellectual concepts prevalent in Rome under Urban VIII of the Pope as poet, and the Pope as Apollo, Marc Fumaroli has thrown considerable light on the picture and on the ideas it advances. The painting clearly conforms in some ways to the kind of images of the poetic process put forward by Renaissance academies and to traditional allegorical representations of Mount Parnassus. Poussin was, however, attempting a redefinition of poetry that would accommodate both Marino's free-thinking approach and the expurgated form of art commended by the Pope and by other advocates of a kind of 'Christian Neo-Classicism'. There could be no such happy medium in reality: the Pope had just put Marino's *L'Adone* on the index, leaving the field open for his own great work, the *Poemata*, published in 1631. *The Inspiration of the Poet* is not just about poetry. It stresses for the first time the connection between poetry, music and painting, and goes further still. Poussin's picture demonstrates the supremacy of painting: unlike the other two arts, painting is not subject to the march of time or constantly superseded by a stream of new sounds or words – it can evoke harmonies which are by their very nature impossible to articulate.

Poussin produced two masterpieces in quick succession as proof of the great power of painting: *The Plague of Ashdod*, now in the Louvre, and *The Empire of Flora*, now in Dresden. Both pictures were bought from the painter in 1631 for 100 crowns each by an odd character – half-merchant, half-swindler – named Fabrizio Valguarnera. In that year Valguarnera was involved in a sensational court case in which Poussin was called to give evidence. The two pictures could not be more different in terms of their subject matter and their source of inspiration, but both reflect a new rigorousness of style.

The Plague of Ashdod was begun in 1630 and delivered to Valguarnera early in 1631, at which point Poussin reworked it. The subject is taken from the first Book of Samuel (V, 1–6): the Philistines have taken the Ark of the Covenant from the Israelites and placed it in the temple of Dagon; the idol falls down on its face in front of the Ark and the people are afflicted with the plague. The choice of subject was far from gratuitous, and was in fact acutely topical (Milan was devastated by the plague in 1629) and had personal associations for Poussin, who had recently recovered from a serious illness. Yves Bonnefoy sees the picture as 'the beginning of modern painting'. It is strikingly new in its composition, and it is from the tension in its structure that the extremely disturbing quality of the picture emanates, and that we get a sense of the intensity of Poussin's own feelings on the subject. The architectural setting is highly ornate, but its lines are unyielding. Caught within them is an orchestrated mass of figures, singly or in groups. The influence of Raphael is clear, and especially of *The Phrygian Plague* engraved by Marcantonio. This is particularly true of the group of men in the foreground trying to turn a child away from his mother's dead body and holding their noses because of the stench. Beyond them mass the Philistines who dare not venture into the temple where their fallen idol lies.

59, 63

François Duquesnoy,
St Susanna,
marble.
Sta Maria di Loreto, Rome.

The Plague of Ashdod,
oil on canvas,
148 x 198 cm (58$\frac{1}{4}$ x 78 in.),
with detail opposite.
Louvre, Paris.

Their agitation is clear: should they return the Ark in order to appease the wrath of the heavens? All around is the town, with only the occasional figure to be seen flitting about on some grisly errand or giving vent to grief. Poussin takes the ideas he explored in *The Death of Germanicus* and *The Massacre of the Innocents* further here, to create his first truly dramatic picture. He succeeds in animating numerous figures in a single urban setting and in displaying their different reactions to the disaster that has befallen them. Poussin's palette is more muted, but as intense as ever, and here and there touches of bright colour and flashes of the East are seen in the occasional gaily striped costumes. A powerful light illuminates the scene from the left, cleverly throwing every figure into sharp relief. With its broken columns, its shattered statue, its streets strewn with corpses and crawling with rats, and its empty vistas bordered with buildings, *The Plague of Ashdod* is a 'metaphysical' picture in the De Chirico sense, and has lost none of its magnetic power. It was both copied and imitated, notably by Mellin (in a drawing in the Louvre, *c.* 1640), Pierre Mignard and Michael Sweerts.

The Empire of Flora has none of the cruel drama of *The Plague of Ashdod*: in this elegiac picture death brings rather beauty and light. Poussin turned once again to Marino for inspiration, finding it particularly in a poem from the *Rime* (1602) and in *Sampogna* (1620). Poussin's picture shows Ovid's legendary heroes and heroines in an idyllic, ethereal setting after their transformation into flowers. With a pergola reminiscent of Primaticcio and Fontainebleau behind her, the goddess of spring showers the recumbent forms of Ajax, Clytie, Narcissus, Hyacinth, Adonis and Smilax around her with riches, while Apollo drives his chariot across the sky. This is a complex picture, perhaps more so than *The Plague of Ashdod*, one which succeeds in juxtaposing radically different characters and events and in creating a fluent and coherent whole. As raw material, the transience of youth and the unhappiness of love do not bode well, and the picture could well have been thoroughly melancholy. The emphasis, however, is on metamorphosis and birth, and this is reflected in the freshness and variety of the colour. The presence of Apollo, Flora and Priapus is a powerful indication of the fecundity of nature, which in this picture is still the rarified garden of literature, where fountains play amid statues and each flower tells its own story. Here sensuality is eliminated thanks to the refining influence of the alexandrine. The legend of Echo and Narcissus, for instance, is encapsulated in the symbolic vase of water in which Narcissus studies his reflection as the nymph looks sadly on. It was a story which Poussin was to treat more movingly in a painting (now in the Louvre) prefiguring Corot and Balthus in its use of subdued pinks and greys.

Control and restraint were becoming the keynotes of Poussin's work in a reaction to the ornate excesses of the Baroque, as a number of less well-known paintings testify. Among these is *The Triumph of David*, in the Prado, similar in its use of colour to *Echo and Narcissus* in the Louvre. Poussin's adolescent David does not conform to our image of a victor, but sits gazing abstractedly at Goliath's severed head and at the huge armour which would dwarf him. Even the classic figure of Victory who crowns him seems to be reflecting on the burden glory brings, and the putti around the harp are reduced to silence. Poussin introduces subtle greys and browns to disturb the harmony he creates elsewhere by counterbalancing warm ochres and pinks and cool blue. The pale tints of the faces and bodies mirror the soft reflections of the armour, drawing them inexorably together. Like *Diana and Endymion* (Detroit) and *Tancred and Erminia* (Leningrad), this picture reveals a new gravity, even though it continues to have the romantic cast first

62

cat. 138

evident in Poussin's early *poesie* in the manner of Titian. The much more cerebral version
65 of *The Triumph of David* (Dulwich Picture Gallery) was completed in 1632 or 1633, but
only, as we now know from X-ray examination, after considerable reworking. It was a
tribute to Domenichino, and in particular to his fresco *The Scourging of St Andrew* in
S. Gregorio Magno. The powerful verticals and horizontals of the architectural setting
emphasize the boldness of the composition. The painting is remarkable for its clarity and
precision: each level within it is quite distinct, each group of figures clearly defined, every
individual gesture and expression finely judged, the pace of the procession perfectly
pitched. It does, however, have the feel of a technical exercise, and this coupled with the
length of time it took to produce, the number of reworkings and the uncharacteristic use
of paint, particularly in the dress, has given rise to an alternative attribution, once again to
Mellin. This version of *The Triumph of David* seems entirely consonant, however, with
the way Poussin's ideas were developing and with his gradual conversion to classicism.

Poussin's chief model from then on was Raphael. Two pictures reveal his influence
particularly clearly: *Apollo and the Muses* (*Parnassus*), in the Prado, which can be dated
68 c. 1632, and *The Adoration of the Magi* of 1633, in Dresden, which is exceptional in being
67 both signed and dated. *Apollo and the Muses* is a variation on Raphael's famous fresco
(Vatican, Stanza della Segnatura). Poussin adopts the same horseshoe composition but in
a gentle landscape setting punctuated by trees which stand out against a blue sky. The original fresco was painted around a door-opening; now this centre foreground is taken up
by the recumbent form of the nymph of the fountain of Castalia and a pair of putti drawing
water from the spring. These largely horizontal elements give a sense of movement to a
composition otherwise dominated by emphatic verticals. The content of the picture, too,
is enriched by other figures. Poets and muses are assembled to see a poet crowned by
Apollo. Some art historians maintain that the kneeling laureate is none other than
Marino, but surely a much more likely identification is with the poet looking out from the
extreme left of the picture. Recent cleaning has brought out a delicate but rich range of
colours reminiscent of *The Empire of Flora*. The picture is certainly formal, but it is one of
Poussin's most brilliant, revealing his ability to adapt his composition and his palette to
suit his subject. *The Adoration of the Magi* seems rather more severe by comparison.
Poussin bases his composition on a painting in one of the Logge di Raffaello, but he
ensures that the impact of his picture will be quite different by varying the ways in which
the kings and their followers respond to the Saviour's birth, ranging from astonishment
and awe to silence and humility. The figures seen in profile in the foreground form a
complex network, linked by the angles of their bodies and by their gestures. The classical
ruin on the left and the distant vista on the right give the picture a spacious feel. *The Adoration of the Shepherds* (London, National Gallery) is a variation on the same theme.
Upright in format, it is generally more decorative and conjures up a much narrower
range of attitudes. The architectural setting establishes a framework for the whole pic-
66 ture, two-thirds of the composition being taken up with a meticulous arrangement of its
perpendiculars and obliques, as well as the grouping of the five cherubs hovering above
– that too is carefully considered.

The time had come for Poussin to make a choice. Rome was being conquered by the
new 'florid' Baroque style. Pietro da Cortona was at the height of his career, and was the
'prince' of the Academy of St Luke from 1634 to 1638. In 1636 he started work on a huge
ceiling painting, full of illusionist effects and teeming with figures, in the Palazzo Barbe-

page 69 ▷

Pietro da Cortona,
The Triumph of Divine Providence,
fresco.
Palazzo Barberini, Rome.

61

Echo and Narcissus,
oil on canvas,
74 x 100 cm (29 x 39^1/$_2$ in.).
Louvre, Paris.

The Triumph of David,
oil on canvas,
100 x 130 cm (39^1/$_2$ x 51 in.).
Prado, Madrid.
See also p. 65.

The Empire of Flora,
oil on canvas,
131 x 181 cm (51$\frac{1}{2}$ x 71$\frac{1}{4}$ in.).
Staatliche Kunstsammlungen, Dresden.

The Triumph of David,
oil on canvas,
117 x 146 cm (46 x 57$\frac{1}{2}$ in.);
with detail opposite.
Dulwich Picture Gallery, London.

The Adoration of the Shepherds,
oil on canvas,
98 x 74 cm (38^1/$_2$ x 29 in.).
National Gallery, London.

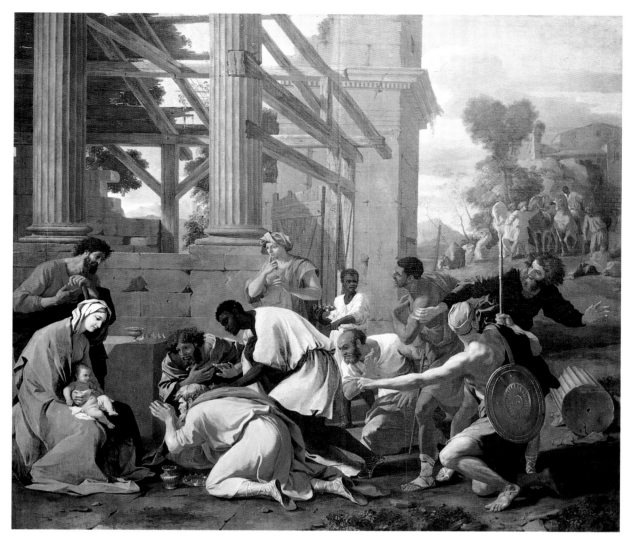

The Adoration of the Magi,
oil on canvas,
161 x 182 cm (63$^1/_2$ x 71$^1/_2$ in.).
Staatliche Kunstsammlungen, Dresden.

Raphael,
The Adoration of the Magi,
fresco.
Logge di Raffaelo, Vatican.

Apollo and the Muses (Parnassus),
oil on canvas,
145 x 197 cm (57 x 77½ in.).
Prado, Madrid.

Raphael,
Parnassus,
fresco.
Stanza della Segnatura, Vatican.

rini: *The Triumph of Divine Providence*. In pledging his rare genius to the service of his important patrons, Pietro da Cortona was opening the door to two centuries of celebratory painting: fine artists from Lebrun to Tiepolo would apply their skills to exalting the great in paintings which transported them out of their true environment and on to a god-like plane. It was a trend which seemed irresistible. Dissenting voices were making themselves heard in Rome as early as 1634, however. Following his troubles in Naples, Domenichino was now back, somewhat wiser for the experience. A heated debate had begun at the Academy between Pietro da Cortona and Sacchi, who championed two rapidly diverging approaches to art. The former was accused of violating the laws of verisimilitude by including so many figures in his paintings and by depicting such exaggerated forms of movement. Sacchi, on the other hand, backed by the little circle around Angeloni who promoted Agucchi's views, were all for simplicity, and for a concentrated effect. The classicist doctrine was undergoing a 'crystallization', as Denis Mahon puts it, even though it had not yet been fully formulated, and would not be so until the publication of two treatises: Dufresnoy's poem *De Arte Graphica* begun in 1640 and finished in 1646; and *L'Idea del Pittore* by Bellori, a zealous admirer of Domenichino and a friend of Poussin's, which appeared only in 1664.

It would be an over-simplification to think of Poussin as an artist who simply followed the latest trend. As always, his response to the current debate was individual and complex. In common with other members of the little coterie that had grown up around Domenichino and Sacchi, he wanted nothing more to do with huge compositions, towering decorative paintings or massive altarpieces. As far as he was concerned, there was no need for painting to be so overblown, and it certainly did not suit his own thoughtful approach. Although he confined himself almost exclusively from then to working on small- or medium-sized canvases, he did not abandon prolixity quite so quickly. The controversy raging in the Academy centred on the optimum number of figures in any picture. Sacchi believed that there should only be a few, as he had recently demonstrated in his ceiling painting of *Divine Wisdom*. However, Poussin's own approach in this period, 1633–5, depends on there being a large number. The scope this offers stimulates him to develop his artistic vocabulary as he strives to find a different stance, gesture and expression for each individual and tackles ambitious scenes, each calling for a particular rhythm of its own. In his hands biblical and classical subjects acquire a new resonance – *The Crossing of the Red Sea* (Melbourne), painted for Amadeo Dal Pozzo, and its pendant, *The Adoration of the Golden Calf* (London), for instance, or *Moses Striking the Rock* (Edinburgh), commissioned by a Parisian art-lover called Melchior Gillier. All three throng with people receding in long winding lines into the background, and all have a common aim: using a carefully chosen moment in a particular episode as their vehicle. Whatever the particular focal point of each scene – a display of divine providence or the lure of a false idol – the variety of response it provokes is what counts. In order to achieve his aim, Poussin places people of all kinds and ages, and from all walks of life, in a staged situation involving the human and the divine. As a result, we have to look at the pictures in a different way, reading them as it were, from one figure to the next, so as to grasp their full import. Poussin has brought about a spectacular and radical change the seeds of which were sown in the orchestrated and morbid pathos of *The Plague of Ashdod*. From now on, nothing will be obvious – it is up to the viewer to decipher the content and to bring an intelligent eye to bear on it. In these paintings there is something arrested, and

The Adoration of the Golden Calf,
oil on canvas,
154 x 214 cm (60$\frac{1}{2}$ x 84$\frac{1}{4}$ in.).
National Gallery, London.

The Crossing of the Red Sea,
oil on canvas,
154 x 210 cm (60$\frac{1}{2}$ x 82$\frac{1}{2}$ in.).
National Gallery of Victoria, Melbourne.

not immediately accessible, about even the broad movements, different as they are in each case; thus, the figures surrounding the Golden Calf, reminiscent of Mantegna and Giulio Romano, conjure up the idea of dance. Here, Poussin is not interested in creating the illusion of movement, but in seeking to fuse poses, patterns and gestures into a coherent whole.

72

The same is true of the first version of *The Rape of the Sabine Women* (New York), an astounding drawing together of straining forms into a single paroxysm of anguish, and

cat. 186

The Saving of the Young Pyrrhus (Louvre), which – thanks to the recent rediscovery of the details of the payment made for it – can now be dated to 1634. A garland of figures vividly evokes the shifts and turns in Plutarch's account: the initial flight and subsequent rearguard action, the terror and despair this inspires, the spirited resistance of the fugitives, and the ultimate saving of the child. Poussin was beginning to take the greatest care in choosing the precise moment in an event he will depict. The supreme moment in tragedy comes, as dramatists like Corneille were beginning to understand, at the point when everything hangs in the balance, and past and future are held in check in a present which is turbulent and uncertain. The famous 'rule' of the three unities of time, place and action does not seem inhibiting when considered in this light; on the contrary, it allows for maximum concentration of emotion.

Poussin's precise way of working was unsuited to large-scale pieces which need to be seen as a whole rather than in detail. Decorative painting on a grand scale must make its point emphatically and needs to dazzle the eye with its richness and the brilliance of the illusion it creates. Poussin, like Domenichino, had tried his hand – and would do so again – at producing such pictures which relied on a number of very calculated elements to be effective at a distance. For him, the point of art was to communicate a message, and painting demanded as much mental effort on the part of the viewer as it did from the artist. Not surprisingly, therefore, he preferred to work within smaller dimensions – canvases about 2 m (6 ft) across and 1.50 m (4 ft 6 in.) high – which could easily accommodate as many figures as the subject required. In the 1630s Poussin was clearly getting to grips with this question of the scale of the setting and of the characters within it. It was an issue which would dictate the future course of his work, and of Western art in general. Poussin was not alone in seeing painting in terms of theatre. At this period there was a general fascination among artists, from Bernini down, with stagecraft and with the theatre's systematic use of gesture and expression. All the great artists, whatever their field, sacred or secular, were trying, each in his own way, to enter into a closer dialogue with their public. Poussin took up where Domenichino left off, and devoted himself to studying *affetti*, the forces which move people, in ever-increasing depth. He was familiar with the writings of Agucchi and his circle, and it was at about this time that he illustrated

75

Leonardo da Vinci's *Treatise on Painting*. Some of the animated figures in these illustrations recur in paintings like *The Saving of the Young Pyrrhus* and *The Rape of the Sabine Women*, clear evidence of his careful consideration of how best to achieve a convincing representation of reality. For Poussin as for Leonardo, painting was first and foremost a cerebral affair, *cosa mentale*, a carefully structured language with a proper syntax and its own vocabulary. His ideas could not have been more different from those of Bernini and the great exponents of the Baroque who sought to conjure up the ineffable in their religious works by plunging the viewer into a kind of trance. They played on all the senses through every medium, and anticipated the Romantic dream of a 'total work of art'.

The Rape of the Sabine Women,
oil on canvas,
104.5 x 210 cm (41 x 82³/₄ in.),
with detail opposite.
The Metropolitan Museum of Art, New York.

Midas Giving Thanks to Bacchus,
oil on canvas,
98 x 130 cm (38^{1}/$_{4}$ x 51 in.).
Alte Pinakothek, Munich.

Illustration for Leonardo's *Treatise on Painting*,
pen and ink and brown wash;
size of illustration 11.4 x 11.8 cm (4½ x 4¾ in.).
Pinacoteca Ambrosiana, Milan.

Meticulousness and strength of character are by no means mutually exclusive. All the early accounts agree that Poussin had a fiery energy – '*fuoco*' and '*furia di diavolo*' are the words used to describe his spirit – and that he was highly sensitive. Certainly this is the impression created by the *Battles*, the early *Bacchanals* or his more or less erotic paintings, many of which are now lost, like the one of *Women Bathing* commissioned by Maréchal de Créquy. Poussin's fiery spirit was soon brought under control, however, his energy tempered by reflection and indeed by disillusionment. His work increasingly reflects a keen awareness of the limiting nature of man's condition and destiny. His was a profound and often painful understanding of the human experience, very likely born of personal trials and tribulations. We should not find it surprising, therefore, that Poussin tackled subjects rarely taken up by other artists before him. The story of King Midas, for instance, which features in three paintings, is a warning against excess of all kinds. Midas asks Bacchus to relieve him of his fearsome ability to turn everything he touches into gold, and so finds liberation and peace. The two smaller pictures, now in New York and Ajaccio respectively, show him washing in the river Pactolus and looking on pensively as a peasant tries to find specks of gold in the water. The third work in Munich, is rather more ambitious and shows the king, surrounded by his entourage, giving thanks to the god. Activity is succeeded by stability and repose, intoxication gives way to calm thought, as – in another context – the two successive versions of *The Inspiration of the Poet* show. The ferocious energy of the early *Battles* is transformed into heroic tension first in *The Death of Germanicus* and then in *The Saving of the Young Pyrrhus*. Poussin's ideas evolved considerably in the course of these ten years of experimentation. Initially, they were rather diverse, but gradually became more sharply focused as the debates on art among the painters in Rome became more heated, and culminating *c*. 1635 in the *Bacchanals* for Cardinal Richelieu and the *Sacraments* for Cassiano Dal Pozzo. Each would inform and enrich the other, and lead to a synthesis of the sacred and the profane.

CHAPTER THREE

Scholarship, Religion and Poetry

POUSSIN AND CASSIANO DAL POZZO.
ANCIENT MYTHOLOGY AS SOURCE MATERIAL.
THE 'TRIUMPHS' FOR CARDINAL RICHELIEU.
MORAL ALLEGORIES.
THE SEVEN 'SACRAMENTS' FOR DAL POZZO.
'THE ISRAELITES GATHERING MANNA'.
THE SEVEN 'SACRAMENTS' FOR CHANTELOU.
THE FIRST LANDSCAPES.

Cornelius Bloemaert,
after Poussin,
illustration for *The Hesperides*,
engraving.

'I am venturing to write to you yet again, since an indisposition prevents me from coming to see you in person, to beseech you with all my might to help me a little; I am so desperate, because most of the time I am ill and I have no way of making a living other than with my hands.' The exact date of this petition, written at a particularly difficult point in Poussin's early days in Rome, is not known. It was addressed to Cassiano Dal Pozzo, one of the most enlightened patrons of the day. He was born in 1588, of an old Piedmontese family. After studying law, he went to Rome where he became private secretary to Cardinal Francesco Barberini, whom he accompanied on his missions. His bearing was solemn, his tastes sober. He preferred the style of Duquesnoy and Sacchi to that of Bernini and Pietro da Cortona. Poussin was presented to him by Marcello Sacchetti. Cassiano Dal Pozzo was responsible for Poussin being given the commission to paint *The Martyrdom of St Erasmus*, and generously assisted him on several occasions. Their friendship really developed from 1635 on, as is clear not only from the numerous pictures Poussin painted for his exacting patron, but also from what survives of their correspondence. Poussin's tone tends, it is true, to be deferential rather than warm, but his feelings are reflected in the tomb he designed following his patron's death in 1657 and in an associated painting, the austerely moving *Annunciation*, now in London.

47

219

Poussin seems to have been even closer to Cassiano's brother, Carlo-Antonio: the artist entrusted the care of his wife and his affairs to him just before leaving for Paris in 1640. Cassiano's cousin, Amadeo, Marchese di Voghera, who lived in Turin, commissioned *The Adoration of the Golden Calf* (London), *The Crossing of the Red Sea* (Melbourne), and perhaps also *St Margaret* (Turin), an altarpiece painted in the late 1630s, exceptional for Poussin in both size and subject. Despite the stiffness and top-heaviness of the composition, and despite Longhi's description of the saint as 'more of an orator than a praying figure', the figure echoes the majestic quality of contemporary sculptures.

70

cat. 101

Cassiano was elected to the Accademia dei Lincei in 1621, and belonged to the intellectual avant-garde of Rome, made up of philosophers and scholars hostile to the free-thinking Frenchmen then closely involved with the Barberini, like Naudé and Bourdelot – whom Poussin later met again in Paris. Although primarily an antiquary and man of letters, Cassiano had wide interests, sharing with his brother a real passion for natural history in general and for ornithology in particular. Several inventories show that he had a number of pictures of birds and quadrupeds painted, but it is not stated by whom. Some art historians have maintained, but without any supporting evidence, that they are by Poussin. There is much argument over the attribution of the strange and rather awkward *Hannibal Crossing the Alps* (Cambridge, Mass.), but it could well fit into this documentary phase in Poussin's work, along with his drawings of elephants and the majestic-looking dromedaries which feature so largely in *Eliezer and Rebecca at the Well*, formerly in the Mahon collection. We know with rather more certainty from a beautiful frontispiece that Poussin was involved in illustrating the *Horti Hesperides* by Father Ferrari (1646), a lavish treatise on lemon-tree cultivation, financed by Dal Pozzo.

cat. 185

For Cassiano Dal Pozzo as for so many other seventeenth-century collectors, history and natural history were equally important. His interest in antiquity was reflected in his collection of statuettes, utilitarian objects and, especially, coins, to which Poussin would have had access. In addition, he had a library of about 4,500 books and manuscripts. The scale of his next great project – a pictorial encyclopaedia of all aspects of classical life – was even vaster. The *Museo Cartaceo*, the 'paper museum', consisted of twenty-three stout volumes filled with hundreds of drawings classified by source – statues, reliefs (especially those on Trajan's Column), objects of all kinds, mosaics (like the one at Palestrina), and so on. The scale of the venture was unprecedented, and Dal Pozzo enlisted a team of artists from among his circle including Pietro da Cortona, Pietro Testa and François Duquesnoy, to produce the mass of drawings needed, Poussin himself is also thought to have had a hand in the project. Until fairly recently he was credited with the albums – owned first by Clement XI, then by Cardinal Albani, and finally by George III – now in the Royal Library at Windsor. Blunt attributes these meticulous, highly finished drawings to Pietro Testa, and although they do not all seem to be by his hand, they have a documentary quality quite unlike what we normally expect from Poussin. Poussin's known pen-and-wash sketches are rapidly executed and luminous, intended as brief reminders for himself. They make up a portfolio of ideas, each page covered with loosely related motifs and frequently annotated. Poussin often made use of works already in published form, such as collections of engravings and Dal Pozzo's *Museo Cartaceo*. However, there was nothing systematic about the source material Poussin compiled.

Above left
Attributed to Pietro Testa,
Hercules and the Tripod of Apollo,
pen and black ink on white paper,
21 x 28 cm (8¼ x 11 in.).
Royal Library, Windsor

Above
Anonymous copy of a sixteenth-century
tripod, from the *Museo Cartaceo*,
pen and black ink on white paper,
20.6 x 12.5 cm (8 x 5 in.).
Royal Library, Windsor.

Bust of Antinoüs,
marble,
second century AD.
Museo Pio Clementino, Vatican.

Like both Testa and Duquesnoy, whose masterpiece *St Susanna* dates from *c*. 1630,   57
Poussin was fully aware of how much there was to be learnt from classical sculpture. He
did his best to explore to the full the expressive range offered by the different models
available to him, from the Belvedere *Antinoüs* to the fake *Dying Seneca*, the Cesi *Juno* to
the *Niobe* group in the Villa Medici, to say nothing of the bas-reliefs. He made judicious
use of a whole stock of different figures and stances, as even a brief study of *The Plague of*   59
Ashdod or *The Israelites Gathering Manna* makes abundantly clear. During the 1630s   103
Poussin gradually developed a more restrained style, exchanging 'Roman' brutality as
exemplified in *The Massacre of the Innocents* for the kind of 'Greek' harmony to be found   55
in the second version of *Et in Arcadia Ego*, and in his designs for the Grande Gallery in   93
the Louvre. Like Duquesnoy's, this was a style which steered clear of emphatic contrasts
and dramatic effects based on lighting and draperies, and concentrated on conveying surface texture rather than three-dimensionality. The modelling of the forms is gentle
(unlike Domenichino's), the composition balanced and flowing. It is easy to see why
Charles Dempsey should categorize this style as already broadly 'Neo-Classical': a sense
of history seems to inform it, though not the nostalgic kind we find at the end of the eighteenth century with Mengs and Winckelmann. Out of all the different stylistic periods
open to them, the artists connected with Giustiniani and Dal Pozzo were drawn to classical antiquity, which fitted most closely with the direction their own art was taking, even
though their access to it was only through later copies and derivative pieces. Through the
different examples of 'classicism' which confronted them in Rome in the 1630s – the kind
espoused by Raphael or Domenichino or the sort epitomized in bas-reliefs of the imperial era or those of Polydorus – they could apprehend the original and shining harmony of ancient Greece, to which the papal city was after all the heir.

Cassiano Dal Pozzo was also interested in art theory, and wanted to publish an illustrated edition of Leonardo da Vinci's *Treatise on Painting*, to be based on an abridged
manuscript in the Barberini library. For this Poussin produced a series of drawings of
figures in movement, now in the Pinacoteca Ambrosiana in Milan (copies in the Hermit-   75
age). The project never materialized, however, at least not in the way intended. An incomplete version, copiously illustrated with engravings, did come out in Paris in 1651.
Leonardo's text was translated by Roland Fréart de Chambray. Poussin's drawings, meanwhile, were adapted by Charles Errard, and Poussin complained vociferously about this
in a letter to Abraham Bosse in 1653. Leonardo's principles sank in, despite all this. Poussin clearly pondered some of them at length, and re-used his compositions in a number
of paintings executed in the 1630s (*The Rape of the Sabine Women*, for instance, and *The
Saving of the Young Pyrrhus*). Poussin implements Leonardo's principles in the most impressive way in the large *Landscape with Pyramus and Thisbe* (Frankfurt), painted for Dal   164
Pozzo in 1651, a picture which reflects twenty years' experimentation in rendering movement and expression.

The description of Dal Pozzo's collection and surviving inventories – notably those
relating to the estates of his brother, Carlo-Antonio, and his nephew, Gabriele – are
inconsistent in places and lack sufficient detail. Most crucial of all, the inventory of Cassiano's effects drawn up after his death is missing. One thing is clear, however: the prepon-
derance of works by Poussin in a collection in which French art was also represented by
the likes of Simon Vouet and Jean Lemaire, and Italian art chiefly by Pietro Testa. Cassiano
seems to have had a particular liking for this tormented painter (who committed

suicide in 1650), and employed him to produce all kinds of pictures, from copies after the antique for the *Museo Cartaceo* to full-blown paintings in the Venetian style which he favoured. Dal Pozzo is thought to have owned between forty and fifty pictures by Poussin, – and insofar as firm identifications are possible – these included every kind of subject: stories from both Old and New Testaments, episodes in the lives of saints, tales from mythology and legend, landscapes recording incidents in history and, of course, the famous set of seven *Sacraments* (Belvoir Castle and Washington, D.C.). The early years of Poussin's career were most fully represented – his later work seems to have had increasingly less appeal for Dal Pozzo, with the important exception of the great *Landscape with Pyramus and Thisbe*, and in addition the artist's services were no doubt increasingly in demand elsewhere. Dal Pozzo remained the most important patron, however, along with Chantelou and Pointel. What impressed him above all in Poussin's work was the passionate quality of the early mythological pictures, and the harking back to antiquity which was beginning to make itself felt in the *Sacraments*. His acquisition of this set shows him to have been one of the most forward-looking patrons of his day, but this should not disguise the fact that his tastes were more eclectic than they might seem.

Cassiano Dal Pozzo was one of a small group of cultivated collectors who demanded a high intellectual content in art. For them, the appeal of a painting lay equally, and perhaps even primarily, in the ideas it encompassed. Under their influence, Poussin became more firmly set on the road he had taken since he first met Marino. Mythology quickly ceased to be simply a source of subject matter and was treated by him in an increasingly esoteric way. The aim was to see beyond the legends about the gods and discover eternal truths. For the majority of the painters of the day, and most notably Pietro da Cortona and Vouet, topics from classical mythology were essentially decorative and agreeable, and meant a warm glow of beautiful bodies harmoniously arranged in a blissful landscape. Poussin had already explored this sensuous approach, one of his finest pictures from that period being *Acis and Galatea* (Dublin) – a revival of the paganism of the second Renaissance with its rich deep colours and glorification of the nude. Poussin's association with Dal Pozzo's circle led him slowly but surely to read Ovid more closely and to digest the learned commentaries that had been written on the *Fastes* and *Metamorphoses*. As a result, he saw the loves of the gods in a more serious, even melancholy light. In *The Empire of Flora* (1631) the themes of unhappy love, violent death and metamorphosis are already inextricably bound up together, and it is just a short step from metamorphosis to redemption. In the very early *Venus and Adonis* (Caen) the use of dark colours creates an elegiac mood. Even here, amid all the lament over the young man's death in the ruddy early evening light, there is nevertheless the promise of rebirth: a spring flower – an anemone – grows on the patch of earth where the hero's blood has been spilt. Eastern religions, ancient mysteries, and the Pythagorean belief in the transmigration of souls all took on a new meaning when looked at from the reasoned and thereby renewed Christian point of view adopted by Dal Pozzo's friends.

It is in the context of such learned, even philosophical thinking that we should consider the mythological subjects painted by Poussin between 1635 and 1640. In *Pan and Syrinx* (Dresden), painted for a fellow artist, Nicolas de la Fleur, Poussin achieves an admirable balance of bodies and trees in what is at once an evocation of physical frustration and a reflection of the poetic process anticipating Mallarmé. Beauty seems to elude capture, certainly, but Syrinx's escape and her subsequent transformation into a reed-bed

82

63

cat. 161

83

Acis and Galatea,
oil on canvas,
98 x 137 cm (38¹/₂ x 54 in.)
National Gallery of Ireland, Dublin.

The Nurture of Jupiter,
oil on canvas,
95 x 118 cm (37¹/₂ x 46¹/₂ in.).
Dulwich Picture Gallery, London.

Pan and Syrinx,
oil on canvas,
106.5 x 82 cm (42 x 32½ in.).
Staatliche Kunstsammlungen,
Dresden.

enable Pan to invent the reed-pipe, and hence music. Earthly love (*Anteros*) is converted, or rather refined, into spiritual love (*Eros*). Pursuit and apparent disappointment were similarly the subject of a lost version of *Apollo and Daphne* painted *c*. 1637, now known *cat. 118* only through an engraving. Poussin had already explored the theme in the version now in Munich (*c*. 1627), and would tackle it one final time in the large unfinished version now in the Louvre (1664–5), a far more complex picture from which all movement is eliminated. Poussin's ideas become more narrowly defined in the two versions of *The Nurture of Jupiter* (Dulwich Picture Gallery and Berlin), painted shortly before 1640, in *82; cat. 145* which the concept of destiny comes to the fore: the infant Zeus, saved from the devouring jaws of his father, Kronos, and nurtured in secret, is destined to become head of the entire Pantheon. As Poussin's thoughts become clearer, so the style of the pictures becomes sharper. The composition is austere: all our attention is focused on the compact group of Curetes and the infant in their charge. Hardly any attempt is made to create a sense of depth. Instead, there is a pattern of arrested, echoing gestures. Colour is kept within carefully defined areas, and the effect is to create beautiful sweeps of blue, yellow and white. There is a sense of premonition in everything: the nymph of the spring who looks on, gnarled trees, the solemn collecting of honey. Very similar in feeling is *Moses* *170* *Saved from the Water* (Louvre) of 1638. It makes little sense to draw an arbitrary distinction between pictures of sacred and profane subjects at this point. The underlying ideas of being chosen or saved, and the emotions that went with them, were the same.

Poussin's new style reached its zenith in *Venus Presenting Arms to Aeneas*, painted *86* for his friend Jacques Stella and now the pride of the museum in Rouen. The picture sums up a passage in the *Aeneid*: on the eve of the battle that will lead to the Trojans establishing themselves in Latium and to the founding of Rome, the goddess shows her son the arms she has asked Vulcan to make for him. The picture is neither narrative nor allegorical: it is a static representation of a symbolic moment, of an individual's acceptance of his destiny. It consists of a juxtaposition of monumental forms, each sharply defined and quite separate from the others, yet contributing to the powerful triple rhythm that runs through the whole. Set against the monochrome backdrop, a landscape of grey-browns and pale greens, are three trees, three river-gods and their three urns, the setting being the banks of the Tiber. These features set off the three main elements, on whose interrelation the work depends for its meaning: the hero, whose gesture conveys both amazement and obedience; the goddess, suspended like a white statue in the sky; and the arms hanging from the oak tree, as compelling in every way as the figures. The objects depicted – the overturned urn in the foreground, the cut reed, the golden lance, the helmet with its scarlet plume and the shield – all assume an extraordinary importance. Symbols rather than accessories, they alert the viewer to all that is implicit in the picture. With the crystallization of Poussin's ideas comes a new hardness and economy in his treatment of his subject. Mythology was giving way to history, and on the occasions when he did tackle classical legends it was in a contemplative spirit and with a seriousness which anticipated his late masterpieces such as *The Birth of Bacchus*, *Landscape with Diana and Orion* and *Apollo and Daphne*. Poussin's rather stilted pictures of the period 1635–40 may not be as profound or display the same astonishing sense of liberation in their touch, composition or thought as his later works, but they are no less ambitious.

It may be because the set of *Triumphs* painted for Cardinal Richelieu fall into this category that these works are less appreciated today. They represent a distinct departure

Opposite
Venus Presenting Arms to Aeneas (detail);
see also p. 86.

Venus Presenting Arms to Aeneas,
oil on canvas,
105 x 142 cm (41¼ x 56 in.).
Musée des Beaux-Arts, Rouen.

from Poussin's earlier work, and in particular from the Bacchic subjects he painted in the late 1620s. Gone is the softness, the warmth of colour, the sensuousness which permeated those first paintings. Poussin was clearly moving in a new direction as early as *cat. 133* c. 1632, as is obvious from *Bacchanal before a Term of Pan* (National Gallery, London). Here, the movement is lively, but frozen. There is no longer any trace of Titian in the figures; solid and slightly thickset, they seem to be inspired instead by the images of classical sculpture conjured up by Mantegna. The rhythm is tight, with rigidly alternating masses and empty spaces. There is a pleasing grace about the work, however, which makes it very much a transitional piece. Everything would change with the large pictures which Richelieu commissioned in 1634 in recognition of the artist's growing celebrity. Poussin's job was to complete the decoration of the King's Chamber in the château the Cardinal had just had built in Poitou. Already in place were a number of clever allegorical pictures by Mantegna, Perugino and Costa, which had come from Isabella d'Este's *studiolo* in Mantua. Poussin sent two paintings in May 1636, *The Triumph of Pan* (London) *cat. 129, 130* and *The Triumph of Bacchus* (Kansas City, Mo). *The Triumph of Silenus*, now known only *91* through an early copy (London), completed the series. *The Triumph of Neptune and Amphitrite* (Philadelphia), almost certainly begun in 1634, also formed part of the same commission, even though it was intended to hang in a different part of the château, in a room celebrating the French navy which Richelieu had re-established. The theme of divine triumphs, beloved of Petrarch, was one which the great Italian Renaissance painters had taken from classical reliefs. In seeking to measure up to them, Poussin was clearly breaking away from the decorative style associated with painting in Rome from Annibale Carracci to Pietro da Cortona. While they strove for exuberant displays of virtuosity, Poussin was refining his art by returning to the available primary sources. His analysis not only of the reliefs, frescoes and mosaics of ancient Rome, but also of the work of the great masters of the *cinquecento* like Raphael, Polidoro da Caravaggio and Giulio Romano, brought him a new expressive range and sense of structure. Armed with these, Poussin was able to translate into pictorial terms the ideas he was then developing with regard to ancient customs and cults.

89

Raphael, *The Triumph of Galatea*,
fresco.
Villa Farnesina, Rome.

    The Triumph of Neptune and Amphitrite is in a category of its own. The first of the four related works, it differs slightly from the other three in style. As to the subject matter of the picture, it has been identified variously as the birth of Venus and the triumph of *Venus genitrix*, the goddess of creation invoked by Lucretius in the opening lines of *De Rerum Natura*. From Poussin's preparatory drawings it is evident that he was working initially on the loosely connected themes of Venus, Galatea and Amphitrite, and it seems likely, therefore, that the Richelieu painting represents an amalgam of marine subjects. Poussin draws skilfully on a number of well-known works to produce a masterpiece of his own. His debt to Raphael's frescoes of *The Marriage of Cupid and Psyche* and especially of his *Galatea* in the Villa Farnesina is obvious. Poussin broadens Raphael's original composition to include a bold Neptune probably inspired by a Roman mosaic. The illusion of dynamic movement so vividly conveyed by the fresco has been intentionally shattered. Instead, everything is emphatically frontal, and the dolphins and sea-horses toss and turn seemingly outside time or space. Poussin was deliberately setting out to make his art static and symmetrical in a conscious response to the movement typical of Roman Baroque. In so doing, he was undoubtedly denying himself the chance to create some exciting effects. In their stead he presents a concentrated composition of inter-

Galatea or *The Birth of Venus*,
brown wash over black chalk, 14.1 x 20 cm (5½ x 8 in.).
National Museum, Stockholm.

(Above) *The Triumph of Pan*,
pen and brown ink,
19.5 x 29.1 cm (7¾ x 11½ in.).
Royal Library, Windsor.

(Above, right) Giovanni Bellini,
The Feast of the Gods,
oil on canvas,
170 x 188 cm (67 x 74 in.).
National Gallery of Art, Washington, D.C.

linked and finely modelled ideal human forms in a huge, airy landscape, half-sea, half-sky, hung with grey clouds which act as a backdrop for a group of cupids. The tripartite structure is very striking. The three carefully balanced central figures form a triangle which is echoed by the blue, peach and yellow draperies behind them, splashes of colour amid the quiet, subdued shades of the rest of the picture which hark back in their simplicity beyond Raphael to the frescoes of ancient Rome. The apparent vastness of the painting belies its moderate size and demands an entire wall for its display.

In the three other *Triumphs* – of Pan, Bacchus and Silenus – Poussin clearly draws on classical art, though his rich warm tones still betray the influence of Venice. The screen of trees in *The Triumph of Pan*, the most beautiful of the three and the only one that is indisputably by Poussin, is borrowed from Giovanni Bellini's *The Feast of the Gods* (*c.*1514), then in the Aldobrandini collection. The composition, however, is entirely Poussin's own and the strict arrangement of figures as if in a bas-relief was the product of long thought. Some preparatory drawings reveal the artist toying with the idea of a composition in depth. Gradually, however, he begins to arrange the figures in parallel bands in the front of the picture and to orchestrate bodies and gestures in an almost abstract way. The links between individuals and groups of characters are purely formal, and have no psychological or dramatic force. None of the *Triumphs* aspires to be much more than

The Triumph of Pan,
oil on canvas, 134 x 145 cm (52³/₄ x 57 in.).
National Gallery, London.

The Triumph of Neptune and Amphitrite,
oil on canvas,
114.5 x 146.5 cm (45 x 57¾ in.),
with detail opposite.
Philadelphia Museum of Art.

decorative, Poussin being keenly aware of the context in which they were to hang. He succeeds in pulling together a wide range of powerful and diverse movements into a balanced and static whole, clearly building on the work both of Mantegna (whose circular *Parnassus* was in Richelieu's collection) and of Giulio Romano, making particular use of his *Sacrifice to Priapus*, which had been engraved by the Master of the Dice.

The stilted style which Poussin adopts here goes hand in hand with an intellectual approach ill-suited to the relaxed Venetian manner. Poussin intended his representation of pagan ceremonies to be accurate, founded on a comparative study of ancient forms of worship. The *Triumphs* painted for Richelieu would never have come into being if Poussin had not been in contact with Cassiano Dal Pozzo's circle and a party to their learned discussions. For them what was being celebrated in the worship of Bacchus and Priapus was the fecundity of nature and the assurance of renewal; the wine of Bacchus also symbolized the blood of Christ, however. All sacrifice could be seen as a source of life, then, be it pagan or Christian. This gave Poussin the opportunity to pursue his own line of thought and for the first time to adopt a grandiose manner. He researched his subject thoroughly, drawing heavily on the *Museo Cartaceo*, then in preparation, but making good use, too, of Guillaume du Choul's great work, *De la religion des anciens Romains* (1556). It was this research which inspired the remarkable props so much in evidence in these pictures, like the masks which form such a striking still-life in the foreground of *The Triumph of Pan*. Ultimately, however, visual concerns prevailed over archaeological accuracy: Bacchus's chariot is drawn not by panthers as it should be, but by two rearing centaurs who inject a strong sense of movement into the procession. **89**

Through the highly literate circle of the Barberini, Poussin had met Cardinal Giulio Rospigliosi (he was elected Pope in 1667, taking the name Clement IX). Rospigliosi was a poet, and had written a number of moralizing plays which had been staged in spectacular fashion in the theatre of the Barberini palace: *Sant'Alessio*, for instance, with sets by Bernini; and *Chi soffre, speri* ('Who suffers, hopes'), whose title alone speaks volumes. Rospigliosi was also a keen art-lover, a patron first of Claude Lorrain, then of Carlo Maratta. He suggested the subjects of four pictures which Poussin painted for him between 1638 and 1640. Two are lost, and known today only through engravings: *The Rest on the Flight into Egypt*, which rather unusually featured an elephant in the background, and *Time Saving Truth from Envy and Discord*, a tense rendering of a theme Poussin was to tackle again on a ceiling in the Palais Cardinal in Paris. The third, *Happiness subdued by Death* (better known under the title of *Et in Arcadia Ego*), now in the Louvre, was painted nearly ten years later than the Chatsworth version. The crude drama of the early version has given way to quiet meditation. The shepherds are no longer thrust forward to confront the death's head which seems to address them from the top of the tomb (an echo of another *memento mori*, painted by Il Guercino). Instead they are grouped around the tomb, lost in thought over its melancholy inscription, *Et in Arcadia Ego*, which harks back to Virgil's *Eclogues* and Jacopo Sannazaro's *L'Arcadia* (1502). Whereas the earlier composition centred on a diagonal, the four figures are now arranged symmetrically in relation to the fateful tomb. The palette is cooler and no longer imposes a unity on the whole; colours are sharply defined, emphatically, rather than gently, leading the eye from figure to figure. Each character has a particular feeling to express. **93**

The fourth in this group of pictures again takes up the theme of the passage of time and the precarious nature of all happiness, but is pedantic rather than elegiac. The *Dance* **94**

Et in Arcadia Ego,
oil on canvas,
85 x 121 cm (33¹/₂ x 47¹/₂ in.).
Louvre, Paris.

The Dance to the Music of Time,
oil on canvas,
83 x 105 cm (32³/₄ x 41¹/₄ in.).
Wallace Collection, London.

to the Music of Time (Wallace Collection) is neither very well known nor particularly well liked, yet the mood of calm contemplation which pervades it makes this one of the most striking moral *poesie* of the period. The picture is polished, and makes skilful use of colour, setting patches of white, yellow and blue against a muted background. The composition is simple, but unusual. Based once again on the triple groupings with which Poussin was so obsessed, it also features strongly symmetrical elements. On the left is a pillar topped by a double-faced head of Janus, with a putto blowing bubbles at its base. On the right, attended by another putto holding an hourglass, sits Time, shown here playing a lyre. In the centre, a man and three women, each differently clothed and wearing a different head-dress, dance to the sound of his music. They are described in the earliest inventories as the Four Seasons. Bellori and Félibien, however, were closer to the mark in seeing them as representations of the four states mankind is fated to experience in an endlessly repeating cycle: Poverty (the male figure), Work, Riches and Pleasure. Apollo, meanwhile, drives across the sky in his chariot, drawn by Aurora and accompanied by the Horae (Seasons).

The allegorical pictures painted for Rospigliosi were unlike anything else Poussin produced. They reflect the sophisticated and highly literary outlook of the man who commissioned them rather than Poussin's own thinking at the time. Allegory as a genre in its own right, with its own language and rules, had never really attracted him. He preferred to convey his own ideas through immediately recognizable subjects familiar to everyone, taking them generally from religious or secular history, as well as from literature. Tasso's *Gerusalemme Liberata*, then still in fashion, provided a number of themes which he tackled at intervals over a period of years. It is interesting to compare the Hermitage version

96   of *Tancred and Erminia*, for instance, painted *c.* 1631, with the one in Birmingham or with *Rinaldo and Armida*, known through a copy in Berlin, both of which date from *c.* 1637. The 'romantic' heat and colour of the first give way to a new, sharper composition which, though less immediately moving, extracts maximum meaning from the subject. Poussin seems to have taken heed of the opening *Allegoria* of Tasso's epic. For Tasso, the many events and characters the poem introduces symbolize the world at large and the power of the human spirit in all its guises. All painting should be centred on the figure of the hero, the epitome of moral strength and the embodiment of the very deepest thoughts and feelings. Henceforward he tended to be the focal point.

Concurrent with the great corpus of allegorical and mythological pictures centred
98–99   on the *Triumphs* for Richelieu was the set of seven *Sacraments* painted for Cassiano Dal
106–7   Pozzo between 1636 and 1642, to be followed shortly by a second set commissioned by Fréart de Chantelou. Poussin was looking at two sides of the same coin at once, researching the earliest Christian practices while deep in a study of pagan worship. He was stimulated in both cases by the same learned coterie, with their overwhelming interest in religious history, or more precisely, perhaps, the comparative history of different religions. In a sense, the mysteries attached to the cult of Bacchus were simply overlaid in Poussin's consciousness by the initiation rites of the primitive Church. The *Sacraments* were not often represented in Italian art. The theme was more popular among artists in Northern Europe, always treated in a contemporary context, and more often than not combined in a single work, as in the famous triptych by Rogier van der Weyden (Antwerp Museum). At Dal Pozzo's request, Poussin tackled each Sacrament individually, depicting in each case a setting and dress supposedly typical of the early days of Christianity. His

Tancred and Erminia,
oil on canvas,
98 x 147 cm (38¼ x 58 in.).
Hermitage, Leningrad.

quest for authenticity led him to go back for the most part to the very origin of each sacrament. Thus, *Baptism* is represented by St John baptizing Jesus, *Penance* by Mary Magdalene with Simon, *Matrimony* by the marriage of the Virgin, *The Eucharist* by the Last Supper, and *Ordination* by Christ giving the keys to St Peter. Through his meticulous scholarship, Poussin manages to bring something new to these scenes from the New Testament, which would have been familiar to all. The remaining two paintings – *Confirmation* and *Extreme Unction* – recall moments in fifth-century Christian life.

Poussin's interpretation was very much in line with current Counter-Reformation thinking, which stressed the need to recapture the original purity of Christian doctrine and practice. The likes of Baronius, Holstenius, Cardinal Massimi, and more particularly Dal Pozzo's friend Paganino Gaudenzi, who were brought up on the writings of the Fathers of the Church, were already beginning to adopt a scientific approach in their study of the early history of the Christian Church. They took into account recent archaeological discoveries. Gaudenzi, for instance, carried out an excavation of the Catacombs and assembled a collection of funerary reliefs, and in 1632 Bosio published a set of engravings entitled *Roma sotterranea* based on palaeo-Christian frescoes. Poussin was in close touch with these developments – both sets of *Sacraments* are full of examples of his attention to detail. One of the most striking instances of his historical accuracy is the *triclinium* which appears in both versions of *Penance* and *The Eucharist*. As a result of much learned debate, in engravings dating from the end of the sixteenth century onwards Jesus and the Apostles were shown reclining on couches to eat. *Tableaux sacrés*, published in Paris in 1601 by the Jesuit priest, Father Richeome, provides a useful and accessible digest of the abstruse scholarly argument. The book was intended to be a Catholic equivalent of Philostratus's *Imagines* (purporting to describe sixty-four works in a Neapolitan gallery), and to serve as a definitive treatise on religious painting. Poussin's quest for accuracy is even more marked in the second set of *Sacraments*, both in the detail of the costumes and in the settings. The shield on the wall of the Chantelou version of *Extreme Unction*, set in the home of a dying soldier, bears the IHS monogram. In *The Eucharist* in the same series the Apostles make their own communion. The setting of the Dal Pozzo version of *Confirmation* is anachronistic: the scene takes place in S. Atanasio dei Greci, a church designed by the contemporary architect Giacomo della Porta and situated near Poussin's house in Rome. The second version, by contrast, is set in a catacomb. The meaning of the picture is enhanced by the inclusion of historical detail, such as the basin used for the baptism of neophytes, seen on the right. This serves as a reminder that in the early Church the ceremonies of baptism and confirmation were often combined, and the funerary backdrop helps unite the ideas of death and resurrection so essential in Poussin's thinking. These references to an ancient liturgy, and to customs no longer current in the seventeenth century, were not merely of anecdotal interest, then, but served a useful purpose. Occasionally they make for some rather odd juxtapositions. The first *Ordination*, for instance, takes place in a rural setting. The backdrop to the second consists of a collection of classical buildings in the midst of which Poussin has inserted a pillar engraved with the letter 'E', an allusion to the *epsilon* at Delphi which, according to Plutarch, proclaimed Apollo's eternity to the world. Rarely have such parallels been drawn between the esotericism of pagan cults and the revealed truths of Christianity.

The first set of *Sacraments* took quite a long time to complete. When compared, the six surviving paintings in the series (*Penance* was lost in a fire in 1816) betray noticeable

Mallery,
The Institution of the Eucharist,
engraving from *Tableaux Sacrés* by Richeome.

Marriage

Ordination

The Eucharist

Confirmation

The first set of *Sacraments*,
oil on canvas, each 95.5 x 121 cm (37$\frac{1}{2}$ x 47$\frac{1}{2}$ in.).
All Belvoir Castle (Collection of the Duke of Rutland)
except *Baptism* in the National Gallery of Art,
Washington, D.C.

The first set of *Sacraments*

Baptism,
National Gallery of Art,
Washington, D.C.

Extreme Unction.
Belvoir Castle
(Collection of the Duke of Rutland).

99

differences in tone and style of composition. The two earliest, *Ordination* and *Matrimony*, feature large numbers of figures arranged quite close together either in a single band or in shallow groups in unremarkable settings which are little more than backdrops and could almost be interchangeable, a wooded landscape in one case and a peristyle in the other. In these two pictures Poussin has succeeded in recreating the majesty of Raphael's *Acts of the Apostles* on a smaller scale; both testify to its influence in the attitudes struck by the figures and in the drapery. Yet again he depicts a range of *affetti*, making each character react differently. *Penance* (known only through an engraving) seems similarly tentative and rather conventional. The arrangement of the figures is much better in *Extreme Unction*, in which a severely geometric setting beings to acquire the depth of a box or a stage. The figures are now grouped rather more loosely than in the the earlier deathbed scene, reminiscent of the one in *The Death of Germanicus*. The empty spaces between them highlight the interlocking sequence of gestures which runs across the picture, culminating in the hand of the priest dressed in yellow. The two young people bustling about the table introduce a charming note of domesticity, although it could be said to detract from the work's dramatic unity. This is not a dramatic picture, however, for despite the evident sadness of the subject, it does not rely on extreme effects, but is remarkable instead for its patches of light colours, soft contours, and graceful, almost lively rhythm.

The Eucharist and *Confirmation* which followed it are far more austere, both in tone and in composition. Both are set at night, and give Poussin an opportunity to explore, as Caravaggio had done, the effects of artificial light. Poussin did so in a different spirit, however, and with rather more of Leonardo's strictness of approach. He looks at what happens when there is more than one light source, and examines the shadow cast on objects. In *The Eucharist* the rigidly symmetrical plan of the *triclinium* leaves very little room for manoeuvre. The scene is lit by two flames flickering overhead, a candle placed on a chest in the foreground and a hidden light source beyond the open door in the background on the left, throwing shafts of light across the floor and bare walls. Surrounded by shade, Jesus and the Apostles are picked out in a narrow strip of light occupying only a small part of the total picture area. The effect could not be more striking: the viewer's attention is drawn to the central figure of Christ as he raises his hand to bless the bread. The arrangement of the figures is considerably more complex in *Confirmation* and generates a sense of solemnity. The figures are seen from various angles – the majority in profile, others from behind or head on. Behind them rise the fluted pilasters of a church plunged in shadow. The Paschal candle has been lit: it is the day before Easter. Just as he did in *Extreme Unction*, Poussin arranges the figures singly or in groups according to need, setting up a pattern of responses and echoes which reverberate in the silent depths of the great edifice. The soft but crisply painted draperies and the interplay of contemplative and smiling faces make this the finest painting in the series.

Baptism is something of an oddity, and needs to be considered separately. Poussin had already started the picture when he left for Paris in 1640. He took it with him, but did not complete it until May 1642. The painting is no longer with its companion pieces in Belvoir Castle: it was sold by the Duke of Rutland and acquired in 1946 by the National Gallery, Washington. The figures are much larger in this picture than in any of the others, and the mountainous landscape in the background is more severe and conjures up a greater sense of depth than the one in *Ordination*. From the surviving preparatory drawings it is clear that Poussin thought long and hard about the composition, which has echoes of both Michelangelo and Raphael. Figures and landscape are more closely integrated than hitherto, demonstrating the great strides Poussin was making in this area. Earlier, *c.* 1635, he had tried to achieve a more unified whole in two versions of *St John Baptizing the People* (Louvre and Malibu, the latter owned originally by Cassiano Dal Pozzo), both still incorporating a linear arrangement of figures across the canvas. In *Baptism* Poussin's approach to modelling and his use of colour are also markedly different, revealing a new boldness. The appeal of the first set of *Sacraments* lies largely in its exquisite attention to detail. Poussin was now abandoning such meticulousness in favour of greater simplicity, and of a sort of harsh grandeur.

102   Poussin was gaining command of a richer, stronger language. *The Israelites Gathering Manna* (Louvre), painted for Paul Fréart de Chantelou in 1638–9, was very much a foretaste of what was to come. Falling between the two sets of *Sacraments* in terms both of subject and of style, it has become famous because of all the critical comment it has aroused: Lebrun, for example, was prompted to give a lecture on it to the Academy in Paris in 1667, and Félibien wrote a commentary on it, published in 1686. It is important to try to set aside everything that has been said and written, and to view the painting as the startling departure it would have seemed to Paris art-lovers in April 1639.

In the seventeenth century the Old Testament story of the manna sent by Jehovah to his starving people in the desert was often seen as a prefiguration of the Eucharist. In Poussin's painting, it provides the vehicle for an all-embracing reflection on divine mercy. In the centre of a great rocky landscape, with the Israelite camp in the distance, Moses stands pointing up to the sky while Aaron prays. Moses's imperious gesture divides the mass of people around him into two groups. Those on the right are thanking him for guiding them there. Those on the left have realized that it is to God that they must give thanks. In the far distance on the left towers a huge rock with a roughly triangular cleft in the middle, which echoes the orientation of the two central figures. Through it shines the morning light. Poussin reinforces the import of the picture by means of a number of groups of figures placed in the foreground. From left to right, the first group is engulfed in misery; the next figure has taken in the miracle; and continuing across the picture people are seen snatching up the manna. Poussin conjures up a whole range of conflicting and changing emotions: resignation, hope, amazement; greed and violence; altruism and charity. Here, the construction is far more systematic than in *The Plague of Ashdod* or *Moses Striking the Rock*. Poussin's aim is to produce a work that can be 'read'. 'Our eye roams over the different parts,' Félibien noted, 'but stops when it comes to the small groups of figures, gradually building up an understanding of the subject.' We start by seeing a unified whole, then a series of different episodes. This technique of subdividing the whole into separate but related incidents allows Poussin to preserve the unity of time, place and subject central to history painting, and yet lose nothing of his meaning. Félibien was full of admiration for this remarkable *tour de force*: 'there is a skilful contrast in the way the different figures are arranged, but their poses and attitudes are uniformly consonant with the story and lend a unity of action and beautiful sense of harmony to the picture.' Shapes, gestures and colours are all finely balanced. Everything is steeped in powerful light suggesting both a physical reality and a spiritual emanation. To demonstrate the deeper levels of meaning within the picture, Poussin places in the left foreground, as close as he could be to the spectator, the figure of a woman comforting but

The Israelites Gathering Manna,
oil on canvas,
149 x 200 cm (58$\frac{1}{2}$ x 78$\frac{3}{4}$ in.),
with detail opposite.
Louvre, Paris.

pushing her own child away as she suckles her famished mother. An old man looks on in amazement: 'such an extraordinary act of charity had to be witnessed by a serious figure who would grasp its full virtue and draw attention to it, so leading people looking at the painting to contemplate it as he does' (Félibien). Rather like the chorus in a Greek tragedy, his role is to comment on the scene and draw the viewer into it by evoking a similar response. From this example of human charity attention moves to the supreme mercy of God which Moses is in the act of explaining to his companions. The interplay of levels and echoes throughout the picture has rarely been paralleled.

Stylistically, the set of *Sacraments* painted for Dal Pozzo lacks unity, and the variety within it betrays an underlying uncertainty of approach. There is nothing tentative or uneven, however, about the series painted for Chantelou between April 1644 and March 1648 after Poussin's return to Rome. The Chantelou *Sacraments* are the best documented of all Poussin's works. Much of the correspondence which Poussin and his friend and client exchanged during the four-year period of their execution has survived. Chantelou had seen works from the Dal Pozzo *Sacraments* in Rome and wanted copies. Dal Pozzo was opposed to the idea. Poussin could not find a copyist he considered competent for the job, and, though highly reluctant to attempt anything twice, decided to 'copy the paintings [himself]... or approach them in a different way'. He took up the challenge with a vengeance: 'This is to be my major work,' he wrote soon after, 'and to it I shall apply all my knowledge and all my talent such as it is.'

The coherence of the second series is particularly remarkable because Poussin never had the chance to see the first set as a whole: each picture was despatched to Paris as soon as it was finished. Chantelou displayed the seven *Sacraments* together in a special room where connoisseurs and distinguished foreign visitors (like Bernini in 1665) were invited to draw aside the curtains covering the paintings and view them one by one. The experience would have been intense, but no less than the austerity and extraordinary profundity of these pictures warranted. What is immediately striking about the pictures is their size and that of the figures within them. The Dal Pozzo pictures measure 95.5 x 121 cm (37 $\frac{1}{2}$ x 47 $\frac{1}{2}$ in.); the Chantelou set is also in landscape format, but larger – 117 x 178 cm (46 x 70 in.). In the second set the figures are still arranged like actors on a stage, but are considerably larger in proportion. The style is bolder, the manner harder. There is noticeably less charm about these pictures and rather more obvious stiffness, particularly in the drapery. The range of gestures and emotions is far richer, however. Every movement and every facial expression is carefully calculated and contributes to the build-up of a solemn evocation of the emotions generated at crucial moments in the course of human life. Poussin offers more here than simply a learned illustration of the *Sacraments*: he brings off a convincing synthesis of Christianity and Stoic philosophy.

These changes were already apparent in the first painting in the series, *Extreme Unction*, begun in April 1644 and finished in October. There is a new tragic dimension, absent in the first version, but already discernible in *The Death of Germanicus*. Set 43 against a dark curtain, figures cluster around the deathbed, and there is a sculptural strength to their forms which comes from the dramatic play of light and shade on the scene. Bright splashes of red and yellow emphasize the otherwise generally sombre tones. Amid the gloom, the figures strike a greater range of attitudes than before. The two young servants on the right have been replaced in this version by a female figure deep in meditation. The figure whose face is almost hidden in her cloak shows an inexpressible sadness echoing a wall painting in Pompeii of *The Sacrifice of Iphigenia*. Gone is the charm and slightly detached quality of the Dal Pozzo version: the solemnity is unrelieved. The following year, Poussin produced *Confirmation* which incorporates no less than twenty-two figures. The scene is a shadowy crypt, furnished with sarcophagi and lit by candles, doubtless intended to represent the interior of a catacomb. The composition is based on two parallel bands of figures, but lacks the great empty spaces which mark the first version. The finely balanced gestures are largely horizontal and connect each figure to the one next to it. There are clear echoes of classical sculpture in the dramatically lit drapery. The repetition of deep folds gives a sober rhythm to the frozen scene which prompted Bernini to exclaim, 'What devotion! What silence!'

In *Baptism*, painted a year later, a row of figures is set off against a landscape, as before. It was an idea Poussin continued to refine in later compositions, aiming at ever greater coherence. The figures are grouped on either side of a central axis defined at one end by St John and at the other by a ruin glimpsed in the distance. Still in evidence on the left is the group of figures getting dressed which Poussin borrowed from *The Battle of Cascina* by Michelangelo. Balancing them on the right are three young people looking up in astonishment at the dove of the Holy Spirit above Jesus's head. The individuals depicted display a wide variety of reactions. There is a convincing sense of depth to the picture, and a freshness which springs from the dawn light that permeates the scene. Chantelou is said to have been disappointed with the picture, which met with considerable criticism in Paris. Compared to the first two, both awesome in their austerity, it could well have seemed 'too mild'. In fact, Poussin was doing his best to vary the effects created and to adapt his style to each subject: 'I am not one of those who always sing the same tune, I know how to vary the rhythm if I choose,' he retorted to his friend on 24 March 1647, giving voice for the first time to the theory of 'modes' which he was later to develop. In the meantime, he reverted to a harsher style with *Penance* (1646–7), one of his most relentlessly symmetrical works. There is a 'metaphysical' quality to the preparatory drawing now in Montpellier: the intense light makes the groups of naked figures look like mannequins. Clearly visible on the left is the figure of Mary Magdalene bent over Jesus's feet. The same crouching pose is echoed by a kneeling servant in the foreground pouring wine from an amphora and seemingly extraneous to the scene. The first version of *Penance* was set in a pleasant peristyle opening onto a garden. Here, by contrast, there is a strong feeling of being enclosed: the rigidly rectangular *triclinium* is boxed in by a curtain and dark, looming pilasters and Ionic columns, creating a sombre mood which the brilliance of the dishes does little to alleviate.

Architecture plays a vital part in this series. As well as bringing a sense of three-dimensionality to the pictures, it takes on a symbolic importance. In *Ordination*, painted exceptionally quickly between June and August 1647, the slender screen of trees in the background of the Dal Pozzo version has given way to towering buildings. The composition is massive and severe: Christ is in the centre, this time, and around him are ranged the Apostles, responding in their different ways to the gesture he makes. The picture has the breadth manifest in Raphael's tapestry designs and at the same time demonstrates a concern for archaeological accuracy, hence the juxtaposition of the bridge, towers, and the temple with its pyramid roof, and the last-minute addition of the column engraved with an 'E', referred to above. The contrast between the two versions is less marked in *The Eucharist*. In the Chantelou picture (September–November 1647) Poussin contents him-

Inspired by the original of Timanthes,
Iphigenia being led to Sacrifice,
fresco.
Museo Nazionale, Naples.

Penance

The second set of Sacraments,
oil on canvas,
each 117 x 178 cm (46 x 70 in.).
National Gallery of Scotland, Edinburgh
(on loan from the Duke of Sutherland).

Opposite: (top left) *Ordination*; (top right) *Extreme Unction*;
(centre left) *Marriage*; (centre right) *The Eucharist*;
(bottom left) *Confirmation*; (bottom right) *Baptism*.

Penance,
pen and brown wash,
21 x 31 cm (8¹/₄ x 12¹/₄ in.).
Musée Fabre, Montpellier.

self with refining the structure of the earlier version, greatly increasing its force by having a single overhead source of light and by grouping the still recumbent Apostles more tightly around the table which now has figures on all four sides. Any monotony the composition might have had is broken up by the marvellous foreshortening of the three figures in the foreground and the slightly off-centre placing of Christ dispensing the bread. A single, acutely moving note interrupts the calm of this close-knit, almost sculptural composition: on the left can be seen the outline of Judas as he breaks away from the others and disappears into the shadows.

Chantelou was apprehensive about *Marriage*, the seventh and last of the *Sacraments*, begun in November 1647 and completed the following March. He did not like the treatment of the subject in the version for Dal Pozzo. The marriage of the Virgin is not a theme which lends itself readily to dramatic effects. Without abandoning the symmetry of the earlier version, Poussin did manage to infuse new life into the composition by placing the three kneeling and seated central figures slightly lower than the rest of the assembled company, thus modulating an otherwise straight line of faces. He emphasizes the joyousness of the occasion by decorating the wall with green garlands tied with red ribbons and by introducing three narrow windows which permit a view of trees, buildings and sky. Here again the lighting is carefully calculated, if a little strange, with dramatic shadows cast on the paved floor. The action takes place within a space defined by four large Corinthian columns mostly in semi-darkness, against which a range of often brilliant colours stand out. The figures are kept deliberately simple and achieve a kind of poetic mystery, e.g. the veiled woman half-hidden behind a column on the left, so admired by Bernini. In this as in all the pictures in the series, the figures deserve close study. Bernini's response sums up their effect. After examining *Extreme Unction* in detail on his knees, he rose and declared that it had 'the same effect as a beautiful sermon to which one listens with rapt attention and after which one is left speechless, for one's innermost being has been moved.'

The *Sacraments* and the *Triumphs* reveal two different but complementary aspects of Poussin's talent. They provide an insight into his methods: the discipline of working on a series fosters his creativity, encouraging him to look for new structures and forms, and to seek ever deeper levels of meaning. Nothing could be more different, on the face of it, than *The Triumph of Pan* and either version of *Confirmation*, yet, beyond the obvious contrasts in rhythm – the energy of the first and the restraint of the other two – a great similarity exists both in the strictness of the compositions and in the effort that went into producing them. The first series of *Sacraments* did not represent a set of definitive statements on Poussin's part. When he tackled the subjects a second time, his ideas were further expanded. The creative process with Poussin involved a slow ripening of ideas requiring both time and patience. It is possible to trace other, less obvious series throughout his work, arising from individual commissions, and consisting of variations on a theme, such as Moses saved from the water and the Holy Family, spread over a span of thirty or forty years. The exhaustive approach demonstrated in Poussin's painting reflected an instinctive need. Partial answers were anathema to Poussin. He strove instead to achieve a complete and final response in which opposites co-exist in a unified whole. Every painting articulates some aspect of contrasting but interrelated concepts – life and death, God and nature, history and eternity.

Detail of *Marriage*
from the second set of *Sacraments*;
see p. 106.

If a letter written by Cassiano Dal Pozzo is to be believed, Poussin was more than able, from as early as 1630, to hold his own with the leading landscape painters then working in Rome, such as Filippo Napoletano and Paul Bril. His earliest surviving draw-

35

207

ings, like the *Ponte Molle* in the Ecole des Beaux-Arts and the brown-wash studies of undergrowth now in the Louvre, are certainly soundly constructed and testify to a keen appreciation of the effects of light. Only ten years later, however, did he really begin to show his mettle in this competitive field, inspired no doubt by the first successes of Claude Lorrain and Gaspard Dughet. In the absence of any landscapes, pure and simple, a number of paintings of mythological subjects help in assessing the way Poussin's talents

cat. 136

evolved. In *Cephalus and Aurora* (London), painted *c*. 1626, the composition of the background is asymmetrical, with strongly delineated trees on the right and hazy vistas on the left. This, like *Bacchanal with a Guitar Player: the Andrians* in the Louvre, reflects the Titianesque style at its height and represents the culmination of a Venetian tradition

88

which began with Giovanni Bellini's *The Feast of the Gods* and in which figures are enveloped in a vibrant atmosphere in harmony with their sorrows or desires. The backgrounds are painted with sweeping strokes and in warm tones. The predominant colour of trees is usually brown rather than green, and leaves are clearly drawn only in places. There are generally clouds in the sky, as if heralding a storm. The languid figures seem gripped by torpor, surrounded by a heavy vapour. It was a style calculated to appeal to a particular clientèle, not least to Dal Pozzo who had quickly recognized Pietro Testa as one of its most talented exponents. Poussin has been credited in the past, and continues to be so today, with some of Testa's best paintings. As an example of pictures that are particularly hard to attribute with certainty, *Landscape with Venus and Adonis* (Montpellier) was originally in the collection of Cassiano Dal Pozzo and possesses all the succulent richness of a bunch of ripe grapes. Equally problematic is the more tightly composed

Landscape with a Man Drinking,
oil on canvas,
63 x 78 cm (25 x 30³/₄ in.).
National Gallery, London.

Landscape with St Jerome,
oil on canvas,
155 x 234 cm (61 x 92 in.).
Prado, Madrid.

110

cat. 227   *Landscape with Numa Pompilius and the Nymph Egeria* (Chantilly), in which the treatment is still broad and somewhat cursory. The trees with their slender overlapping trunks resemble studies from nature. Poussin embarked on a more intensive phase of landscape study in 1631, when the young Gaspard Dughet moved into his house, and the two began their rambles around the Roman countryside with Claude Lorrain. A keen hunter with a passion for the woods and mountains he conjured up so vividly, Dughet was a committed landscape painter from the start. His brother-in-law, meanwhile, continued to see man as the *raison d'être* of his art for a long time.

It was the artists of the Bolognese school who really perfected the art of 'historical' landscape painting, and the influence of one artist in particular almost certainly set Poussin firmly on this path. Domenichino returned unexpectedly from Naples in the summer of 1634, and was taken in by the Aldobrandini, first in Frascati, then in Rome. In the Palazzo Aldobrandini he saw the famous pair of lunettes, *The Flight into Egypt* and *The Entombment*, by Annibale Carracci, and was inspired to produce the most tightly constructed of his landscapes, in which figures, trees, rivers, mountains and buildings are all assembled in a clear order. In this Domenichino was following the advice of Agucchi who advocated 'a rational organization of the elements in a landscape' in which everything from man down had its proper place. The Bolognese approach was more coolly logical than the Venetian, while eliciting a similarly emotional response from the viewer. Instead of the uneasy edge characteristic of Venetian painting, the keynotes of the Bolognese style are an intensity to which every detail contributes, and a sureness of hand which springs from the new harmony which exists between the figures and their setting. Poussin, for his part, was showing signs of succumbing to this trend. In *The Return from Egypt* (Cleveland), painted *c.* 1634 and apparently after a rather more cursory first version (Dulwich), the different planes are no longer so harshly defined or plunged in shade, and lead the eye smoothly through the landscape to the far distance. The very subject of the picture is typical of the Bolognese school. Poussin's *Landscape with Juno and Argus* (Berlin), which illustrates a passage from Ovid's *Metamorphoses*, is even more ambitious, but clumsy in parts. The main figures, for instance, are too small in context and are lined up

cat. 67
cat. 66

cat. 218

symmetrically in the foreground. There is a new breadth in the handling of the trees, however, and a sense of depth in the terrain disappearing into the horizon.

This interest in nature was more marked in the late 1630s. *The Virgin Protecting the City of Spoleto*, now known as *St Rita of Cascia* (Dulwich), which probably dates from around 1636–8, is exceptional in Poussin's oeuvre in depicting a view of a city: the grey-brown walls are alternately brightly lit and plunged into shadow, while spectacular clouds gather overhead. There is a wildness about *Landscape with Travellers at Rest* and *Landscape with a Man Drinking* (both in London), and the *Landscape with a Man Pursued by a Serpent* (Montreal), reminiscent of the Roman countryside. The *Landscape with St Jerome* (Prado) must date from 1636–7, having been one of a series of paintings commissioned by Philip IV of Spain for the Landscape Gallery in his palace, Buen Retiro. Claude and Dughet both contributed to the series, and in terms of style Poussin's picture clearly owes much to his brother-in-law. The anchorite is shown in the midst of a dense landscape punctuated by the slender, sometimes overlapping tree-trunks typical of Dughet. An opening in the trees on the left lets some light into this otherwise austere scene of retreat. Soon after this Poussin explored further the idea of a saint musing alone in a large landscape. His first two masterpieces in this genre were *Landscape with St John on Patmos* (Chicago) and *Landscape with St Matthew* (Berlin), both executed 1640–1. Poussin charged a mere 40 crowns apiece for these two pictures as a favour to Giovanni-Maria Roscioli, the young ecclesiastic from Siena who commissioned them, along with *The Saving of the Young Pyrrhus* (1634), now in the Louvre, and *The Continence of Scipio* (1640), now in Moscow. In Cesare Gnudi's terms, the changes in Poussin's approach to space can be seen as a move away from a 'continuous melody' and towards a 'definite beat' and 'strong scansion'. The background landscape in the version of *Moses Saved from the Water* (Louvre) painted for André Le Nôtre in 1638, with its stretch of still water punctuated by the reflections of an aqueduct and a pyramid, is the most accomplished example of this new rhythmic clarity. From now on it is the precision with which a painting is executed and the consideration given to the respective weight of its different components which ensure that each element remains quite distinct. The blur of vegetation recedes into the distance and rivers, roads and man-made monuments take its place, creating a measurable and coherent space and easily comprehensible surroundings in which one can readily imagine oneself.

The *Landscape with St John on Patmos* and *Landscape with St Matthew* were probably designed as pendants. The two Evangelists appear in symmetrical positions in the respective foregrounds. They sit, accompanied by their attributes, writing the New Law. In *Landscape with St John on Patmos* the juxtaposition of the cross-shaped plinth in the foreground and the obelisk in the distance emphasizes the new order arising out of the old. The figures occupy only a tiny part of the canvas, however. A Mediterranean landscape stretches out behind St John: the pinky-grey reflections of an ancient city peep out from behind the trees, and beyond them is the sunlit sea. Behind St Matthew a river meanders between heavily wooded banks towards a ruined tower and distant mountains. In both works Poussin relies on artifice of different sorts to suggest depth and to connect foreground to background. There is a solemn majesty about them both, however, which springs from the beauty of the sharply defined masses, the symmetry of the trees, and the light, radiant in one, mysterious in the other, of Revelation which permeates both scenes. Most important of all – and it is here that Poussin differs from Claude or the artists of the

Bolognese school – each picture has its own particular tone. The *Landscape with St John on Patmos* anticipates Cézanne, while the *Landscape with St Matthew* has a more romantic quality. On the eve of his journey to Paris, Poussin was very much his own man. The early questioning and preoccupation with opposites had given way to a new, thoughtful harmony.

Wooded River-bank along the Tiber,
pen and brown wash,
16.4 x 12.8 cm (6$^1/_2$ x 5 in.).
Musée Fabre, Montpellier.

Landscape with St Matthew,
oil on canvas,
99 x 1356 cm (39 x 53 in.).
Staatliche Museen, Berlin-Dahlem.

Landscape with St John on Patmos,
oil on canvas,
102 x 133 cm (40 x 52¼ in.).
Art Institute of Chicago.

CHAPTER FOUR

Interlude in Paris; the Court of Louis XIII

ARTISTIC AIMS OF THE KING AND HIS MINISTER.
POUSSIN'S ARRIVAL IN PARIS IN 1640.
ALTARPIECES AND INTERIOR SCHEMES.
THE GRANDE GALERIE OF THE LOUVRE.
FRIENDS AND PATRONS.
POUSSIN'S RETURN TO ROME.
CARDINAL CAMILLO MASSIMI.

By the late 1630s Poussin was much in demand in Rome. Paris was beginning to take an increasing interest in him, however. The *Triumphs* painted for Cardinal Richelieu had proved a great success, as had a number of pictures painted for private collectors there. It was a time when the future of the French monarchy at last seemed secure, thanks to the long-awaited birth of the Dauphin, the future Louis XIV, in 1638; and France was trying to establish itself as an international force – not a conspicuously easy task. Not surprisingly, increasing attention was paid to the arts, not only as a means of manifesting power, but on account of the great prestige which accrues to those who promote them. Louis XIII took a keen interest in painting, having himself painted since childhood. The king was more than surpassed in sumptuousness, however, by his minister, Richelieu, whose building projects included the Palais Cardinal and the châteaux at Richelieu and Rueil; he could offer more than just personal patronage, being also the representative of the State. Earlier, while at Marie de Médicis's side, he had recommended Rubens as a painter and supervised the decoration of the gallery in the Palais du Luxembourg. He was acutely aware of the value of art and the part painters could play in ensuring the lasting fame of a particular reign. His protégés included Claude Vignon and, more particularly, Philippe de Champaigne. Richelieu was also responsible for recalling Vouet and Stella from Italy, in 1627 and 1634 respectively, to serve the king. Finally, of course, he engaged Poussin to produce the *Triumphs* as part of the decorative scheme for his own château.

In 1638 François Sublet de Noyers was appointed Surintendant des Bâtiments du Roi. The construction and maintenance of Crown buildings ceased to be the province of the Surintendant des Finances – an office which would be quite separate in future. From this point it was Sublet's job to draw up plans, agree prices and authorize expenditure. Richelieu's innovations had opened up new areas of responsibility, and he also had to oversee fortifications, the minting of coins and medals, and the royal presses. Major works were already in hand or about to start. The restoration and conservation of Fontainebleau, the decoration of Saint-Germain-en-Laye and the recently built Palace of Versailles, and the internal arrangement of the Louvre were all projects which needed to be directed by men whose authority and prestige were universally recognized. Vouet, as First Painter to the King, could not do everything, even with all the assistance he could muster from his enormous studio. He clearly preferred, anyway, to work on lucrative commissions for rich private patrons. Sublet cast about in Europe, therefore, for an artist of at least similar standing. Prominent Italian painters, such Pietro da Cortona, declined the offer. The negotiations with Poussin were carried out by Sublet de Noyers's cousins and closest advisers, the Fréart brothers, who were members of the provincial gentry: Roland was lord of Chambray and Paul of Chantelou. It was these two, rather than the small-minded Sublet, who understood Richelieu's grand designs and set his ideas in motion. As the political centre of the Christian world, Paris must also become its artistic capital, Inevitably, then, they looked to Rome, where so many relics of classical civilization, so many fine masterpieces and great men were to be found.

The impetus the Fréart brothers gave to art was astonishingly long-lasting, given how briefly they enjoyed their position of influence. Richelieu's death in 1642, followed by Sublet's disgrace in 1643, and his death in 1645, soon stripped them of any direct power. Richelieu's successor, the shrewd 'second Cardinal', Mazarin, had simply to continue, however, along the lines they had already established. During his period of office a number of the ideas they had put forward were finally realized, most notably the Académie Royale for the teaching of painting and sculpture, founded in 1648. Although not in any real sense doctrinaire, the Fréart brothers believed firmly in education and advocated a return to a greater purity and discipline in art. They assembled a collection of moulds and casts of classical sculpture for young artists to learn from. Roland published several treatises, first on architecture, in 1650, and then on painting, in 1662. Raphael and Poussin were the idols of both brothers. They were the stars of Paul's outstanding collection of classicist art, graced with a visit from Bernini during his stay in France in 1665. Poussin's seven *Sacraments* and his *Self-Portrait* of 1650 dominated the collection, which also included other masterpieces such as *The Israelites Gathering Manna*.

106–7, 149
102

Poussin's association with Chantelou dated back to the summer of 1640, when the Fréart brothers came to Rome charged with persuading the reluctant painter to comply with Sublet de Noyers's instructions and obey the king's commands. Poussin had been flattered initially when in January 1639 he began to receive letters first from the superintendent and then from the king himself, and was no doubt tempted by the terms proposed: a limited stay of only five years, 1,000 crowns for the journey, an annual salary of 1,000 crowns and accommodation in a lodge in the Tuileries Gardens. There were as many good reasons for staying in Rome as there were for leaving, however: pictures to be finished, the after-effects of his illness, and his young wife who was not remotely keen to accompany him. He was loath to leave a city where he had found the peace of mind so necessary to him. He was probably worried, too, about all the scheming which went on in Paris and at court, and about the constraints he would encounter in working for the king. Lastly, he did not see himself fitting readily into the role of great decorator at the head of a vast team. He had stipulated that he should not be required 'to paint ceilings or vaults', but there was always a chance his wishes might not be respected. After two years of procrastination, he set off with the Fréart brothers on 28 November 1640. They went by sea from Civita Vecchia to Genoa, and thence to Marseilles, and then made their way up the Rhône valley. It was altogether a rather pleasant journey, culminating in a V.I.P. welcome in Paris. By the end of the year, he was comfortably settled in and presented to Louis XIII. Delighted at last to have two painters to play off one against the other, the king made his feelings plain in his now famous quip, 'That will teach Vouet a lesson!'

Poussin's first letters from Paris convey genuine contentment, and with good reason. As well as the pleasure of meeting old friends, Paris afforded him honour and prosperity. During his stay his earnings were between 16,000 and 20,000 livres. His accommodation in the Tuileries – his 'little palace' as he called it – was a delight. There was another side to the coin, however, for the duties of First Painter turned out to include 'the general supervision of all works of art or decoration connected with the royal houses'. In the space of a few months, he went from producing designs for tapestries to painting altarpieces and from designing architectural ornament to drawing the frontispieces of books. His time was chiefly taken up, however, with the management of the project which was the king's prime concern: the decoration of the Grande Gallery in the

The Institution of the Eucharist,
oil on canvas,
325 x 250 cm (128 x 98½ in.).
Louvre, Paris.

Michel Dorigny,
The Virgin Giving the Society of Jesus her Protection,
engraving after Simon Vouet.

Opposite
The Miracle of St Francis Xavier
(detail); see also p. 123.

Louvre. There was no question of easel-painting now; Richelieu and the king allowed him barely a moment's respite. He was only barely able to finish *Baptism*, the last of the *Sacraments* commissioned by Dal Pozzo, which he had brought with him from Rome, and likewise *The Holy Family* (Detroit) for the art dealer Stefano Roccatagliata. Despite its modest size, the latter is striking in its restraint and memorable for the way in which the three figures are complemented by the purely geometrical elements around them.

Poussin's first task meant trying his hand again at a kind of painting he had not attempted since *The Martyrdom of St Erasmus* and *The Virgin Appearing to St James* – an altarpiece. On Poussin's arrival, the king commissioned a painting to adorn the chapel of the château at Saint-Germain. Poussin worked on the picture until September 1641. Both the king and the queen were pleased with the result, even though Poussin's austere *Institution of the Eucharist* could hardly be more different in character from the elegant style and light palette they had come to expect from Vouet. Poussin skilfully adapts his subject to the upright format and huge scale of the canvas – over 3 m (10 ft) high – and makes no attempt to produce a historically accurate reconstruction of the scene. Unlike the Dal Pozzo *Eucharist*, which focuses on Jesus blessing the bread and the wine, Christ is about to give communion. Instead of showing the Apostles reclining on a *triclinium* as Judas steals away, Poussin now paints all twelve kneeling or standing in a confined space closed off by a very restrained row of Ionic columns. He avoids any possible monotony by breaking up the symmetry and throwing the composition off centre, the hand of Jesus raised in blessing being at the true centre of the picture. Both the lamp and the chalice are slightly out of line with it, and the figure of Christ is on the right. The fact that the faces of the Apostles in the middle ground are all more or less aligned is more than compensated for by the position of the kneeling figures in the foreground who act as repoussoirs. The expressions and attitudes, finally, are more varied and more revealing than those in the Dal Pozzo picture and prefigure the dramatic feel of the Chantelou version. Forms seem almost to grow out of the semi-darkness, illuminated only by the twin flames of the lamp. The picture is something of an oddity, curiously close to the art of Georges de La Tour, who was then well-known in Paris and particularly highly regarded by the king. It took a certain amount of daring to produce so austere and undecorative a picture, especially as an altarpiece.

Poussin's major achievement during his stay in Paris must be *The Miracle of St Francis Xavier* (Louvre), commissioned by the superintendent in 1641 for the high altar of the Jesuit Noviciate, founded by him ten years earlier. Conceived by Father Martellange, the church was a shining example of the new style of architecture advocated by Sublet de Noyers and Fréart de Chambray. Its regularity of line and restrained decoration had been celebrated in poems and engravings. In entrusting the most important picture in the church to Poussin (rather than to Vouet or Stella, whose works were relegated to chapels in the transepts), the superintendent clearly wanted a painting to match the architecture. Poussin, for his part, resumed his association with the Jesuits. As he had done in his early years, he scoured the lives of the Society's founders for a suitable subject, finally choosing one which, on the face of it, seemed scarcely suited to his talents: while on their evangelizing mission to Japan, St Francis Xavier and his companion Juan Fernandez revive the daughter of an inhabitant of Cangoxima. To cope with a canvas nearly 4.50 m (14 ft 6 in.) in height Poussin introduces two levels into the composition: below, the dead girl surrounded by her family and the two priests; above, Jesus appearing in a glory in the sky,

99

cat. 37

119

98

123

Jacques Stella,
Jesus Discovered in the Temple,
oil on canvas,
234 x 200 cm (92¼ x 78¾ in.).
Church of Notre Dame, Les Andelys.

flanked by two angels. The composition of the upper part, featuring all the strictness of a painting by Raphael, recalls a spandrel in some Romanesque church, the calm majesty of the representation of Christ contrasting sharply with the human drama taking place below. There are echoes of the Dal Pozzo version of *Extreme Unction*, but here the   99 deathbed is placed at an angle and the figures around it form a far more compact group, in which attention is focused on the yellow dress of the woman supporting the girl's head and on the white surplices of Francis Xavier and Fernandez. Both priests gaze skywards, while the rest of the assembled company display a wide range of emotions: some are distraught, some register surprise or joy, others give thanks to God. There is little local colour to suggest the Orient, save the almost completely shaven heads of the Japanese men. The carefully calculated arrangement of gestures and expressions, however, amply illumines the scene.

It was this analysis of extremes of emotion which made the picture the success it was. Poussin was teased about his Christ in Majesty, though: people said it looked more like 'a Thundering Jove than a God of mercy'. Never one to mince words, Poussin retorted that he did not see 'Christ as stiff-necked or as some molly-coddling parent'. The most striking, and the most disappointing, aspect of the picture is its ambiguity: it is neither wholly an altarpiece nor really a history painting. The image Poussin creates is diffuse. Because he included so many disparate figures, he could not hope to rival the direct intensity which both Vouet and Stella displayed in their work for the same church. Vouet's painting of *The Virgin Giving the Society of Jesus her Protection*, now lost, but   120 known through an engraving, achieved its effect by heaping pathos on pathos in a polished whole, while Stella's approach in *Jesus Discovered in the Temple* (now in the church at Les Andelys) was more severe, and relied for its effects on a striking simplicity very much in tune with the architectural setting. Recent cleaning has altered our perception of the Poussin work, however, by revealing the glory of its original colours. Where his altarpiece for Saint-Germain was dark and sober, the colours in this picture are bright and pure, as befitted a light, new church – yellows and pale greens, strong blues and oranges, brilliant whites heightened by touches of red and black. The detail of the copper bed-leg reflecting the light is a masterly touch.

Nowhere else in Poussin's work do the circumstances of a particular commission have a more marked effect than in *The Institution of the Eucharist* and *The Miracle of St*   119, 123 *Francis Xavier*. Poussin seems constrained, ill at ease even, in these two large altarpieces. At the same time, however, he was getting to grips with the form itself, and the two pictures represent a convincing alternative both to the animated Roman style and to the expansive, virtuoso approach adopted by Vouet in this sort of painting. Poussin's is a very studied approach. His compositions are deliberately frontal, and the figures given a static, monumental quality. There is a dynamic sense of perspective and a skilful use of colour and light. Finally, there is a study of different *affetti* in the Domenichino manner. Poussin's art had a profound effect on young Parisian artists like Le Sueur and La Hyre, but did not inspire any real followers.

In terms of decorative work, Poussin was faced with two decorative projects quite unmatched in scale: a chamber in the Palais Cardinal, and the entire Grande Gallery in the Louvre. Richelieu commissioned Poussin to paint two pictures for his 'Grand Cabinet', *Moses before the Burning Bush* (now in Copenhagen) to hang above the fireplace,   *cat. 15* and a circular *Time and Truth Destroying Envy and Discord* (Louvre) for the ceiling.   123

Time and Truth Destroying Envy and Discord,
oil on canvas,
diameter 297 cm (117 in.).
Louvre, Paris.

The Miracle of St Francis Xavier,
oil on canvas,
444 x 234 cm (174³/₄ x 92 in.).
Louvre, Paris.

Both were painted on canvas and Poussin had to work to predetermined formats. The subjects, too, were stipulated by Richelieu. There were fitting similarities between the story of Moses being chosen by God to deliver the Israelites and that of Richelieu's own mission as cardinal and minister and his struggle against the Reformation. The allegorical ceiling subject celebrates his political career and points uncompromisingly to the obstacles he encountered and the calumnies he endured during his period of office. The oval *Moses before the Burning Bush*, finished some time before November 1641, features the severe 'Thundering Jove' of a God also seen in *The Miracle of St Francis Xavier*, the composition being simple but slightly stiff. Poussin deemed his skills quite unsuited to ceiling painting and he never attempted another. The painted lunette through which the cloudy sky and the foreshortened allegorical figures perched on its rim are seen reflect the illusionist works that Vouet and his followers were busy creating in houses all over Paris, for example that of Chancellor Séguier. Poussin's figures have a much stronger sculptural quality, however. The shadows are dramatic, the colours intense, the gestures almost frozen. Poussin is clearly no more at home with allegory here than he was in the pictures commissioned by Giulio Rospigliosi, finding it limiting as a genre with its accepted forms of personification and standard sets of attributes. His two female fiends, however, are a far cry from the kindly figures generally in vogue; they have a powerful wild-eyed presence not readily dismissed, particularly evident in Discord with her serpent locks and chilling expression.

The Grande Galerie of the Louvre was Poussin's first and last experience of working on a massive project. In tackling it he was vying with the great names in Italian art, like Annibale Carracci, and with contemporary painters like Pietro da Cortona and Romanelli. The enormous waterside wing linking the Louvre to the Tuileries had been the centrepiece of Henri IV's grand scheme. At the time of his death, its upper floor was still undecorated. No other gallery in any of the royal residences could compare with it in size, not even those at Fontainebleau and Saint-Germain. The Petite Galerie had been filled with portraits of all the kings of France, and the intention was to incorporate views of the most important cities in the kingdom on the piers of the Grande Galerie. The landscape painter Jacques Foucquières was commissioned in 1626 to produce the 96 views required, but in the event completed only two. An inauspicious political climate halted the project, and it was resumed only after the birth of Louis XIII's heir and the appointment of Sublet as Surintendant des Bâtiments du Roi. It was decided that the work should be completed as quickly as possible, and Poussin's role was to oversee this process. He soon lost heart, and his letters during the period 1641–2 show signs of embarrassment, weariness, even anger. On top of the sheer difficulty of the artisitc conception, Poussin was faced with all sorts of other problems, like having to manage a team and coping with the caustic comments of his rivals. Despite all this he duly began, reluctantly or otherwise, to produce drawings and cartoons for the project.

The chosen theme of the Grande Galerie was Hercules, a perfectly fitting subject for the palace of the French King. Hercules was after all a founder of dynasties, among them that of Navarre. The Valois had appropriated him, and Henri IV who succeeded them had himself portrayed as a *Gallic Hercules*. Furthermore, the life of Hercules provided a fount of adventures and labours with which to fill up and articulate what was a far from easy space. If anything, the gallery was restricting: disproportionately long in relation to its width – over 400 m (1,300 ft) long by only 8 m (26 ft) wide – with many windows on both sides and a vaulted ceiling. In a letter Poussin complained of 'the melancholy, mean, cold feel of it all'. The scheme finally accepted by Sublet sought to respect the lines of Lemercier's architecture on the one hand, while doing its utmost to fulfil its task of glorifying the king on the other. Foucquières was expected to carry on the work commissioned in 1626, to paint views of the cities of France on the wall spaces between windows. He soon fell out with the project's new manager, however. The springs of the arches were to be decorated with scenes from the life of Hercules, painted *en grisaille* to resemble bas-reliefs, rectangular in format over the piers, and within medallions supported by atlantes over the windows. The vault, divided along its entire length by a moulding, was to be covered with stucco copies of reliefs and other classical pieces selected by the Fréart brothers when on their mission to Italy in 1640. The scheme was a composite one, then, but one in which every detail was designed to celebrate the Bourbons: it combined a 'catalogue' of the territories under their dominion with a more direct tribute to the royal family and Louis XIII in particular. Clearly inspired by Rome, the scheme was distinctly classicist and purist in feeling, and was intended to trumpet Richelieu's new cultural policy to the world at large.

Poussin began to outline the general structure of the scheme, deciding on the distribution of the paintings, and to produce cartoons for his associates to work from. He started by designing the purely decorative elements like the atlantes and terms, before setting to work on the scenes from the life of Hercules, for which he drew inspiration from Natale Conti's *Mythologie*. The surviving studies for the scheme fall into three distinct groups: firstly, there are sketches by Poussin himself (like the ones in the Louvre and at Bayonne, for instance), which show him working out different ideas for pairs of pictures; then there are more elaborate drawings in which he begins to develop his ideas; and finally there are very finished drawings, sometimes incorporating a grid, by Poussin's associates like Rémy Vuibert and Jean and Pierre Lemaire (many of them now in the Hermitage). There would also have been large working drawings, now lost, used for transferring the designs. The vault was painted in oils, directly on to the plaster. Poussin gave his workforce minute instructions, never content with what they did. Based as it was on ornamental motifs and 'bas-reliefs' painted *en grisaille*, Poussin's design ran counter to all contemporary notions of decorative painting. Instead of trying to break up the lines of the vault by creating the illusion of a sky with flying figures, in the manner of Pietro da Cortona or Vouet, Poussin refused to interfere with the architectural framework or even to countenance over-emphatic projections: 'Everything I have set out for this vault,' he wrote, 'should be considered as laid on to its surface. Nothing should break through this skin, figures should not be allowed to jut out beyond or be embedded deep into it. Instead, everything on the surface should reinforce the form and structure of the vault.' Art should obey the laws of reason, and respect true perspectives and actual viewpoints. While other painters created an 'aspect' immediately pleasing to the eye, Poussin held that art should present a 'prospect', a coherent view, applied to the entire composition. It is little wonder that Poussin's uncompromising attitude and contradictory thinking should have provoked criticism from Vouet, Lemercier and others, who protested that the paintings were too small, the decoration too sparse, the whole design lacking in splendour. Such comments added to Poussin's disenchantment with this great venture, and very likely influenced his decision to return to Rome. Although he continued to despatch designs from there to Vuibert and the Lemaires who had taken charge of the team

Hercules and Theseus Fighting the Amazons, pen and brown wash, 13.2 x 13.6 cm (5¼ x 5½ in.). Royal Library, Windsor.

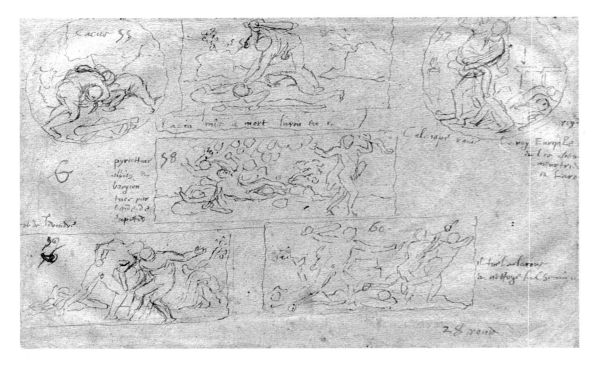

The Labours of Hercules,
pen and brown ink,
18.7 x 30.2 cm (7½ x 12 in.).
Musée Bonnat, Bayonne.

Assistant of Poussin,
Hercules Learning to Play the Lyre,
pen and ink and brown wash,
highlighted with white chalk,
18 x 42.3 cm (7 x 16½ in.).
Louvre, Paris.

Louis van Blarenberghe,
snuff-box with decoration showing
the Duc de Choiseul visiting
the Grande Galerie of the Louvre.
Private Collection.

working on the gallery, Poussin was able to complete only a small part of the scheme: probably no more than ten rectangular paintings and as many medallions.

Work on the project ceased as early as 1643. The deaths first of Richelieu and then of the king, as well as the disgrace of Sublet, put an end to it once and for all. Neither Mazarin nor Colbert was able to resurrect the project, though some decorative work was done in 1668. The gallery ceased to have a *raison d'être* after Louis XIV abandoned the Louvre for Versailles in 1678. The decoration, left unfinished and subsequently neglected, gradually disappeared during the eighteenth century. Evidence of it is seen on the side of a snuff-box (private collection) by Van Blarenberghe, showing the Duc de Choiseul on a visit to what was thereafter the Map Gallery. The gallery remained largely untouched until Hubert Robert was taken on by the Museum to try to articulate the long and unwieldy space and to improve the lighting. When work stopped on the project in 1643, the Italian style of decoration held sway: from the Palais Mazarin, decorated 1645–7 by Romanelli, to Lebrun's masterpiece, the Hall of Mirrors at Versailles (1679–84), the emphasis was on great vaults divided into broad scenes. It was a style which, with its penchant for illusions, its use of rich colour, its displays of virtuosity and its swirling movement, focused on 'aspects', not 'prospects'.

Frontispiece for an edition of the works of Horace, engraving by Claude Mellan after Poussin.

While in the service of the king, Poussin had to be able to turn his hand to anything, even designs for tapestries and frontispieces for books. He had no time to mull over compositions at length and, being accustomed to working slowly and alone, he found it difficult not to betray the panic into which the never-ending stream of orders threw him: 'I have only one pair of hands and a single feeble brain, with no-one to help me or lessen the load.' Indeed, Sublet seems to have been insatiable in his demands. Whatever the project – the sculpting of Sublet's arms on the pediment of the Jesuit church, the decoration of his private apartments in a town-house in the Rue Saint Honoré, or the building of a chapel in the Château de Dangu, his country residence near Gisors – Poussin was required to provide both drawings and advice. Not only did he have to produce designs for these projects, like the Council staircase or the Orangerie in the Palais du Luxembourg, but he had to take a personal hand in their execution, seeing to details like gilding, fireplaces and ceiling cornices, and the ornamentation of reception rooms and bedrooms alike. In the process, he hit out at Lemercier, whose design for Sublet's office he thought mean, 'just right for a haberdasher's shop'. Where artists like Vouet, Charles Errard, and later Lebrun, were able to generate an inexhaustible supply of ideas for decoration and impose a style of their own, the man who painted *The Israelites Gathering Manna* was quick to throw up his hands in despair. To his mind, the decorative scheme for the Louvre and the preparation of a set of cartoons for a series of tapestries depicting the seven *Sacraments* were more than enough to keep him busy. When the Surintendant asked him in July 1642 to come to Fontainebleau 'to see if it would be possible to restore Primaticcio's paintings, virtually destroyed by the ravages of time, or at least to find some way of saving the best-preserved examples', Poussin took the opportunity to ask to be allowed to return to Italy, ostensibly so that he could fetch his wife. He was given permission to go, on condition that he 'put in order … everything he had begun' and return the following spring.

Poussin was slightly happier when asked to design frontispieces for books printed by the royal press, established in 1640. Claude Mellan engraved three of his designs for editions of the works of Virgil and Horace, and of the Bible, capturing with his customary clarity and breadth a monumental grandeur similar to that found in Poussin's paintings of the period. They are not, perhaps, the most inspired of designs. Their conception was slow and shrouded in a certain amount of gloom. 'We are too far from the sun,' wrote Poussin to Chantelou on 20 March 1642, 'for there to be any question of finding anything delightful here. As long as I am not confronted with anything actually hideous, however, I can rely on what remains of my memories of real beauty to provide me, as it has for the frontispiece for the Horace, with some sort of an idea which will just about pass muster.' The frontispieces for both Horace and Virgil have their roots in *The Inspiration of the Poet* (Louvre): Virgil is being crowned by Apollo, while Horace is having a mask put on him by the Muse. The figure of God on the frontispiece of the Bible is taken straight from *The Miracle of St Francis Xavier*. The winged woman stands for History. Her veiled counterpart, accompanied by a sphinx, symbolizing 'the obscurity of things enigmatic', represents Prophecy. In these frontispieces the figures are arranged symmetrically and stand out like statues against the light backgrounds with their simple hatching. Poussin respected the constraints of the frame and of the format and whiteness of the paper in exactly the same way as he respected the architectural context in the Louvre. Instead of choosing this or that episode and making a real illustration of it, as most of his contemporaries would have done, Poussin opts for an allegorical approach, and turns books into monuments not limited by time or space. This innovation in the world of fine books never really took off, however, the results being far too abstract and bald to be commercially successful.

54

123

Brief though it was, and despite the problems he encountered, Poussin's stay in Paris at least gave him the opportunity to renew old friendships, for example with Champaigne and Stella, and establish new ones, and more importantly, to extend his public following. He was fêted from the moment he arrived. Poussin allowed himself some 'wild living' – jaunts into the country and evenings, like the one Abbé Bourdelot described to Cassiano Dal Pozzo in a letter dated 1 May 1642, spent energetically eating and drinking. His companions on these occasions were painters like Jean Lemaire and Rémy Vuibert, his assistants on the Louvre project, and, more commonly, doctors and philosophers like Gabriel Naudé, Guy Patin, Pierre Richer and Pierre Gassendi. Poussin must have felt reasonably at home. After all, he had got to know Bourdelot and Naudé in Rome through the Barberini. Bourdelot had stood up for Galileo and helped Campanella to escape from the Inquisition. Naudé, who was then Richelieu's librarian, was also fiercely opposed to superstition of any kind. Both doctors like them, the Parisians Richer and Patin were also of a literary bent. Richer tried his hand at Latin verse, while Patin was a brilliant letter-writer whose account of the Fronde was the fullest and liveliest of the day. Gassendi's philosophy was essentially Epicurean and diametrically opposed to that of Descartes, and he was a humanist in outlook. Other associates included Tristan l'Hermite and Saint-Amant, both poets, the Dupuy brothers, both scientists, and Jacques de Thou, Parliamentary President and later French ambassador to the Netherlands.

All these associates, from Poussin's friends of long standing to his more recent contacts, belonged to the 'Literary Republic' which was taking shape from Rome to Paris, and were united in their often forceful rejection of dogma and the principle of absolute authority. Although for the most part they maintained at least an outward show of being good Christians, they could hardly have been called devout. In terms of the religious beliefs and practices of the day, they were quite beyond the pale: frequently free both in behaviour and in intention, they were rationalist thinkers who propounded a 'natural' philosophy and upheld a system of moral values based on Stoic principles. This is not to say that Poussin was himself one of the 'the Libertines', one of the growing number of fully-fledged free-thinkers described by René Pintard as representing such a significant force in the seventeenth century. In choosing to keep the company he did, however, Poussin revealed himself as independently minded and capable of critical judgment and informed opinion, and aloof from both Church and State. Although Poussin worked in Paris both for the Jesuits and for that most pious of kings, Louis XIII, his paintings are by no means mystical outpourings and are well-nigh devoid of religious feeling. Like many of the finest thinkers of his day, Poussin had been trying for several years, in the pictures he painted for Cassiano Dal Pozzo onwards, to combine what he saw as the best aspects of ancient, pagan civilization and of Christianity into a coherent whole in art. This does not mean that he and his friends went in for interminable philosophical and theological discussions. By all accounts, their Paris get-togethers were anything but earnest.

Because of the many contacts he made during his stay in Paris, Poussin was able to build on his existing clientèle and expand his circle of devotees. He now had a band of followers in France as well as in Rome, membership of which depended on being proposed and accepted, as in a club. Poussin's character and method of working were such that his relations with his buying public were unusual for an artist at this period. Obstinate and unyielding by nature, he was at once mistrustful and demanding. His rate of progress was slow and made slower still by ill-health – as early as 1642 he complains in a letter about his 'trembling hand'. Poussin preferred to work for a small group of private patrons of a clearly defined type, some of whom had to wait several years for delivery of a painting. The image he projected was of an exceptional talent, ownership of his slowly matured masterpieces being the privilege of only a happy few.

Poussin's return to Rome in 1642 saw an end to his dealings with princes and ministers, churches and religious orders, and from now on he did little work for members of the nobility. A few ambassadors to the Holy See were honoured with paintings, however. In 1653 Sublet's first assistant, Monsieur de Mauroy, obtained a version of *The Adoration of the Shepherds* (now lost, but known through an engraving). Henri d'Etampes-Valençay managed to obtain *The Assumption of the Virgin* (now in the Louvre) of 1650, a work purchased shortly after by Mauroy. The Duc de Créquy is reputed to have bought two paintings of *The Holy Family* sometime in the 1650s, one of which – featuring eleven figures – is now owned jointly by the Norton Simon Museum in Pasadena and the Getty Museum in Malibu, California. The duke's grandfather, Maréchal de Créquy, himself a great collector, had earlier commissioned Poussin to paint two pictures when he was ambassador to Rome in 1633–4: *The Rape of the Sabine Women* (New York) and *Women Bathing* (now lost). Poussin's last commission of this kind came late in his career, from the Duc de Richelieu, the Cardinal's nephew. This was the important set of *Four Seasons* (1660–4), sold on almost immediately by the duke to Louis XIV.

Equally, Poussin's work was evidently not destined to reach many of the high-ranking ministers or financiers in whom, for reasons either of ostentation or personal taste, artists working in Paris in the seventeenth century found their chief patrons. There was Richelieu, of course, whose association with Poussin began with the *Triumphs* and ended with the decoration of the Palais Cardinal. Mazarin, too, commissioned work from him, but on nothing like the same scale. Three paintings are listed under the name Pous-

cat. 58
183

178

72; *cat. 171*

38–9, 246–7

sin in the inventory of his effects drawn up in 1653, all apparently executed before 1640: *Four Naked Children and Two Dogs, Apollo with a Muse and a Poet Crowned with Laurel Leaves* (generally identified with the *The Inspiration of the Poet* in the Louvre) and *The Fable of Endymion with the Chariot of the Sun* (possibly the marvellous picture in Detroit). For the Surintendant des Finances, Nicolas Fouquet, Poussin designed in 1655 a set of terms intended for the gardens of his château, Vaux-le-Vicomte, near Melun (these are now at Versailles). This came about, however, as a result of friendly pressure from Abbé Louis Fouquet, the minister's brother and himself a collector of antiquities. For Mme Fouquet Poussin painted a version of *The Holy Family with St Elizabeth and St John the Baptist* (now in the Louvre). We should not forget, of course, the large picture painted much earlier, in 1637, for the Secretary of State, Louis Phélypeaulx de la Vrillière, who was then filling the magnificent gallery in his town-house with Italian masterpieces. *Camillus and the Schoolmaster of Falerii*, now in the Louvre, is tense and stoical in feeling and tackles a theme Poussin had explored several years earlier in a smaller version, now in Pasadena, painted for Michel Passart, the Maître des Comptes.

178

141

With Passart we come to the big names in administration and finance who constituted the most important part of Poussin's following by far. Royal advisers jostle with bankers and merchants. Such people were Poussin's most consistently loyal clients, and it was they who owned the most varied and significant collections of his works. In addition to *Camillus and the Schoolmaster of Falerii*, Passart had acquired the *Landscape with a Woman Washing her Feet* (1650), now in Ottawa, and the moving *Landscape with Diana and Orion* (1658), now in New York. He also owned one of Poussin's 'stoical' masterpieces, *The Testament of Eudamidas* (*c.* 1653, Copenhagen). With Passart, a small section of Parisian society had found in Poussin an artist perfectly in tune with their strict tastes, treating serious moral and philosophical subjects, in the same way that François Mansart and Louis Le Vau were in tune with their ideas on architecture. Also worthy of mention in this context are Melchior Gillier, one of the king's advisers, who acquired *Moses Striking the Rock* (Edinburgh) while in Rome in 1634 as steward to the then ambassador, Maréchal de Créquy; the Parliamentary President, Jacques de Thou, who in 1646 bought the rather severe but striking *Crucifixion*, now in Hartford, Conn.; and Hennequin du Fresne, Master of the Royal Hunt, for whom Poussin painted in 1648 one of his most astounding pictures, *The Madonna of the Steps* (Cleveland).

cat. 232
229

140

cat. 19

cat. 78

179

Poussin's friends from Lyons were his most impressive supporters. This group included bankers and rich merchants who were often in Paris and Rome on business. Between them, they owned a sizable part of Poussin's output and helped push up its value to heights rarely reached in the seventeenth century. In the forefront of this group were Jean Pointel, who had settled in Paris, and his associate Jacques Serisier (or Cérisiers): to them he entrusted for safekeeping a large proportion of the money he amassed during his stay in Paris, and when he made his will in September 1642 before departing for Rome he appointed them as his executors. By all accounts they were serious-minded, hardworking men of integrity with a bent for order. Judging by the works which Poussin reserved for them, they seem to have shared something of the artist's moral and political outlook.

The inventory of Pointel's effects drawn up after his death, and published a few years ago, lists twenty-one paintings and eighty drawings by Poussin. It was an austere selection of his works which featured only paintings from his later years, beginning with the large

Moses Saved from the Water (1647) and *Eliezer and Rebecca at the Well* (1648), both now
in the Louvre, and ending with a monumental version of *The Holy Family* with four
149   figures painted in 1655, possibly the work now in Sarasota, and encompassing the *Self-*
145   *Portrait* (Berlin) of 1649 and *The Judgment of Solomon* (Louvre) of the same year. The
collection also included a number of other works every bit the equal of these masterpieces: *Landscape with a Man Killed by a Snake* (London) and *Landscape with Orpheus*
162   *and Eurydice* (Louvre), both painted *c.* 1648; *Landscape – a Calm* (Sudeley Castle) and
163   its pendant, *Landscape – a Storm* (Rouen), both painted in 1651; and finally, and most
159   importantly, the *Landscape with Polyphemus* (Hermitage, Leningrad), painted in 1649.
Valued by Pointel himself at 60,000 livres and by Philippe de Champaigne, who drew up
the inventory, at the rather more modest figure of 15,000, the collection was eventually
sold at auction. Prices rocketed as investors began to take a speculative interest in Poussin, which trend reached its peak in the 1680s. In Poussin's own lifetime, even though the
prices he charged were relatively low, his finest pictures were in great demand. Félibien
recounts that one lady of his acquaintance was 'so taken' with *Eliezer and Rebecca at the*
Well, then in Pointel's possession, that she offered him 'anything he should want: but he
was so passionately attached to his friend's paintings that, far from wanting to sell them,
he could not bear to be without them for even a single day.' By refusing to part with his
pictures, this most exclusive of collectors was helping to turn works by Poussin into a
rare, hence very expensive, commodity.

    Serisier, the wealthy mercer, commissioned only four paintings, which count
215   among the finest – *Esther before Ahasuerus* (1655), now in the Hermitage; *The Flight into*
cat. 61   *Egypt with a Traveller at Rest* (1658), a version of which has recently come to light; and
above all, two huge landscapes painted in 1648 (in Cardiff and Liverpool respectively),
154,155   *Landscape with the Funeral of Phocion* and *Landscape with Gathering of the Ashes of Pho-*
cion, both revealing an unforgettable precision. Serisier continued to expand his collection by timely purchases, and when Bernini visited his Paris residence in 1665, he saw as
many as a dozen paintings by Poussin, several of which had come from Pointel. The great
banker and industrialist Lumague (or Lumagne), one of the richest men of his day, owned
158   only one work by Poussin, but one of the very best – the *Landscape with Diogenes*
(*c.* 1648), now in the Louvre. Two other, lesser figures from Lyons were also quick to sup-
cat. 73   port Poussin: a manufacturer of silk and brocade called Reynon acquired *Christ Healing*
the Sick (Louvre) in 1651, while the 'treasurer' and merchant Mercier bought the second
cat. 96   version of *St Peter Healing a Sick Man* (New York) in 1655. According to the records,
Poussin was well represented by the end of the seventeenth century in many collections
in Lyons. These men of money knew a good investment when they saw one, but they were
also attracted to the high-minded restraint in Poussin's works, a quality to which they
almost certainly aspired themselves. They were the French equivalent of the patrons who
helped Poussin during his early days in Rome, and supported him in the direction he was
taking counter to contemporary Italian and French trends.

    Compared with a man like Pointel, Paul Fréart de Chantelou, Poussin's devoted
friend and regular correspondent, might seem rather insignificant. It was his collection,
however, much more than Pointel's, which had already begun to be dispersed before
1660, which so enhanced Poussin's reputation in Paris. According to the inventory drawn
up after his death in 1694, Chantelou owned twelve paintings by Poussin. Chantelou had
102   sold *The Israelites Gathering Manna* to Fouquet a good many years earlier, but the list of

Gérard Audran,
Hercules and Deianira,
engraving after Poussin.

N. Poussin In . A Paris Chez Audran . Avec Privilege du Roy . P. mariette 1692

106–7 course includes the seven *Sacraments*, which were valued at 70,000 livres. They passed to Roland Fréart and then to his nephews, before being bought by the Duc d'Orléans in 1716. They remained in Paris until the Revolution, and in 1798 they came to England. In

149 addition, there was the famous *Self-Portrait* (Louvre) of 1650, the large five-figure *Holy Family with St Elizabeth and St John the Baptist* (Hermitage) completed in 1655, and a small picture of *The Ecstasy of St Paul* (Sarasota) painted in 1643 as a pendant to another jewel in Chantelou's collection, *The Vision of Ezekiel*, thought at the time to be by

132 Raphael. There were also two other pictures, both now lost: *Hercules and Deianira*, known through a number of drawings and an engraving, which is reputed to have been

cat. 72 painted *c.* 1637 for Jacques Stella; and *Christ and the Woman of Samaria* also engraved, painted in 1662 for Madame de Chantelou, for whom – as Madame de Montmort – Pous-

cat. 63 sin had painted *The Rest on the Flight into Egypt* (now in the Hermitage) in 1655, the year before her marriage to Chantelou. Chantelou's collection contained the very best of the new classicist movement in art, and was typical of the most enlightened Parisian connoisseurs of the 1640s and 1650s. Original paintings by the great masters being already beyond his means, Chantelou bought copies, often of a very high standard, of works by Raphael, Leonardo da Vinci, Annibale Carracci, Domenichino, and even Poussin himself, His collection included, among others, copies of three of Richelieu's *Triumphs*. When he visited Chantelou in 1655, Bernini exclaimed admiringly as he viewed one of them, 'What a brilliant storyteller!'

Poussin did little work for writers, though they are, of course not generally known for their wealth, nor is there any special reason why they should be drawn to the visual arts. He painted nothing, apparently, for Saint-Amant, who sang Poussin's praises in his great epic, *Moïse sauvé*. Apart from the Cavaliere Marino, Poussin had virtually no professional writers among his clients. With Chantelou's backing, Paul Scarron, whose burlesques were then very much in fashion in Paris, wrote to Poussin in 1645 asking him to paint a picture. Poussin was repelled by both the man and his work, and kept him plead-

183 ing for five years. Having thought first of a *Bacchanal*, he finally painted *The Ecstasy of St Paul* (Louvre) for him in 1650, a morally elevating picture acquired shortly afterwards by the rich collector Evrard Jabach. St Paul is the patron saint of poets, and it is possible that in this work Poussin was making something of a point about poetic dignity to the man who wrote *Virgile travesti*. Poussin served his painter friends rather better, from the little-

83 known Nicolas-Guillaume de La Fleur, for whom he painted *Pan and Syrinx* (Dresden) *c.* 1637, to the already famous Charles Lebrun, whom he had met in Paris. Lebrun returned to Rome with Poussin in 1642 and stayed for three years, absorbing all the advice he could and almost mirroring his style at that stage. He later expressed his gratitude to Poussin for having 'opened his eyes to the mysteries and finer points of his art with his comments' (Nivelon). Poussin is also credited with advising him to go back to

228 France. The *Landscape with Two Nymphs and a Snake Attacking a Bird* (Chantilly) may be the picture Poussin is known to have painted for his follower in 1659. André Le Nôtre, near whom Poussin had his lodgings in the Tuileries Gardens, owned two paintings by Poussin, both of which he bequeathed to the king and are now in the Louvre: the sensitive

170.198 *Moses Saved from the Water* (*c.* 1638) and the rather more severe *Christ and the Woman Taken in Adultery*, the latter commissioned by him in 1653. Jacques Stella, perhaps the closest of all Poussin's fellow artists, did best; he owned five works spanning twenty years

cat. 194 – two executed in the late 1630s in Rome, *Rinaldo and Armida* (Berlin) and *Venus Pre-*

senting Arms to Aeneas (Rouen), as well as *Moses Striking the Rock* (Leningrad) and *The Exposition of Moses* (Oxford), painted in 1649 and 1654 respectively, and finally one of the last great mythological paintings, *The Birth of Bacchus* (Cambridge, Mass.), painted in 1657. All five pictures bear witness to the closeness of the emotional and creative ties between the two painters, and to the degree of inspiration shared by both men. They had known each other since the early days in Italy, and had worked on the same projects for Richelieu and Louis XIII, notably the Palais Cardinal, the Jesuit church and designs for the royal press. Moreover, ever since his return to France in 1534, Stella had made it his business to promote his friend's work both in Lyons, his native city, and in Paris, where he had lodgings in the Louvre. On Stella's death in 1657, the works by Poussin in his collection passed to his nephews and nieces named Bouzonnet, two of whom were painters. Claudine made engravings after the paintings, thus helping to make these compositions even better known, and the elderly Poussin took Antoine under his wing and gave him advice when he came to Rome.

Once settled into his house in the Via Paolina and into his old ways after his return to Rome in 1642, Poussin resumed work. He carried on supervising the Louvre project, entrusted since his departure to Rémy Vuibert, and he was burdened with a mass of jobs for Chantelou. With the demise both of the king and of his minister, however, Poussin found himself gradually released from his official commitments. He could now devote himself once more to his private patrons and work at his own pace, producing a mere handful of paintings each year. His clientèle was largely French, as we have seen. Cassiano Dal Pozzo commissioned only one more painting from him, *Landscape with Pyramus and Thisbe* (1651) now in Frankfurt, though he did also have copies made of three of Poussin's most famous 'heroic' landscapes, *Landscape with a Woman Washing her Feet*, *Landscape with a Man Killed by a Snake* and *Landscape with the Funeral of Phocion*. If Dal Pozzo was no longer one of the leading patrons of art in Rome, it was not due to any change of heart on his part, but because the situaton had changed in Rome. Following the death of Urban VIII in July 1644, the succession of Innocent X Pamphili brought with it the downfall of the Barberini, who, having been all-powerful, were now forced to flee to France. Poussin had been working on an idea for a painting of *Scipio and the Pirates* for Cardinal Francesco Barberini (preparatory drawings for which are in the Royal Library), and with him he lost one of his most influential supporters. The new pope was far from francophile, his taste inclining rather to Spain. Poussin was to find his last great Italian patron, however, in the papal entourage.

Camillo Massimi, born in 1620 of a distinguished Roman family, had a very chequered career, prospering or failing as he fell in or out of papal favour. Having been sent off to Spain as a Nuncio by Innocent X, he was recalled to Rome in 1658. He was then free to devote himself to the studies that were so dear to him. With his library of Latin, Greek and Hebrew manuscripts, and his collection of antiquities, he was a fitting successor to Dal Pozzo, who died in 1657. Created a cardinal in 1670 by Clement X, he died seven years later. He painted in his spare time, and was a great collector of pictures, becoming a friend of Velázquez, and patron first of Claude Lorrain, who painted *Coral Hue*, one of his last and most lyrical pictures, for him, and later of Carlo Maratta. Massimi already had Poussin's drawings for Marino in his collection in 1647, when he commissioned the monumental and severe pair of pictures typical of Poussin's new manner – *Moses Trampling on Pharaoh's Crown* and *Moses and Aaron before Pharaoh* (both now in the Louvre). He

86; cat. 20
171
cat. 122

164

cat. 232

cat. 13
cat. 16

cat. 152   later acquired two early works, both with moral overtones – *Midas Washing in the Pacto-*
92   *lus* (New York) and the first version of *The Arcadian Shepherds: 'Et in Arcadia Ego'*
            (Chatsworth). Poussin had great faith in his patron and, towards the end of his life, may
            well have asked his advice before tackling a number of somewhat esoteric subjects.

232   Shortly before his death, Poussin gave Massimi his last, unfinished painting, *Apollo and*
            Daphne (Louvre). Bellori conjures up the familiarity between the two men when he
            describes how once, as an elderly sage, Poussin, lamp in hand, escorted the Monsignore
            through the gloom of his simple house: 'Thinking of the inconvenience of his having to
            carry the lamp, the great man remarked: "I pity you for having only one servant." To
            which Poussin retorted, "And I pity your lordship all the more for having so many."'

Austere and outspoken: such was the image future generations would have of Poussin, a far cry from the concept of the 'noble painter' which had slowly been emerging
since the Renaissance. Artists like Rubens, Velázquez, Guido Reni and later Lebrun, all
adopted a life style very like that of the great lords and prelates for whom they worked.
Their clothes were beautiful, their studios sumptuous, their conversation sparkling:
artists were gaining in social status and aspired to new and greater heights. Poussin, by
contrast, never went in for such ostentation, even during his time at the French court. His
home in the Via Paolina, Rome, was comfortable enough, but hardly the last word in fine
furnishing. Poussin may have boasted a few paintings and antiquities, but nothing like the
full-blown collections owned by so many of his fellow artists. No silver or jewellery is
listed in the inventory drawn up after his death, but there is no suggestion, either, of
poverty or of a fringe existence. Poussin was no Caravaggio. Although he may have had
his bohemian moments early on in his career, his life had long been settled and regular,
and generally comfortable. From all the available documentary evidence – and particularly from Poussin's own series of wills – it seems that he enjoyed a life of quiet prosperity. He could afford to work in the slow, measured way which his art dictated. Poussin has
been fondly pictured taking an evening stroll under the trees along the Pincio or in the
Piazza di Spagna 'surrounded by a retinue of intimate admirers' (Bellori). It conjures up a
serene, peaceful, almost magical image, but a rather misleading one, which makes Poussin seem somehow removed from ordinary life, almost as if he is making his final bows
before leaving this world. In fact, when he returned to Rome Poussin had a long period of
slow, and often difficult, work ahead of him. In the twenty-odd years he lived there he
produced his most accomplished works. It seemed as if, after all the early uncertainties,
Poussin had returned from Paris firmly set on a course which he would diligently pursue
to the very end.

CHAPTER FIVE

Wisdom and Fortune

The ten years following Poussin's return to Rome in 1642 were without doubt the most productive of his career, both in terms of output and of profundity of thought. In the 1630s Poussin had applied a strict scholarly approach to a variety of subjects. Now, his work centred on the exploration of a number of favourite themes. It was almost certainly the close understanding which existed between Poussin and his patrons, like Pointel and Chantelou, which made this possible. The second set of *Sacraments* for Chantelou dominated the years 1644–8, so much so that Poussin had to postpone other projects. Chantelou was an excellent but demanding patron who constantly burdened Poussin with tasks, some of them trivial in the extreme – he was even asked to obtain particular perfumes and soaps, and those scented gloves which were all the rage in Parisian polite society. Others were more serious. Sublet de Noyers's former colleague was eager to add to his own collection and also to provide French artists with examples of great art to work from. He wanted copies made of all the great masterpieces in Rome like Raphael's *Transfiguration* or the Carracci frescoes in the Palazzo Farnese, and planned to assemble a collection of copies of classical statues or, failing that, busts. The scheme was an endless source of trouble for Poussin, who was never happy with the copyists hired to do the job – young Frenchmen who happened to be available, like Reynaud Levieux, Charles Errard, Pierre Mignard, Jean Nocret and Pierre Lemaire, brother of Jean, with whom Poussin had worked on the Louvre project. Obtaining originals was no easy matter, for the new pope had put a ban on the export of antiquities. The situation called for ever more devious tactics, and Poussin found himself with various busts on his hands, as is evident from his letters to his French patron. These provide an interesting, and at times harsh and grating, counterpoint to the majesty of the actual pictures. In providing an insight into Poussin the man, they are unparalleled, conveying as they do a strong sense of his quest for perfection, or indeed his impatience and confusion. Sometimes he becomes quite heated. When Chantelou complains, for instance, that Pointel has been better served than he, Poussin takes him to task for being so ungrateful: 'why have I spent so much of my precious time running errands for you all over the place and in all weathers, if not to show how greatly I respect you? I will say no more about it – how can I when I have sworn to be your loyal servant? Believe me when I tell you that I have done for you what I would do for no other living soul, and when I say that I will always continue to serve you with all my heart.' Chantelou conceded and good relations were restored.

In his letters to Chantelou, Poussin talked in detail about his art, as will be seen in the next chapter, but he also wrote at considerable length about political events. From the safety of Rome, which remained mercifully unscathed, Poussin watched in horror as the rest of Europe suffered enormous upheavals. Although the Thirty Years' War, the most immediate danger to stability in France, ended with the signing of the Treaty of Westphalia in 1648, other troubles were flaring up here, there and everywhere. A popular rebellion led by Masaniello broke out in Naples in 1647, threatening to overthrow Spanish rule. The revolt was soon crushed, however, and Henri de Guise's claims to Campania

were quickly quashed. Franco-Spanish relations, already not at their best, rapidly deterio-
rated. In Rome, too, the anti-French faction was gaining ground after the election of Innocent X and subsequent fall of the Barberini. 'People have nothing but contempt for us,
and no-one will feel remotely sorry whatever ill may befall us. We are considered on a par
with the Neapolitans, and we will be treated just the same,' wrote Poussin on 24 May 1649.
Just as the Civil War in England ended in 1649 with the execution of Charles I, so rebellion broke out in Poland, with the revolt of the Cossacks. Poussin seems relieved, in
the face of all this wild bloodshed, to be no more than an observer watching from the
sidelines: 'It is a great pleasure to live in such an eventful century – provided you have a
nice little secluded spot somewhere in which to sit back and watch the drama,' he noted
on 17 January 1649. Poussin was of course more directly affected by events in France. In
1648, while Louis XIV was still a minor, the revolt known as the Fronde posed a serious
threat to the throne, and Mazarin was forced to flee Paris. For Poussin, Mazarin's downfall
was something of a cause for celebration – he thought him corrupt and dishonest. He was
anxious, however, about the state of 'our poor country' and worried lest it fall into
decline. Poussin had little faith in the French character, believing that a strong, stable central power-base was necessary to stop the rabble getting out of hand. When, in August
1649, king, court and Mazarin were all reinstated, he could hardly contain his disgust:
'Those who recognize the stupidity and fickleness of the masses will not be remotely surprised by anything they do.' It was to be only a temporary lull, for all that. The princes
launched a second offensive, and the Fronde continued until 1653.

Poussin's thinking was in line here with the neo-Stoical philosophy so dear to theoreticians and parliamentarians at the end of the sixteenth century. The likes of Montaigne, Pierre Charron and Guillaume Du Vair expressed themselves in just the same way.
In fact, Poussin now delved into the works of his favourite authors, Livy and Plutarch in
particular, in a bid to reflect on present events by reference to past history. The force of
many of Poussin's paintings of classical subjects springs primarily from his reaction to his
own troubled times – the two Phocion landscapes, for instance, and *Coriolanus*, which
articulates a range of responses with a grandeur and an economy worthy of Corneille.
Poussin's pessimism had its roots, too, in his own recent experience in Paris. Although he
was reluctant to give up the advantages he had gained, like his lodgings in the Tuileries
Gardens, and missed, or affected to miss, his position at court, Poussin realized, as events
unfolded, that he would not return to Paris. Even in Rome, he remained somewhat aloof,
being critical of his young fellow artists and of the great rivalries within the art world, and
having no interest in honour for its own sake; he therefore turned down the job of principal of the Academy of St Luke when it was offered to him in 1657. There was nothing
superficial or acquired about his detachment, however. His experience of death, illness
and increasing infirmity engendered in him a dread which he often expressed with heart-
felt sincerity, yet it seems also to have reinforced his artistic outlook: 'Whatever my final
fate,' he wrote on 9 June 1643, 'I am resolved to accept whatever good and endure whatever evil may be in store for me. Misfortune and disgrace are such common features of
human life that I wonder that any intelligent person should allow himself to be roused by
them . . . We own nothing outright, all possession is merely temporary.' The tone is set,
and it is Seneca's – the Seneca of *De Consolatione*, the *Letters to Lucilius*, and the treatise
rendered as *La tranquillité de l'âme* by Montaigne, from which Poussin takes his last sen-
tence verbatim. Poussin's letters rehearse the basic tenets of Stoic philosophy over and

154–5, 144

Opposite
Camillus and the Schoolmaster of Falerii,
oil on canvas,
252 x 268 cm (99¹⁄₄ x 105¹⁄₂ in.).
Louvre, Paris.

The Testament of Eudamidas,
oil on canvas,
110.5 x 138.5 cm (43¹⁄₂ x 54¹⁄₂ in.).
Statens Museum for Kunst, Copenhagen.

The Continence of Scipio,
oil on canvas,
114.5 x 163.5 cm (45 x 64¹⁄₂ in.).
Pushkin Museum, Moscow.

over again: good fortune is inevitably followed by misfortune, which must be endured with fortitude; illness and death must be faced with equanimity; envy should be seen as absurd, criticism as something from which to learn; only 'true' riches are worth pursuing, i.e. 'peace and tranquillity of mind'; nothing should ever be undertaken precipitately – 'the tortoise can never keep up with the eagle'.

Poussin illustrated such well-worn precepts with examples from history. *The Death of Germanicus* was the first of a series of pictures in this vein, to be followed as early as the late 1630s by *Camillus and the Schoolmaster of Falerii* (Louvre), painted for Louis de La Vrillière in 1637, and *The Continence of Scipio* (Moscow), bought by Roscioli in 1640. Both episodes are prominently treated by Plutarch, Livy and Valerius Maximus. Both testify to the magnanimity of 'souls of noble birth'. While besieging the Etruscan town of Falerii, Camillus punishes a schoolmaster who betrays his pupils by offering them as hostages. Scipio, for his part, renounces his share of the booty and restores a captive to her betrothed. In both pictures the hero is shown in profile, seated in a commanding position on a throne. The first is turbulent and jarring: Camillus, draped in red, conveys grandeur and authority with his every gesture, while the schoolmaster appears abject and almost bestial. Of the two versions the smaller, and probably slightly earlier, one now in Pasadena more effectively conjures up the sense of a bas-relief. The sculptural quality of the group formed by the *magister* and his pupils (with its echoes of the *Laocoön* group) in the La Vrillière version, however, together with the harsh and compelling presence of standard-bearing soldiers, reminiscent of Mantegna, and the elimination of all background detail, makes it the stronger and more monumental of the two. By contrast, *The Continence of Scipio* is airy and calm: the principal characters are seen face to face, with the generous conqueror being crowned with laurels by a young girl as Allucius gives thanks to him. For Poussin as for Corneille in *Cinna*, written at the same time, the greatest victory a man can aspire to is to conquer his own passions.

A number of other ideas failed to make headway, and perhaps were never intended to be developed. Poussin made a sketch showing Cato falling on his sword (now in the Royal Library), for instance, but it probably amounts to little more than a casual note jotted down while reading. The immediacy of the horror involved makes it an unlikely subject for Poussin to have wanted to tackle, though Lebrun did just this in 1646 (his painting is now in the museum at Arras). Poussin was not interested in provoking extremes of emotion with a sensationalist display of gore and death, but preferred to create an image which required thought both in the making and in the viewing. *Mucius Scaevola*, on the other hand, was obviously intended to be the subject of a finished painting, as a preparatory drawing now in the Hermitage makes plain. The sketch has the shakiness characteristic of Poussin's last years. Begun at an uncertain date, the painting, which reappeared some time ago, respects its strictly perpendicular composition, but was completed by one of Poussin's followers. The subject was one of the most popular *exempla virtutis* in the seventeenth century, and demonstrates the hero's steadfastness and contempt for suffering and death.

Poussin may well have found the common run of subjects, so often used by painters and playwrights, somewhat hackneyed, and may therefore have tried to seek more abstruse instances of virtue. *The Testament of Eudamidas* (Copenhagen) is one such, inspired by a story taken by Montaigne from Lucian's dialogue on friendship entitled *Toxaris*. From his deathbed the impoverished Eudamidas dictates his will, bequeathing his

43

141

140

Camillus and the Schoolmaster of Falerii
(detail); see p. 141.

The Death of Cato,
pen and brown ink,
9.6 x 14.9 cm (3³/₄ x 6 in.).
Royal Library, Windsor.

mother and daughter to his two best friends, charging them to provide food for the first and a dowry for the second. The friends did as they were bid, and went down in Corinthian history. The painting enjoyed enormous success, especially during the Neo-Classical era. It spawned even more copies, engravings and imitations than *The Death of Germanicus*. The composition is derived from the Chantelou version of *Extreme Unction*, but has been simplified, with only five figures brought much closer to the viewer. The rarified, oppressive silence that dominates the scene is typical of Poussin's later work, suggesting a date well after 1650. The work in Copenhagen is rather unexceptional, however, and this has given rise to suggestions that it is only a copy. Arguably the most severe picture Poussin ever produced, it remains for all its fame a difficult work to assess.

The large and more complex *Coriolanus* now at Les Andelys was probably painted at about the same time. The story has obvious parallels with the revolt led by the princes during the Fronde (1650–3), but it is incidental to a reflection on wider issues. The defeated leader Coriolanus, preparing to take up arms against his own country, is swayed by the entreaties of his wife and mother, and sheathes his sword. Coriolanus's humanity and sense of duty towards Rome (the impassive female warrior on the left) ultimately triumph over his anger and desire for vengeance. In a sequence of criss-crossing gestures, outstretched arms and straining hands, Poussin manages to articulate an extraordinary intensity of meaning with an economy rare in painting. He does so, all the more remarkably, without setting out to prettify his subject. The figures are little more than props supporting simplified tragic masks reminiscent of Greek theatre, and the use of colour is strident, with blues, reds and greens harshly juxtaposed. Poussin is seeking in this picture to lead the viewer step by step past each figure, with its particular stance and expression, through every stage in Plutarch's account and every argument advanced by the women in their attempt to sway Coriolanus. The composition is unashamedly artificial, aiming to

Follower of Poussin *Mucius Scaevola*,
oil on canvas, 154 x 119 cm (60¹/₂ x 46³/₄ in.).
Commerce d'Art, Paris.

Coriolanus,
oil on canvas,
112 x 198.5 cm (44 x 78 in.).
Musée Municipal,
Les Andelys.

The Judgment of Solomon,
pen and brown wash over black chalk,
24.8 x 38.4 cm (9³⁄₄ x 15¹⁄₄ in.).
Ecole des Beaux-Arts, Paris.

The Judgment of Solomon,
oil on canvas,
101 x 150 cm (39¾ x 59 in.).
Louvre, Paris.

present a rational analysis rather than a realistic account of events. Poussin includes the ultimate artifice, the allegorical figure of Rome, to emphasize to the full the pressures on Coriolanus. Every detail is an integral part of the whole, more so than in *The Israelites*   102 *Gathering Manna*, in which a number of discrete episodes can be observed. *Coriolanus* was not rated very highly in the past, but to those living in a century which has seen the rise of artists like Fernand Léger and Picasso, this powerful exposition of a man's triumph over his passions is perhaps less shockingly stark. Despite the obvious differences, it does make sense to compare it with *Guernica*, as Jacques Thuillier has done. Both works feature the bristle of lethal weaponry, the criss-cross of outstretched arms, the gaping mouths and wild, staring eyes. What we have is a stark portrayal of the horrors of civil war, with no anecdotal content, no historical colour, no background landscape to speak of.

Not long before, Poussin had created a similar tension in *The Judgment of Solomon*   145 (Louvre), painted in 1649 for Pointel. According to Bellori, Poussin considered this his best work. Though biblical, the theme has features in common with the Roman and Stoical subjects Poussin tackles elsewhere. Solomon is the epitome of wisdom, inspired by God and called upon to confront the unbridled passions of human beings. As the crowd looks on with a mixture of hope and fear, the king sits on his golden throne above the two disputing mothers, about to announce his decision which will tip the scales in favour of justice. Counterbalancing the calm of Solomon's pose, the sweeping drapery and the symmetry of his hands are the telling lines on his brow at the apex of he triangle on which the whole composition is based. The impact of the painting is unforgettable: it depicts a crisis at its peak, a build-up of tension which Solomon's decision is about to dispel. Here, Poussin's customary clarity and simplicity reach new heights, even though by an odd quirk he appears to have granted the dead baby to the wrong mother. The architectural setting is dark and muted in colour and strictly geometric in line, suggesting the kind of generalized antechamber used as a backdrop in classical tragedy. The treatment of the principal figures is markedly different from that of the onlookers. Their gestures are expansive, those of the background figures more restrained. The crowd is much smaller in the finished painting than in a preparatory drawing (now in the Ecole des Beaux-Arts,   144 Paris), in which Solomon towers above the assembled company like some vaguely monstrous idol. Poussin positively shouts his message, by distorting bodies and faces to such an extent that they become caricatures and by topping the feverish scene with jarring yellows and reds. Yet again, however, the economy and coherence of the composition are such that the painting, whatever its demerits, is altogether convincing.

While battling to capture in a single image the quintessence of wisdom, Poussin was persuaded, after repeated petitioning by both Pointel and Chantelou, to attempt his own likeness. He was far from happy about the project: he had no experience of portraitpainting and capturing likenesses was not his forte. Only the dearth of talented portrait painters in Rome made him agree to undertake the task: 'I would have had my portrait painted and sent to you before now, as I know you would have liked,' he wrote to Chantelou on 2 August 1648, 'but I cannot bring myself to spend a dozen pistoles to have my head coldly pummelled and painted up by the likes of Mr Mignard, who – although he is the best practitioner I know – is as untalented as he is undisciplined.' The drawing (Brit-   147 ish Museum), which shows him at the age of thirty-six convalescent but still in pain, is uncompromisingly candid. The two oils executed in 1649–50, though far less blunt, reveal the same rigorous frankness. The *Self-Portrait* in Berlin is universally acknowl-   148 edged to be the painting sent to Pointel in June 1650, even though by comparison with the engraving by Pesne, it appears too have been slightly trimmed along the top and sides. In this half-length view, Poussin is shown soberly but not particularly elegantly dressed, his head gently tilted back, his hands crossed, a pencil-holder in his left and his right resting on a book entitled *De lumine et colore*. A thick garland of laurel leaves behind him is supported at either end by a Duquesnoy-style putto. Framed by the putti is a stone tablet inscribed with details of Poussin's Normandy origins, his age and his qualifications. Poussin's expression – half-smiling, half-melancholy – is far more fluid in this picture than in the second portrait (Louvre) intended for Chantelou and completed in May 1650. The Chantelou work has provided posterity with its definitive image of Poussin at the height of his career, his toga-type dress reminiscent of the great men of ancient Rome. The artist is still seen from the waist up, but here he faces the viewer more squarely, his high forehead is deeply furrowed and his gaze intent. Only his right hand is visible, resting on a portfolio tied with a ribbon, and the light catches a tiny pyramid-shaped diamond set in a ring on his finger. There are no tools in evidence this time. Instead, the setting features the everyday attributes of an artist – a stack of frames and pictures against a dark ground – in his studio. Jutting out from behind the stretchers and gilded mouldings is part of a painting including a half-length portrait of a woman seen in profile, crowned with a diadem decorated with an eye, and a pair of hands reaching out to enfold her. According to Bellori, this represent an allegory of Painting welcomed by Friendship, and is surely one of the finest tributes ever paid by a painter to his patron. Here, as in the *Self-Portrait* for Pointel, there is a prominently placed inscription, this time on a blank canvas, which gives only his place of birth, his age – fifty-six – and the date, a Jubilee year, 1650.

149

Although produced at roughly the same time, the two oils show Poussin in quite different guises and reveal quite different aspects of his art. They effectively take the place, therefore, of the treatise on painting which he never wrote. The first is in the style of a memorial, and sets the living painter against a stone bearing an 'epitaph'. There are allusions to sculpture and to the different elements of painting – drawing, and the use and appreciation of light and colour. The emphasis is on the conditions necessary to an artist's vision and the process by which a fully rounded reality can be created in two dimensions. The Louvre portrait goes further, and is much more confident in tone. The painter is now subordinated to the concept of Painting. Because of its ambivalence, the portrait for Pointel arguably conveys a more convincing sense of a human being, but we know that Poussin himself preferred the Chantelou portrait, and Bernini, who saw both works in Paris the year Poussin died, thought it a better likeness. It is important that the apparently impassive face of the wise sage of painting should not be allowed to mask the power of thought and the unique mixture of symbolism and realism which underpin this portrait.

Shortly before he sent his self-portrait to Chantelou, Poussin suggested that he paint for him a set illustrating the principles of Stoic thought which would constitute both a sequel and a counterpart to the seven *Sacraments*. He outlined his proposal in a rather curious letter datd 22 June 1648: 'I would like, if possible, to adapt these seven Sacraments by illustrating seven different situations, conjuring up as vividly as I can the most distressing tricks of Fortune ever inflicted on man, especially on those who have shown their contempt for her doings. There would be nothing idle or haphazard about these ex-

Self-Portrait,
red chalk,
37.5 x 25 cm (14³/₄ x 10 in.).
British Museum.

Self-portrait,
oil on canvas,
78 x 65 cm (30³/₄ x 25¹/₂ in.).
Staatliche Museen zu Berlin:
Gemäldegalerie (Bodemuseum).

EFFIGIES NICOLAI POVSSINI ANDEL
YENSIS PICTORIS. ANNO ÆTATIS.
ROMÆ ANNO IVBILEI
1650.

Self-Portrait,
oil on canvas,
98 x 74 cm (38½ x 29 in.).
Louvre, Paris.

amples. They would remind people of the moral strength and the wisdom they must develop in order to be able to remain steadfast and resolute in the face of the very worst which that blind madwoman can do to them.' Chantelou appears not to have responded to this suggestion. Richard Verdi maintains nevertheless that a new cycle was at least partially completed. Whatever the truth, it is the case that in a number of pictures painted at this time Poussin dealt with themes very similar to the ones he outlined to Chantelou, focusing on man's powerlessness to alter destiny, and on the need to be firm and constant in order to withstand its battering. 'Only the very wise and the very foolish can remain unaffected by the buffeting [of Fortune] – the first stand quite aloof from it, while the second are oblivious to its existence. All those in between, however, are doomed to feel its harsh blows', noted Poussin, paraphrasing Montaigne.

Poussin's paintings reflect different kinds of wisdom, ranging from the sort embodied by Solomon, who combines thought with action and demonstrates the power of decisiveness, to the rather more detached variety which he himself strives to achieve and which is bred of pessimism. In *Landscape with the Funeral of Phocion* and *Landscape with Diogenes* (1648) human events pale almost into insignificance in a vast landscape. [154, 158] Man is no longer thrust into prominence by some heroic act but retreats into the background, part of a natural order which henceforward tends to dominate the scene. Poussin takes up and refines the techniques of his predecessors, the Carracci and Domenichino, attaining a degree of perfection never paralleled. These ideal landscapes, with their combination of figures and nature, also aim to instruct. Subsequently, Poussin would incorporate a larger number of figures and man-made elements in this kind of composition and impose a much tighter, yet noble, structure on his material: henceforth, truth to nature would have to be subordinate to the demands of a lofty moral exposition.

Poussin's *Landscape with a Roman Road* (Dulwich Picture Gallery) and *Landscape with a Man Washing his Feet* (National Gallery, London) are both to some extent tech- [151] nical exercises, but fascinating for all that. Poussin is beginning to handle depth with a new authority, creating the illusion of receding space by introducing a road – straight in one case, winding in the other – which disappears into the distance partly hidden by trees. The works are deliberately antithetical, and it is tempting to interpret them as contrasting nature and culture, the rustic world and the civilized world. Instancing both Cato and Varro, Anthony Blunt even saw in the arms hung on the tree in the background of *Landscape with a Man Washing his Feet* an allusion to Horace's lines about the old soldier retiring from active service. With travellers moving along the roads and other figures resting by their sides, the content of these landscapes provides a direct metaphor for man's journey through life, at times calm, at times hazardous. Neither work represents any clearly recognizable subject, but this does not mean that they lack a purpose. Poussin looks at landscape neither through poetic eyes like Claude, nor with Dughet's passion for naturalism. His paintings are recollections of nature, restructured in the light of his own ideas about man and destiny. In the dramatic *Landscape with a Man Killed by a Snake* [152] (London) painted for Pointel, Poussin depicts just such a fatal encounter with destiny. The idea for this theme may have come, as has been argued, from the infestation by snakes of the area around Fondi – it is possible that Poussin visited Fondi in 1641 while on a trip to Naples with Pointel. The snake is only of peripheral importance, however, as it sets in motion a train of different reactions, as Félibien realized when he called the work *The Effects of Terror*. Fénelon, who described the painting, also analyzed its meaning. The

*Landscape with a Man
Washing his Feet*,
oil on canvas,
74.5 x 100 cm (29¼ x 39½ in.).
National Gallery, London.

Landscape with a Roman Road,
oil on canvas,
78 x 99 cm (30¾ x 39 in.).
Dulwich Picture Gallery, London.

Landscape with a Man Killed by a Snake,
oil on canvas,
119 x 198.5 cm (47 x 78 in.).
National Gallery, London.

sharp angles of the road and the alternating areas of light and dark draw the eye in an abrupt zigzag through the composition – from the man choked by the snake in the foreground to the passer-by who flees in terror towards a woman in the middle distance, her reaction being merely one of surprise, since she cannot see the cause of his fear, and finally to the figures in the distance, who remain unmoved. The structure links one gesture with another. The horror is no longer immediate as it is, for instance, in *The Massacre of the Innocents* or *The Plague of Ashdod*. It does not dominate the scene and, seen in a wider context, its effects become entirely relative and local: fear touches a small core of people directly, but its impact decreases with distance. The world moves on, regardless, steered by a stoical *logos* that metes out the good and the bad indiscriminately.

Nowhere else does Poussin convey the insignificance of human lives and actions more forcefully than in *Landscape with the Funeral of Phocion* (Cardiff) and *Landscape with the Gathering of the Ashes of Phocion* (Liverpool), both painted for Serisier. Plutarch describes how the Athenian general, famous for being upright and outspoken, was falsely accused of treason and condemned to death by an assembly of the people. His body, banned from the city, was taken secretly to Megara, where it was burnt and the ashes gathered up by his widow. This was a subject whch had not been tackled before, but one which had special significance for Poussin. Recent political events, not least the Fronde, had heightened his contempt for 'the stupidity and fickleness of the masses', and would have made him identify all the more keenly with the wrongly maligned hero. In a way which runs strikingly counter to expectation, Poussin boils the entire story down to a handful of figures seen in the foreground. More remarkably still, the figure of the hero is almost non-existent: in one case he is present as a corpse covered in a shroud, and in the other all that remains are his ashes. Phocion's death is ignominious, and the last respects paid to him are poignantly pathetic, yet by underlining the contrast between the meanness of the event and the majesty of the world which carries on all around, Poussin manages to convey a sense of the sublime. In *Landscape with the Funeral of Phocion*, winding tracks and sinuous stretches of water lead the viewer's eye to the city of Athens, with its acropolis, its temples, and its square little houses; countless tiny figures go about their business, oblivious to the drama now unfolding. In the distance on the right a procession is in progress: this was an annual event in honour of Zeus held on 19 March, and Poussin follows Plutarch meticulously in his depiction of it. In this taut composition, Poussin confines his palette to greens and browns and uses horizontal lines of walls and stone blocks to conjure up what Blunt calls a 'closed' space within which every figure and every object is carefully placed. Such precision is even more marked in *Landscape with the Gathering of the Ashes of Phocion*, where the trees are denser, but the composition more symmetrical. The picture is constructed around a central vertical axis, from the woman standing in the foreground, up through the pediment of the temple seen from the front, to the steep rocks and cloud beyond. The dark areas of the trees on either side help to focus attention on the central event. Here, Poussin uses foliage and structures in a way which captured the imagination of English garden designers in the eighteenth century. Palladian edifices appeared between lawns and behind clumps of trees, providing landmarks while satisfying a sentimental desire to achieve a harmonious union of man and nature. The same sense of balance is conveyed in Poussin's painting, but in his later landscapes the balance shifts and wilderness begins to encroach on an ordered, civilized world. In the two episodes from the Phocion story, however, town and country merge, as was true of Rome as

55
59

154, 155

Landscape with the Funeral of Phocion,
oil on canvas,
114 x 175 cm (45 x 67 in.).
National Museum of Wales, Cardiff
(on loan from the Earl of Plymouth).

Landscape with the Gathering of the Ashes of Phocion,
oil on canvas,
116 x 176 cm (45⁵/₄ x 69¹/₄ in.).
Walker Art Gallery, Liverpool.

Poussin knew it in the seventeenth century. Poussin conjures up a vision of life which is at once ideal and rustic, achieving his effects with the texture of a wall, a mass of foliage, a flock of sheep, a shaft of sunlight on the grass, a group of bathers in a boat, and what emanates from these paintings is, paradoxically, a great, and almost palpable, simplicity.

Poussin's best picture of 1648 was undoubtedly *Landscape with Diogenes* (Louvre). Denis Mahon believes that it is too free in style to have been painted as early as this, but in fact it fits in well with the series of landscapes painted by Poussin in the late 1640s. Gone is the emphatic geometry of the Phocion pictures; the lines are now softer and the landscape unfurls smoothly. Poussin still makes use of a winding road, clumps of trees, stretches of water and outcrops of rock, but is more subtle in his handling of these devices. The composition remains as clear and readable as ever. In the foreground, in an incident related by Diogenes Laertius. Diogenes, who lived in extreme poverty in the fourth century BC, on seeing a young man drinking from a spring using his cupped hands, casts aside his drinking bowl, the last of his worldly possessions, and so reaches a state even closer to nature. The backs of the two figures are turned to the rest of the composition, and on the left a dense thicket of trees and bushes forms a screen. The landscape unfolds behind them. Tiny figures can be glimpsed on the banks of a river that flows through a city strung out on the hills beyond. Unassuming houses and great defences, temples and palaces are seen side by side – on the left, for instance, is a scaled-down version of Bramante's Belvedere. This is a strange, half-Norman, half-Roman version of Athens; a beautiful summer afternoon light plays over the scene, picking out all the elements in it, shadowy in the foreground but more and more brightly lit as they recede into the distance. This picture illustrates clearly how different Poussin's approach is from that of Claude Lorrain, who is fanciful and manipulates light to create arresting effects. For Poussin no poetic statement is possible without a firm grounding in reality. The work is aptly titled: most of the picture is taken up with trees and tracts of land, and painted in greens, greys and browns. Light, shimmering sky and water counterbalance the dull textures of these areas and help to create the airiness that permeates the whole. By his simple act, Diogenes seems not only to have renounced one form of life and acquiesced in another, but to have freed the world from all constraint and menace.

There was scope, then, in Stoic though for the kind of harmony attained by Diogenes, in which a man of great wisdom becomes at one with the natural world, knowing himself to be an integral part of it. Poussin pursued this line of thought a little later, *c*. 1650, in the *Landscape with Polyphemus* for Pointel (Hermitage) and the virtually unknown *Landscape with Three Monks* in Belgrade, an awesome and mysterious work celebrating peace and solitude, which Charles Sterling sees as a contrasting pendant to *Landscape with a Man Killed by a Snake*. Religion and mythology as described by Ovid simply provide Poussin with the germ of an idea. From a few simple figures he generates a great vision. This was not the first time he had tackled the story of Polyphemus, the cyclops in love with the nymph Galatea and jealous of her handsome lover Acis. A youthful rendering occurs in a dramatic and brutal drawing now in the Royal Library. *Acis and Galatea* (Dublin) reveals an exaggerated sensuousness – the various lovers reach out for each other as if in a feverish quest. By contrast, the tone of the work now in the Hermitage is serene. No more story-telling, but a musical sensation – like the stirring of the still air as suggested in the Pastorals of Beethoven and Berlioz. The landscape is vast and profuse, encompassing trees, mountains and even the sea, just visible in the distance; the scattered

158

159
cat. 212

152

26, 82

figures merge into their surroundings. Three nymphs cluster in the foreground. A pair of satyrs spy on them from one side, while a river-god meditates on the other. In the far distance, the lovelorn cyclops seems almost to be a part of the rock on which he sits idly composing tunes on his pipe. The men working the land on the plain below him appear minute compared with the legendary beings. This is the golden age of Virgil, in which all life follows the rhythm of nature and harmony prevails, a balance soon to be upset, however, as men take over the land of the gods. The pantheistic vision which underlies this painting found a more complete expression in works painted late in Poussin's life, like *Landscape with Hercules and Cacus* (Moscow) and *Landscape with Diana and Orion* (New York). In the present work, however, it is simply implicit in the vastness and abundance of nature. In terms of its subject, *Landscape with a Woman Washing her Feet* (Ottawa), painted *c.* 1650, remains something of a mystery, but it is obviously in a similar vein. Sturdy tree-trunks towering in the foreground give way to isolated, wispy trees as the landscape fades into the distance. The satyr spying on the woman is reminiscent of those present in *Landscape with Polyphemus*, thus introducing a note of sensuality far removed from the sensuous intoxication of Poussin's early mythological scenes. Although well composed, the painting achieves none of the grandeur of the slightly earlier landscapes. The same is true of *Landscape with Three Men* (Prado) which, according to Charles Dempsey, represents Diogenes leaving Sparta for Athens, another popular Stoical subject. The influence of the Carracci and of Domenichino is clear at every turn: carefully balanced lines, foreground designed to lead the eye inwards, different areas punctuated by sharply defined buildings and figures alternately active and contemplative.

 Repetition of a well-tried formula was, however, alien to Poussin. In one painting he represents human events as minute and almost imperceptible, scarcely causing a ripple in the order of the universe. In the next he shows nature in action as a central force. Already in *Landscape with Orpheus and Eurydice* (Louvre), there is evidence of a fire in the background. Smoke belches from the Castel Sant'Angelo and the sky darkens as Eurydice draws back in fear from the snake barely visible in the lush grass. In a second Orpheus's playing to the tranquil group in the foreground will be rudely interrupted and she will be dead. The obvious contrast between the figures conjures up a sense of disquiet, but there is as much ominous tension in the landscape as there is in the arrangement of the figures. Poussin goes even further, however, in *Landscape – a Calm* (Sudeley Castle) and its pendant *Landscape – a Storm* (Rouen), both painted in 1651. He is attempting to achieve in the supposedly inferior genre of landscape painting what he so successfully does in works with more immediately noble subjects. His aim is to articulate sharply contrasting emotions and generate similarly contrasting feelings in the viewer by painting in an appropriate 'key', using structure and rhythm to evoke a particular mood. The composition of *Landscape – a Calm* is symmetrical, arranged in calm horizontal lines around a gleaming expanse of water. The colours are light, the blues of the pool subtly reflecting those of the sky, and the execution polished. By contrast, in *Landscape – a Storm* the composition is harsh, the lines jagged, the colours muted. A great tree just struck by lightning seems ready to eclipse everything, from the terrified travellers in the foreground to the ghostly looking town momentarily lit up by another flash. The romantic quality of the painting has led to it being attributed to Dughet. Although it is in a sorry state, its clarity and strength of purpose are unmistakable, and Poussin's hand is obvious

228, 229

cat. 232

cat. 237

161

162
163

157

Landscape with Diogenes,
oil on canvas,
160 x 221 cm (63 x 87 in.).
Louvre, Paris.

Landscape with Polyphemus,
oil on canvas,
150 x 198 cm (59 x 78 in.).
Hermitage, Leningrad.

in the nightmarish precision of details like the shadows cast by tiny figures as they scurry past the starkly illuminated section of wall in the background on the right.

The awesome *Landscape with Pyramus and Thisbe* (Frankfurt), painted for Cassiano Dal Pozzo in 1651, combines all these elements. Poussin explained the content in a letter to Jacques Stella, later quoted by Félibien: 'I have tried to depict a storm on land, and have done my best to conjure up the sense of a raging wind, of a dark, charged atmosphere heavy with rain, and of lightning striking in several places at once, creating a certain disorder. All the figures in the picture react in character to the weather: some let the driving wind whip them along through the dust; others struggle to walk into the wind, shielding their eyes with their hands. On one side, a shepherd runs off abandoning his flock as he catches sight of a lion wreaking havoc with a herd of cattle. It has already felled a number of herdsmen and is busy attacking others. Some defend themselves, others goad their cattle and try to escape. Dust swirls around as the chaos mounts. Some way off, a dog barks and his hackles rise, but he is too frightened to come nearer. In the foreground Pyramus lies dead, and close by him Thisbe gives vent to her grief.'

Stormy landscapes, a popular subject with artists since classical times, continued to be so with many painters in Rome in Poussin's day, from Paul Bril and Agostino Tassi to Gaspard Dughet. Poussin rose to the challenge set by Apelles, according to Pliny the Elder, and strove – as he apparently had done – to paint the unpaintable – thunder, lightning, tornadoes. Poussin is likely to have been most influenced, however, by Leonardo da Vinci, who describes how to render a storm (*'una fortuna'*, as he calls it) on canvas. The term would have appealed to Poussin and may have led him to choose the story of Pyramus and Thisbe as the subject of, or rather an excuse for, this particular painting. Related by Ovid and dramatized by Théophile de Viau in 1621, the story is based on a series of misunderstandings, and so comes firmly within the orbit of that 'blind madwoman', Fortune. As Poussin's letter to Stella makes clear, however, the hapless lovers are only one detail among many. They are mentioned only at the end of his description, and are in a sense emblematic of the whole: they illustrate how inconsequential human events are by comparison with the natural phenomenon of the storm. Whatever the turmoil of the subject, the composition is as taut as ever, and the amount of thought and effort Poussin put into the painting is clear from the number of changes he made. Looming trees, rocky outcrops and an entire unearthly looking town straggle around a surprisingly still stretch of water. These untroubled waters have been variously interpreted. Thus, for Louis Marin they symbolize the dispassionate eye of the artist who, god-like, remains calm and clear-sighted in the very thick of the storm he himself has caused. Whatever the truth, *Landscape with Pyramus and Thisbe* is certainly a compelling illustration of the 'Sublime' style normally associated with rhetoric but here applied to painting. The Sublime, according to the treatise *Longinus on the Sublime* (dating from the first or second century AD), 'is not about persuasion, but overpowers and transports us, inspiring in us a mixture of wonder, astonishment and surprise, not content simply to convince or to please … Judiciously used where necessary, it strikes like a flash of lightning, in which all the forces of Oratory are massed together, and overturns all before it.' With this definitive storm picture Poussin opened up a whole new range of possible meaning in landscape painting, using it as he had previously used history painting to articulate emotion at a time of crisis. Markedly different from the rather more sensational, even fantastic, approach adopted by his contemporary Salvator Rosa, it was a way of tackling landscape which would remain

164

page 165 ▷

Landscape with Orpheus and Eurydice,
oil on canvas,
120 x 200 cm (47¼ x 78¾ in.).
Louvre, Paris.

Landscape – a Calm,
oil on canvas,
97 x 131.5 cm (38¹/₄ x 51³/₄ in.).
Sudeley Castle, Gloucestershire
(The Morrison Trustees).

Landscape – a Storm,
oil on canvas,
99 x 132 cm (39 x 52 in.).
Musée des Beaux-Arts, Rouen.

Landscape with Pyramus and Thisbe,
oil on canvas
192.5 x 273.5 cm (75³/₄ 107³/₄ in.).
Städelsches Kunstinstitut, Frankfurt.

unexploited until the end of the eighteenth century. Then it was taken up with a vengeance by Joseph Vernet and so many others. Henceforward, however, the aim would no longer be to delight the viewer, but to overwhelm him with a delicious sense of terror engendered by the vastness and monstrosity of nature in action.

It is impossible to divorce these great landscapes, in which Poussin hoped to conjure up a sense of destiny, from his overtly Christian works. As a painter of religious subjects, Poussin was something of an exception, for his personal beliefs remain unclear. He certainly does not fit into the same obvious category as either Philippe de Champaigne, who was closely involved with the radical Jansenist movement in France, or the extremely devout Guido Reni, whose faith bordered on morbid superstition. The idea put forward, most recently by Paola Santucci, that Poussin was some kind of propaganda painter for the Jesuits seems absurdly narrow and simplistic. He could just as well have been one of that vast number of lukewarm believers who were good Christians largely out of habit, and barely concerned with mysticism or theology. Alternatively, perhaps the image of the 'artist-philosopher', so authoritatively endorsed by Blunt, is the most apposite, for Poussin was a free-thinker, often only just on the right side of the divide between what was acceptable and what was not, whose 'wisdom' was way ahead of the beliefs and mediocre piety of the day. What is certain is that Poussin did paint religious paintings, for churches and individuals alike, in circumstances and in a way sufficiently out of the ordinary to be worthy of mention.

Although in the seventeenth century artists relied on their secular patrons for a regular flow of lucrative work (though destined to be less well preserved than their religious paintings, the numbers of seculur works produced was clearly enormous), it was from the Church, both in France and Italy, that they received their most important commissions. Size, location, and effect were all guaranteed to be bigger and better; even if religious orders and parishes did not pay well, the exposure they offered was especially valuable. Like all his contemporaries of any competence, Poussin deliberately sought

27opportunities to get himself noticed, first in Paris (with *The Death of the Virgin*), and later

47, 46in Rome (with *The Martyrdom of St Erasmus* and *The Virgin Appearing to St James*). Notre Dame in Paris and St Peter's in Rome were no more to be sneezed at than was, say, the church of S. Luigi dei Francesi, for which Mellin was chosen in preference to Poussin. The situation changed with Poussin's brief stay in Paris. The two large altarpieces he was called upon to paint for the king and for the Jesuit church made his name: everybody went to see them, everybody talked about them. Poussin could well have made altar paintings his speciality, like so many before him. However, the visions, martyrdoms and miracles which constituted their subject matter and the spectacular simplified style demanded were alien to him, and would have prevented him from pursuing his own ideas. He was infinitely happier painting on a more modest scale for private individuals. It was a time when religious subjects were in great demand and painters were churning out versions of *The Holy Family*, *The Virgin and Child*, and depicting a host of different saints, as well as episodes from the Old Testament. History, and more particularly the history of the Church, was all-important. The range of subject matter varied from artist to artist, some having a preference for the unusual, and tending to specialize in less familiar stories from the Bible and forms of worship peculiar to particular regions or environments. By comparison, Poussin's repertoire seems narrow: his handful of preferred themes, all firmly canonical and seldom obscure, illustrate the basic tenets of Christianity, notably the story of Moses and the lives of Christ and of the Virgin. The Acts of the Apostles figure in his work to a lesser extent, and the lives of saints scarcely at all. It is as if, with every new picture he painted, Poussin became increasingly aware of the richness of meaning inherent even in apparently hackneyed subjects. There are at least three versions of the Moses story, for instance, two of Eliezer and Rebecca and close on thirty of the Holy Family. Another key factor was rivalry among patrons – the sight of a highly acclaimed picture in one collector's hands could prompt another to covet a second, even more beautiful version. Poussin, who hated mere repetition, was faced with having to outdo himself. The theme of the Holy Family reveals his method of tackling the problem. From a nucleus of predetermined elements, Poussin generates a range of variations, each distinct and an entity in its own right, in terms as much of style as of content, be it the number of figures, the handling of forms and overall composition, or a particular spiritual message.

Religious painting was expected to be very precise in its iconography. Ever since the publication of Emile Mâle's seminal book on religious art after the Council of Trent, art historians have been eager to rediscover, for every commission of any significance, evidence of a programme – a set of guidelines provided by the clergy anxious to ensure not only that the message reached the faithful but also that it was presented in an orthodox manner. The more one studies seventeenth-century painting and the underlying circumstances, however, the clearer it becomes that the great artists of the day were anything but theologians. At the other end of the scale the mass of uninventive, third-rate painters or 'illustrators' who spent their lives turning out stock images or producing engravings for publication, and who had to work to a very tight brief, were at best willing technicians. Painters of whatever status – whether artists of the first rank or mere imitators – were left relatively free to do as they saw fit. Different religious orders favoured particular subjects (Elijah, for instance, was popular with the Carmelites, and St Bruno with the Carthusians), but the Church generally did no more than fix the subject and ensure that the proprieties were observed. Painters could, if they wanted, seek guidance and refer to specialist works, as Poussin was more than ready to do. The meaning of many pictures becomes far clearer when they are looked at in the light of the various apologetics of his day. It certainly helps to know, for instance, that the story of the gathering of manna by the Israelites was regarded as a prefiguration of the Eucharist, and that, as Lebrun later emphasized, the colours of the robes of the three angels who bear St Paul up to heaven in the Paris version of *The Ecstasy of St Paul* symbolized the 'three different states of grace' – 'efficacious', 182 'helping' and 'triumphant'.

There was nothing particularly remarkable, then, about the iconographic freedom which Poussin appears to have enjoyed. There was an accepted visual language with a recognized set of conventions which could help them to make their message more accessible. What set Poussin apart as a religious painter was the erudition he displayed and the kind of people for whom he worked and whose interests and ideas he came to share. We have seen how much he disliked the overpowering, but popularizing, Baroque approach, with its martyrdoms and ecstasies, subjects he avoided as far as possible. He also steered clear of displays of virtue *per se*. Even Charity, a concept so central to miltant Counter-Reformation Christian thought, features in his painting only rarely, e.g. in *The Israelites Gathering Manna*. Miracles, too, are largely absent in Poussin's work, though 102 some scenes from the life of Moses and paintings like *Christ Healing the Sick* were prob- cat. 73 ably regarded, at least by the clients for whom they were painted, as depicting miracles.

Poussin's religious paintings do not rely on dramatic effects; the keynotes are rather elucidation and quiet meditation. The *Sacraments* were geared to the tastes of Cassiano Dal Pozzo and his circle. In anyone else's hands, they might have been little more than an illustration of the *Annals* of Baronius. In Poussin's, however, the emphasis is not on theology but on history and, particularly in the second set, moral example. Poussin was no more interested in turning the *Sacraments* into an elaborate allegory in the manner of Father Richeome than he was in putting them forward in the context of contemporary religious debate, as Rubens did with his *Triumph of Divine Love*. However different they may appear at first sight, the *Sacraments* are not a case apart from other series like the *Triumphs* painted for Richelieu and the great heroic landscapes; the different series reverberate with echoes of each other, and have a far greater resonance as a result.

For Poussin, then, both the sacred and the profane are bound up in a single universe. He gradually developed his own 'religion', incorporating all manner of apparently contradictory concepts. Paris was, as we have seen, a city where the extremely devout were to be found cheek by jowl with the most radical free-thinkers, and where atheists openly declared their beliefs. It is known that in both Paris and Rome he was involved with 'libertines', learned thinkers, at any rate, critical in varying degrees of the Church's authority. Poussin's attitude is manifest in a letter to Chantelou dated 8 May 1650, in which the only part of the Jubilee celebrations he chooses to describe is the entry of a wooden crucifix, the effigy 'now endowed with a beard, and with hair that grows over three inches [*quatre doigts*] a day – they say the Pope is going to give it a ceremonial crop one of these

Rubens,
The Triumph of Divine Love,
oil on canvas,
87 x 91 cm (34¼ x 36 in.).
Prado, Madrid.

days.' Yet despite his obvious scepticism about miracles, 'which happen so frequently that it's a marvel', and his contempt for superstition, he had a genuine respect for Christian values. His thinking owed its final direction to the devout humanists and the Jesuits he encountered in Paris and to the learned members of Dal Pozzo's circle in Rome. Poussin gradually established his own vision, linking Christianity firmly to paganism, seeing the one as a continuation and development of the other, and finding clear parallels between classical philosophy and Holy Writ. His study of primary sources, embarked upon early on in his career, lies at the root of this outlook. Researches into the early Church and into ancient cults and mysteries reinforced his sense of the way the two worlds were related and interconnected. As a result of upheavals in Europe in his own time, Poussin turned more and more to historians and Stoical thinkers, and moral issues began to dominate his own thinking. Having to switch from one sort of subject to another with successive commisions meant that Poussin never let either strand of thought drop, and that the two became fused as his work focused jointly on man's destiny and his place in the universe. Poussin's austere outlook had little in common with religious conventions and led eventually to a synthesis of God, nature and human history.

Poussin's originality began to show itself in *The Crucifixion* (1645–6), now in Hart- *cat. 78* ford. The picture has suffered and is therefore not easy to decipher: the paint surface is worn and the browns and reds have darkened. Despite this, Poussin's harrowing interpretation of the theme comes through forcefully. As Poussin wrote in 1646 in answer to Stella, who was pressing him for a depiction of Christ carrying the cross, 'I am no longer in good enough health or spirits to get involved with gloomy subjects. The Crucifixion has made me ill and given me a great deal of heartache, but [painting] the bearing of the cross would finish me off. I would not be able to withstand the deep and distressing thoughts with which one has to fill one's mind and heart in order to paint such a bleak and dismal subject with any conviction. Do not insist, I beg you.' In the event, the painting never materialized, but Poussin did jot down a rough idea for it in a wash drawing now in Dijon. In general Poussin preferred to tackle the Crucifixion indirectly, concentrating on scenes of lamentation around Christ's dead body. Here, exceptionally, he chooses to depict the event itself and, moreover, to follow the most dramatic account, that of Matthew. Darkness has fallen, the earth shakes and the dead rise up. Poussin opts for a landscape format: it enables him to stretch a band of figures, powerfully punctuated by the three crosses, across the picture, and gives him scope to orchestrate a complex sequence of looks and gestures. In the foreground the seated soldiers and the semi-recumbent dead man rising from his grave add to the intensity of the drama, and at the same time strike a primitive, almost medieval note. Poussin seems to have cast his mind back to techniques used in decorating cathedral portals when trying to find an alternative to the whirling excesses of the Baroque. Poussin undoubtedly wanted to make the viewer experience the same pain and distress as he had felt while working on the picture. In this respect the painting is unique in his œuvre.

In the ten years following his spell in Paris, Poussin built up several quite distinct sets of paintings. The most obvious example is the set of *Sacraments*, painted for Chantelou. There were also the scenes from the life of Moses and the various paintings of the Holy Family. Poussin's fascination with Moses as a subject is apparent from the fact that he devoted just under twenty paintings, or about a tenth of his total known output, to him. In a rather strange and obscure passage in Loménie de Brienne, the child destined to lead

Christ Carrying the Cross,
brown wash and black chalk,
16 x 25 cm (6¹/₂ x 10 in.).
Musée des Beaux-Arts, Dijon.

the Israelites becomes a major figure in a syncretic roll-call of the gods: 'It is Moses – Moshe to the Israelites, Pan in Arcady, Priapus in the Hellespont, Anubis to the Egyptians – whom I pull from the waters and he alone who warrants the name of Moshe (pulled from the waters) which I give him.' There are echoes here of Dal Pozzo and his friends, and of their interest in comparative religion. In neo-Platonic thought, Moses was linked with St Paul (who features in several of Poussin's paintings), the two being considered the supreme embodiments of the word of God. Lastly, in an interpretation first formulated by Philo of Alexandria in his *Vita Mosis*, Moses was paired with Aaron, and together they represented – as they do in *The Israelites Gathering Manna* and *The Adoration of the Golden Calf* – the epitome of eloquence, divine on the one hand, human on the other. Running through all the episodes treated by Poussin, however, is the rather more straightforward idea of divine choice and salvation. Hidden on the banks of the Nile, the infant Moses is saved by Pharaoh's daughter, and later spared by Pharaoh himself after trampling on his crown, an act seen as betokening the subsequent deliverance of the Israelites from Egyptian rule. Moses in turn saves his people from thirst and starvation by sweetening the bitter waters of Marah, striking the rock to produce water and causing manna to fall from heaven. Water is a key element in all the paintings, serving as a metaphor for baptism. It also features in other biblical paintings, like *Moses Defending the Daughters of Jethro* (lost, but known from a surviving drawing), *Eliezer and Rebecca at the Well* (Cambridge, with Rebecca offering water; and Louvre, with Eliezer offering jewels) and *Christ and the Woman of Samaria* (lost). Poussin chose these subjects, then, because each touches on a basic theme which he would tackle more directly in various depictions of *The Baptism of Christ* (including the two versions of *Baptism* from the *Sacraments*) and in a number of the portrayals of the Holy Family, all of which include a basin and amphora with their obvious symbolic significance.

102,70

cat. 14

222, 175
cat. 72

Moses Saved from the Water (1638),
oil on canvas,
93 x 120 cm (36½ x 47¼ in.).
Louvre, Paris.

Moses Saved from the Water (1647),
oil on canvas,
121 x 195 cm (47½ x 76¾ in.).
Louvre, Paris.

The Exposition of Moses (1654),
oil on canvas,
150 x 204 cm (59 x 80¼ in.).
Ashmolean Museum, Oxford.

Overleaf
Details from
Eliezer and Rebecca at the Well (1648);
see p. 175.

Guido Reni,
The Sewing School,
oil on canvas,
146 x 205 cm (57½ x 80¾ in.).
Hermitage, Leningrad.

These are true variations on a theme: each brings a new dimension to the same basic idea. Each subject calls for its own style. The two versions of *Moses Trampling on Pharaoh's Crown* (Louvre and Woburn Abbey) and *Moses and Aaron before Pharaoh* (Louvre) are dramatic and severe, similar in tone to the last of the *Sacraments*. To accommodate the miraculous, as he did in 1637 and 1649 in the two versions of *Moses Striking the Rock* (Edinburgh and the Hermitage respectively), Poussin adopts a complex narrative style. Young women predominate in his treatments of *Moses Saved from the Water*, imparting a sense of joy and grace. Poussin painted at least three such pictures, the first in 1638 (Louvre), the second for Pointel in 1647 (Louvre), and the third for Reynon in 1651 (London/Cardiff). The three versions are strikingly different. The first is light, graceful, uncluttered and altogether more unassuming than the second, which includes more figures and is set in a landscape bounded on the horizon by temples, pyramids and obelisks. The lines have become harder in the second picture and the colours darker. The composition centres on the essentially static figure of Pharaoh's daughter standing slightly to the left of centre looking down on a circle of other, equally static figures. The Reynon version seeks to achieve greater variety. The figures are no longer neatly separated, but crowd in a single animated movement around a central axis, and the composition is based on sweeping concentric curves. The colours are bright and a little harsh. In *The Exposition of Moses* (Oxford), painted three years later for Stella, the tone is one of solemn grief: the colours are muted, the faces heavy, the expressions at once pained and abstracted; there are few gestures – the figures, wrapped in their own thoughts, are isolated one from another. A bizarre half-classical, half-medieval fort looms out of the background, contributing a strange tension to this large composition. It is not bursting with obvious emotion. The feeling, though intense, filters slowly from the silent, solid-looking figures who seem to have no connection with one another and to find themselves arbitrarily juxtaposed. The gesture of the standing woman in the centre echoes that of the women kneeling at the river's edge. Although Brienne blames the artist for including the river-god on their right, this figure acts primarily as a counterbalance to the king on their left, the former rapt in contemplation of the future, the latter lost in grief. The trees and river-banks, too, contribute to the overall balance, reinforcing the structure of the picture with strong vertical and horizontal lines. The figure of the Nile, like the seers so often included on the pediments of Greek temples, serves not so much to identify the location as to turn the event into an *exemplum*, lifting it out of the temporal realm and pointing to the eternal truths it illustrates. Poussin thus conveys the literal scene and its deeper meaning in a single image.

Eliezer and Rebecca at the Well (Louvre), painted in 1648, is one of his most brilliant works. Pointel was greatly taken with *The Adolescence of the Virgin*, or *The Sewing School*, by Guido Reni, in which Mary sits sewing, surrounded by young women. He was especially moved by the great variety of 'expression manifest on these noble and graceful countenances' and by the 'delightful costumes', and asked Poussin to paint him a picture 'filled, like that one, with young women embodying different kinds of beauty' (Félibien). It should be stressed that Pointel did not specify the subject, and that the subject itself was relatively unimportant. He merely stipulated that the painting should match the character and quality of a particular well-known work. Pointel was calling the tune like any other patron, but he was careful not to restrict Poussin's artistic freedom by imposing too rigid a brief. The resulting picture more than satisfied Pointel's simple requirements and went

cat. 13

cat. 16

cat. 19, 20

170, *cat. 11*

cat. 8

175

Eliezer and Rebecca at the Well,
oil on canvas,
118 x 197 cm (46$\frac{1}{2}$ x 77$\frac{1}{2}$ in.).
Louvre, Paris.
For details see pp. 172, 173.

beyond what he had requested – a series of young beauties displaying a range of emotions. This particular subject appealed to Poussin because it afforded interesting possibilities in terms of composition and provided the focus for the exploration of a deeper meaning. In simple terms, fourteen principal figures are grouped harmoniously in a landscape dotted with architectural elements. Twelve young women shown in varied poses are disposed around the two central figures. The painting brings to mind a passage in a letter from Poussin to Chantelou dated 20 March 1642: 'I am sure you will have found the young women you must have seen around Nîmes no less inspiring than the ravishing columns of the Maison Carrée [first century BC] – after all, the columns are just classical recreations of their living beauty.' Sphere and cylinder are the essential forms to which everything is related: the sculptural-looking bodies, the necks, the heads, the eyes, the stone ball, Eliezer's turban, the amphorae. All these rounded forms are contained in an equally pronounced linear architectural setting. Bright, lively colours permeate the scene, as Poussin juxtaposes complementary shades in various ways. In this lively, clear composition which anticipates artists as diverse as Ingres and Picasso, every individual occupies a carefully calculated place, quite separate from, yet linked to the adjacent figure. The rhythm is alternately measured and hurried as emphatic verticals punctuate the scene at varying intervals: the figures are like columns here, articulating the space between them as they come closer or draw apart. It is not just the 'music' of the picture which makes it remarkable. Each face registers a different emotion in response to Eliezer's choice – curiosity or excitement, uneasiness or jealousy. Although the viewer's eye may range over them, it is drawn back to the central, compelling event – the silent dialogue conjured up by Eliezer's raised index finger and the hand Rebecca modestly lays on her breast. Poussin manages to convey the incomprehensible yet irresistible nature of Providence, and his evocation of the subject illustrates why in the seventeenth century it was so commonly considered to prefigure the Annunciation.

Another masterpiece dating from 1648 is *The Madonna of the Steps*. Two versions [179] exist (National Gallery, Washington, D.C., and Cleveland, Ohio) and considerable controversy existed as to which was the earlier until X-ray examination gave the Cleveland picture precedence. The treatment is quite unlike Poussin's earlier paintings on similar themes, which tended to be charming and lyrical. The versions of *The Holy Family with St John the Baptist* in the Heineman Collection in New York and in Karlsruhe, both *c*. 1629, for instance, feature a warm, Venetian palette, like the delicate *The Rest on the Flight into* [cat. 62] *Egypt* (1632–3), now in the Oskar Reinhart Collection in Winterthur, though a new harshness of touch began to suggest itself in a work painted in Paris in 1641–2, *The Holy Family* (*The Roccatagliata Madonna*), now in Detroit. These early works were all in upright format and rather loose in structure, relying on the vertical edge of the picture for support. In *The Madonna of the Steps*, by contrast, which is in landscape format, Poussin arranges the five figures slightly off-centre in a pyramid-like formation culminating in Mary's head. There are clear echoes of High Renaissance art, and in particular of Raphael's *Madonna of the Fish* (Prado), Andrea del Sarto's *Madonna del Sacco* in Florence, and one of the lunettes in the Sistine Chapel. Walter Friedländer points out that there are similarities, too, with *The Aldobrandini Wedding*, the famous copy of a Hellenistic wall-painting in Rome, and instances the proud figures and the way the composition is arranged on several parallel planes. The foreshortened perspective is remarkable and so too is the almost strident use of the three primary colours, red, yellow and blue. Despite its masterly simplicity, this painting abounds with symbols: gold and incense as a reminder of the Magi, apples of original sin, and a basin of cleansing. For Howard Hibbert the painting illustrates the encounter of the Old and the New Law. According to him, Joseph, who appears half-lying in the shadow with his ruler and compass, harks back to the architects of the Temple in Jerusalem, and Mary, seen triumphantly showing the infant Jesus to Elizabeth and the young St John, represents the way to heaven and salvation, the *scala coelestis*. The scene works as a religious metaphor and provides an uncompromisingly linear counterpoint to the massive forms which Poussin sets so powerfully upon it. Never again did he produce anything as imposing and never again would he seem so much at ease. He takes an obvious delight – as two preparatory drawings demonstrate – in fitting together forms which are themselves uncomplicated – framing the infant Jesus's head inside two pillars, for instance – so giving them a whole new significance.

cat. 49   The ten-figure *Holy Family* (Dublin), painted the following year, is imbued with greater warmth. Mary is still at the centre of the composition as all the others focus their gaze upon her. Mary's expression, however, now reveals a faraway look and a hint of sadness. Her presentiment of the Passion to come is emphasized by Jesus, shown sitting on his mother's knee with arms outstretched in the shape of a cross. The cluster of putti laden with flowers lighten the tone, but the dominant mood is one of solemn stillness, and this is emphasized by the monumental, hieratic figures of Joseph in red and St Anne in white, and by the towers rising up out of the almost monochrome landscape. The composition must have been met with general approval because Poussin re-used it, with modifications, several times in the early 1650s. Again and again we find a number of figures – five in the Louvre picture, nine in the one in Cambridge, Mass., and eleven in the one jointly owned by the museums in Pasadena and Malibu – grouped around a central

178   axis formed by trees or an architectural feature. The painting in the Louvre, *The Holy Family with St Elizabeth and St John the Baptist in a Landscape*, which, like Raphael's *Canigiani Madonna*, shows the young St John playing with the infant Jesus, is more intimate in feeling than the other two. In both versions of *The Holy Family with St Elizabeth and St John the Baptist* the emphasis is on baptism and redemption, as groups of rather interchangeable-looking putti bring the Virgin a large copper basin in which to bathe Jesus. The landscape in each case continues the main theme, with calm, glassy waters and grey buildings on their banks. In each case, the poses and the relationship between the individual figures are slightly different – but the intensity of the looks they exchange does not change, and the thoughtful silence takes on an almost agonizing feeling.

cat. 45   Poussin's treatment of the theme became increasingly monumental. In June 1655 he completed a large, five-figure version of *The Holy Family with St Elizabeth and St John the Baptist* (now in Leningrad) for Chantelou, a work which he had been planning for a considerable time. Poussin's aim was to create an image to rival Raphael's *Holy Family of Francis I* (1518; Louvre) – but harder in feeling, and he reverted to the use of an upright format. Here the figures occupy almost the entire surface, while the landscape is relegated to the background. The stiffness of their postures is emphasized by the crisp draperies; their heads are mask-like, their features etched with mathematical precision, their eyes large and lacking in expression. The palette is muted, with only the odd dash of pink to alleviate the dull blues and brick-reds. Poussin adopted a similar approach in at least

178   two other works, *The Holy Family with the Infant St John the Baptist* (Sarasota) and *The Holy Family with St Elizabeth and St John the Baptist* (Louvre), where the central axis of

The Madonna of the Steps,
oil on canvas,
72.5 x 111.5 cm (28¹/₂ x 44 in.).
Cleveland Museum of Art, Cleveland, Ohio.

Opposite
Various treatments of the Holy Family theme.

(Above left) *The Holy Family with St Elizabeth
and St John the Baptist*,
oil on canvas, 94 x 122 cm (37 x 48 in.).
Louvre, Paris.

(Below left) *The Holy Family with the Infant
St John the Baptist*,
oil on canvas, 198 x 131 cm (78 x 51¹/₂ in.).
The John and Mable Ringling Museum of Art,
Sarasota, Fla.

(Above right) *The Holy Family*,
oil on canvas, 96.5 x 133 cm (38 x 52¹/₄ in.).
J. Paul Getty Museum, Malibu, Cal.,
and the Norton Simon Museum, Pasadena, Cal.

(Below right) *The Holy Family with St Elizabeth
and St John the Baptist in a Landscape*,
oil on canvas, 68 x 51 cm (26³/₄ x 20 in.).
Louvre, Paris.

Architectural features seen in details from six paintings.

Landscape with Pyramus and Thisbe (see p. 164).

Landscape – a Storm (see p. 163).

Landscape with Diogenes (see p. 158).

Christ Healing the Sick (see cat. no. 73).

Baptism, from the second set of *Sacraments* (see p. 106).

Ordination, from the second set of *Sacraments* (see p.106).

the picture is the figure of Joseph as he stands meditating or praying. As he grew older, Poussin was primarily concerned to convey the stature of his subjects and to combine breadth of form with compactness of composition. There is something quintessential about the static, almost primitive presences he conjures up, and it is tempting to regard them as examples of universal, timeless imagery.

Poussin's choice of subjects always had a certain logic. The Holy Family appealed to him because of the structural possibilities. He clearly enjoyed wrestling with composition, even if in this case the final result betrays a certain stiffness. The paintings are severe, and in the past were not only not much liked, as is still the case today, but sometimes simply misunderstood. Bernini, for instance, was utterly taken aback by a painting of the Holy Family (probably the version now in Dublin) which he saw in Serisier's house in 1665. 'He asked who it was by. I was surprised by the question. I said, "Poussin". He replied that he would never have thought it, that he could not possibly have painted those children.' It would undoubtedly have been difficult for an Italian to relate easily to these pictures: the subject was one which Italian artists had made their own and into which they poured all their emotive energy; Poussin, by contrast, was not interested in arousing emotion, except perhaps through the harsh majesty of his compositions. Poussin's approach to the theme of the Holy Family was unique in its time and ran increasingly counter to the trend towards sentimentality and prettiness epitomized by an artist like Mignard. Poussin is equally uncompromising in the way he handles his subject in the

183, 182 small *Assumption of the Virgin* (Louvre), painted in 1650, and in *The Ecstasy of St Paul* (also in the Louvre), painted in 1649–50 for Paul Scarron. Poussin was influenced by the work of the Bolognese artists of the early part of the century. His figures are undoubtedly rather leaden, but the complex, sculptural groupings are perfectly balanced. A distant landscape appears framed within the severe lines of the architectural background in the lower half of *The Ecstasy of St Paul*; in front of it, the sword resting on a book provides a perfect example of precision and perspective. The picture is similar in these respects to

179 *The Madonna of the Steps*, which dates from roughly the same time. It is at once a scholarly work, in every sense of the word – its complex symbolism was the subject of a series of lectures given at the Académie Royale in 1670 – and a powerfully majestic one. Poussin

cat. 134 had reached a peak of severity in his work, and this was to be reflected in *Bacchanal before a Temple*, painted c. 1650. Though the painting itself is lost, some twenty copies of an engraving of it survive: with its massive forms and frozen gestures, the work no longer embodies the feverish heat of Poussin's early paintings.

Poussin's form of religious belief was neither simple nor cosy. he did not share in the seventeenth-century idea of 'mystical invasion', by which the presence of God was made manifest through particular, unique individuals, nor was he part of the school of painting that had grown up with Caravaggio and sought to capture the poetry of an immanent God. He hoped instead, by looking at the nature of man and by using the simplest and most *general* forms, to re-create a sense of continuity with the past and to get back to basic values. Poussin's 'wisdom' lay here, in this unstinting and lucid pursuit of truth, underpinned as it was by a thorough command of his medium.

The Ecstasy of St Paul,
oil on canvas,
148 x 120 cm (58$\frac{1}{4}$ x 47$\frac{1}{4}$ in.).
Louvre, Paris.

The Assumption of the Virgin,
oil on canvas,
57 x 40 cm (22½ x 15¾ in.).
Louvre, Paris.

CHAPTER SIX

The Theory and Practice of Painting

POUSSIN'S WRITINGS ON ART.
THE RHYTHM OF WORK.
USE OF SKETCHES AND MODELS.
SPACE AND THE DISPOSITION OF FIGURES.
THE RHETORIC OF GESTURE.
THE THEORY OF MODES.
COLOUR AND LIGHT.

*'It is very hard to be a good judge of this art
if one does not have a profound experience of both the
theory and practice of it.'*
(Poussin to Chantelou, 24 November 1647)

In any museum Poussin's paintings are clearly distinguishable from the works of other painters. It is not that they are visually stunning or that their technique is captivating. They are more likely to seem the opposite, stern and flat. In a recent exhibition held in Paris *Camillus and the Schoolmaster of Falerii* stood out among other Italian masterpieces of the *seicento* in the reconstituted Galerie La Vrillière, not only because of the sort of grim restraint which characterizes it, but also because it conveys a sense of absolute inevitability, a world in which chance seems to play no part. Poussin was already thought of by his more enlightened contemporaries as being in a class of his own. Félibien makes it clear that Poussin was not content simply to 'know the world through his senses' or to imitate the great masters. The standard seventeenth-century approach of drawing from nature and copying recognized works was not enough for him. He needed to comprehend the underlying principles: 'He was particularly keen to grasp the reason for of the different sorts of beauty discernible in art.' He supplemented a practical training based on his reading and on discussions with leading thinkers in Rome.

Poussin himself wrote surprisingly little about his art. In about 1650 he had the idea of writing a book on painting, and got as far as collecting notes and copying out passages of interest from learned treatises on the subject. A dozen of Poussin's statements on art were published by Bellori as an appendix to his biography (1672). Writing did not come easily to Poussin, however. At their best his letters tend to be lively, abrupt even, but full of banter. Equally often, however, they can be laboured, especially when his correspondent was not well known to him. As he told Sublet de Noyers, he 'was used to living among people who understood him through his work, knowing how to write well not being his special skill'. Hence, for us his letters can never be anything more then second best; his thoughts were primarily expressed in conversation, and the devotees who accompanied him on his evening strolls would have been best placed to glean his ideas. According to Bellori, 'He would often talk about art, and with such expertise that not just painters but cultivated people in general came to hear him discourse on the supreme purpose of painting, not to educate [his listeners], but simply as ideas came to him.'

Poussin's major treatise never materialized, so we have to rely on discovering his ideas on art from a handful of odd fragments. His ideas were hardly new, nor was there anything doctrinal about his thinking – it was made up of well-worn commonplaces familiar to Rome and Florence since the Renaissance. His famous letter of 1 March 1665 to Fréart de Chambray is not in fact the artistic testament it has so often been considered, but a reply to *L'Idée de la perfection de la peinture* published three years earlier, and an amalgam of ideas culled from different sources. He starts by stating essential prerequisites for seeing and representing an object: light, a transparent medium, a defined space, colour, distance, an instrument. They are derived from a popular treatise on optics by Vitellion based on the learned research of the eleventh-century Arab scholar Alhazen. Poussin goes on to list the 'elements' which a painter brings to his 'material', i.e. his subject: order, ornament, decorum (or propriety), beauty, grace, vividness, costume (or historical detail), verisimilitude and judgment. The terms have a rhetorical flavour, and are drawn from seventeenth-century Italian treatises, like those of Paolo Aresi and Agostino Mascardi, and from Ludovico Castelvetro's commentary on Aristotle's *Poetics*, published in 1572 but still in regular use in Poussin's day. Anyone familiar with the subject would immediately have connected them with the art of poetry and thought of Horace's maxim, then widely endorsed, *Ut pictura poesis* ('as painting, so poetry').

Poussin's stated views are identical in the twelve Observations published as a set by Bellori and in his letters. On all questions of technique, he turns to the established authorities, whose treatises he would have been able to read either in printed or in manuscript form. He makes liberal use of the works of Alberti, Peregrino Viator or Father Zaccolini on perspective, Dürer on proportion in the human body, and, as we have already seen, Vitellion on optics. Poussin was commissioned by Cassiano Dal Pozzo to illustrate Leonardo da Vinci's *Treatise on Painting*, the source of his theories about the human body in motion. Poussin does not limit himself to the technical principles, however, but looks beyond the realm of art to literature and oratory. Thus, he quotes, in a more or less adapted or abbreviated form, from Aristotle, Quintilian and Tasso, whose *Discourse on Epic Poetry* he cites extensively, and he also includes extracts from a variety of basically Aristotelian treatises on poetry and rhetoric. Poussin's art is essentially experimental, however, and strives above all to be exact. he is tireless, humble and painstaking in his pursuit of perfection – 'I have overlooked nothing', he wrote. For him, theory had only a small part to play in the whole arduous process. Art was as much a practical as a cerebral activity, and his ideas continued to evolve throughout his life.

Compared with many of his peers, Poussin worked slowly and produced little, about 230 paintings (including those now lost) in the course of a career spanning more than forty years, i.e. an average of between five and six a year. His rate varied, however. The early years were prolific, for he had to sell his works in order to live, and therefore had to paint quickly, even resorting to repeating subjects that proved commercially successful. There are at least three versions, for instance, of a composition depicting a *Nymph and Satyr Drinking* (in Dublin, Madrid and Moscow). Much less preparation went into the paintings of the 1620s and 1630s than into Poussin's later work, and as a result alterations were frequent. His rate of work gradually slowed down, particularly after the Paris interlude. When people complained about his slowness, he would blame it on the summer heat, illness and, later, the infirmities of old age. The marked decline in Poussin's output in the last years of his life is undoubtedly attributable in large measure to his increasingly shaky hand. The constraints were not only physical, however: equally powerful in determining his rate of progress was his perfectionist approach. Without being in any way exceptional, Poussin was able in his youth to work quickly, launching straight into a painting. He quickly abandoned the speedy, *fa presto* method then common in both France and Italy. Haste of any sort was anathema to him, and he was contemptuous of those 'Paris painters' who could 'whip up' a picture overnight. Human figures, and arranging them, created special difficulties, and Poussin complained to Chantelou that it sometimes took him a whole day to paint a single head. This may help to explain his variable output from year to year. According to the records, he produced only four paintings in 1647, but of these three are large works each incorporating more than twenty figures. By comparison, the following year seems to have been enormously productive. Of the eleven known works, however, six consist essentially of landscapes in which the figures are much smaller and are therefore less time-consuming. It was not just the execution which took so long, and increasingly, as his career drew to a close, Poussin would not even begin painting until he had completed painstaking preparations in which he would pay scrupulous attention to the principles of 'order and . . . the manner in which . . . things are arranged'.

At the beginning of his career Poussin was governed entirely by his patrons and by the commissions he received. All his early pictures – *Battle* pictures, scenes from mythology, love scenes and religious paintings alike – were geared to particular commissions or needs. The altarpieces like *The Martyrdom of St Erasmus* and *The Virgin Appearing to St James* had to conform to strict specifications, the subject, format and number of figures being predetermined. Gradually Poussin became more his own master, but until the end of the 1630s his patrons continued to dictate in general terms what he should paint: Dal Pozzo wanted *Sacraments*, Rospigliosi allegories, Richelieu *Triumphs*. The trip to Paris, with all the constraints it entailed, was a turning point. There he met a new breed of middle-class collectors, demanding, certainly, but prepared to trust him and give him free rein in his choice of subject and way of treating it. With success came more custom and a degree of material ease: Poussin could work at own pace and on his own ideas. From then on, he and his patrons became partners. To judge from some of the letters, it seems there was even a complete reversal of their traditional roles. Quite often patrons would start out without any very clear idea of what they wanted, stipulating a large landscape, for instance, or a picture of the Holy Family, and the painting would evolve from there. Pointel wanted a picture featuring a certain number of beautiful young women, and ended up with *Eliezer and Rebecca at the Well* (Louvre). Poussin would 'chew over' an idea, as he did in the case of 'two topics' suggested to him by Madame de Montmort in 1665. He often dictated the final subject, and could be quite mischievous about imposing his will on his patrons: we know what a song and dance he led Scarron, who had wanted a 'Bacchic subject' but who ended up with *The Ecstasy of St Paul* (Louvre).

Poussin was a *history painter*. His concept of art was very much in the Renaissance tradition, but his own definition of art changed somewhat over the years. The idea, borrowed from Aristotle's *Poetics*, that art should *imitate*, remained central to his thinking. But what should it imitate? In one of the notes quoted by Bellori, Poussin applies Tasso's thoughts on poetry to painting, and states categorically that 'painting is nothing more than an imitation of human actions'. Everything else – 'the actions of animals' and 'all natural things' – is incidental. By 1665, however, the scope of painting had widened, and Poussin asserts that 'with the use of line and colour, [it is] an imitation on a flat surface of all that is to be seen under the sun'. In the interim, landscape had begun to assume greater importance, with human history reduced to one element among many in the broader history of the universe. Despite this, Poussin is remembered for the first of the two statements, not the second. Even in his own day, the painters of the Académie Royale read in it a rejection of all but the most noble of subject matter. In the letter he wrote to Fréart de Chambray on 1 March 1665, Poussin states that the 'subject matter . . . should be noble' and 'admit the finest form possible'. He is rejecting the sort of crude scenes of everyday life churned out by the followers of Caravaggio and the *bamboccianti*. Genre painting was generally out of favour at the time. Sacchi and Albani rejected it on grounds of impropriety. Félibien, for his part, was critical of the Le Nain brothers for depicting nothing but scenes of 'low life, bordering on the ridiculous'. The Bible, ancient history and myth-

47, 46

175

182

ology, on the other hand, were seen as providing subjects satisfying to both the eye and the mind.

By using his discretion in imitating 'all that is to be seen under the sun', the painter-poet could rise above the particular and deal, instead, with the universal. Such was the conclusion to which Agucchi's search for a happy medium between the artifice of the Mannerists and the crude realism advocated by the followers of Caravaggio had led him: while remaining true to reality, painting should interpret it; similarly, it should depict nature, but only from a 'beautiful' angle. The conflicting notions of beauty propounded by Plato and Aristotle were being brought together in a new *Idea della bellezza*. The Platonic ideal was no longer something which belonged to the realm of metaphysics; on the contrary, it was now firmly rooted in the real world. Poussin's thoughts on 'the idea of Beauty', as expressed in the brief extract quoted by Bellori, are clearly coloured by this new line of thinking: 'painting is none other then a perception of incorporeal things, and when it depicts bodies it merely represents the order and the measure in which these things are arranged, paying greater heed to the idea of beauty than to anything else.' To achieve this '*idea delle cose incorporee*' – a phrase coined by Marsilio Flicino, and taken up by Lomazzo in his *Idea del tempio della pittura* (1590) – the artist has to structure and modify the raw material nature gives him according to the three principles of *order*, *measure* and *aspect* (or form). 'Order' is the correct spacing of the different elements in a picture, 'measure' their harmonious relative proportions, and 'aspect' the judicious arrangement of lines and colours.

Art, then, refines and improves upon nature. The painter must aim for simplicity and clarity, the latter, according to Aristotle, being 'best achieved on a relatively small scale'. This is why Poussin believed so firmly in the need for 'moderation' in art, and why he was so convinced that it was vital for an artist to restrict size – the notion of 'moderateness' was central to the debate which raged in the Academy of St Luke in 1636 between Pietro da Cortona and Andrea Sacchi. Pietro da Cortona and his followers maintained that painting should have an epic quality: while illustrating essentially one event, a work should include a series of minor episodes designed to comment on and draw attention to the central action, incorporating many figures and a wealth of beautiful detail, and using a rich palette. Sacchi, by contrast, argued that painting should limit its range and concentrate its effects with an economy of line suggestive of tragedy. Poussin, as we know, sided with Sacchi, going even further than him. Sacchi subscribed to the idea that history painting was a branch of decorative painting, and continued to cover huge surfaces, whereas Poussin confined himself more or less exclusively to easel-painting. Even when he tackled scenes that called for large numbers of figures, and where the action was broken down into several 'episodes', Poussin was rigorous in his pursuit of clarity, carefully considering the disposition of the different elements and paying scrupulous attention to scale. He developed his own method of working.

It was a question first of defining the subject. Poussin made a habit of jotting down notes based on what he saw as well as on what he read. Félibien states that 'He took every opportunity to study, wherever he happened to be', and goes on to describe how 'as he walked through the streets he would watch everyone around him, and if he saw anything remarkable he would note it down in a book he always carried expressly for this purpose.' Hardly any of these studies have survived – they were probably destroyed either by Poussin himself or by his family. The study of a seated woman (Royal Library, Windsor)

189

Study of a Seated Woman,
pen and brown ink,
11.4 x 7.7 cm (4½ x 3 in.).
Royal Library, Windsor.

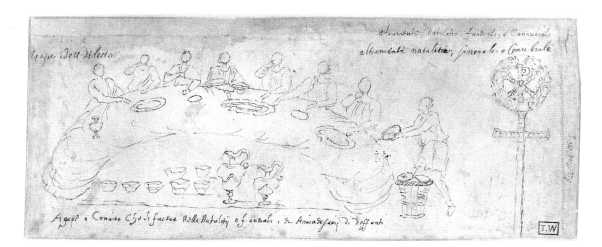

A Funeral Banquet,
pen and brown ink,
12.2 x 29.5 cm (4³/₄ x 11¹/₂ in.).
Private Collection, Paris.

does, however, have the look of one such quick sketch quite possibly executed while Poussin was out walking. *The Death of Cato* (also in the Royal Library; see p.143) captures the emotions generated by a reading of Plutarch, and a pen-and-ink drawing of *A Funeral Banquet* (private collection) is based on an engraving in Bosio's *Roma sotterranea*. Poussin would preserve such miscellaneous items for future use. Thus, for *The Rape of the Sabine Women*, he started with the works of Livy, Plutarch and Virgil, selecting certain elements from their accounts. In illustrating these, he utilized his own stock of visual material, while referring equally to Giovanni da Bologna's famous sculpture of the same subject and the bas-relief on its plinth, as well as to his own quick sketches from life. The basic idea of the picture gradually began to take shape, as much the product of chance experiences as of a sustained line of thought.

'He would consider the subject carefully, and then dash off two or three sketches outlining the composition', wrote Sandrart. For Poussin, drawing was both a physical and an intellectual process, involving the literal and mental drafting of an idea. His initial jottings were cursory, with the aim of establishing the broad outline of a composition and its main rhythm. These were governed by the number of figures required to tell the 'story', the choice of format, and the proportions of the canvas, generally calculated on the basis of the 'golden mean' or some other given ratio. Poussin gradually worked out the size and shape best suited to his needs, permitting him to incorporate not only a good number of figures but also a town or landscape in the background. Painting for Poussin was not just about imposing order on a plane surface or even about creating the illusion of depth. Above all, it was about meeting the challenge of filling a hitherto empty space with forms of all kinds. The preliminary sketches were essentially to do with the organization of mass and space, using lines and, more importantly, light and shade to conjure up a sense of volume. Initially, Poussin's method was to use thick hatching (studies for *The Massacre of the Innocents* and *The Martyrdom of St Erasmus*, for instance); later, he adopted the much faster technique of using wash (e.g. in the studies for the *Sacraments*). There are no details, and none of the fine lines or sweeps and flourishes present in the work of so many other artists. Poussin thinks in terms primarily of light and volume.

From the late 1620s on, sketching was no longer adequate. Increasingly, Poussin wanted to be able to construct entire compositions and needed, as it were, to 'feel' how they would work. To this end he resorted to a device popular in the sixteenth century

53
191
192

The Martyrdom of St Erasmus,
pen and brown ink, 20.4 x 13.2 cm (8 x 5¼ in.).
Uffizi, Florence.

Baptism, pen and brown wash,
15.7 x 25.5 cm (6¹/₈ x 10 in.).
Louvre, Paris.

Baptism, pen and brown wash,
16.5 x 25.4 cm (6¹/₂ x 10 in.).
Louvre, Paris.

Baptism, pen and brown wash,
12.3 x 19.1 cm (5 x 7¹/₂ in.).
Uffizi, Florence.

Baptism, pen and brown wash,
16.4 x 25.5 cm (6¹/₂ x 10 in.).
Hermitage, Leningrad.

with painters like Tintoretto, Barocci and El Greco, but no longer in current use: a three-dimensional model or miniature set populated with tiny figures representing those to be included in the painting. Poussin brought his own refinements to the technique, and his methods are described at length by Sandrart, Bellori and Le Blond de La Tour. He would start off with a board, marked with a grid, representing the ground. On this he would set out a series of little wax figures dressed in fine material or paper, fixing them by means of pegs, and arranging them within a given perspective established by converging threads stretched out above the base. The board was then covered with a backless box of the same size. By making slits in the top and sides Poussin could adjust and direct the lighting at will, and he could build up the 'stage set' by introducing wax props or drawings of scenery at the sides. Having done all this, he would make peep-hole in the front of the box to enable him to gauge the effect of the composition. He would then draw what he saw through the hole, moving the different elements about until he achieved the desired result. Although none of these constructions has survived, it is still possible to get some idea of their nature by reference to various extant series of working drawings, which in some cases clearly illustrate the gradual process of correction and improvement. This is particularly true of the series of preparatory drawings for *Baptism* in the second set of *Sacraments* (see p. 192).

Above all, the models helped Poussin to structure three-dimensional space. They seem to have made their appearance at the very moment when he was seeking to open up his compositions and apply the rules of linear perspective drawn up by Alberti, Dürer and, rather nearer to Poussin's own time, Father Matteo Zaccolini, under whom Domeni-

59, 72, 194

chino studied. *The Plague of Ashdod* and both versions of *The Rape of the Sabine Women* marked a turning point in Poussin's approach. Up till then, his compositions were essentially linear, and the figures placed more or less parallel to the picture plane, or set one

47, 43

above the other, as in *The Martyrdom of St Erasmus*. Even in *The Death of Germanicus*, where space begins to take on a three-dimensional quality, the composition conforms to the rules governing bas-reliefs. If we look at the pictures Poussin painted after 1630, however, it is clear that he has fully mastered Alberti's principles and has succeeded in applying them without losing anything of the surface density he achieved earlier. A detailed study of the second version of *The Rape of the Sabine Women* (?1637–8), now in the Louvre, led Avigdor Arikha to note that two focal points exist in the picture. The vanishing point falls centrally and is marked by an arch, but the obliques in the picture all radiate out from a point slightly below and to the left, on the mounted soldier's helmet, the lines having been traced out on the prepared canvas. Against the strict geometry of the architectural context is set a vortex of frenetic gesture. Despite the fact that both figures and buildings are properly scaled down as they recede into the distance, the viewer's eye is not free to travel far in that direction, but is compelled instead to move end-

179

lessly from side to side. In *The Madonna of the Steps* (1648), a work in a quite different vein, Poussin manages to create the illusion of perspective – with some spectacular foreshortening – while respecting the picture plane. The figures are grouped as if in one line and form a triangle which stands out clearly against the perpendicular lines of the architectural background.

Poussin would be uncompromising in his rejection of *quadratura* and of absolute illusionism in his work on the Grande Gallery in the Louvre. He did not pander to the eye and obliterate the lines of the vault with a painted sky complete with flying figures. On the

The Rape of the Sabine Women,
oil on canvas,
159 x 206 cm (62$\frac{1}{2}$ x 81 in.),
with detail opposite.
Louvre, Paris.

One of the marble terms,
after a design by Poussin,
for the gardens of Vaux-le-Vicomte
(now at Versailles).

contrary, he refused to include in his scheme anything which looked in any way implausible and was not suited to the layout and dimensions of the gallery. Instead, he sought to emphasize the fabric of the building by decorating the surfaces in imitation of bas-reliefs. He believed that art should present a 'prospect', a coherent picture which allowed the spectator to understand what was being represented, rather than an 'aspect' designed to make no more than a superficial impression. This preoccupation led Poussin increasingly in his later easel-paintings to marry the setting to the subject matter. Here architecture and landscape are no longer used primarily to convey a precise sense of depth, but to illuminate the action. The setting in *The Plague of Ashdod*, for instance, simply provides a platform for the action, a *scaena tragica* of the kind advocated by Vitruvius and given material form by Serlio. There was nothing rigid about such settings: with their imposing buildings, they would do for any 'serious' subjects. In *Christ and the*   198
Woman Taken in Adultery (Louvre), however, painted over twenty years later, the interplay of inanimate forms and lines in the background mirrors the dumbshow being enacted in the foreground. The great diagonal of the staircase in the distance emphasizes the gesture made by Christ in the centre of the picture. The buildings in the foreground, meanwhile, are introduced like flats in a stage set and echo the dramatic gestures of the groups of supernumeraries on either side.

Poussin's landscapes follow a similar pattern. They, too, were essentially interchangeable to begin with, and tended to be built around the sort of oblique view long favoured for landscapes. The great works of the late 1640s, like *Landscape with a Man*   152
Killed by a Snake, Landscape with the Funeral of Phocion and *Landscape with the Gather-*   154, 155
ing of the Ashes of Phocion, and *Landscape with Diogenes*, were much more precisely   158
constructed, and were in the Vitruvian mould. By concentrating the action in the foreground, breaking up the landscape beyond into a series of different planes stretching into the middle distance, the figures becoming smaller and the colours lighter, Poussin was creating a finite, measurable space. In the later works, however, like *Landscape with*   229
Diana and Orion, The Birth of Bacchus and *The Four Seasons*, the central figures, al-   *cat. 122*
though placed in the foreground, seem to merge into the dense weave of the landscape   238–9, 246–7
around them. Gone is the clarity of the intellectual three-dimensional approach. Instead, the emphasis is on the emotion that the painting's surface can convey. Poussin made his final views absolutely clear in 1665 in the definition of painting, when he emphasized that it was 'on a flat surface'. To the modern eye, Poussin's last great masterpieces, like *Winter*
and *Apollo and Daphne*, which were quite unparalleled in their day, have the shallow   247, 232
look of frescoes. The inspiration to paint in this way could have come from either French painting or classical wall-painting. It was not its decorative quality, however, but its expressive force which attracted Poussin to this genre. His precise meaning may become more mysterious, but his desire to capture 'the ineffable' remains unchanged, and it is this which the rich surface textures and subtle rhythms of his late landscapes convey.

The key element in history painting was the human figure: it introduced both a yardstick and a catalyst, hence the great care taken in getting it right. Normally, artists relied on drawing, both from life (academy figures) and after the most celebrated examples of classical sculpture. Poussin did both. However, none of his life drawings or studies of drapery survives, whereas a very different state of affairs obtains in the case of Annibale Carracci and Simon Vouet, whose numerous extant drawings give us a very good idea of their abilities. Some of Poussin's drawings after the antique and his study of *Castor and*   197

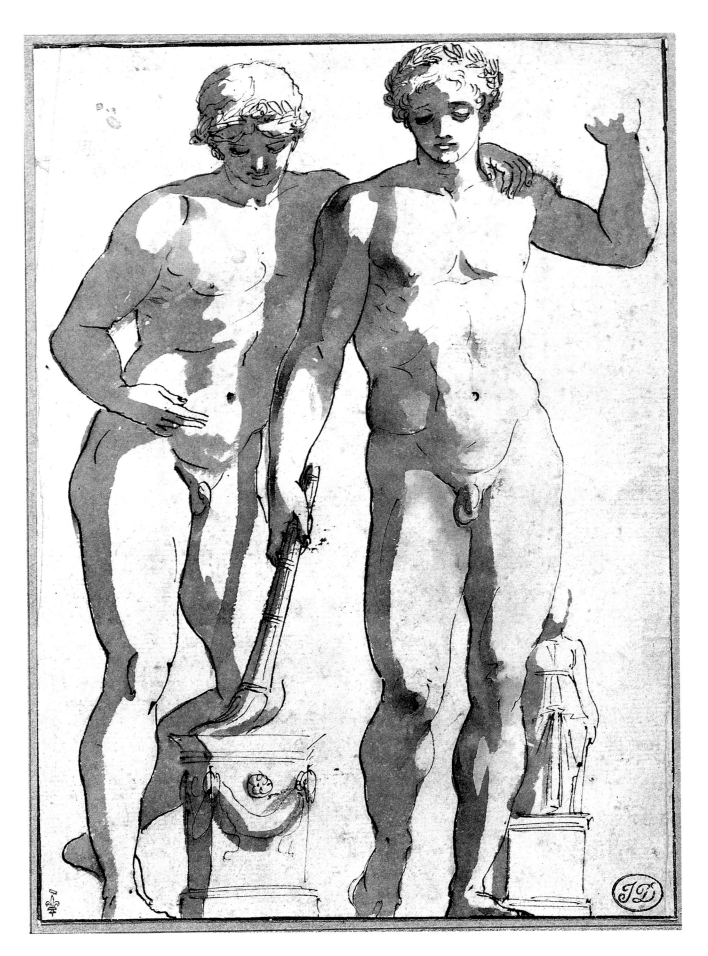

Two Athletes,
pen and brown wash,
24.6 x 17.1 cm (9³/₄ x 6³/₄ in.).
Musée Condé, Chantilly.

197

Christ and the Woman Taken in Adultery,
oil on canvas,
122 x 195 cm (48 x 76¾ in.),
with detail opposite.
Louvre, Paris.

Pollux at Chantilly and various studies of bas-reliefs (to be found in Bayonne, among other places) reflect a keen interest in sculpture. Bellori reproduced his study of the proportions of the Belvedere *Antinoüs* complete with detailed supporting measurements.   80 Drawing was not enough for him, however. He wanted to see his figures move in three-dimensional space, hence needed to feel them come to life in his hands. He had done some clay and wax modelling with Duquesnoy, and indeed he has been variously credited with a number of statuettes of children and with the sculpture of *Ariadne Asleep* now in the Louvre. Be this as it may, he must have established a reputation as a three-dimensional artist by the time Abbé Louis Fouquet commissioned him to produce models for a series of terms and urns for the gardens at Vaux-le-Vicomte. Poussin's biog-   196 raphers all emphasize how skilful he was in his handling of wax, and in the way he dressed his models and altered their poses.

Poussin's method of composition, though laborious, did have at least two distinct advantages: it enabled him to get an instant sense of the the overall effect a painting would have, and to modify elements within it quickly and easily. Instead of working on individual elements in isolation and then trying to combine them in a drawing or on the final canvas, he could plan the whole composition at once, grouping his figures and moving them about, bearing in mind the distances between them and how they were to be lit. As noted above, his methods can be seen in the working drawings for the Chantelou version of *Baptism* and the two versions of *The Rape of the Sabine Women*, for instance. As well as being moved about, any figure could be remodelled as necessary, so as to fit better into the whole. The danger, as Leonardo da Vinci had pointed out, was that the results could appear uniform and contrived. It comes as no surprise that model figures capable of being contorted at will should have found particular favour with the Mannerists. For his part, Poussin was more than master of his technique, the model sets that he constructed being intended not to provide miniature wax *tableaux vivants* to be precisely copied on canvas, but to permit reflection. Despite their solidity, the lighting lent the model figures an unearthly quality, as if they were part of another universe which suddenly stood revealed, and their frozen dance took on the vividness of a dream. Poussin would set to work, expanding and modifying the image as necessary. He would constantly refer back to nature, and almost certainly had recourse to the living model for particular details.

Poussin's human figures have an unmistakably studied and forced quality. In the later works his approach is essentially analytical. Every moment is broken down, every gesture frozen, as if suspended. Poussin did his best to do as Leonardo and others recommended by making each character clearly recognizable as to age, sex and station in life. He was similarly precise in the way he chose to dress his figures. Having carefully sorted out all these details, he was left, at the final painting stage, with the difficult task of giving each individual distinctive features. With the help, perhaps, of treatises on physiognomy like the one by Porta, Poussin set about doing as Domenichino did, portraying a variety of *affetti* or emotions. The faces tend to resemble masks whose function is to express a particular reaction – anger, terror, pity and so on. The various expressions seen in *The Massacre of the Innocents* and the two versions of *The Rape of the Sabine Women* –   55, 72, 194 the silent howl which so riveted Francis Bacon – call to mind Greek tragedy. Each of the young women in *Eliezer and Rebecca at the Well* has the same kind of features, round,   175 full face and large thick-lidded eyes. The colouring and hairstyles change, however, the angle of the neck differs, the mouth opens or closes a fraction, a crease appearing or disappearing at its corner as it does so, and each casts her gaze in a slightly different direction. Through these tiny details, Poussin evokes not fully rounded characters or even specific individuals, but the entire range of reactions that a display of divine will might engender in the human heart. There is something absolute, even disturbing about these majestic, Junoesque heads. Through them, as through the bodies, Poussin is determined to make manifest and give independent form to what would otherwise remain hidden.

72, 194, 214 Marc Fumaroli has attempted to show that in a number of paintings, ranging from the two versions of *The Rape of the Sabine Women* to *The Death of Sapphira*, Poussin was drawing on a precise code of gestures formulated by both classical and later orators. Quintilian and later Agostino Mascardi both stressed the part played by *action* in oratory, stating that without it *diction* was ineffective. Poussin proclaims the importance of body language in one of the observations collected by Bellori: 'Quintilian attributes such importance and vigour to it, that he considers concepts, trials and affections pointless without it, just as lines and colour are pointless without it.' The gestures of the orator-hero are measured, at once noble and commanding. By contrast, the common people, to whom his words are directed, do little more than gesticulate: they express themselves in a dis-
141 organized manner. The contrast is particularly marked in works like *Camillus and the*
198 *Schoolmaster of Falerii* and *Christ and the Woman Taken in Adultery*. On one side we are presented with straight backs, harmonious poses, fingers firmly pointing; on the other, with awkward attitudes, bowed figures, a welter of movement and faces distorted with emotion. The hero, be he Jesus or Romulus, becomes the interpreter of the Word. His commanding gesture renders his meaning unequivocal and visible, activating the other participants; this gives rise to a frenzy, as in *The Rape of the Sabine Women*, or brings a
cat. 73 sense of calm revelation, as in *Christ Healing the Sick*. Gesture in Poussin carries with it a hidden meaning which the viewer must decipher, just as he does the mysterious characters traced on the ground which Christ points out to the Pharisees in *Christ and the Woman Taken in Adultery*. The interlocking sequence of gestures made by the suppliant
145 women in *Coriolanus* helps explain the import of the figure of Rome on the left – the personification of the fatherland confronting the rebel general. As already noted in the case
102 of *The Israelites Gathering Manna*, all the figures are arranged singly or in groups so as to project the implicit meaning of the subject. A full understanding of the picture depends on reading and digesting every line, i.e. studying each and every figure in context.

However different and jarring they may appear, every pose and gesture are closely dictated and governed by an overall rhythm, so lending a work its particular force. Even paintings as turbulent as the two versions of *The Rape of the Sabine Women* are underpinned by order and balance: figures mirror each other, groups answer one another. There is a carefully orchestrated pattern of echoes running from one side to the other, and from one plane to another. The apparently chaotic scene is in fact as precisely judged as the tranquillity and harmony of any version of *The Holy Family* or of *Christ and the Woman Taken in Adultery*. Poussin's painstaking search for the right form for every subject sets him firmly apart from his contemporaries. His aims were not always appreciated, and patrons and friends were sometimes surprised, even disappointed, by his seemingly gratuitous changes of tone. Chantelou, for instance, was somewhat dissatisfied with his version of *Baptism*. It did not, he felt, match up to *Moses Saved from the Water*, which Poussin had just painted for Pointel, and he accused Poussin of serving him less well than his rival patron. Poussin wasted no time in replying: 'Do you not see that it is the nature of the subject which is the cause of this, and your mood, and that the subjects which I undertake for you have to be represented in a different way? Therein lies all the skill of painting.' Every painting called for a particular *mode*, and Poussin strove to temper his form of expression to each subject, and to choose a central rhythm when he came to arrange lines and colour. In the somewhat obscure and confused letter he wrote to Chantelou on 24 November 1647, he talks of 'moderation' and 'moderateness'. This was his way of describing the kind of measured approach which was so central to his work.

The concept of modes was derived largely from music. Poussin writes admiringly of the 'fine old ancient Greeks' who invented the various modes, in effect the forerunners of modern tonalities: *Dorian* – 'steady, solemn and severe'; *Phrygian* – 'vehement, violent'; *Lydian* – thought appropriate 'for the pitiful'; *Hypolydian* – possessing 'a certain sweetness and softness'; and *Ionian* – 'of a joyous nature'. Poussin is merely reproducing more or less accurately a passage from Giuseppe Zarlino's treatise *Istituzioni Harmoniche*, published in Venice in 1558, which summarized the different theories propounded, starting with the Pythagoreans and concluding with Glareanus, whose *Dodecachordon*, published in 1547, listed twelve different 'modes', each with a Greek epithet. Poussin probably became acquainted with such learned works through Domenichino, who had a passion for music and even invented musical instruments. Poussin was likely, however, to give these modes new slants. They were reminiscent of the five orders of architecture – Tuscan, Doric, Ionic, Corinthian and Composite – devised by Vitruvius. The terms were later taken up by Serlio and used to define the three major categories of drama: tragedy, comedy and satirical drama. Poetry, according to Aristotelian thought, fell into two broad categories, and was either solemn and heroic (the *modus gravis*), or quick and light (the *modus levis*). Classical oratory, meanwhile, was based on a universally accepted hierarchy of styles: the mean (*humilis*), the moderate (*mediocris*) and the sublime (*gravis*). Poussin was almost certainly more conversant with these literary ideas than with musical theory. Later in the same letter to Chantelou he cites Virgil in his defence of the use of modes. Virgil, he asserts, whether he speaks of love or war 'is so skilful in giving each line the sound appropriate to its subject matter that in truth it seems he can make us see the things he describes, simply through the sound of the words he uses.'

Attempts have been made to ascribe a particular mode to each of Poussin's paintings. Just as a poet constructs word patterns and sounds, and a musician successions of notes, intervals and rhythms, a painter plays with lines, sometimes horizontal, sometimes vertical, gestures, solids and hollows, and colour – harsh, soft, light, dark – in order to achieve a particular harmony and set of effects in each of his works. Examples of the categorization of Poussin's pictures by mode are: *Landscape with the Funeral of Phocion* and *Landscape with the Gathering of the Ashes of Phocion*, both broad, severe and static, are supposed to represent the Dorian mode; *The Rape of the Sabine Women*, with its vehemence and its violent, repeated movements, is associated with the Phrygian mode, which Poussin also considered appropriate to battle scenes; because each in its own way constitutes a lament, *Landscape with Pyramus and Thisbe* and the touching *Lamentation over the Dead Christ* (Dublin) are both reckoned to be in the Lydian mode; the two versions of *The Ecstasy of St Paul*, it is argued, are in the Hypolydian, which 'is suitable for religious subjects, glories and images of heaven'; scenes of feasting and dancing as depicted in the *Bacchanals* can only fall within the Ionian mode. These categories are highly debatable, however, not least because their definitions are so skimpy. Some of

154, 155

194

164, 223

182

229, 232   Poussin's late works, such as the *Landscape with Diana and Orion* and *Apollo and Daphne*, do not fit readily into any of these categories, however loosely interpreted.

102   Internal contrast plays a crucial part in other paintings, hence a whole group of works –
152   encompassing *The Israelites Gathering Manna*, the *Landscape with a Man Killed by a*
228   *Snake* and finally the *Landscape with Hercules and Cacus* – cannot be seen in terms of any one mode. Poussin originally took up the concept of modes in a metaphorical sense to clarify his explanation to a disgruntled patron. He never saw it as a system to be followed rigidly, but rather as a general principle, reflecting the need to keep within certain limits and to subordinate the diction to the subject. Central to Stoic philosophy is the notion of a higher rational order. The virtue of the later works lies in this order: nothing seems redundant, everything has its place and its *raison d'être*.

In any examination of *ideas* in art there is some risk of overlooking the physical aspect of painting. 'Fine craftsmanship', it has to be said, its not what we look for primarily in Poussin, and he certainly could not match the technical excellence of a Rubens or a Guido Reni. He had none of the panache, either, of painters like Vouet and Luca Giordano. Critics have concluded from this, somewhat over-hastily, that Poussin never yielded to the pure thrill of painting in the way so many artists did in the seventeenth cen-

47, 44   tury. Many of his early works, however, like *The Martyrdom of St Erasmus* and *The Triumph of Flora*, not to mention some of the *Bacchanals*, betray a genuine enjoyment of the chosen medium. In those early days Poussin would launch straight into the canvas, often making false starts: X-ray examination has revealed not only that he made alterations but also that he re-used canvases. Dark, briskly painted grounds are overlaid and highlighted with warm or bright colours: golden yellows, plums, deep blues, creamy whites. The brush-strokes are vigorous, sometimes rather thick, and conceal a basic, even clumsy, sketch, together with some fairly weak modelling which tends to flatten forms. It is too facile to attribute the dry, restricted style which followed simply to Poussin's increasing unsteadiness of hand. It must be remembered that he had a deliberate policy of 'moderation', and that from the 1640s onwards, he had to respond to new demands. Just as a subject had to be pondered over at length and a composition meticulously worked out with the help of drawings and models, a canvas too called for lengthy preparation. It had first to be carefully primed, then coated with a reddish-brown *imprimatura*. The next stage was to add guide lines, scored with a stylus or simply using chalk. Poussin normally marked out either squares or oblique lines radiating from a central point. The grid enabled the drawing to be transferred. Poussin seems not to have been in the habit of making full-scale drawings, only one such being known, and only a

65   fragment at that – for *The Triumph of David* (Dulwich Picture Gallery). Even this is not a cartoon in the conventional sense, however, and was occasioned by Poussin's desire to move one group within the overall composition. He did not begin painting until he had come to a precise and satisfactory solution. X-ray examination of his later works has revealed very few changes of heart. The outline drawings which show up under the glaze, or *velatura*, tend, on the contrary, to be firm and decisive. All the indications are that Poussin worked slowly, one stage at a time, in a manner quite different from the *fa presto* approach adopted by painters of the Baroque. As he grew older, Poussin was less able to conjure up form with the same ease and exactness as he once had. He made the most of each brush-stroke, adding to the sense of volume, the colour and the meaning with every

touch. The broad, sensuous manner of the early years gave way to an entirely different approach, as Poussin turned his failing powers to good account.

Today, it is very difficult to pronounce with any authority on the purely pictorial qualities of Poussin's work. The brownish ground has often come through to the surface, and the colours darkened. The later works, with their mat surfaces, frequently rough texture and painting *en camaïeu*, have suffered particularly from the ravages of time, and look distinctly unattractive. Restoration, if well done, vividly confutes the harsh comments which generations of critics have levelled at Poussin. In his *Balance des peintres* (1708), Roger de Piles gives Poussin a mere six out of twenty for colour, compared with considerably higher marks for drawing (seventeen), composition (fifteen) and expression (fifteen). In his *Abrégé de la vie des peintres* (1699), he deplores the fact that Poussin uses 'only general tones instead of imitating the colours of nature', that he has no 'notion' of chiaroscuro, and that instead of 'grouping objects and light together to good effect', he disperses them to such an extent that 'the eye often does not know which way to look'. Piles was writing at a time when the 'Colourist' faction was gaining strength, and the champions of drawing and restraint were being outnumbered by followers of Rubens and the Venetian school. It is not surprising, therefore, that he preferred Poussin's early works, still showing the influence of Titian and his rich harmonious tones.

It is certainly true that for Poussin colour was secondary to drawing, and in terms of the painting as a whole, it was definitely subordinate to the idea depicted, to what Poussin wanted to express. 'Colour in painting,' he once remarked, paraphrasing Tasso, 'is a lure designed to attract the eye, in the same way that in poetry the beauty of the lines of verse do.' Only drawing appeals to the mind. Poussin was as dependent on these 'lures' as the orator and poet, however. In the Berlin *Self-Portrait* the prominently placed book on   148
which his hand rests is entitled *De lumine et colore*. In his most successful works, Poussin does not see colour as useless decoration, nor, however, does he revel in it for its own sake, as Rubens does with his warm flesh tones or Velázquez with his silvery greys. For him, both the choice of colour and how it was used were dictated by the subject. Its function was essentially expressive, like the sound of words. In the Hartford *Crucifixion*, for   *cat. 78*
instance, the colours are gloomy, while in the Dublin *Lamentation over the Dead Christ*   223
they are harsh and shrill, and light and joyful in *Eliezer and Rebecca at the Well* and *Christ*   175, *cat. 73*
Healing the Sick. Colour can also have a symbolic meaning: the character and motives may be conveyed by the colour of an individual's clothes. In *The Judgment of Solomon*,   144
for example, the bad mother is depicted in dull green and red, while the good mother wears blue, yellow and white, and Solomon white and bright red. To Roger de Piles, as later to Eugène Delacroix, this preoccupation with making the artist's meaning plain got in the way of harmony, and prevented Poussin from achieving a pleasing integration of colour. Poussin rejected not only the idea of total unity favoured by the Venetian school, but also the chiaroscuro technique adopted by Flemish painters, and the manipulation of shades within a particular range so brilliantly exemplified in the work of Rembrandt. Avigdor Arikha has observed, apropos *The Rape of the Sabine Women* (Louvre), that   194
Poussin thinks of colour as ranging from cold to warm rather than from light to dark, and that when painting shadows he uses warmer, rather than darker, shades. He uses very little black, but relies heavily instead on ochres and earth colours which provide a foil for brilliant dashes of ultramarine, deep yellow and vermilion. In paintings such as *The*   214
Death of Sapphira and *Christ and the Woman Taken in Adultery* the colours can seem   198

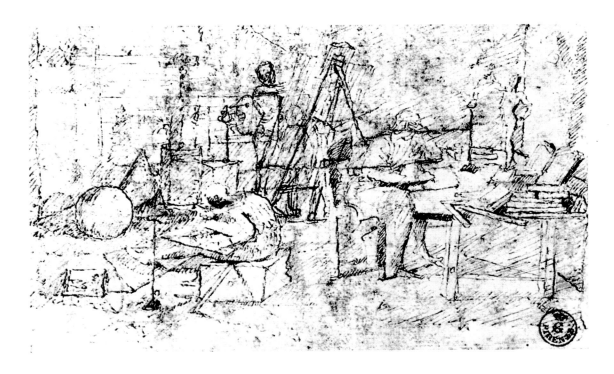

Artists Sketching,
pen and brown ink,
118 x 194 cm (46 ¼ x 76½ in.).
Uffizi, Florence.

rather discordant; the stark reds, yellows and blues are uncompromising, without sub-
tlety. Poussin takes his cue from mediaeval stained glass and considers colour in terms of
relative intensity. He applies it in patches of varying brightness, repeating colours at different points in the composition to point to echoes in the poses of the figures.

Before he left for Paris in 1640, Poussin got Jean Dughet to copy out passages from a
treatise by Father Zaccolini on how to depict light and shade. Zaccolini's manuscript was
rediscovered in the Biblioteca Medicea-Laurenziana in Florence, and Elizabeth Cropper
has recently pointed out the bearing it has on Poussin's work. It is illustrated with drawings of solid geometric forms lit in different ways by artificial light from one or more
sources. Originally formulated by Leonardo da Vinci, these practical exercises were of
particular relevance to Poussin at one stage in his career, and he was clearly familiar with
them, as a drawing in the Uffizi shows: three artists are shown in a studio drawing a
sphere, a cone and a cylinder, working by the light of lamps fitted with reflectors. It is
obvious from the way Poussin depicts the different light sources and the accuracy with
which he paints shadows in works like the Dal Pozzo *Eucharist* and the Chantelou
Extreme Unction that he has a thorough knowledge of the subject. There are reminders
of the theory, too, in the sphere and in the form of the vases and structures seen in the
Louvre version of *Eliezer and Rebecca at the Well*, painted a little later. Natural light has
taken the place of artificial, however, and Poussin's concern is with colour and reflected
light rather than sharply defined shadows. Gone are the dawns and dusks of his early,
Venetian mode, with their quivering shadows and shimmering waters. Instead he opts
for an even light which brings out the forms without creating an excessive contrast between light and shade. The exaggerated light and shade of the three-dimensional models
gave Poussin a preliminary, outline view of volumes: he could establish with certainty
which part of a form was most brilliantly lit and which was plunged in darkness. For the
subtle detail he turned to nature. Brienne owned a landscape drawing by Poussin dating

98
106

175

View of the Aventine Hill, brown wash over black chalk.
13.4 x 31.2 cm (5½ x 12½ in.).
Uffizi, Florence.

Claude Lorrain,
Landscape with a Shepherd,
oil on canvas.
Private collection, New York.

Gaspard Dughet,
Landscape with a Herdsman and his Goats,
oil on canvas,
68 x 120.4 cm (26³/₄ x 47¹/₂ in.).
Art Institute of Chicago.

Study of Undergrowth,
brown wash over black chalk,
25.4 x 18.5 cm (10 x 7½ in.).
Louvre, Paris.

back to the days when he went on trips into the countryside around Rome with Claude and Sandrart. It showed 'all the streaks of light which occur as day breaks', and on it Poussin had apparently scribbled, 'I would like this to be dawn'. The few known landscape drawings known to be by Poussin reveal a special awareness of light, focusing not on the way it affects surfaces but on the way it defines and animates form. In the *View of the Aventine Hill* in the Uffizi, brilliant sunlight falls directly on the trees, creating a pale halo around the dark mass of leaves and making them stand out clearly in the stillness of the Roman heat. Unlike Claude Lorrain, who was so keen on early morning and evening mists and sea vapours, Poussin's backgrounds are always distinct, his clouds almost palpable, his stretches of water precise and mirror-like: his is the art of the immutable. On the rare occasions when he attempted the impossible – depicting the blast of a storm, swirls of dust, flashes of lightning, sheets of rain – he was only following Leonardo's lead. His brother-in-law Gaspard Dughet was much more successful in this field, doubtless because he had a much keener eye for 'meteors' and natural phenomena of all kinds.

205

206

Poussin's aims were quite different: he wanted to make nature comprehensible by presenting it in a restructured form. Roger de Piles judged Poussin's work in terms of its ability to create an immediate 'effect at first sight', and as a result failed to appreciate his skilful use of colour and light. Félibien, on the other hand, in his long accounts of *The Israelites Gathering Manna* and *Eliezer and Rebecca at the Well*, clearly understood Poussin's purpose and realized that his pictures are designed to be expositions of events. He comments first on the appropriateness of the time of day: a cloudy morning for *the Israelites Gathering Manna* and a brilliant late afternoon for *Eliezer and Rebecca at the Well*. He praises 'the pleasing range of light and shade' in the former, and even identifies three different sorts of lighting or 'effects', all emanating from the sun as its rays break through the cloud here and there like a searchlight. A 'sovereign' light strikes the parts closest to the viewer, such as the upper halves of the figures in the foreground. A 'glancing light plays over the parts that are more in shade, like the lower halves of the same figures. Lastly, a 'spent' or 'dead' light covers the parts furthest from the viewer, in accordance with the rules of atmospheric perspective – the 'vaporous' morning air hangs like a veil. The same principles govern the use of colour: the most brightly lit figures – the young woman suckling her mother and the kneeling woman on the right – are swathed in yellow and blue, the colours 'which partake most of light and air'. The same approach is manifest in *Eliezer and Rebecca at the Well*, where 'the sun is beginning to sink below the horizon'. The light is 'gentler and softer than during daytime'. As befits a hot dry climate, the air is not 'charged with vapours', but the flesh-tints gradually 'die' the further away the young women are. The light and reflections are finely judged, neither too strong nor too weak, and perfectly balanced: 'the colours keep to their allotted space, without encroaching on others or being encroached upon, and without undermining each other'. Poussin steered clear of the dramatic contrast between great expanses of light and shade so beloved of the Venetians. Everything remains clear and readable. As Félibien stresses, the lighting is perfectly suited to the subject. In interior scenes like *Moses Trampling on Pharaoh's Crown* and the Chantelou version of *Extreme Unction*, for instance, the flesh-tints are ruddier, light and shade more pronounced, the glints of reflected light sharper, the different parts 'more powerfully expressed, more clearly defined'. Conditioned as we are by the concept of 'complete' harmony propounded by Piles, responding to such an alien and in many ways bewildering way of painting is not easy, and requires considerable

102,175

cat. 13

106

effort if we are to understand Poussin's approach, but the pleasure such understanding brings more than compensates for the struggle.

There has been much discussion – still unresolved – about precisely what Poussin meant when, just before his death, he stated that his art set out to 'delight'. According to Horace, who took the idea from Aristotle, poetry has a twin goal, *'docere et delectare'*, to instruct and to please. It should imitate in an idealized way, creating a better, more beautiful version of reality that is both mentally improving and aesthetically satisfying. Poussin seems ultimately to have attached more importance to the second of Horace's goals – in itself altogether surprising. Not only did Poussin himself have a Stoical turn of mind and believe in the importance of the 'imitation of human actions' and of moral examples in art, but since the Counter-Reformation an entire school of thought had grown up which believed firmly with Armenini and Lomazzo that the purpose of art was to edify. Advocates of classical idealism like Bellori, Félibien, and the members of the Académie in Paris, too, stressed the educational nature of art. In fact, however, in his last few works, like the *Four Seasons*, Poussin distanced himself from the flat didacticism of theoreticians like Lomazzo who believed that painting should be strictly moral in character and 'constantly show the true path leading from the eyes to the soul'. In 1642 he was clearly already adopting a quite different stance when, in a letter to Chantelou, he talked of the spirit being delighted by the sight of beautiful young women and beautiful columns in equal measure. For Poussin, the balanced arrangement and perfect proportions of the different elements within a painting, in short the order which he brings to his material, lead to an apprehension of the truth rather than to a coolly rational absorption of it. In this sense, as Blunt has pointed out, Poussin's notion of delight comes close to St Augustine's concept of *delectatio boni* and to the ideas of St Bonaventura, who believed that we come close to divine truth through 'the order, measure, beauty and arrangement of things'.

Poussin thus no longer agreed unequivocally with the generally held belief that painting, poetry and oratory are all broadly equivalent. Already in *The Inspiration of the Poet* he senses that painting has something different, richer to offer. The development of his art proves it: from a painstaking unravelling and minute analysis of his subject (*The Israelites Gathering Manna* being perhaps the best example), he moves on to a delicious evocation of a timeless, harmonious world, designed to gladden the soul through the eye. We are closer here to architecture or music, both of which are founded on the 'accord' of the constituent parts. The subject and its literal meaning are now only of incidental importance. Instead the emphasis is on congruity and harmony: every element has to fit perfectly with the others and with the whole. The scene has, of course, still to be plausible from a geographical and historical point of view – the 'costume' is as important as ever. Primarily, however, it is an excuse for a 'new and beautiful arrangement' (Ninth Observation on Painting). Writing in 1658 of the 'appurtenances' in *The Rest on the Flight into Egypt* (Hermitage), Poussin declared: 'I have included all these things ... in order to provoke delight through innovation and variety and to show that the Virgin depicted here is in Egypt.' Poussin's words conjure up an image of a composer like J. S. Bach: he must have felt something of Poussin's 'delight through innovation and variety' when composing his Fugues, infinitely varied yet centred around a single theme. Poussin is not, on the other hand, one of those people 'who always sing the same tune'. The pleasure his work generates results largely from the modulations he creates, from the interplay of theme and variation, the mixture of the expected and the unexpected.

54

102

cat. 65

CHAPTER SEVEN

The Fruits of Old Age

THE ARTIST'S DECLINING PHYSICAL POWERS.
THE LAST RELIGIOUS WORKS.
LANDSCAPE PAINTING REDEFINED: ALLEGORY AND MYTHOLOGY.
'APOLLO AND DAPHNE' AS POUSSIN'S LAST TESTAMENT.
THE FINAL MAJOR UNDERTAKING: THE 'SEASONS'.

The last ten years of Poussin's life were marked by death and suffering. Gradually he lost his closest friends: Cassiano Dal Pozzo and Jacques Stella both died in 1657, and Pointel in 1660; Jacques Dughet, who had taken him in and nursed him so many years before, had previously died in 1650, survived by his wife for nine years. Very soon, all Poussin had left were a few nephews, on both the Norman and Roman sides of the family, and his wife, Anne-Marie. She succumbed in October 1664 to 'a consumptive cough', and Poussin was left in despair: 'She has gone, just when I needed her help most, leaving me stricken in years, half paralyzed, a prey to infirmities of all kinds, a foreigner on my own without friends (for they do not exist in this town).' His hands became shakier and refused to transcribe the ideas his mind continued to generate. The pen-strokes in his drawings and letters are halting and jerky, the brush-strokes in his paintings fine, stipple-like. His output slowed down, and there were long periods of enforced inactivity. In August 1660 he wrote to Chantelou: 'I am never free from pain for a single day, and the shaking of my limbs increases with the years. The excessive heat of the present season is taking its toll, hence I have been obliged to give up all work and lay my paints and brushes aside.' Early in 1665 he told Félibien, 'I am now too infirm, and too paralyzed to work. I stopped using my brushes some time since, my only thoughts now being to prepare myself for death. I can feel it in my bones, life is over for me.'

However hard he was assailed by dread and even despair, Poussin remained doggedly determined to try to work, steadfast in his pursuit of an increasingly particular goal. He was, of course, distinguished and respected. In 1657 he declined an invitation to become head of the Academy of St Luke, and in 1664 Colbert thought of him as a possible director for the newly opened Académie de France in Rome. He had an endless stream of visitors: collectors eager to have their pictures authenticated by the artist (fake Poussins were already springing up), young artists like Antoine Bouzonnet, Jacques Stella's nephew, whom he took under his wing. There were not many of the older generation left: Pietro da Cortona was ill, Sacchi died in 1661. The one survivor was Claude Lorrain, with whom Poussin was still in the habit of drinking a 'drop of good wine for pleasure', according to a letter written by the painter Abraham Brueghel on 22 April 1665. Although he continued to be surrounded by admirers, Poussin became increasingly insulated and apparently indifferent to events, whether of a political or an artistic nature. He was no longer interested in the way art was developing, in France with Lebrun and Mignard, or in Rome with Maratta. There is nothing else in the entire seventeenth century to compare with the extraordinary, uncharacteristic masterpieces of Poussin's last years, such as the *Lamentation over the Dead Christ* or the *Four Seasons*

Poussin had attained a balance in his work *c.* 1655 which it was difficult to surpass. *The Death of Sapphira* (Louvre) and *St Peter Healing a Sick Man* (Metropolitan Museum, New York) are the finest examples of this 'magnificent manner', a harder version of the style adopted by Raphael in *The Acts of the Apostles*. These pictures are very carefully constructed, with figures arranged either in a pyramid or in a horizontal band. The relation-

214, cat. 96

Opposite
The Death of Sapphira (detail);
see also p. 214.

The Death of Sapphira,
oil on canvas,
122 x 199 cm (48 x 78¹/₂ in.).
Louvre, Paris.

Achilles among the Daughters of Lycomedes,
oil on canvas,
97 x 129.5 cm (38¹/₄ x 51 in.).
Museum of Fine Arts, Boston.

Esther before Ahasuerus,
oil on canvas,
119 x 155 cm (47 x 61 in.).
Hermitage, Leningrad.

215

Raphael,
The Death of Ananias, tapestry.
Vatican Museums.

ship between the figures and the setting is perfectly judged, and the solemn lines of the architecture reflect the profundity of the scene. The background in *The Death of Sapphira* is unforgettable. Framed by lines of palaces and steps, a still pool glimmers in the middle distance. In a small square in front of it, a charitable scene is taking place, a faint echo of the main action so strikingly underlined by St Peter's pointing finger. The principal and subsidiary characters are carefully positioned throughout, with every detail meticulously calculated and planned – and it shows. There is arguably more feeling in *Esther before* **215** *Abasuerus* (Hermitage), a work reminiscent of *The Judgment of Solomon*, but with less **144** contortion and more grandeur in the figures. The composition is based on an inverted triangle, with two obliques opening out and an empty space in between. There is a dramatic contrast between the group of women on the left and the group of men on the right, and between the king seated majestically on his throne and Esther collapsing before him in a crumpled mass of heavy fabric and supported by her attendants. Bernini admired the sheer expressive force of the picture, which reminded him of Raphael. There is the same intensity in *The Baptism of Christ* (Johnson Collection, Philadelphia), *cat. 71* the last of a series on this theme. The composition is simple: six large figures, all turned to the left, are ranged in a band seen against a rudimentary landscape. There are none of the hallmarks of Poussin's earlier treatments of the subject: the skilful lining of figures, the semi-naked forms, the varied poses. Here expressions, gestures, attitudes all lead in a single direction, to the heart of the picture: the Holy Spirit descending to men now in a state of peace. There is an intensity, too, in the colour which enhances the emotional force of the picture: the darker flesh tones cause the brilliance of the light-coloured draperies to stand out even more.

A comparison of the two versions of *Achilles among the Daughters of Lycomedes* is even more revealing. The first (Museum of Fine Arts, Boston), was painted shortly after **215**

1650. In choosing this subject, Poussin was perhaps seeking to emulate the great painters of antiquity who had tackled it, according to Pausanias and Pliny. What attracted Poussin initially was the dramatic aspect of the scene – a single event involving a number of very different individuals each of whom could be expected to behave in a very different way. Ulysses's cunning, Achilles's rapture, and Deidamia's astonishment are each clearly conveyed by the way the figures are arranged – their gestures converge, their eyes light on each other. In the second version (Richmond) painted *c.* 1656 for the Duc de Créquy, the action is frozen. The figures are now all separate and distinct, and seen head-on as if posing for a family photograph. Achilles, now fully armed, is looking at himself in a mirror, while the three girls, the two Greeks and the old servant woman all have their eyes firmly fixed on him. Their very stillness seems to be a comment on the scene. The emphasis throughout is on verticals – in the figures themselves, the architectural details, the mountainous landscape in the background. A heavy silence prevails. Achilles has been found out despite all the efforts made to conceal his identity, but there is a moment's respite for the hero before the story unfolds.

Poussin seems to have embarked *c.* 1655 on a set of religious pictures based on traditional iconography, but stripped of all superfluous detail. The four small pictures, engraved by Pietro del Po – *The Annunciation* and *The Nativity* (both Munich), *Lamentation over the Dead Christ* (lost) and *Noli me tangere* (Prado) – are neither sketches for larger paintings nor reduced versions of earlier pictures. They undoubtedly incorporate elements which appeared in a more finished form in the roughly contemporary *The*

219
223

Annunciation (1657; London) and the Dublin version of *Lamentation over the Dead Christ*. These four panels do, nevertheless, appear to form a coherent set, or at least two pairs of meditations on the birth and death of Christ respectively. They have traditionally been thought to be very late. Félibien, however, mentions 1653 as the date of *Noli me tangere*, and this work, together with *Lamentation over the Dead Christ*, is listed in the inventory of Jean Pointel's effects drawn up after his death in 1660; since Pointel's last visit to Rome occurred in 1657, all the evidence tends to suggest an earlier date. The handling of the paint is still firm, and the modelling of the figures has the sculptural quality of the large *Holy Family* painting of 1655. These pictures are often brushed aside – even in the late seventeenth century Brienne, for instance, described *Noli me tangere* as 'a trifle.' They do, however, clearly illustrate Poussin's increasing leanness of style: great religious subjects are reduced to two or three figures set very close together and occupying almost the entire picture area. All sentimentality is eliminated, yet there is a wealth of feeling.

In 1657 Poussin took up a form he had not attempted since his stay in Paris – the altarpiece; he now adopts an entirely new approach, however. There is no mention in any of the sources of his altarpiece entitled *The Annunciation* (London), though a cartouche near the bottom of the picture bears an inscription which is quite explicit: POVSSIN.FACIEBAT./ANNO.SALVTIS.MDCLVII./ALEX.SEPT.PONT.MAX.REGNANTE./ROMA. Art historians inferred from this that the picture was painted for Pope Alexander VII's private chapel. Jane Costello has argued convincingly, however, that it is in fact the work that Poussin alludes to in a letter to Chantelou of 24 December 1657 when he says of Cassiano Dal Pozzo, 'Our good friend . . . is dead and we are working on his tomb.' Dal Pozzo had died two months earlier, on 22 October, and was buried in Sta Maria sopra Minerva. This accounts for the square format and the inclusion of the inscription, neither feature being characteristic of Poussin: *The Annunciation* was intended to hang above an altar and to

Bernini,
The Ecstasy of St Theresa,
marble group,
Sta Maria della Vittoria, Rome.

Opposite
The Annunciation,
oil on canvas,
105 x 103 cm (41$\frac{1}{4}$ x 40$\frac{1}{2}$ in.).
National Gallery, London

POVSSIN·FACIEBAT·
ANNO·SALVTIS·MDCLVII·
ALEX·SEPT·PONT·MAX·REGNANTE·
·ROMA·

The Vision of St Francesca Romana,
engraving by Gérard Audran
after a lost painting by Poussin.

be incorporated in a monument, which was in fact never built. In its austerity it is quite unlike the usual treatment of the theme. The Virgin is shown sitting cross-legged on a cushion on a very low dais in an attitude of perfect humility. The dove of the Holy Spirit appears in an aureole above her. Mary's open arms complement Gabriel's gestures as, genuflecting slightly, he points to her with one hand and to heaven with the other. There is no setting to speak of, only a bare floor and a large green curtain, with a bed just visible beyond it in the background on the right. According to Friedländer, the prominently placed book serves to remind us of Mary's wisdom and to treat her as a latter-day Minerva, on the site of whose temple stands the church in which Dal Pozzo was buried.

Seen now well lit in the National Gallery, though originally designed for a dark chapel, the picture has a strikingly sculptural quality. The light is intense, like a spotlight throwing particular areas into sharp relief – the top half of the angel's body, Mary's face, the upper part of her legs and knees – and making the figures stand out clearly against the background. The colours are light, even bright in places, and there is a marked contrast between Gabriel's coloured wings and his white tunic. Mary's clothes fall in loose folds, the angel's in tighter creases. When viewing this silent dialogue between woman and angel, it is difficult not to be reminded of Bernini's *Ecstasy of St Theresa*, only slightly earlier in date, which Poussin would almost certainly have seen in the church of Sta Maria della Vittoria. It would be interesting to know what he thought of it – perhaps *The Annunciation* was intended in some way to be a reply to it. Bernini's work speaks of graceful abandon, with flowing lines and a shifting light playing on the polished marble surface. Poussin's, by contrast, is severe and hieratic. Where Bernini draws on the expressive possibilities of all the arts to create an effect which leaves the viewer almost spellbound, Poussin relies on painting alone to convey a message which is quite unequivocal. Nothing could be more explicit or more direct than the finger Gabriel points towards Mary, or the dove hovering above her head. There is nothing sensuous about her attitude. All trace of a smile, of prettiness has disappeared. Instead, she expresses an acceptance of destiny. The picture has never enjoyed the popular acclaim accorded to *The Ecstasy of St Theresa*, and indeed it is not particularly well-known even today. Poussin presents neither a pious image nor a display of virtuosity, yet the painting has extraordinary qualities, and is a measure of Poussin's distinctive individuality in the Roman art scene of the 1650s.

The Vision of St Francesca Romana, now lost but known through a seventeenth-century engraving, was commissioned by Cardinal Rospigliosi, probably *c*. 1657. It is not known whether this was an altarpiece (as its upright format would seem to suggest) or a work of smaller dimensions. The year before, Rome had been gripped by the plague, and Poussin had lost a sister-in-law and a niece. The picture is very different in concept from *The Plague of Ashdod* of 1630, and is more of a commemorative piece. The Virgin appears on a cloud to St Francesca, who begs her to avert the plague. The body of a woman wrapped in a shroud lies on the ground, and in the background the Plague is shown carrying off a dead child and being chased away by an angel. This is an entirely symbolic depiction, quite unlike the dramatic images of death and terror so well conveyed by Italian painters of the *seicento*, particularly the Neapolitans. The language is the most economical possible. As in *The Annunciation*, the emphasis is on an encounter between two principal figures, each treated like a statue, in an austere architectural setting. Here, too, the absence of pathos is somewhat disconcerting, yet it makes clear just how far Poussin has come as an artist in this, his second rendering of the the theme.

218

220

59

The fruits of old age

223   There is undoubtedly more feeling in the *Lamentation over the Dead Christ* (Dublin), the greatest of Poussin's last religious pictures, painted some time after 1657. It is not difficult to imagine the 'deep and distressing thoughts' which the aging Poussin put into the picture. In the small *Lamentation over the Dead Christ* engraved by Pietro del Po, Poussin was clearly influenced by Sebastiano del Piombo's impressive *Pietà* and Marcantonio Raimondi's engraving of the *Mater Dolorosa*. He adopts the same striking outline composition here, setting the horizontal form of Christ against the strictly vertical mass of Mary. He fleshes this out by placing Joseph of Arimathaea, St John and the other two Marys in a kind of bas-relief across the picture. The figures are commanding, not least because they have been brought to the front of the picture parallel with the picture plane. Although the figures fit together tightly and their different poses echo one another, each seems locked in private suffering. The strain in the gestures is almost unbearable, and the palette strident, jarring, with strong passages of blue, white and red, and touches of violet, salmon-pink and green against a hushed dusk sky. The setting is austere, the few details all the more disquieting: a withered tree with only a few leaves to indicate the coming Resurrection, a bowl and urn on the left, the gaping opening of the sepulchre on the

cat. 81   right. A comparison of this *Lamentation over the Dead Christ* with the Munich version painted some thirty years earlier clearly shows how radically Poussin's approach has changed. The diffusion of the early version, with its reliance on visible emotion, has given way to concentration, to a relentless threnody which returns continually to the same painful note. There is no place now for pretty details or beauty – nothing must be allowed to detract from the depth and range of emotion – and there is no escape; the viewer is thrust into this oppressive atmosphere by the use of the close-up technique.

    Poussin could not hope to achieve a sparer, more intense image than this, but he could seek to vary its effects. Other religious pictures of the late 1650s are intended to be more directly appealing. The last two variations on the theme of the Holy Family are

cat. 63   deliberately designed to arouse the spectator's curiosity. *The Rest on the Flight into Egypt* (Hermitage), painted between November 1655 and December 1657 for Madame de Montmort, later Madame de Chantelou, has all the customary characteristics of pictures of this period: figures in static, almost stilted, poses concentrated in a group in the foreground; a perfect weaving together of gestures and figures; and a powerful background landscape. Poussin uses the same basic structure perfected in his earlier works in landscape format depicting the *Holy Family*, and adds local colour. Poussin's Egypt consists essentially of a few 'exotic' figures – where we would expect to see angels, two Nubian women and a young boy appear on the right offering food and drink – and of a remarkable background filled with monuments of all kinds and complete with a procession of the priests of Isis bearing objects associated with their cult. The obelisk, the canopy-shaped building, the tower on the right 'with the concave roof and great vase for collecting the dew' and the 'little building designed as a retreat for the bird Ibis' are all taken from the Palestrina mosaic which Dal Pozzo had had copied. All this betokens an interest in archaeology, but this was nothing new: Poussin was passionately interested in syncretism and, like many learned men of his day, was fascinated by 'hieroglyphics', which were thought to express some forgotten wisdom. Although it was the product of long deliberation, the Leningrad picture, unlike the seven *Sacraments* which were also minutely researched, is less unified, with a distracting number and variety of props

222   (or 'appurtenances'). Equally strange is *The Flight into Egypt* engraved by Pietro del Po,

The Flight into Egypt with a Traveller at Rest,
engraving by Pietro del Po
after Poussin.

almost certainly after the painting executed for Serisier in 1658. It was this picture which prompted Bernini to remark while visiting the Paris collector, 'People should stop working when they reach a certain age; their powers inevitably decline.' This work betrays an odd mixture of movement and static elements. The couple are shown walking in the direction in which the angel points them so commandingly. As she walks with Jesus in her arms, Mary turns to look back. Lying by the road observing them is a traveller. Here again, destiny must untimately follow its inevitable course. The beautiful landscape in the background reinforces the structure of the composition, albeit without lending it much sense of depth. The principal figures are confined to the centre by the mountain on the left and the beginnings of a portico on the right. They have a momumental quality, emphasized by the deep, parallel folds in the drapery.

Poussin's two last religious works, *Christ and the Woman of Samaria* and the Fitz-   *cat. 72* william version of *Eliezer and Rebecca at the Well*, again depict a powerfully moving encounter between two individuals. The composition in each case is disconcertingly simple, and based on a severe linear pattern, the figures being balanced and weighty. The first (now lost and known only through an engraving by Jean Pesne and an early copy) was completed for Madame de Chantelou in 1662. Poussin's treatment of this subject is in the same tradition as Annibale Carracci's before him (1604, Vienna) and Pierre Mignard's after him (1681, Raleigh; and 1690, Louvre), and gives equal prominence to figures and landscape. The solid forms of the background – the well, the ramparts and the rocky outcrops – provide a fittingly severe setting for the dialogue between the two figures. The version of *Eliezer and Rebecca at the Well* now in Cambridge could well be expected to compare unfavourably with the one in the Louvre. This is far from being the case, however. It is certainly true that Poussin no longer shows the same ease in handling paint, and at first sight the picture, which may in fact be unfinished, seems drab and somehow stiff. The moment Poussin has chosen to represent here is the one just before Eliezer speaks and offers her jewels, and the picture centres on Rebecca giving Abraham's servant water from her jar. Instead of an analysis of different 'passions' and a set of graceful and varied poses, Poussin offers us a silent line of figures, a delicately coloured frieze in which the different shades – pale green and pink, sandy yellow and lavender blue – seem to melt into one another. In the place of the order and rhythm of the earlier version he substitutes a quite different sort of structure. The groups of figures are no longer exquisitely orchestrated. Here Poussin simply alternates contrasting angles and attitudes: the figures are seen alternately head-on and in profile, bent over and upright, against a background of mountains and buildings which screen the horizon. A slow, rightward movement is checked in the centre, which is almost static, before resuming on the right-hand side. Two young women prepare to leave the scene on the right, their jars full, and are counterbalanced by the figure of the servant leading the camels in from the left. Here, as in other late works like *Landscape with Diana and Orion, Autumn* and *Landscape with*   *229, 246* *Hagar and the Angel*, Poussin's figures file across the picture, following the course allotted to them by destiny, in the midst of a hushed, twilight world.

There has been speculation over why Poussin should have reverted to landscape painting at the end of his life, after a fairly long break – six years elapsed between *Land-*   *164* *scape with Pyramus and Thisbe* and *The Birth of Bacchus*. The explanation generally   *cat. 122* given is that for a man of his age it was easier than history painting, which involved huge numbers of figures and a complex construction, and required a tension and precision the

Eliezer and Rebecca at the Well,
oil on canvas, 96.5 x 138 cm (38 x 54¼ in.).
Fitzwilliam Museum, Cambridge.

Lamentation over the Dead Christ,
oil on canvas,
94 x 130 cm (37 x 51¼ in.).
National Gallery of Ireland, Dublin.

infirm Poussin was no longer able to provide. His increasing shakiness meant that he could no longer delineate form with a sure hand. Landscape painting allowed for a much looser technique, and it was quite possible to conjure up texture and light with broken, even jerky strokes. Poussin turned his physical limitations to advantage – so much so that some writers have even sought to compare his last works to those of Corot, Vuillard and the Impressionists. For others, these paintings speak of a release from all restraint, and reveal a spirit finally rebelling against a highly mechanical approach to art. By the end of his life, they maintain, Poussin, like Titian and Rembrandt, had arrived at that state of detachment, of aloofness which men of genius so often reach in old age. This is a rather romantic image of Poussin, and one which it is difficult to reconcile with the man who painted the *Seasons*. It is certainly true that Poussin abandoned and broke away from the normal field of art in the seventeenth century. It is true, too, that landscape painting as a genre was less demanding and less time-consuming, and that Poussin could express himself freely through it. *Landscape with Diana and Orion* and *Landscape with Hercules and Cacus* cannot be separated, however, from everything that has gone before them. Although they may seem more direct, less calculated in their construction, they are in fact just as complex and successful as his earlier works, and reveal the same relentless pursuit and development of an idea.

In *Landscape with Pyramus and Thisbe* all the forces of nature were unleashed and carefully studied in the best tragic tradition. Human existence, subject as it is to the whims of fortune, came across as paltrier than ever. With *The Birth of Bacchus* (Cambridge, Mass.), painted in 1657 for Stella, the world of mortals gives way to the world of the gods, and drama to allegory. Mercury has just plucked Bacchus from Jupiter's thigh and is shown handing him over to the nymphs who are to take care of him. Jupiter, meanwhile, can be seen lying resting on a couch in the clouds attended by Hebe, while Pan plays his pipes in the shade of the trees. In the foreground on the right is a surprising scene: Narcissus lies dying by his pool, as Echo weeps for him. In fact their presence makes perfect sense in the overall context of Poussin's rather esoteric vision. The Stoics attempted to give a rational interpretation of classical legends, analyzing the gods in terms of natural forces, and myths in terms of physical phenomena and moral truths. Poussin drew heavily on a learned sixteenth-century commentary along these lines, that of Natale Conti on Ovid's *Metamorphoses* and Philostratus's *Imagines*. Bacchus and Narcissus represent the two extremes of fertility and sterility, life and death. A preparatory drawing (Fogg Art Museum) makes the allegory even more explicit: included in the sky are the figures of Apollo and Venus who symbolize the fecundity of the plant and animal kingdoms. Venus also appears with all her attributes in a drawing of the same date, 1657, of *Venus with a Bowl* (Louvre).

The Birth of Bacchus is a difficult painting, but manages to avoid being turgidly didactic thanks to the sense of rhythm which permeates it and because it represents an entirely new approach to landscape. The figures are arranged in three main groups. On the left are the nymphs, half-immersed in crystal-clear water (as they are in the Palestrina mosaic). In the centre, handing over the infant to two other nymphs, is the pivotal figure of Mercury, whose outstretched arms link sky and earth. On the right, treated in isolation, are the sad figures of Echo and Narcissus. A grotto topped with trees and strewn with vines and ivy stretches across almost the entire width of the picture behind the figures, shutting out everything else, and filtering the light emanating from an invisible source

The Birth of Bacchus,
oil on canvas,
122 x 179 cm (48 x 70½ in.).
Fogg Art Museum, Cambridge, Mass.

Venus by a Fountain,
pen and brown wash,
25 x 23 cm (10 x 9 in.).
Louvre, Paris.

beyond. For Poussin, the scene involves not just the actors, the gods who feature in the story, but the whole of nature: earth and water, air and sun, plants and clouds. Poussin's vision goes beyond Conti's laborious analyses and partakes of Campanella's 'panpsychism'. Tommaso Campanella, a Dominican, was a protégé of the Barberini family and of Cassiano Dal Pozzo; he had links with French free-thinkers, was hounded by the Inquisition, and put forward some extraordinarily bold ideas. According to him, the universe sprang from a marriage of opposites. It was governed by a warm life-giving element, an immanent force, or *spiritus* (rather like the *pneuma* in Stoic philosophy), which originated in the sun. This fused with the cold earth, which was the source of all decay, to create life, in an endless cycle of birth and destruction.

The life-enhancing character of the sun is also illustrated in *Landscape with Diana and Orion* (Metropolitan Museum) painted at about the same time for Michel Passart. Poussin may have got the idea for this from a passage in Lucian describing a picture. The

229

theme was highly unusual. It was taken up by Campanella in his *City of the Sun* (1623): it is the subject of one of the pictures on the walls of the ideal city he conjures up. Poussin seems to have combined several different versions of this complex myth, as E. H. Gombrich has shown, and as before to have relied heavily on Conti's laborious explanations. The giant Orion had three fathers: Neptune, Jupiter and Apollo. He was blinded by Diana for wanting to rape a nymph called Aerope, and later cured by Apollo. The classical legend apparently admits of a meteorological interpretation. Orion's three parents symbolize water, air and sun, and these, when combined, produce clouds. The rape of Aerope is therefore supposed to be represented in the clouds climbing up into the sky, and the punishment inflicted by Diana, goddess of the moon, in the clouds falling to earth in the form of rain. The healing of Orion by Apollo is a reminder that the sun dries up the rain and the whole cycle is ready to begin again. The huge hunter strides across the picture, preceded by a mass of thick cloud which functions both as his *alter ego* and as a metaphor for his blindness. As he feels his way towards the warm healing light, he is helped by Cedalion, seen perched on his shoulders, and Vulcan, at his feet, while Diana looks on from high above in the sky. A precise esoteric meaning is inherent, then, in this myth, and the story of Orion illustrates 'the cyclical and reciprocal way the elements generate and then destroy life' (Conti).

Poussin's painting – one of his most powerful – is not readily explained, for it is neither landscape nor allegory, and is quite exceptional. It makes no concessions to conventional notions of composition: the rules of perspective are ignored and the outsize figure of Orion merges into the wild nature from which he springs. Everything about it is strikingly bold: the disproportion of the figures, the powerful arch formed by the trees, giant and cloud, the textured mass of the rocks and leaves, the muffled harmony of muted browns and greens, the way the sun's rays are stopped by the clouds and light up their edges. Poussin's depiction of blind Orion has a visionary power which not even the most extreme examples of Romantic painting have ever been able to match. Claude Simon described it recently as an image of the poet groping along 'the creative path'. The painting has to be seen in the context of its own time, however. This picture, like *The Birth of Bacchus* before it, follows a sixteenth-century humanist approach continued by the Jesuits, and reflects a belief that waiting to be uncovered in the symbols and legends of classical mythology were a primordial wisdom and knowledge long since obscured by both pagan and Christian religions. The *Landscape with Diana and Orion* is itself a kind of hieroglyph, a vivid and striking image which hints at the 'deep, dark unity' of the world through a tight network of parallels and analogies. It was an age which took a keen interest in emblems and in the *ars memoriae*, and in which, therefore, lengthy description was far inferior to painting in conveying complex reality because painting could combine apparently disparate and even contradictory elements in a single picture. Painting demanded more than just an understanding of this developing language, however: it called for an equal, if not greater, measure of poetic intuition if its full force was to be appreciated.

There is also a degree of mystery in the *Landscape with two Nymphs and a Snake*
cat. 225   *Attacking a Bird* (Chantilly), even though the composition is far more open and the world it conjures up rather more familiar. This may, according to Félibien, be the work
158   painted in 1659 for Lebrun. It has the same quiet grandeur as *Landscape with Diogenes*, but here man is far less obtrusive a presence, and it seems that the scene lacks any moral

Landscape with Hercules and Cacus,
oil on canvas,
156.5 x 202 cm (61^1/$_2$ x 79^1/$_2$ in.).
Pushkin Museum, Moscow.

Landscape with Diana and Orion,
oil on canvas,
119 x 183 cm (47 x 72 in.).
The Metropolitan Museum of Art, New York.

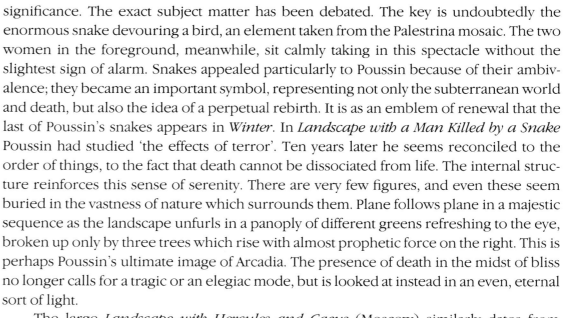

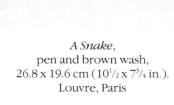

A Snake,
pen and brown wash,
26.8 x 19.6 cm (10¹/₂ x 7³/₄ in.).
Louvre, Paris

significance. The exact subject matter has been debated. The key is undoubtedly the enormous snake devouring a bird, an element taken from the Palestrina mosaic. The two women in the foreground, meanwhile, sit calmly taking in this spectacle without the slightest sign of alarm. Snakes appealed particularly to Poussin because of their ambivalence; they became an important symbol, representing not only the subterranean world and death, but also the idea of a perpetual rebirth. It is as an emblem of renewal that the last of Poussin's snakes appears in *Winter*. In *Landscape with a Man Killed by a Snake* 152 Poussin had studied 'the effects of terror'. Ten years later he seems reconciled to the order of things, to the fact that death cannot be dissociated from life. The internal structure reinforces this sense of serenity. There are very few figures, and even these seem buried in the vastness of nature which surrounds them. Plane follows plane in a majestic sequence as the landscape unfurls in a panoply of different greens refreshing to the eye, broken up only by three trees which rise with almost prophetic force on the right. This is perhaps Poussin's ultimate image of Arcadia. The presence of death in the midst of bliss no longer calls for a tragic or an elegiac mode, but is looked at instead in an even, eternal sort of light.

The large *Landscape with Hercules and Cacus* (Moscow) similarly dates from 228 *c*. 1660. It has sometimes been seen as a pendant to *Landscape with Polyphemus* (Lenin- 159 grad) of 1649, but seems to be considerably later, not least because of the style and the broken, almost fuzzy strokes. Instead of being based on a network of lines intersecting at right or acute angles, the composition relies on a number of very unequal masses being brought into balance and is deliberately asymmetrical: the right half is dense and impenetrable, the left, by contrast, more open. Rocks, river, bushes and trees all run into each other in fairly wild swirls to create what is perhaps the most lyrical of all Poussin's landscapes. It is not difficult to see how its theme relates to Poussin's thinking at the time and to other pictures in which he seems eager to fend off despair: Hercules's victory over the cattle-rustling Cacus, whom he is shown dragging from his cave after a violent struggle, is the triumph of light over darkness, and of good over evil. Poussin has chosen to depict only the closing moments of the scene recounted so dramatically by Evander to Aeneas in Book VIII of *The Aeneid*, and consigns the hero and the monster to the background. Peace returns, the river is calm, the cattle quietly chew the cud, and an inevitable trio of nymphs in the foreground comment on the action. Virgil's story gave Poussin the opportunity to conjure up a vision of the site on which Rome was built, of the Aventine Hill, the Tiber and Latium as the wild places they would have been in the early days of human history. In the far distance, an intangible, dream-like citadel stands before a range of bluish mountains, an intimation perhaps of the city to come. The painting is exceptionally rich in detail, and deceptively modern in feeling because of Poussin's new looseness of style. The quivers and vases in the foreground, the clefts in the rock, the reflections in the water and that strange willow perched high up on the left all combine to conjure up a mood which looks forward to the Sublime style of the next century. Only Poussin, however, could have created the sense of some primordial tapestry or wall-painting which is present here.

The same is true of *Landscape with Hagar and the Angel* (private collection, Rome). *cat. 210* This work was first brought to public attention in 1960 by André Chastel and is thought to be the right-hand part of a larger unfinished work, although its composition makes sense as it stands. Poussin has chosen to depict the moment when the pregnant Hagar is summoned back to Abraham by Jehovah's messenger, in another variation on the theme of destiny. The two figures are placed off-centre, and occupy only a small part of this obviously late landscape. The wildness of the setting is reminiscent of *Landscape with Hercules and Cacus*. There are echoes of *Landscape with Diana and Orion* in the clouds edged with light, the painful but determined way Hagar plods on, and the angel shown in a blaze of sunlight. The painting is moving in its conciseness and in the very personal vision of the world that it presents. The irregular outlines of rocks and trees and of the clouds which echo them are the hallmarks of late Poussin. His representation of nature can no longer be accurate, and as a result his landscapes become at once imaginary and more direct.

232   *Apollo and Daphne* (Louvre) is generally seen as Poussin's last artistic testament, presented by him, unfinished, to Camillo Massimi in 1664 because his hand was so shaky that he could no longer work on it. It was indeed one of his last works, painted at exactly the same time as the *Seasons*. The fact that it is unfinished gives it an extra dimension. It is an ambitious work in terms of both size and subject matter, and sums up all the major preoccupations of Poussin's life. In it Poussin brings together a group of mythological figures close to his heart and places them in a pastoral setting such as he has used often before, full of rocks, trees and springs, in one of those rich, motionless, powerfully constructed compositions in which he excelled. Two groups, centred squarely on the two main characters, face each other in the foreground. On the left, is seated Apollo on a knoll under an oak tree, surrounded by wood- and water-nymphs. Behind him Mercury steals an arrow from his quiver, and in front, Cupid strains his bow, pointing it towards Daphne opposite, who has taken refuge beside her father, the river-god Peneus, and four other nymphs. In the background is a herd of oxen together with some dogs, and to the right, mourned by two shepherds, the figure of Hyacinthus, the young prince once loved by Apollo and accidentally killed by him. The figures are convincingly placed – whether sitting, standing or lying – to form an oval, empty in the middle. Here, as in other pictures, the effect of the arbitrary and uninterrupted line of figures is to create a flat picture rather to conjure up any sense of depth – the only place the picture opens out at all, and even then only slightly, is in the centre with a view of a distant mountain. The main thrust of the picture is lateral, created by the look that Apollo gives Daphne, both doomed to remain forever apart.

    The traditional title of *Apollo in Love with Daphne* reflects this emphasis. Poussin had already depicted Apollo's hapless love for Daphne early on in his career in rather

cat. 117   more commonplace fashion. The Munich version of *Apollo and Daphne* showed Apollo finally attaining the object of his desire after a long pursuit, only to see her instantly turn into a laurel tree. Here Poussin depicts an earlier episode in the story, related by Ovid in his *Metamorphoses*. Apollo makes fun of Cupid's weapons, whereupon Cupid wounds him with a sharp-pointed arrow designed to induce love and Daphne with a blunt one designed to repel love. We see their combined fates taking shape in an ominous calm. Once again Poussin prefers a static image to a dynamic one, a meditative approach to a narrative one. The god and nymph who confront one another provide a perfect focus for all his thoughts and ideas, and give him a good basis on which to construct his picture. The concept of opposites, as all critics from Friedländer and Panofsky onwards agree, is

cat. 122   central to Poussin's late work (previously noted in the case of *The Birth of Bacchus*). Here Apollo and Daphne are like opposite poles, one positive, the other negative, representing desire and repulsion, fecundity and sterility, and an endless charge is set up between

Apollo and Daphne,
oil on canvas,
155 x 200 cm (61 x 78¾ in.),
with details opposite and overleaf.
Louvre, Paris.

Apollo Guarding the Flocks of Admetus,
pen and brown ink,
29 x 42.3 cm (11½ x 16½ in.).
Biblioteca Reale, Turin.

Apollo and Daphne,
pen and brown wash over black chalk,
31 x 43 cm (12¼ x 17 in.).
Louvre, Paris.

them which remains as vividly mysterious and powerful as ever. Impossible love may be the main theme, but it is supplemented and enriched by a host of secondary and related themes, so much so that the title could just as well be, as has been suggested, *The Misfortunes of Apollo*.

The extant preparatory drawings for this painting reveal that Poussin tried out various ideas, adding and eliminating different elements. He started out with the central image of Apollo guarding Admetus's herd and gradually included more and more: a group of nymphs, the serpent Python, Mercury in his guise as stealer of arrows, and so on. Cupid's revenge and Daphne's refusal feature for the first time in the large wash drawing (Louvre) which marks a fairly late stage in the development of the composition. Poussin seems to have been toying with a variety of different conventional ways of representing Apollo, as herdsman, serpent slayer and musician, for instance. He finally chose to focus on Apollo in love – and, more particularly, disappointed in love – but without losing sight of his other roles and their inherent significance. Hyacinthus's death and Mercury's act of theft are much more than interesting but extraneous details. They give the picture its half-tragic, half-mocking tone. Apollo's very situation harks back to the theme of the capriciousness of Fortune: here, after all, is a god banished from Olympus and condemned to mind the King of Thessaly's cattle herds. There is a vestige of the disillusionment of the 1640s here. The great painting in the Louvre adds up to a cryptic whole which reflects both wisdom and knowledge, and offers both a moral perspective and a picture of world order. Anthony Blunt systematically set about illuminating this enigmatic picture. Not only has he identified all the sources Poussin is likely to have used – Lucian and Philostratus as well as the more obvious Ovid, all three reworked by Blaise de Vigenère – but he undertakes an exhaustive analysis of the picture itself.

According to Blunt, Poussin draws not only on Campanella's concept of opposites but on ancient philosophy and contemporary scientific theory. It was in order to accommodate such complex levels of thought that he divided his final composition so strikingly in two – the figures on the left, centred on Apollo, conjuring up life and fertility in contrast to those on the right, grouped around Daphne, who evoke sterility and death. Poussin looked beyond Campanella and his heliocentric view of the world, to Heraclitus, for whom the universe was a harmonious entity which sprang from the balanced co-existence of opposites like love and repulsion, hot and cold, and wet and dry, and from an endless transmutation of the three basic elements, water, earth and fire, each represented by different figures. Apollo's lyre and Cupid's bow are both symbols of this continuous state of tension. Sixteenth-century mythographers had helped promulgate these ideas, often in a somewhat garbled form, under the guise of allegory. Poussin's painting also includes an allusion, according to Blunt, to the discoveries of Kepler and Galileo. Commentators had been puzzled up till then by the incident of Mercury stealing an arrow from Apollo's quiver – Bellori, for instance, saw it as a mere *scherzo*, unrelated to anything else. For Blunt, it illustrates the then newly discovered fact that the planets merely reflect light from the sun. To the Church these ideas were heretical. Could it be that Poussin was at the forefront of a new movement and was deliberately using mythology as a vehicle for propagating the most daring ideas of his day? Could it be, too, that Massimi, the learned churchman, was perfectly aware of this and understood all the implications of Poussin's seemingly esoteric approach? We must guard against over-interpretation, however. It is by no means certain that Poussin had all these concepts clearly in mind when he developed the idea for this picture. It is not remotely certain, either, that he had direct access to all the relevant texts. He is more likely to have come across the potted versions by Conti or de Vigenère. However complicated the composition may be, moreover, it is prevented from being pedantic not only by the tone, which is detached and slightly mocking, and the presence of various familiar or incongruous details, but also by its sheer originality and its highly personal, even private, character. The 'misfortunes of Apollo' are the same that dog all human existence. The painting is as much an allegory of the artist as of the world: as he sits in the twilight of his life no longer a prey to vicissitudes of any kind and surrounded by his works, the wise creator knows that he will never achieve the beauty he has always striven to reach and sometimes almost did, and con-

54 templates this fact with equanimity. Poussin had already depicted Apollo in *The Inspira-*
68 *tion of the Poet* and *Apollo and the Muses* (*Parnassus*), and it is significant that he should have chosen to depict him again here. Apollo has now laid down his lyre, but, though still, it strains to catch some primordial, enduring harmony, and through its very immobility, the mere fact of its enchanted presence, it conjures up everything Poussin thought painting should achieve. Painting was for him primarily about poetry and music, and sprang more from inspiration than craft. 'It is the golden bough in Virgil which cannot be found or picked except by those who are led to it by fate', the elderly Poussin wrote to Fréart de Chambray in March 1665. More than ever he refused to adopt a stock formula here. He worked long and hard to establish the right composition – the early drawings are markedly less well balanced than the final result. The figures gradually fell into place to form a kind of charmed circle which a single unfortunate gesture would be enough to break. Alert or relaxed, they are linked together by the line of their bodies and the angle of their gaze. Some are perhaps less successful than others. There is a degree of stiffness, for instance, about the nymph dressed in yellow awkwardly perched in a tree and Daphne who sits clasping her father to her. By contrast the dryad dressed in blue who looks down at Mercury has something of the mysterious quality of Vermeer's Clio in his painting of *The Artist's Studio*. There is a touch of voluptuousness in every detail of the recumbent naiads who form a gentle arc in the centre – the way one twists her hair, another leans on her elbow, a third curves her hip – which contrasts with the sleepy heaviness of the cattle. In the two naked women, finally, standing on the right, one facing, the other with her back to the viewer, Poussin is clearly revelling one last time in the sheer glory of the human form and the incomparable power of pure rhythm. Another painter would later be fired by these amber and pink bodies and try to recreate them: Ingres's *Golden Age*, painted on a wall of the Château de Dampierre, also remained unfinished. Such is the fate of the most beautiful dreams.

The four *Seasons*, painted between 1660 and 1664 for the Duc de Richelieu, were the major undertaking of the tail-end of Poussin's life, and represented an effort to put landscape painting once and for all on a par with history painting and to demonstrate its expressive range to the full. Like the *Triumphs* and the *Sacraments*, the *Seasons* were the product of a sustained and coherent train of thought. Like *The Birth of Bacchus* and *Landscape with Diana and Orion*, they incorporate layers of different meaning, but in a clearer way. The *Seasons* go way beyond the conventional language of allegory. Poussin had no desire to do as Pietro Testa had done in his engraved series of the *Seasons* (1642–4), and depict, often in a highly complicated form, the courageous artist's struggle against the tyranny of time, the elements and his own passions. He did not choose either

page 242 ▷

Spring,
oil on canvas,
117 x 160 cm (46 x 63 in.).
Louvre, Paris.

Summer,
oil on canvas,
119 x 160 cm (47 x 63 in.),
with details overleaf.
Louvre, Paris.

to personify the seasons or to illustrate them through scenes of everyday life. Instead he turned to the Old Testament. *Spring* takes the form of Adam and Eve in the garden of 238 Eden, before the Fall (Genesis, ch. 2); *Summer*, of Boaz allowing Ruth to glean in his 239 fields (Ruth, ch. 2); *Autumn*, of Moses's messengers returning from the Promised Land 246 with an enormous bunch of grapes (Numbers, ch. 13); and finally *Winter*, of the Flood 247 (Genesis, ch. 7). Willibald Sauerländer has proposed a very scholarly analysis of the religious significance of the series. He bases his account on the assumption that Poussin would have learnt about the subject from exegetes like the Jesuit Serarius, who published a commentary on the Book of Ruth in 1611, and from ecclesiastics in his circle like the Abbé Claude Nicaise, who was canon of the Sainte Chapelle in Dijon. Poussin would also have been familiar with the view, popular from the Stoics to the Church Fathers, that the seasons symbolized life, death and the salvation of man. In this sense, the four paintings in the Louvre can be said, he argues, to complement the seven *Sacraments* which illustrate the institutions and rites of the early Christian Church. In *Spring* we have a picture of the state of man before the Law: implicit in Paradise is the coming of the Church, while Adam prefigures Christ. The meeting of Ruth and Boaz in *Summer* represents the union of Christ and his bride, the Church, and the harvesting of the wheat the consecrated bread and the sacrifice of the mass. The choice of subject is more understandable when one remembers that it was from the marriage of Ruth and Boaz that the line which ended in Christ first issued. The Eucharist also features in the next painting, *Autumn*, symbolized by the huge bunch of grapes. The two trees juxtaposed in the picture, one barren, the other laden with fruit, symbolize the Synagogue and the Church. The Flood in *Winter* stands for the Last Judgment; Noah's Ark, floating on the waters in the distance, represents the Church once again, this time saving the faithful.

An interpretation like this gets nowhere near the heart of these pictures, however, and everything we know about Poussin seems to argue against it. Friedländer, Blunt and Thuillier all stress in turn that the richness of the *Seasons* comes from Poussin's talent for synthesis. The theme of the series is vast enough to allow Poussin to bring together different orders and levels of meaning: he takes up and re-works the oldest allegorical traditions, combining readily understandable allusions with a more complex system in which pagan and Christian symbols are united. It would be easy to take one look at these landscapes and immediately start thinking of them in terms of other series topical in the seventeenth century: the four times of day, the four ages of man, the four elements, the four ages of the world. Although Poussin does play on these associations, he avoids drawing precise parallels in the systematic way so beloved of his contemporaries. We know nothing at all about the process of composition of the *Seasons* – there are no surviving preparatory drawings, no references in any known letters. Each of the four episodes encompasses the same ideas as *The Birth of Bacchus* and *Landscape with two Nymphs* cat. 122, 2 *and a Snake Attacking a Bird*. Once again Poussin explores the dual concepts of fertility and sterility, life and death, and focuses on the complementary power of the sun, water and earth. More than ever here, he conveys a sense of wonder at the never-ending bounty of the earth, at the succession of leafy trees, ripe wheat, and delectable fruit it brings forth. Behind the biblical figures we always sense the gods of antiquity – Apollo, Ceres, Bacchus and Pluto. The cataclysm of the Flood in *Winter* constitutes not so much a divine punishment as the climax of a cycle which could begin again – as the presence of the powerful twisting snake in the foreground, far more prominent than the ark drowned in mist, makes clear. The four *Seasons* are 'historical' landscapes in which three different stories are fused in a single image embracing mankind, nature and the march of life. Never before, perhaps, in the history of Western painting, had so many different and often difficult things been stated with such simplicity. Never before had a painter had such a sense of the universe as a whole. Poussin was neither projecting a personal view of the world nor imbuing it with his own feelings, however: his sense of the universe is impersonal, and it is in this fact, seen by some as a defect, that his greatness lies.

Outwardly different, the four *Seasons* form an extremely coherent series, whose hallmark is strength of composition based on the golden section. The composition hinges in each case on the rocks or trees which appear on the left and help direct the eye to the view which disappears either into the centre (as in *Summer* and *Winter*) or to the right (as in *Spring* and *Autumn*). The figures are for the most part arranged in the lower third of each composition. They are pushed into the foreground by a whole range of screens; trees and bushes, rocks and waterfalls, fields of wheat. Their size varies: in *Spring* Poussin presents a panoramic view, while in *Summer* and *Winter*, which have the largest number of figures, attention is focused on the middle distance, and in *Autumn* the size of the principal figures seen in close-up relates to the massive bunch of grapes they are carrying. The lighting is carefully considered, and the different atmospheric effects – clouds, back-lighting, sheets of rain – are designed to conjure up the four times of day: morning, noon, evening and night. Poussin was emulating Claude Lorrain, who took great pleasure in producing pairs of landscapes for his clients and pitching the light accordingly.

With its lush vegetation, *Spring* is the freshest and, as it were, the most naive of the four paintings, and in it Poussin seems to hark back to his native Normandy. In the middle of this leafy nest, this fertile Arcadia, Adam and Eve wake and feast their eyes on one another. As she points to the Tree of Knowledge in the early morning light, however, Eve signals the end of this innocent world of boundless green lawns and stretches of calm water, and shady bowers full of birds. The light is mysteriously introduced from the left through a narrow opening between two rocks above a waterfall in much the same way as it is in *The Israelites Gathering Manna* and *The Birth of Bacchus*. Poussin's fine strokes are used to great effect: every leaf is picked out, the trees are dotted with tiny white flowers and fruit, and the horizons melt into a blissful bluish haze.

Summer is more rigorous in construction, and includes a large number of figures, set mainly in profile against the backdrop of a wheatfield at harvest time. The light catches the pale stalks and ears of wheat, creating a delicate ripple through the field. The sturdy tree on the left, partly clipped by the edge of the picture, provides an anchor for this essentially frontal composition. It is answered in the distance on the right by a second, less solid tree, in an echo of Boaz and Ruth, and of the contrast between masculine and feminine. The boundary-stone in the bottom right corner and the buildings in the distance help convey a sense of space. Beyond the fields mountains are visible. A strong noon light plays on the whole scene, diffused by a few clouds: this suggests the middle of life, the moment of decision when fates are sealed. With a freedom worthy of the *Georgics*, Poussin combines elements drawn from classical sources – like the servant with the lance and the team of horses trampling on the grain, taken from a relief on the Arch of Titus – with images culled from everyday life – like the women busy preparing food, the reapers quenching their thirst and the people binding sheaves. The stocky, coarse figures, spread out singly or in groups, together form a loose band, drawing attention to

03, *cat. 122*

Overleaf
Details from *Autumn* and *Winter*;
see pp. 246, 247.

page 248 ▷

Autumn,
oil on canvas,
117 x 160 cm (46 x 63 in.).
Louvre, Paris.

Winter,
oil on canvas,
118 x 160 cm (46¹/₂ x 63 in.).
Louvre, Paris.

the central episode, the encounter between Boaz and Ruth, reminiscent, in its opposition of majesty and humility, of some Annunciation scene. Because of its structure and richness of meaning, *Summer* remains an archetype of so-called classical landscape. More than this, the sense of warmth and eternal power which radiate from it make it the emblem of Poussin's genius.

Autumn is less immediately attractive, with its muted shades, its vista of grey mountains and crags crowned with a town, its rather scraggy vegetation. There are a number of strange elements which cannot wholly be explained by the subject: the determined way in which Moses's two messengers walk with their heavy burden, for instance; the two women with their backs turned, one perched on a ladder picking fruit, minute by comparison with the men, the other walking off to the right with a basket on her head; finally, the contrasting of the barren and fertile trees on the left. Poussin has chosen not to conjure up the rich colours of autumn or to explore the tragic quality often attributed to that season. Instead he offers a very restrained view of the slow but steady march of time, of the end of the day, of the close but also the fruits of a man's life. It is surely not too far-fetched to see in the wheat of *Summer* and the wine of *Autumn* a metaphor for the work an artist produces and refines and then is done with.

People have wondered why Poussin did not illustrate *Winter* with a snow scene, in accordance with convention. It has been suggested that what he is depicting is a Mediterranean winter, complete with torrential rains. Poussin, however, had always steered clear of the picturesque, and the Flood offered far more dramatic potential. Both Michelangelo in the Sistine Chapel and Antonio Carracci in the Palazzo del Quirinale had depicted huge numbers of figures being swept away in great swirling movement. Poussin, as usual, was restrained in his approach. His composition is steady, even calm. Two expanses of water are linked by a cataract. Their emphatically horizontal lines are reinforced by the line of the boat on the right and the two men in the water in the foreground. Rocks and dead trees are brought in like flats to create a kind of fore-stage, while in the far distance can be seen the dim shapes of mountains and towns doomed to be engulfed by the waters. The main dynamic feature is the streak of lightning which rips through the sky. It is echoed by the other obliques around it – the angle of the trees and of the upturned boat. The small number of figures serves to heighten the emotion; a few poses and gestures say it all. All the force of the picture is concentrated in two powerful verticals formed by the last remaining figures as they strain to save themselves from inevitable doom. A man in a boat about to capsize stretches his hands up to heaven in prayer. A family forms a human chain in a desperate bid to reach safety, with the child being passed from one parent to another, a precious bundle swathed in red fated to perish with the rest. This fragile, primordial human chain was later taken up and re-used in a melodramatic vein by Girodet in his *Flood Scene* of 1806 (also in the Louvre). The wan light of the sun just discernible in the distance as a faint disc under a veil of rain is quite exceptional in Poussin's œuvre, and indeed in seventeenth-century painting. It illustrates his relentless quest for the perfect means of expression. He went to the very heart of his subject and in this case wanted to create a picture of gloom, with hardly any colour, an image of night approaching in a world of dark grey. This does not mean that the work is pessimistic. As Chateaubriand wrote in a now famous passage in the *Vie de Rancé*, it 'has something of the stamp of the old man's former days. How extraordinary is the pitch and toss of time! Men of genius often signal their end with a masterpiece: it is their soul taking wing.' Ac cording to one Romantic school of thought, still current, *Winter* represents a premonition of approaching death. This is to disregard the three *Seasons* which have gone before and to ignore the cyclical nature of existence conjured up by the zigzag of the snake which echoes the flash of lightning, and by the ark in the distance. In the infinite cycle of birth, life and death, illustrated by nature, the elements and the seasons, man is swept away without reprieve, but the world carries on: such is the divine order of things.

The arrival of all four paintings in Paris in 1664 was greeted as something of an event by the small world of connoisseurs there. Loménie de Brienne relates that 'We gathered together at the Duc de Richelieu's. Everyone of any worth in the painting field then in Paris was there. The discussion which took place was long and learned. Bourdon and Lebrun both spoke and said some good things. I spoke too, and declared myself in favour of *The Deluge*. M. Passart shared my views. M. Lebrun did not rate either *Spring* or *Winter* very highly, but praised *Summer* to the skies. Bourdon, however, thought *Terrestrial Paradise* the best, and would not be swayed from his opinion.' Reflected in these differences of opinion are the contrasting 'modes' which Poussin adopts in these paintings. Here, yet again, he alternates strong and weak, drama and calm for our 'delight'. It is not clear if Poussin's admirers sensed anything more than this. The *Seasons* amount to a symphony in four movements incorporating all the key figures developed in the course of a lifetime's work, now complete, and expressing them in an ever-changing rhythm and light. Countless elements from earlier works reappear here, and are given a new, richer resonance. *Winter*, for instance, owes a great deal both to the second version of *Extreme Unction* and to *Landscape with Pyramus and Thisbe*. We sense in it, subdued after 'the pitch and toss of time', the violence of *The Massacre of the Innocents* and *The Plague of Ashdod*. Brienne believed that 'the intention is beautiful, but the execution does not match up to it', but these pictures are surely too accomplished as statements to be in any way diminished by a slight lack of technical dexterity. It seems nonsensical to try to relate them to the rest of seventeenth-century painting: they convey with the most overwhelming force, but with apparent simplicity and limited means, all that many others have attempted to express with greater technical resources, but without success. The beauty and power of nature, man's beginnings and his inevitable end, the religious simplicity which characterizes the great moments in life, the strength and weakness inherent in human feeling, the heroic yet derisory nature of human action, are all articulated in the *Seasons* and given breath one last time in a kind of inner world and slowly fading light. Imperceptibly, the colours darken as they do in Rome at sunset, when the roofs turn from the colour of burning coals to the colour of ash, faintly tinged with pink. There is no sense of despair in this slow fading into darkness. Poussin has bequeathed us his vision, a legacy that is as inimitable as it is valuable.

106
164
55, 59

Thematic Catalogue
of Paintings

This is not a *catalogue raisonné*, but an illustrated list providing brief details about each work, either extant or known through a copy, drawing or engraving. The information includes ownership, support, dimensions, provenance, references to the most recent *catalogues raisonnés* and to major exhibitions. In addition there are occasional bibliographical citations, to which the reader is referred for a discussion of the work in question. Any questions of attribution and dating are noted briefly in individual entries. Several works have been included, the authorship of which I regard as doubtful, but which have been listed by well-known art historians at one time or another within the corpus of Poussin's œuvre. The thematic grouping of the works permits a comparison of successive versions of the same themes, and draws attention to various recurring features.

Dimensions are given in centimetres and inches, height preceding width.

Catalogues
The *catalogues raisonnés* cited are those by Blunt (1966), Thuillier (1974), Wild (1980), Wright (1985) and, for Poussin's early years, Oberhuber (1988). In the case of engravings, the *catalogues raisonnés* by Andresen (1863) and particularly Wildenstein (1957) are cited. Full details of all the works are given in part II of the bibliography.

The names of collectors and others for whom an entry appears in the biographical list (pp. 298–307) are identified by the symbol*. The principal sources are cited in parentheses in abridged form; for full details see part I of the bibliography.

1   *Self-Portrait*
Berlin, Staatliche Museen (Bodemuseum)
Canvas, 78 x 65 (30³/₄ x 25¹/₂)
Inscription (at top): NICOLAVS POVSSINVS
ANDELYENSIS ACADEMICVS ROMANVS PRIMVS
PICTOR ORDINARIVS LVDOVICI IVSTI REGIS
GALLIAE. ANNO DOMINI 1649. ROMAE. AETATIS
SVAE. 55. Title of book: DE LVMINE ET COLORE.
Prov.: Painted for Pointel* 1649 (correspondence);
Serisier*; acquired by the museum in 1821.
Cat.: Blunt 1; Thuillier 163; Wild 147; Wright 144.
Exh.: Paris 1960, 89 *bis*.
Bibl.: Winner 1987.
This work is considered to be the first of several
versions; by comparison with the engraving after
it by J. Pesne, the canvas appears to have been
slightly cropped, especially at the top.
See p. 148.

2   *Self-Portrait*
Paris, Louvre
Canvas, 98 x 74 (38¹/₂ x 29)
Inscription: EFFIGIES NICOLAI POVSSINI
ANDELYENSIS PICTORIS. ANNO AETATIS. 56.
ROMAE ANNO IVBILEI 1650.
Prov.: Painted in 1649–50 for Chantelou*
(correspondence); entered the French national
collections in 1797.
Cat.: Blunt 2; Thuillier 170; Wild 161; Wright 167.
Exh.: Paris 1960, 90.
Bibl.: Winner 1983.
See p. 149.

3   *The Sacrifice of Noah*
Tatton Park, Cheshire, The National Trust
Canvas, 99 x 134.5 (39 x 53)
Prov.: Siad to have come from the Corsini
collection in Rome.
Cat.: Blunt R.7; Thuiller 44c; Wild R.3; Wright 52;
Oberhuber 17.
In spite of the poor condition of the work and its
unknown history, it can be dated 1627–8 (rather
than Oberhuber's estimate of 1626).

4   *Eliezer and Rebecca at the Well*
Private collection
Canvas, 93 x 117 (36¹/₂ x 46)
Prov.: Dal Pozzo* (?); Private collection, England, until 1960; Denis Mahon.
Cat.: Thuillier B.18; Wright 32; Oberhuber 42.
Exh.: Fort Worth, Texas 1988, 42.
Bibl.: Mahon 1965.
The attribution is still disputed, notably by Thuillier. The work can be dated between 1627 (Oberhuber) and 1629 (Mahon).

6   *Eliezer and Rebecca at the Well*
Cambridge, Fitzwilliam Museum
Canvas, 96.5 x 138 (38 x 54¹/₂)
Prov.: Acquired by Anthony Blunt, London, 1933; acquired by the museum from his estate, 1984.
Cat.: Blunt 9; Thuillier 217; Wild 194; Wright 196.
Exh.: Paris 1960, 100; Rome-Düsseldorf 1977–8, 46.
A late work (*c.* 1664?), possibly unfinished.
See p. 222.

8   *The Exposition of Moses*
Oxford, Ashmolean Museum
Canvas, 150 x 204 (59 x 80¹/₄)
Prov.: Painted in 1654 for Jacques Stella* (Félibien); Claudine Bouzonnet-Stella; the Duc d'Orléans (before 1727); in England by the end of the eighteenth century; acquired by the museum from a private collection, 1950.
Cat.: Blunt 11; Thuillier 190a; Wild 180; Wright 182.
Exh.: Paris 1960, 105; Rome-Düsseldorf 1977–8, 39.
See p. 171.

5   *Eliezer and Rebecca at the Well*
Paris, Louvre
Canvas, 118 x 197 (46¹/₂ x 77¹/₂)
Prov.: Painted in 1648 for Pointel* (Félibien); the Duc de Richelieu*; acquired by Louis XIV in 1665.
Cat.: Blunt 8; Thuillier 154; Wild 145; Wright 138.
Exh.: Paris 1960, 79; Rome-Düsseldorf 1977–8, 31.
See p. 175.

7   *The Exposition of Moses*
Dresden, Staatliche Kunstsammlungen: Gemäldegalerie
Canvas, 114 x 196 (44⁵/₄ x 77¹/₄)
Prov.: Acquired in Paris by Augustus III of Saxony, 1742.
Cat.: Blunt 10; Thuillier 9; Wild M.9; Wright 7; Oberhuber 60.
Generally dated between 1627 and 1629, except by Thuillier, who dates this work to 1624, pointing out several awkward compositional features.

9   *Moses Saved from the Water*
Paris, Louvre (inv. no. 7271)
Canvas, 93 x 120 (36¹/₂ x 47¹/₄)
Prov.: Painted in 1638 (Félibien); André Le Nôtre*; bequeathed by him to Louis XIV in 1693.
Cat.: Blunt 12; Thuillier 117; Wild 81; Wright 103.
Exh.: Paris 1960, 57.
See p. 170

10 *Moses Saved from the Water*
Paris, Louvre (inv. no. 7272)
Canvas, 121 x 195 (47½ x 76¾)
Prov.: Painted in 1647 for Pointel*
(correspondence); the Duc de Richelieu*;
acquired by Louis XIV in 1665.
Cat.: Blunt 13; Thuillier 148; Wild 132; Wright 134.
Exh.; Paris 1960, 78; Rome-Düsseldorf 1977–8, 30.
See p. 170.

12 *Moses Trampling on Pharaoh's Crown*
Woburn Abbey, Bedfordshire, Collection of the
Marquess of Tavistock and the Trustees of the
Bedford Estates.
Canvas, 99 x 142 (39 x 56)
Prov.: Painted in 1645 for Pointel* (inventory of
1660); Brienne*; Cotteblanche*; the Marquis de
Seignelay; collection of the Duc d'Orléans;
entered the collection of the Dukes of Bedford at
the end of the eighteenth century.
Cat.: Blunt 16; Thuillier 138; Wild 124; Wright 133.

14 *Moses Defending the Daughters of Jethro*
Lost
Engravings: A. Trouvain (Wildenstein 14); G.
Vallet.
Drawings: Several preparatory drawings are
extant, two of which are in the Cabinet des
Dessins at the Louvre (inv. nos. 32432 and RF 747).
Cat.: Blunt 17; Thuillier 149; Wild 145.
According to Thuillier, the original painting
(which is not listed in the known sources) should
be dated *c*. 1647–8.

11 *Moses Saved from the Water*
London, National Gallery, and Cardiff, National
Museum of Wales
Canvas, 116 x 177.5 (45¾ x 70)
Prov.: Painted in 1651 for Reynon* (Félibien);
passed through several French and then English
collections (at the end of the eighteenth century);
Derek Schreiber, Bellasis House, Dorking, Surrey;
acquired jointly by the two museums, 1988.
Cat.: Blunt 14; Thuillier 178; Wild 166; Wright 176.

13 *Moses Trampling on Pharaoh's Crown*
Paris, Louvre
Canvas, 92 x 128 (36¼ x 50½)
Prov.: Painted for Cardinal Massimi* (Bellori);
acquired by Louis XIV in 1683.
Cat.: Blunt 15; Thuillier 150; Wild 117; Wright 136.
Exh.: Paris 1960, 76.
Pendant of No. 16; to be dated later than the
version for Pointel, *c*. 1647–8.

15 *Moses before the Burning Bush*
Copenhagen, Statens Museum for Kunst
Canvas (oval), 193 x 158 (76 x 62¼)
Prov.: Completed in 1641 for Cardinal Richelieu*
(to hang over a chimney-piece in the Grand
Cabinet of the Palais Cardinal); royal collections;
first recorded in the collection of the King of
Denmark in 1761.
Cat.: Blunt 18; Thuillier 127; Wild 101; Wright 118.

16 *Moses and Aaron before Pharaoh*
    (also known as *Moses Changing the Staff of
    Aaron into a Snake*)
Paris, Louvre
Canvas, 92 x 128 (36¼ x 50½)
Prov.: See No. 13.
Cat.: Blunt 19; Thuillier 151; Wild 118; Wright 137.
Exh.: Paris 1960, 77.
Pendant of No. 13; this painting must also date
from *c*. 1647–8.

18 *The Israelites Gathering Manna*
Paris, Louvre
Canvas, 149 x 200 (58½ x 78¾)
Prov.: Completed in 1639 for Chantelou*
(correspondence); Fouquet*; entered Louis XIV's
collections by 1661.
Cat.: Blunt 21; Thuillier 118; Wild 85; Wright 113.
Exh.: Paris 1960, 56; Rome-Düsseldorf 1977–8, 26.
See p. 102.

20 *Moses Striking the Rock*
Leningrad, Hermitage Museum
Canvas, 122.5 x 193 (48¼ x 76)
Prov.: Painted in 1649 for Jacques Stella*
(Félibien); Claudine Bouzonnet-Stella*; Sir Robert
Walpole; acquired in 1779 by Catherine the Great
of Russia.
Cat.: Blunt 23; Thuillier 161; Wild 151; Wright 141.
Exh.: Paris 1960, 88; Düsseldorf 1978, 33a.

17 *The Crossing of the Red Sea*
Melbourne, National Gallery of Victoria
Canvas, 154 x 210 (60½ x 82¾)
Prov.: Painted for Amadeo Dal Pozzo*, Marchese
di Voghera (Bellori); the Chevalier de Lorraine;
Sir Jacob Bouverie; collection of the Earls of
Radnor; acquired by the museum in 1945.
Cat.: Blunt 20; Thuillier 82; Wild 63; Wright 87.
Exh.: Paris 1960, 37.
Dated between 1633 and 1637 by different
authors; doubtless contemporary with the
Triumphs for Cardinal Richelieu, this painting and
its pendant, *The Adoration of the Golden Calf*
(No. 21), became separated in 1945.
See p. 70.

19 *Moses Striking the Rock*
Edinburgh, National Gallery of Scotland
(on loan from the Duke of Sutherland)
Canvas, 97 x 133 (38¼ x 52¾)
Prov.: Collection of Melchior Gillier* (Félibien);
various French collections, including those of the
Marquis de Seignelay and the Duc d'Orléans;
collection of the Duke of Bridgewater; on loan to
the museum since 1946.
Cat.: Blunt 22; Thuillier 87; Wild 56; Wright 88.
Exh.: Edinburgh 1981, 28.
Félibien, who cites the work before mentioning
Camillus and the Schoolmaster of Falerii
(No. 181), suggests a date *c*. 1633–5.

21 *The Adoration of the Golden Calf*
London, National Gallery
Canvas, 154 x 214 (60½ x 84¼)
Prov.: See No. 17; acquired by the National Gallery
in 1945.
Cat.: Blunt 26; Thuillier 83; Wild 64; Wright 86.
Exh.: Paris, 1960, 38.
Datable, like its pendant, to between 1633 and
1637.
See p. 70.

22 The Adoration of the Golden Calf
Lost
Engraving: J.-B. de Poilly (Andresen 74)
Copy: San Francisco, Cal., The Fine Arts Museums,
M. H. De Young Memorial Museum.
Cat.: Blunt 25; Thuillier 63; Wild 23; Wright L.5;
Oberhuber 82.
Exh.: Fort Worth, Texas 1988, 82 (San Francisco
copy).
The painting in San Francisco is now universally
regarded as a copy; the original would be datable
to *c.* 1629–30.

24 Moses Sweetening the Bitter Waters of Marah
Baltimore, Md, Museum of Art
Canvas, 152 x 210 (59³/₄ x 82³/₄)
Prov.: Acquired in England by the first Earl
Harcourt in 1755; entered the museum in 1958.
Cat.: Blunt 28; Thuillier B.23; Wild M.1; Wright A.3;
Oberhuber 48.
Exh.: Paris 1960, 11.
'Repainted and disfigured', according to Thuillier,
this work has sometimes been attributed to
Mellin. The style is reminiscent of the *The Virgin
Appearing to St James* (No. 93), which dates from
1629–30.

26 The Battle of Joshua against the Amorites
Moscow, Pushkin Museum
Canvas, 97.5 x 134 (38¹/₂ x 52³/₄)
Prov.: See previous entry; sent to Moscow in 1927.
Cat.: Blunt 30; Thuillier 12; Wild 17; Wright 4;
Oberhuber 2.
Exh.: Paris 1960, 3.
Pendant of No. 25.

23 The Adoration of the Golden Calf
(fragment: heads of two women)
Southwell, Nottinghamshire, Booth collection
Canvas, 32 x 45.5 (12¹/₂ x 17³/₄)
Prov.: Fragment of a work painted for a Neapolitan
client, cut into pieces in 1647 during the
Masaniello revolt (Félibien); went to Rome, then
England; the Earls of Carlisle.
Cat.: Blunt 27; Thuillier 64A; Wright L.4;
Oberhuber 70.
Exh.: Edinburgh 1981, 3.
Wright is alone in refusing to attribute this work to
Poussin. His argument is based on an X-ray
examination (which reveals overpainting of part
of a landscape with ruins). The style would seem
to indicate a date slightly earlier than 1630.

25 The Battle of Joshua against the Amalechites
Leningrad, Hermitage Museum
Canvas, 97.5 x 134 (38¹/₂ x 52³/₄)
Prov.: Acquired, like its pendant, No. 26, by
Catherine the Great of Russia in 1774.
Cat.: Blunt 29; Thuillier 11; Wild 16; Wright 3;
Oberhuber 1.
Exh.: Paris 1960, 2.
One of the very first works painted in Rome
(*c.* 1625), rather than in Paris (*c.* 1622–3), as
Oberhuber suggests.

27 The Battle of Gideon against the Midianites
Rome, Vatican Museums
Canvas, 98 x 137 (38¹/₂ x 54)
Prov.: Unknown
Cat.: Blunt 31; Thuillier 13; Wild M.4; Wright 5;
Oberhuber 11.
Exh.: Rouen 1961, 73; Fort Worth, Texas 1988, 11.
Bibl.: Thuillier in *Colloque Poussin*, 1960, II,
p. 264.
This work was discovered by Thuillier in the
Vatican collections and first published by him.
Closely linked to the two previous entries, it can
be dated, like them, *c.* 1625–6.
See p. 37.

28 *The Plague of Ashdod*
Paris, Louvre
Canvas, 148 x 198 (58¼ x 78)
Prov.: Acquired from the artist in early 1631 by
Fabrizio Valguarnera* (documented); the Duc de
Richelieu*; acquired by Louis XIV in 1665.
Cat.: Blunt 32; Thuillier 65; Wild 31; Wright 30;
Oberhuber 84.
Exh.: Paris 1960, 23; Rouen 1961, 76; Bologna
1962, 57.
See p. 59.

30 *The Triumph of David*
London, Dulwich Picture Gallery
Canvas, 117 x 146 (46 x 57½)
Prov.: Lord Carysfort, 1776; C. A. de Calonne,
c. 1787; acquired in 1795 by Noël Desenfans; Sir
Francis Bourgeois; bequeathed by him to Dulwich
College in 1811.
Cat.: Blunt 33; Thuillier B.26; Wild 41; Wright 68.
Exh.: Paris 1960, 9; Edinburgh 1981, 13.
This is one of Poussin's most controversial works,
since there is no mention of it at all in the early
source material and X-ray examination has
revealed some reworking. Some art historians
have questioned its attribution and date (certainly
completed *c.* 1632–3).
See p. 65.

32 *Esther before Ahasuerus*
Leningrad, Hermitage Museum
Canvas, 119 x 155 (47 x 61)
Prov.: Serisier* (Chantelou, *Voyage du Bernin*);
the Marquis de Seignelay; the Duc d'Orléans;
acquired between 1763 and 1774 by Catherine the
Great of Russia.
Cat.: Blunt 36; Thuillier 193; Wild 123; Wright 185.
Exh.: Düsseldorf 1978, 37a.
Datable to *c.* 1655.

29 *The Triumph of David*
Madrid, Prado
Canvas, 100 x 130 (39½ x 51)
Prov.: In the collection of Girolamo Casanatta* by
1664 (Bellori); Carlo Maratta; acquired by Philip V
of Spain.
Cat.: Blunt 34; Thuillier 66; Wild 20; Wright 61;
Oberhuber 72.
Exh.: Rouen 1961, 74; Edinburgh 1981, 11.
Datable to *c.* 1630–1.
See p. 62.

31 *The Judgment of Solomon*
Paris, Louvre
Canvas, 101 x 150 (39¾ x 59)
Prov.: Painted in 1649 for Pointel* (Félibien);
Achille de Harlay; acquired by Louis XIV in 1685.
Cat.: Blunt 35; Thuillier 162; Wild 148; Wright 142.
Exh.: Paris 1960, 87; Rome-Düsseldorf 1977–8, 33.
See p. 145.

33 *The Capture of Jerusalem by Titus*
Vienna, Kunsthistorisches Museum
Canvas, 147 x 198.5 (58½ x 78¼)
Signed: NI. PVSIN FEC.
Prov.: Commissioned by Cardinal Francesco
Barberini* (Bellori), who gave the painting to
Prince von Eggenberg, the Holy Roman Emperor's
ambassador to Pope Urban VIII; recorded in the
Imperial Collection in Vienna from 1718.
Cat.: Blunt 37; Thuillier 115; Wild 84; Wright 102.
Exh.: Paris 1960, 39; Rome-Düsseldorf 1977–8, 25.
Datable to 1638, the year of the Eggenberg
embassy and of the payment for the frame.
Cardinal Francesco Barberini paid the artist for a
first version in 1626. It subsequently belonged to
Cardinal Richelieu and then to his niece, the
Duchesse d'Aiguillon. See Blunt L.9; Thuillier 26;
Wild 10; Wright L.16.

NEW TESTAMENT THEMES

THE VIRGIN AND CHILD
AND
THE HOLY FAMILY

35 *The Virgin and Child*
Lost
Engraving: J. Pesne (Wildenstein 41)
Cat.: Blunt 45; Thuillier 153; Wild 181; Wright L.8.
Associated by Blunt with a work seen by Bernini at
Serisier's* in 1665 (Chantelou). Dated by Thuillier
c. 1648–50.

37 *The Holy Family*
(*The Roccatagliata Madonna*)
Detroit Institute of Arts
Canvas, 71 x 55.5 (28 x 21³/₄)
Prov.: Painted in 1641–2 in Paris for Giovanni
Stefano Roccatagliata* (correspondence); in the
collection of the Bailiff of Breteuil during the
eighteenth century; donated to the Institute in
1954.
Cat.: Blunt 46; Thuillier 130; Wild 106; Wright 121.
Exh.: Paris 1960, 65.

34 *The Virgin and Child*
Brighton, Sussex, Preston Manor
Canvas, 58.5 x 49.5 (23 x 19¹/₂)
Prov.: Cassiano dal Pozzo* (inventories);
reappeared in Paris in 1819.
Cat.: Thuillier 21; Wild R.54a; Wright 9; Oberhuber
26.
Exh.: Rome-Düsseldorf 1977–8, 8.
The garland of flowers is said to be by Daniel
Seghers, who was in Paris *c.* 1625–7; see also
No. 80.
See p. 42.

36 *The Holy Family*
Lost
Engraving: J. Pesne (Wildenstein 42)
Cat.: Blunt 47; Thuillier 201; Wild 127; Wright L.9.
A late work (*c.* 1656–8?).

38 *The Holy Family with St John the Baptist*
Karlsruhe, Staatliche Kunsthalle
Canvas, 101 x 75.5 (39³/₄ x 29¹/₄)
Prov.: In several English collections during the
nineteenth century; Thyssen collection.
Exh.: Paris 1960, 17.
In spite of Wild's opinion (he attributes it to
Mellin), the work fits well into Poussin's output at
the end of the 1620s.

39 *The Holy Family with St John the Baptist*
Toledo, Ohio, Museum of Art
Canvas, 169.5 x 127 (66¼ x 50)
Prov.: In the Vittore Zanetti collection at the
beginning of the nineteenth century; English
private collection; acquired by the museum in
1976.
Cat.: Blunt 49; Thuillier B.30; Wild R.46; Wright
A.30; Oberhuber 10.
Exh.: Fort Worth, Texas 1988, 10.
The attribution is still very much in dispute: this
work is variously thought to date from very early
in Poussin's Roman period (1625, according to
Oberhuber) or *c.* 1630 (Blunt, Wright), whereas
Thuillier regards it as possibly one of his late
works.

41 *The Holy Family with St John the Baptist*
Lost
Engraving: S. Vouillemont (Wildenstein 45)
Cat.: Blunt 50; Thuillier 195; Wild R.51; Wright
L.10.
Dated before 1640 by Blunt, but *c.* 1655 by
Thuillier.

43 *The Holy Family with St Elizabeth and St John
the Baptist*
Paris, Louvre
Canvas, 94 x 122 (37 x 48)
Prov.: Painted for Mme Fouquet* (Brienne);
acquired in 1685 by Louis XIV.
Cat.: Blunt 55; Thuillier 177; Wild 169; Wright 171.
Exh.: Paris 1960, 104.
Generally thought to date from the early 1650s.
See p. 178.

40 *The Holy Family with the Infant St John the
Baptist*
Sarasota, Fla, The John and Mable Ringling
Musuem of Art
Canvas, 198 x 131 (78 x 51½)
Prov.: Undoubtedly the work painted for the Duc
de Créquy* in 1655 (correspondence); Pointel*
(Chantelou); Sir Richard Worsley; the Earls of
Yarborough.
Cat.: Blunt 51; Thuillier 196; Wild 183; Wright 174.
Exh.: Paris 1960, 107; Rome-Düsseldorf 1977–8,
40.
See p. 178.

42 *The Madonna of the Steps*
Cleveland, Ohio, Museum of Art
Canvas, 72.5 x 111.5 (28½ x 44)
Prov.: Painted in 1648 for Hennequin du Fresne*
(Félibien); Lord Ashburton(?); Lerolle; Bertin-
Mourot; acquired by the museum in 1981.
Cat.: Blunt 53 (as copy of the Washington version –
see note below); Thuillier 152; Wild 138; Wright
140b.
Bibl.: A. Tzeutschler-Lurie, 1982.
Now regarded as the original, following much
detailed research. The Washington version,
formerly in the collection of the Dukes of
Sutherland, is an excellent seventeenth-century
copy, oil on canvas, 68.5 x 97.8 (27 x 38½).
See p. 179.

44 *The Holy Family with St Elizabeth and St John
the Baptist in a Landscape*
Paris, Louvre
Canvas, 68 x 51 (26¾ x 20)
Prov.: Possibly painted in 1656 'for a private
person' (Félibien); acquired in 1685 by Louis XIV.
Cat.: Blunt 57; Thuillier 198; Wild 186; Wright 187.
Exh.: Paris 1960, 112.
See p. 178.

45 *The Holy Family with St Elizabeth and St John the Baptist*
Leningrad, Hermitage Museum
Canvas, 172 x 133.5 (67³/₄ x 52¹/₂)
Prov.: Intended for Chantelou*, planned as early as 1647, but only completed in 1655 (correspondence); Sir Robert Walpole; acquired in 1779 by Catherine the Great of Russia.
Cat.: Blunt 56; Thuillier 194; Wild 182; Wright 175.

47 *The Holy Family with St Elizabeth and St John the Baptist*
Chantilly, Musée Condé
Canvas, 67 x 49 (26¹/₂ x 19¹/₄)
Prov.: Rospigliosi* collection in Rome (inventory of 1713); Fesch; Reiset; acquired in 1879 by the Duc d'Aumale.
Cat.: Blunt 52; Thuillier B.41; Wild R.42; Wright 122.
Generally accepted as being by Poussin, in spite of Thuillier's reservations (he considers it to be by Charles Errard).

49 *The Holy Family with St Anne, St Elizabeth and St John the Baptist*
Dublin, National Gallery of Ireland
Canvas, 79 x 106 (31¹/₄ x 41³/₄)
Prov.: Painted in 1649 for Pointel* (Félibien); in 1665 in the Serisier* collection (Chantelou, *Voyage du Bernin*); the Earls of Milltown; date of accession 1902 (Milltown gift).
Cat.: Blunt 59; Thuillier 164 (copy); Wild 150; Wright 143.
Exh.: Dublin 1985, 35.
An inferior version is in the De Young Memorial Museum, San Francisco, Cal.; this was exhibited in Paris in 1960 (No. 82).

46 *The Holy Family with St Elizabeth and St John the Baptist*
Moscow, Pushkin Museum
Canvas, 64 x 50.5 (25¹/₄ x 19⁵/₄)
Prov.: Stroganoff collection.
Cat.: Blunt R.31; Thuillier R.28; Oberhuber 75.
Bibl.: Thuillier 1978, p. 160.
Attributed by Thuillier to Charles Errard*, but not universally accepted as such.

48 *The Holy Family with St Elizabeth and St John the Baptist*
Cambridge, Mass., Fogg Art Museum
Canvas, 98 x 129.5 (38¹/₂ x 50¹/₂)
Prov.: Fromont de Venne (engraving by J. Pesne); several French collections; in England at the beginning of the nineteenth century; donated to the museum in 1942 by Mrs Samuel Sachs.
Cat.: Blunt 54; Thuillier 176; Wild 167; Wright 172.
Exh.: Paris 1960, 101.
Datable to *c.* 1650–1.

50 *The Holy Family with St Elizabeth and St John the Baptist*
Malibu, Cal., The J. Paul Getty Museum; and Pasadena, Cal., The Norton Simon Museum.
Canvas, 96.5 x 133 (38 x 52¹/₄)
Prov.: Undoubtedly the work painted for the Duc de Créquy* in 1651 (Félibien); collection of the Dukes of Devonshire at Chatsworth; acquired by the two museums in 1981.
Cat.: Blunt 58; Thuillier 179; Wild 168; Wright 173.
See p. 178.

THE LIFE
OF CHRIST

51   *The Holy Family with St John the Baptist*
     (*The Rest on the Flight into Egypt*)
New York, Heineman collection
Canvas, 76 x 63 (30 x 24⁵/₄)
Prov.: Possibly from the Della Torre collection in
Naples.
Cat.: Blunt 63; Thuillier 57; Wild M.11; Wright 59;
Oberhuber 36.
Exh.: Paris 1960, 27; Fort Worth, Texas 1988, 36.
In poor condition, this small painting is usually
dated *c*. 1627 (1629 by Thuillier).

53   *The Annunciation*
Munich, Alte Pinakothek
Panel, 47.5 x 38 (18⁵/₄ x 15)
Prov.: Antoine Benoit(?); mentioned in the
Düsseldorf Gallery inventory in 1778; entered the
gallery in 1806.
Cat.: Thuillier 218; Wild 187a; Wright 193.
Exh.: Rome-Düsseldorf 1977–8, 43.
Bibl.: Blunt 1960 (*Poussin Studies*, XI).
One of a series of four paintings (see also Nos. 55,
83, 84) executed *c*. 1655.

52   *The Annunciation*
London, National Gallery
Canvas, 105 x 103 (41¹/₄ x 40¹/₂)
Inscription: POVSSIN. FACIEBAT. ANNO. SALVTIS.
MDCLVII. ALEX. SEPT. PONT. MAX. REGNANTE.
ROMA.
Prov.: Painted in 1657 to adorn the tomb of
Cassiano Dal Pozzo* in Sta Maria sopra Minerva,
Rome (correspondence); in England at the
beginning of the nineteenth century – various
owners; given to the gallery in 1944.
Cat.: Blunt: 39; Thuillier 203; Wild 192; Wright 188.
Exh.: Bologna 1962, 59a.
Bibl.: Costello 1965.
See p. 219.

54   *The Annunciation*
Chantilly, Musée Condé
Canvas, 75 x 95 (29¹/₂ x 37¹/₂)
Prov.: Reiset collection; acquired in 1879 by the
Duc d'Aumale.
Cat.: Blunt 38; Thuillier B.21; Wild M.12; Wright
A.6, Oberhuber 65.
Engraved, as a work by Poussin, in 1661. Dated
1627 by Blunt, and 1628 by Oberhuber. Attributed
to Mellin* by Thuillier and Wild.

55   *The Nativity*
Munich, Alte Pinakothek
Panel, 45.5 x 38 (18 x 15³/₄)
Prov.: See No. 53
Cat.: Blunt R.19; Thuillier 219; Wild 187b; Wright 194.
Exh.: Rome-Düsseldorf 1977–8, 44.
See Nos. 53, 83 and 84.

57   *The Adoration of the Shepherds*
Munich, Alte Pinakothek (Bayerische Staatsgemäldesammlungen; in store at Schloss Schleissheim).
Canvas, 97.5 x 131.5 (38¹/₄ x 51⁵/₈)
Prov.: Palatine Electors, Mannheim; passed in 1777 by inheritance into the collection of the Electors of Bavaria.
Exh.: Rome-Düsseldorf 1977–8, 41.
Regarded by Rosenberg (1977–8) as a good early copy, Blunt dates this painting *c.* 1655, slightly earlier than Thuillier, who proposes a date between 1652 and 1654. It is sometimes confused with No. 58.

59   *The Adoration of the Magi*
Dresden, Staatliche Kunstsammlungen: Gemäldegalerie
Canvas, 161 x 182 (63¹/₂ x 71¹/₂)
Signed and dated: Accad. rom. NICOLAVS PVSIN faciebat Romae. 1633.
Prov.: M. de Charmois*; in the Cotteblanche* collection in 1665 (Chantelou, *Voyage du Bernin*); acquired in Paris by Augustus III of Saxony in 1742.
Cat.: Blunt 44; Thuillier 75; Wild 51; Wright 63.
Exh.: Bologna 1962, 59b.
See p. 67.

56   *The Adoration of the Shepherds*
London, National Gallery
Canvas, 98 x 74 (38¹/₂ x 29)
Signed on the stone in the foreground: N. Pussin fe.
Prov.: Sir Joshua Reynolds; Beauchamp collection; acquired by the gallery in 1957.
Cat.: Blunt 40; Thuillier 72; Wild 50; Wright 74.
Datable to *c.* 1631–3.
See p. 66.

58   *The Adoration of the Shepherds*
Lost
Engraving: J Pesne (Wildenstein 33).
Prov.: Painted between 1650 and 1653 for M. de Mauroy* (correspondence, Félibien) (?).
Cat.: Blunt 42; Thuillier 185; Wild 178; Wright 181.
Sometimes confused with No. 57. Wright notes that Blunt later entertained doubts, about the authenticity of a painting in a Texas private collection, suggested as being the original.

60   *The Rest on the Flight into Egypt with an Elephant*
Lost
Engraving: Anonymous, seventeenth century (Wildenstein 58).
Prov.: Undoubtedly the work commissioned by Cardinal Rospigliosi* (Bellori).
Cat.: Blunt 62; Thuillier 125; Wild 119; Wright L.12.
There was a version (the original?) in Cardinal Fesch's collection, which was sold in 1840. Dates from 1638–40.

61 *The Flight into Egypt with a Traveller at Rest*
Lost
Engraving: P. del Po (Wildenstein 57)
Prov.: Undoubtedly a work painted for Serisier* in 1658 (Félibien).
Cat.: Blunt 61; Thuillier 207; Wild 198; Wright L.11.
Two versions, which have recently reappeared, claim to be original: the one recently shown at the Galerie Pardo in Paris (*Thèmes de l'âge classique*, May-June 1989, pp. 50f.) measures 97 x 133 cm (38¼ x 52½ in.) and is said to have come from the Lethière collection, sold in 1829; and the smaller one – oil on canvas, 73.5 x 97 cm (29 x 38¼ in.), in a Swiss private collection – was published by Blunt (*Burlington Magazine*, April 1982, pp. 208–13). Neither has received unanimous acceptance.

63 *The Rest on the Flight into Egypt*
Leningrad, Hermitage Museum
Canvas, 105 x 145 (41¼ x 57)
Prov.: Painted between 1655 and late 1657 for Mme de Montmort* (correspondence); during the nineteenth century in the Stroganoff collection; entered the Hermitage in 1931.
Cat.: Blunt 65; Thuillier 200; Wild 195; Wright 189.
Exh.: Paris 1960, 109.

65 *The Massacre of the Innocents*
Paris, Musée du Petit-Palais
Canvas, 98 x 133 (38½ x 52¼)
Prov.: Mentioned in the Altieri collection, Rome (guides, from 1686 to 1794); Auguste Dutuit; bequeathed to the museum in 1902.
Cat.: Blunt 66; Thuillier B.7; Wild 45; Wright 70; Oberhuber 32.
Exh.: Paris 1960, 4.
The painting has suffered greatly and its attribution has been doubted. Dated 1627 by Oberhuber, *c.* 1630 by Wild and Wright.

62 *The Rest on the Flight into Egypt*
Winterthur, Oskar Reinhart collection
Canvas, 88 x 67 (34¾ x 26½)
Prov.: Possibly in the Crozat collection before 1740; during the nineteenth century in the collection of the Earls Grosvenor (from 1874 the Dukes of Westminster); acquired in 1926.
Cat.: Blunt 64; Thuillier 73; Wild 40: Wright 76.
Datable to between 1632 and 1634.

64 *The Massacre of the Innocents*
Chantilly, Musée Condé
Canvas, 147 x 171 (58 x 67½)
Prov.: Marchese Vincenzo Giustiniani* (inventory of 1638); Lucien Bonaparte; various English collections; acquired in London by the Duc d'Aumale in 1854.
Cat.: Blunt 67; Thuillier 25; Wild 59; Wright 41; Oberhuber 83.
Dated 1625 by Thuillier, but later (between 1628 and 1630) by all other experts.
See p. 55.

66 *The Return from Egypt*
London, Dulwich Picture Gallery
Canvas, 112 x 94 (44 x 37)
Prov.: First recorded in England in 1792; Noël Desenfans; Sir Francis Bourgeois; bequeathed by him to Dulwich College.
Cat.: Blunt 68; Thuillier 60; Wild M.38; Wright 75; Oberhuber 78.
Datable to *c.* 1629–30.

67   *The Return from Egypt*
Cleveland, Ohio, Museum of Art
Canvas, 134 x 99 (52³/₄ x 39)
Prov.: In the collection of the Princes of
Liechtenstein since 1733; acquired by the museum
in 1952.
Cat.: Blunt (rejected, unnumbered, pp. 48–50);
Thuillier 76; Wild M.39; Wright 77.
Exh.: Paris 1960, 52.
Although Blunt claimed that this was a copy or
imitation of a lost original, the painting is now
generally accepted as being by Poussin, and dated
c. 1633–4, several years later than the Dulwich
version (No. 66).

69   *St John Baptizing the People*
Paris, Louvre
Canvas, 94 x 120 (37 x 47¹/₄)
Prov.: André le Nôtre* (Félibien); bequeathed by
him to Louis XIV in 1693.
Cat.: Blunt 69; Thuillier 78; Wild 42; Wright 96.
Exh.: Paris 1960, 55; Bologna 1962, 61; Edinburgh
1981, 30.
Dated *c.* 1633–5 by Thuillier, *c* 1636–7 by Blunt,
which seems more likely.

71   *The Baptism of Christ*
Philadelphia, Pa, Museum of Art
(The John G. Johnson collection)
Canvas, 92 x 129 (36¹/₄ x 50⁵/₄)
Prov.: Unknown until 1911, when the work
entered the Johnson collection.
Cat.: Blunt 72; Thuillier 192; Wild 189; Wright 184.
Exh.: Paris 1960, 110.
A late work, datable to *c.* 1655.

68   *St John Baptizing the People*
Mailbu, Cal., The J. Paul Getty Museum
Canvas, 95.5 x 121 (37¹/₂ x 47)
Prov.: Cassiano Dal Pozzo* (Bellori); collection of
the Dukes of Rutland, 1785–1958; Bührle, Zurich;
acquired by the museum in 1971.
Cat.: Blunt 70; Thuillier 85; Wild M.14; Wright 95.
Exh.: Bologna 1962, 62.
Dated by Blunt between 1636 and 1640,
considerably earlier by Thuillier (*c.* 1633–5), this
work would appear to be much earlier than the
version in the Louvre (No. 69).

70   *The Baptism of Christ*
Switzerland, private collection
Panel, 30 x 23 (11³/₄ x 9)
Prov.: Commissioned in 1645 by Jean Fréart de
Chantelou* and executed in 1648
(correspondence); Czernin collection, Vienna;
Wildenstein, New York.
Cat.: Blunt 71; Thuillier 147; Wild 137; Wright 132.
Exh.: Paris 1960, 85.

72   *Christ and the Woman of Samaria*
Lost
Engraving: J. Pesne (Wildenstein 64).
Prov.: Painted in 1662 for Mme de Chantelou
(formerly Mme de Montmort*; correspondence).
Cat.: Blunt 73; Thuillier 216; Wild 203; Wright L.14.

73 *Christ Healing the Sick*
Paris, Louvre
Canvas, 119 x 176 (46⁵/₄ x 69¹/₄)
Prov.: Painted in 1650 for Reynon* (Félibien); the
Duc de Richelieu*; acquired in 1665 by Louis XIV.
Cat.: Blunt 74; Thuillier 174; Wild 162; Wright 168.
Exh.: Paris 1960, 94.

75 *The Entry of Christ into Jerusalem*
Nancy, Musée des Beaux-Arts
Canvas, 98 x 134 (38¹/₂ x 52³/₄)
Prov.: Owned by the sculptor Etienne Maurice
Falconet in the eighteenth century; bequeathed to
the museum by his granddaughter, Baroness
Jankowitz, in 1886.
Cat.: Blunt 77; Thuillier B.27; Wild M.15; Wright 71.
In poor condition (incomplete according to
Wright), this work is in a style close to that of the
Dulwich *Triumph of David* (No. 30); as in that
case, the attribution has been much debated
(Thuillier and Wild see it as a mature work by
Charles Mellin).

77 *Christ in the Garden of Gethsemane*
Private collection
Canvas, 62 x 49 (24¹/₂ x 19¹/₄)
Inscribed on the back: SALVATORIS IN HORTO
GETSEMANI A NICOLAO POVSSIN COLORIBVS
EXPRESSA.
Prov.: Possibly the painting from the Dal Pozzo*
collection mentioned by Sandrart.
Cat.: Blunt L.30; Thuillier 79; Wild M.13; Wright
L.13; Oberhuber 39.
Bibl.: T. J. Standring, 1985.
Dated 1627 by Oberhuber and *c.* 1630–5 by
Thuillier (based on two drawings, in the
Hermitage and the Royal Library at Windsor, of a
very different composition). Another version – on
copper, 63 x 51 (24⁵/₄ x 20) – said to have come
from the Barberini collection is reported to be in
a private collection (Oberhuber 40).

74 *Christ and the Woman Taken in Adultery*
Paris, Louvre
Canvas, 122 x 195 (48 x 76⁵/₄)
Prov.: Painted in 1653 for Le Nôtre* (Félibien);
bequeathed by him to Louis XIV in 1693.
Cat.: Blunt 76; Thuillier 188; Wild 177; Wright 178.
Exh.: Paris 1960, 103; Bologna 1962, 82.
See p. 198.

76 *The Institution of the Eucharist*
Paris, Louvre
Canvas, 325 x 250 (128 x 98¹/₂)
Prov.: Commissioned in December 1640 by Louis
XIII for the chapel of the Château de Saint-
Germain-en-Laye; hung by 20 September 1641
(correspondence); entered the Louvre in 1792.
Cat.: Blunt 78; Thuillier 126; Wild 100; Wright 117.
See p. 119.

78 *The Crucifixion*
Hartford, Conn., The Wadsworth Atheneum
Canvas, 148.5 x 218.5 (58¹/₂ x 86)
Prov.: Commissioned in 1644 by Jacques de Thou*
and executed in 1645–6 (correspondence);
Jacques Stella* and his heirs; in England by the
mid-eighteenth century; acquired by the museum
in 1935.
Cat.: Blunt 79; Thuillier 139; Wild 28; Wright 131.
Exh.: Rome-Düsseldorf 1977–8, 29.

79   *The Deposition from the Cross*
Leningrad, Hermitage Museum
Prov.: Count Brühl, minister of Augustus III of
Saxony; acquired by Catherine the Great of Russia
in 1769.
Cat.: Blunt 80; Thuillier 17; Wild M.3; Wright 39;
Oberhuber 24.
Exh.: Paris 1960, 24.
Datable to the very early years in Rome, *c.* 1627 or
slightly earlier.

81   *Lamentation over the Dead Christ*
Munich, Alte Pinakothek
Canvas, 102.7 x 146 (40^1/$_2$ x 57^1/$_2$)
Prov.: the Electors of Bavaria from the eighteenth
century.
Cat.: Blunt 82; Thuillier 18; Wild 12; Wright 40;
Oberhuber 64.
Dated very early (1625–6) by Thuillier, later by
most authorities.
See p. 42.

83   *Lamentation over the Dead Christ*
Lost
Engraving: P. del Po (Wildenstein 71)
Prov.: Pointel* (inventory of 1660).
Cat.: Thuillier 220; Wild 187c; Wright 192.
The original was one of a series of four paintings
on panel (see Nos. 53, 55 and 84). A version on
canvas (47 x 37 cm; 18^1/$_2$ x 14^1/$_2$ in.) in a London
private collection is probably a copy.

80   *Pietà*
Cherbourg, Musée Thomas Henry
Canvas, 49 x 40 (19^1/$_2$ x 15^3/$_4$)
Prov.: Cassiano Dal Pozzo*; Boccapaduli
collection; Dufourny collection; sold in 1819;
Thomas Henry collection; bequeathed by him to
the museum in 1835.
Cat.: Blunt 81; Thuillier 20; Wild R.54b; Wright 8;
Oberhuber 25.
Exh.: Rouen 1961, 100; Rome-Düsseldorf 1977–8,
7; Fort Worth, Texas 1988, 25.
See also the *Virgin and Child* (No. 34) which also
features a garland of flowers by Daniel Seghers.
Datable to *c.* 1625–7.
See p. 42.

82   *Lamentation over the Dead Christ*
Dublin, National Gallery of Ireland
Canvas, 94 x 130 (37 x 51^1/$_4$)
Prov.: the Dukes of Hamilton; acquired by the
gallery in 1882.
Cat.: Blunt 83; Thuillier 206; Wild 190; Wright 191.
Exh.: Paris 1960, 96; Bologna 1962, 84; Rome-
Düsseldorf 1977–8, 42.
Datable to *c.* 1656–7, possibly even slightly later.

84   *Noli me tangere*
Madrid, Prado
Panel, 47 x 39 (18^1/$_2$ x 15^1/$_2$)
Prov.: Pointel* (inventory of 1660); inventoried in
the Spanish royal collection from 1746.
Cat.: Blunt R.41 (and L.32); Thuillier 221; Wild
187d; Wright 195.
Exh.: Rome-Düsseldorf 1977–8, 45.
One of a series of four paintings on panel (see
Nos. 53, 55 and 83).

86   *The Assumption of the Virgin*
Washington, D.C., National Gallery of Art
Canvas, 134.5 x 98 (53 x 38½)
Prov.: Quite possibly in the collection of Vincenzo
Giustiniani* (inventory of 1638); Soderini
collection in 1750; the Earls (later Marquesses) of
Exeter, Burghley House; acquired by the gallery in
1963.
Cat.: Blunt 92; Thuillier B.28; Wild M.27; Wright 72;
Oberhuber 68.
Exh.: Paris 1960, 7; Paris-New York-Chicago 1982,
88; Fort Worth, Texas 1988, 68.
Attributed to Mellin* by Thuillier and Wild.
Sometimes dated after 1630 (Mahon), sometimes
slightly earlier.

85   *The Death of the Virgin*
Lost
Canvas(?), 200 x 140 (78¾ x 55)
Prov.: Painted *c.* 1623 for one of the chapels in the
Cathedral of Notre Dame, Paris (Bellori, Félibien);
sent to the Petits-Augustins store in 1793, then in
1797 to the Louvre and in 1803 to the museum in
Brussels; there is no trace of it after 1815.
Cat.: Blunt 90–91; Thuillier 8; Wild 3; Wright 1;
Oberhuber D.1.
Exh.: Fort Worth, Texas 1988, D.1 (*modello*).
A watercolour version (Hovingham Hall,
Yorkshire, Worsley collection) of this composition
is sometimes regarded as the original *modello*,
and sometimes as a copy.

87   *The Assumption of the Virgin*
Paris, Louvre
Canvas, 57 x 40 (22½ x 15¾)
Prov.: Completed in 1650 for Henri d'Etampes-
Valençay* (correspondence); various private
owners (including M. de Mauroy); acquired by
Louis XIV in 1685.
Cat.: Blunt 93; Thuillier 168; Wild 159; Wright 169.
Exh.: Paris 1960, 95.
See p. 183.

88   *St Denis Crowned by an Angel*
Rouen, Musée des Beaux-Arts
Canvas, 177 x 110 (69¾ x 43¼)
Prov.: Seized from the church of Saint-Germain-
l'Auxerrois in Paris in 1793; sent to the museum in
1803.
Cat.: Blunt R.51; Thuillier B.2.
Exh.: Rouen 1961, 92.
Bibl.: Thuillier in *Colloque Poussin*, 1960, II, p. 33.
Rejected by most writers, this painting could,
according to Thuillier, be one of the rare works
from Poussin's very early beginnings (*c.* 1618–
20?). The background is similar to that of No. 89.

89 *St Denis Terrifying his Executioners*
La Meilleraye-de-Bretagne, Abbey of Notre Dame
Canvas, 68 x 82 (26³/₄ x 32¹/₂)
Prov.: Abbey of Saint-Denis; seized during the
Revolution; given to the Abbey at La Meilleraye by
Louis XVIII in 1821.
Cat.: Blunt R.52; Thuillier B.1.
Exh.: Rouen 1961, 93.
Bibl.: Thuillier in *Colloque Poussin*, 1960, II, p. 34.
Rejected by the majority of writers, this painting
(of which at least two other versions are known)
could, according to Thuillier, be one of Poussin's
earliest works, dating from *c*. 1621–3.
See p. 23.

91 *The Martyrdom of St Erasmus*
Rome, Vatican Museums
Canvas, 320 x 186 (126 x 73¹/₄)
Signed bottom left: Nicolaus Pusin fecit.
Prov.: Commissioned for St Peter's Basilica in
Rome in February 1628; paid for June-October
1629.
Cat.: Blunt 97; Thuillier 54; Wild 22; Wright 28;
Oberhuber 67.
See p. 47.

93 *The Virgin Appearing to St James*
Paris, Louvre
Canvas, 301 x 242 (118¹/₂ x 95¹/₄)
Prov.: Painted *c*. 1629–30 for a church in
Valenciennes (Bellori, Félibien); the Duc de
Richelieu*; acquired by Louis XIV in 1665.
Cat.: Blunt 102; Thuillier 59; Wild 25; Wright 29;
Oberhuber 77.
Exh.: Paris 1960, 15.
See p. 46.

90 *The Martyrdom of St Erasmus*
Ottawa, National Gallery of Canada
Canvas, 99 x 74 (39 x 29)
Prov.: Sciarra collection, Rome; Fairfax-Murray
collection; Ugo Ojetti; accession date 1972.
Cat.: Blunt 98; Thuillier 53; Wild 22a; Wright 27;
Oberhuber 66.
Exh.: Fort Worth, Texas 1988, 66.
Bibl.: Costello, 1975.

92 *The Miracle of St Francis Xavier*
Paris, Louvre
Canvas, 444 x 234 (175¹/₄ x 92)
Prov.: Commissioned by Sublet de Noyers* in
1641, for the high altar of the Jesuit Noviciate in
Paris (correspondence); entered the royal
collections in 1763.
Cat.: Blunt 101; Thuillier 128; Wild 103; Wright
119.
Exh.: Paris 1960, 62.
See p. 123.

94 *The Ecstasy of St Paul*
Sarasota, Fla, The John and Mable Ringling
Museum of Art
Panel, 41.5 x 30 (16¹/₄ x 11³/₄)
Prov.: Painted in 1643 for Chantelou*
(correspondence, Félibien); in the collection of
the Ducs d'Orléans during the eighteenth century;
in England at the end of the eighteenth century;
acquired by the museum in 1956.
Cat.: Blunt 88; Thuillier 134; Wild 116; Wright 123.
Exh.: Paris 1960, 67.
Painted as a pendant to a *Vision of Ezekiel*, which
Chantelou believed to be an original by Raphael.

95   *The Ecstasy of St Paul*
Paris, Louvre
Canvas, 148 x 120 (58¹/₄ x 47¹/₄)
Prov.: Painted in 1649–50 for Paul Scarron*
(correspondence); Jabach* collection; collection
of the Duc de Richelieu*; acquired by Louis XIV in
1665.
Cat.: Blunt 89; Thuillier 169; Wild 160; Wright 170.
Exh.: Paris 1960, 92; Bologna 1962, 80.
See p. 182.

97   *The Death of Sapphira*
Paris, Louvre
Canvas, 122 x 199 (48 x 78¹/₂)
Prov.: Fromont de Vennes* (Félibien); acquired by
Louis XIV in 1685.
Cat.: Blunt 85; Thuillier 191; Wild 179; Wright 179.
Exh.: Paris 1960, 106; Rome-Düsseldorf 1977–8,
38; Dublin 1985, 37.
Dated *c*. 1654–56 by Blunt and Thuillier, *c*. 1652 by
Mahon and Rosenberg.
See p. 214.

99   *St Cecilia*
Madrid, Prado
Canvas, 118 x 88 (46¹/₂ x 34⁵/₄)
Prov.: First recorded in 1734 at the Alcazar in
Madrid.
Cat.: Blunt 93; Thuillier B.25; Wild M.32; Wright 57;
Oberhuber 74.
Exh.: Fort Worth, Texas 1988, 74.
Attributed to Mellin by Wild and Thuillier. Datable
to between 1627 and 1630.

96   *St Peter Healing a Sick Man*
New York, The Metropolitan Museum of Art
Canvas, 126 x 165 (49¹/₂ x 65)
Prov.: Painted in 1655 for Mercier* (Félibien);
Jacques Stella*; collection of the Princes of
Liechtenstein; acquired by the museum in 1924.
Cat.: Blunt 84; Thuillier 197; Wild 184; Wright 186.

98   *The Mystic Marriage of St Catherine*
Edinburgh, National Gallery of Scotland
Wood, 127 x 167.5 (50 x 66)
Prov.: Cassiano Dal Pozzo*(?); Cook collection;
Heathcoat Amory collection; bequeathed to the
gallery in 1973.
Cat.: Blunt 95; Thuillier B.24; Wild M.29; Wright 57;
Oberhuber 69.
Exh.: Edinburgh 1981, 9.
Attributed to Mellin by Thuillier and Wild, but
accepted by other authorities and dated between
1627 and 1630.
See p. 50.

100   *The Vision of St Francesca Romana*
Lost
Engraving: P. del Po (Wildenstein 89); Audran.
Prov.: Commissioned by Cardinal Rospigliosi* (to
whom the engraving by Pietro del Po is
dedicated); disappeared at the beginning of the
nineteenth century.
Cat.: Blunt 99; Thuillier 202; Wild 120; Wright L.20
Must date from *c*. 1656–8.

THE SEVEN SACRAMENTS

102–108
FIRST SERIES
FOR DAL POZZO

101 *St Margaret*
Turin, Galleria Sabauda
Canvas, 213 x 145 (83¼ x 57)
Prov.: Commissioned by Cassiano Dal Pozzo*, or his cousin, Amadeo dal Pozzo, Marchese di Voghera*; in the collection of the House of Savoy from 1741.
Cat.: Blunt 104; Thuillier 100; Wild 80; Wright 100.
Exh.: Paris 1960, 58; Bologna 1962, 70; Rome-Düsseldorf 1977–8, 23.
Generally dated a little earlier than 1640 (1636–7 according to Thuillier).

All canvas, 95.5 x 121 (37½ x 47½)

103 *Penance*
Lost (destroyed by fire at Belvoir Castle, 1816).
Engraving: L. de Châtillon (Wildenstein 93).
Cat.: Blunt 108; Thuillier 107; Wild 87; Wright 105.
Exh.: Edinburgh 1981, 39 (engraving).

102 *Ordination*
Belvoir Castle, Grantham, Leicestershire, the Duke of Rutland.
Prov.: Painted between 1636 and 1640 for Cassiano Dal Pozzo* (Bellori, etc.); sold to the Duke of Rutland by the Boccapaduli family in 1785.
Cat.: Blunt 110; Thuillier 111; Wild 76; Wright 109.
Exh.: Edinburgh 1981, 31.
See p. 98.

104 *Marriage*
Present ownership and provenance, as for No. 102.
Cat.: Blunt 111; Thuillier 108; Wild 43; Wright 106.
Exh.: Edinburgh 1981, 32.
See p. 98.

105 *Extreme Unction*
Present ownership and provenance, as for
No. 102.
Cat.: Blunt 109; Thuillier 109; Wild 44; Wright 107.
Exh.: Bologna 1962, 68; Edinburgh 1981, 33.
See p. 99.

107 *Confirmation*
Present ownership and provenance, as for
No. 102.
Cat.: Blunt 106; Thuillier 110; Wild 87; Wright 108.
Exh.: Paris 1960, 61; Bologna 1962, 69; Edinburgh
1981, 35.
See p. 98.

Edinburgh, National Gallery of Scotland
(on loan from the Duke of Sutherland).
All canvas, 117 x 178 (46 x 70)

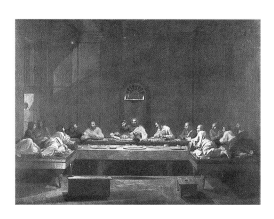

106 *The Eucharist*
Present ownership and provenance, as for
No. 102.
Cat.: Blunt 107; Thuillier 112; Wild 89; Wright 110.
Exh.: Edinburgh 1981, 34.
See p. 98.

108 *Baptism*
Washington, D.C., National Gallery of Art
(Samuel H. Kress Collection)
Prov.: See No. 102; sold c. 1939 by the Duke of
Rutland, then passed into the Kress collection.
Cat.: Blunt 105; Thuillier 113; Wild 105; Wright
111.
Incomplete at the end of 1640, the painting was
finished by Poussin in Paris, and despatched to
Cassiano Dal Pozzo in May 1642.
See p. 99.

109 *Extreme Unction*
Prov.: The set of seven paintings was
commissioned by Paul Fréart de Chantelou*
(correspondence, etc.); this work was begun on
14 April 1644, completed on 20 October and
despatched on 30 October; Chantelou collection,
Paris; the Duc d'Orléans in 1716; sold in 1798 in
London (with the Galerie d'Orléans) to the Duke
of Bridgewater; passed to the Duke of Sutherland
by inheritance.
Cat.: Blunt 116; Thuillier 140; Wild 121; Wright
124.
Exh.: Paris 1960, 69; Edinburgh 1981, 40.
See p. 106.

110 *Confirmation*
See No. 109. Begun on 30 April 1645, completed on 10 December.
Cat.: Blunt 113; Thuillier 141; Wild 125; Wright 125.
Exh.: Paris 1960, 70; Edinburgh 1981, 41.
See p. 106.

112 *Penance*
See No. 109. Begun before 4 February 1647, completed on 3 June.
Cat.: Blunt 115; Thuillier 143; Wild 131; Wright 127.
Exh.: Paris 1960, 72; Edinburgh 1981, 52.
See p. 107.

114 *The Eucharist*
See No. 109. Begun before 1 September 1647, finished by 3 November.
Cat.: Blunt 114; Thuillier 145; Wild 134; Wright 129.
Exh.: Paris 1960, 74; Edinburgh 1981, 54.
See p. 106.

111 *Baptism*
See No. 109. Completed on 18 November 1646.
Cat.: Blunt 112; Thuillier 142; Wild 130; Wright 126.
Exh.: Paris 1960, 71; Edinburgh 1981, 47.
See p. 106.

113 *Ordination*
See No. 109. Begun on 3 June 1647, despatched before 19 August.
Cat.: Blunt 117; Thuillier 144; Wild 133; Wright 128.
Exh.: Paris 1960, 73; Edinburgh 1981, 53.
See p. 106.

115 *Marriage*
See No. 109. Begun before 24 November 1647; finished by 23 March 1648.
Cat.: Blunt 118; Thuillier 146; Wild 135; Wright 130.
Exh.: Paris 1960, 75; Edinburgh 1981, 55.
See p. 106.

CLASSICAL SUBJECTS

MYTHOLOGY

117 *Apollo and Daphne*
Munich, Alte Pinakothek
Canvas, 97 x 131 (38¼ x 51½)
Prov.: Collection of the Electors of Bavaria from 1781.
Cat.: Blunt 130; Thuillier 22; Wild R.44; Wright 14; Oberhuber 19.
Félibien and Sandrart cite several versions of this subject. Details of provenance in this instance are uncertain. Dated by Thuillier *c*. 1625, it is certainly earlier than *The Death of Germanicus* (No. 184).

119 *Apollo and Daphne*
Paris, Louvre
Canvas, 155 x 200 (61 x 78¾)
Prov.: Left unfinished by Poussin shortly before his death, and given to Cardinal Camillo Massimi* (Bellori); Massimi collection during the eighteenth century; Lethière collection; acquired by Napoleon III in 1869.
Cat.: Blunt 141; Thuillier 222; Wild 205; Wright 204.
Bibl.: Panofsky 1950; Friedländer 1965; Blunt 1966.
See p. 232.

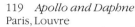

116 *Acis and Galatea*
Dublin, National Gallery of Ireland
Canvas, 98 x 137 (38½ x 54)
Prov.: In England by the eighteenth century; Spencer collection, Althorp; Leslie collection; Lane collection; bequeathed to the gallery in 1918.
Cat.: Blunt 128; Thuillier 46; Wild 37; Wright 46; Oberhuber 58.
Exh.: Rome-Düsseldorf 1977–8, 19; Edinburgh 1981, 7; Dublin 1985, 34; Fort Worth, Texas 1988, 58.
Datable to *c*. 1630 (Mahon, Rosenberg), or slightly later (Thuillier, Oberhuber).
See p. 82.

118 *Apollo and Daphne*
Lost
Engravings: Two drawings engraved during the eighteenth century, one by P. Mariette (published by Audran).
Prov.: Possibly the painting mentioned by Félibien as being in the Stella* collection, and described by Bellori.
Cat.: Blunt (under No. 130); Thuillier 105; Wild 74; Wright L.21.
Dated by Thuillier *c*. 1637.

120 *Apolla and Phaeton*
Berlin: Dahlem Museum
Canvas, 122 x 153 (48 x 60¼)
Prov.: Jean-Michel Picart in 1674 (appraised by the Académie Royale de Peinture); first recorded as being in Potsdam in 1773.
Cat.: Blunt 172; Thuillier 41; Wild 27; Wright 50; Oberhuber 59.
Exh.: Paris 1960, 40; Bologna 1962, 58.
Generally dated, after Thuillier, between 1627 and 1630.

121   *Apollo and the Muses (Parnassus)*
Madrid, Prado
Canvas, 145 x 197 (57 x 77$\frac{1}{2}$)
Prov.: Spanish royal collection, first recorded in
1746.
Cat.: Blunt 129; Thuillier 69; Wild 26; Wright 67.
Exh.: Paris 1960, 6 *bis*.
Painted *c.* 1631–3 (Mahon, Thuillier), later than
Blunt's proposed date of 1626–7.
See p. 68.

123   *The Nurture of Bacchus*
       (also known as *The Childhood of Bacchus*)
London, National Gallery
Canvas, 75 x 97 (29$\frac{1}{2}$ x 38$\frac{1}{4}$)
Prov.: Mariette collection (sold in 1775)(?);
various English collections; G. J. Cholmondeley
bequest, 1831.
Cat.: Blunt 133; Thuillier 31; Wild R.26; Wright 16;
Oberhuber 27.
Exh.: Paris 1960, 29; Rouen, 1961, 77; Rome-
Düsseldorf 1977–8, 10; Fort Worth, Texas 1988, 27.
Datable to *c.* 1626.

125   *The Nurture of Bacchus*
Chantilly, Musée Condé
Canvas, 135 x 168 (53 x 66)
Prov.: Bought in 1859 at the Northwick Sale by the
Duc d'Aumale.
Cat.: Blunt 134; Thuillier 40; Wild R.28; Wright 45;
Oberhuber 14.
Dated *c.* 1627 by Thuillier, earlier by Oberhuber
(1625), and later (in all probability too late) by
Blunt and Wright (1630–5).

122   *The Birth of Bacchus*
Cambridge, Mass., Fogg Art Museum
Canvas, 122 x 179 (48 x 70$\frac{1}{2}$)
Prov.: Painted in 1657 for Jacques Stella*
(Félibien); the Duc d'Orléans; sold, London, in
1798; Samuel Sachs, who donated it to the
museum in 1942.
Cat.: Blunt 132; Thuillier 204; Wild 193; Wright
190.
Another version (Thuillier 209), with some
variations and a little later in date, was engraved
c. 1660 by J. Verini (Wildenstein 127).
See p. 225.

124   *The Nurture of Bacchus*
       (also known as *The Childhood of Bacchus*)
Paris, Louvre
Canvas, 97 x 136 (38$\frac{1}{4}$ x 53$\frac{1}{2}$)
Prov.: Acquired by Louis XIV before 1683.
Cat.: Blunt (under No. 133: copy) and R. 64;
Thuillier 37; Wild R.27; Wright 23; Oberhuber 23.
Exh.: Paris 1960, 29; Rome-Düsseldorf 1977–8, 11;
Dublin 1985, 33; Fort Worth, Texas 1988, 23.
Rejected by Blunt, the work has since been
generally accepted as authentic and dated
c. 1626–7.
See p. 41.

126   *Bacchus/Apollo*
       (*Bacchus and Erigone*)
Stockholm, National Museum
Canvas, 98 x 73.5 ((38$\frac{1}{2}$ x 29)
Prov.: In England in the eighteenth century;
acquired by the museum in 1928.
Cat.: Blunt 135; Thuillier 33; Wild 30; Wright 20.
Exh.: Paris 1960, 12.
Bibl.: Panofsky, 1960; Grate, 1988, no. 26, pp. 56–9.
An earlier version (corresponding to a sketch in
the Fitzwilliam Museum, Cambridge) has been
revealed by X-ray examination under seventeenth-
century reworkings not by Poussin and not
reflecting – as Panofsky maintained – an alteration
of the subject from Bacchus and Erigone to
Bacchus/Apollo. The original version is datable to
1626–7.

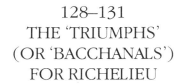

**128–131
THE 'TRIUMPHS'
(OR 'BACCHANALS')
FOR RICHELIEU**

127 *Bacchus and Ariadne*
Madrid, Prado
Canvas, 122 x 169 (48 x 66½)
Prov.: In the Spanish royal collection from 1746;
entered the museum in 1829.
Cat.: Blunt R.66; Thuillier B.8; Wild R.45; Wright
15; Oberhuber 18.
Exh.: Rome-Düsseldorf 1977–8, 1.
Possibly from the Dal Pozzo* collection. Rejected
by Blunt and Thuillier, this is, according to
Rosenberg, an original in poor condition, datable
to *c.* 1625–6.

129 *The Triumph of Bacchus*
Kansas City, Mo, Nelson-Atkins Museum of Art
Canvas, 128.5 x 151 (50½ x 59½)
Prov.: See previous entry; Ashburnham collection;
Lord Carlisle; acquired by the museum in 1932.
Cat.: Blunt 137 (copy); Thuillier 91 (copy); Wild
68; Wright 81.
Exh.: Rome-Düsseldorf 1977–8, 22; Edinburgh
1981, 24.
Regarded by Blunt and Thuillier as a copy,
reinstated by Rosenberg in 1977. This could be a
worn and over-cleaned original.

128 *The Triumph of Pan*
London, National Gallery
Canvas, 134 x 145 (52¾ x 57)
Prov.: Commissioned, perhaps in 1634, by
Cardinal Richelieu* for his château in Poitou, and
delivered in 1636; passed to Richelieu's great-
nephew, Armand; sold in the eighteenth century
(replaced by a copy) and arrived in England at an
unknown date; Ashburnham collection; Morrison
collection until 1982.
Cat.: Blunt 136; Thuillier 90b; Wild 67; Wright 82.
Exh.: Paris 1960, 45; Edinburgh 1981, 18.
Now accepted as the original (a version
bequeathed to the Louvre by P. Jamot being
regarded as a good early copy). The *Triumphs*
were frequently copied, notably for Chantelou*.

130 *The Triumph of Silenus*
Lost
Copy: See note below.
Prov.: See No. 128; the original disappeared
without trace in the eighteenth century.
Cat.: Blunt 138; Thuillier 92; Wright 83.
Exh.: Edinburgh 1981, 26 (copy).
The National Gallery in London acquired an early
copy – canvas, 143.5 x 121.5 (56½ x 47¾) – in 1824
as part of the Angerstein collection.

131 *The Triumph of Neptune and Amphitrite*
Philadelphia, Pa, Museum of Art
Canvas, 114.5 x 146.5 (45 x 57³/₄)
Prov.: See No. 128; Fromont de Brevannes
collection in 1700; Crozat collection; acquired in
1771 by Catherine the Great of Russia; sold in
1932 by the Soviet Government, and acquired by
the museum.
Cat.: Blunt 167; Thuillier 93; Wild 66; Wright 80.
Exh.: Paris 1960, 47; Edinburgh 1981, 27; Paris-
New York-Chicago 1982, 89.
Separated from the three other *Triumphs* in
Richelieu's château, this work had a different later
history. According to Thuillier, this was the
earliest of the series (1634).
See p. 91.

133 *Bacchanal before a Term of Pan*
London, National Gallery
Canvas, 100 x 142 (39¹/₄ x 56)
Prov.: In the Randon de Boisset collection, sold in
1777; was in England by the end of the eighteenth
century; various owners; purchased by the gallery
in 1826.
Cat.: Blunt 141; Thuillier 71; Wild 49; Wright 79.
Exh.: Paris 1960, 50; Edinburgh 1981, 15.
There is some controversy over dating; on
grounds of style a date in the early 1630s seems
likely.

135 *Cephalus and Aurora*
Hovingham Hall, Yorkshire, Worsley collection
Canvas, 79 x 152 (31 x 59³/₄)
Prov.; Cassiano Dal Pozzo* (?); from 1770 in the
Worsley collection.
Cat.: Blunt 145; Thuillier 15; Wild 5; Wright 6;
Oberhuber 4.
Exh. Edinburgh 1981, 1.
One of the earliest works of the Roman period
(c. 1624–5).
See p. 40

132 *Bacchanal with a Guitar Player: the
Andrians*
Paris, Louvre
Canvas, 121 175 (47³/₄ x 69)
Prov.: Duc de Richelieu*; acquired in 1665 by
Louis XIV.
Cat.: Blunt 139; Thuillier 47; Wild R.33a; Wright 43;
Oberhuber 55.
Exh.: Paris 1960, 30; Rome-Düsseldorf 1977–8, 15;
Edinburgh 1981, 4; Fort Worth, Texas 1988, 55.
Generally dated c. 1627–8

134 *Bacchanal before a Temple*
Lost; for other versions see note below
Engraving: Mariette (Wildenstein 131).
Prov.: Commissioned (in 1649?) by M. du Fresne*
(Félibien).
Cat.: Blunt 140; Thuillier 167; Wild 48; Wright A.2
(copy, private collection, Australia).
Exh.: Paris 1960, 98 (copy in San Francisco).
A very well-known works, of which around twenty
known copies were recorded by Blunt; one of
these is now in the De Young Memorial Museum,
San Francisco, Cal. The version formerly in a
private collection in Australia has been tentatively
suggested by Wright as a possible original. The
work (perhaps based on an earlier composition)
must have been executed c. 1650.

136 *Cephalus and Aurora*
London, National Gallery
Canvas, 96 x 130 (37³/₄ x 51¹/₄)
Prov.: Uncertain provenance (sold in France in
1750?); G. J. Cholmondeley Bequest, 1831.
Cat.: Blunt 144; Thuillier 30; Wild 8; Wright 24;
Oberhuber 61.
Exh.: Edinburgh 1981, 12.
This work is generally dated 1630 or slightly
earlier. Thuillier believes it was painted c. 1625–6
and altered a little later (there is evidence of many
reworkings).

137   *Diana and Endymion*
Detroit Institute of Arts
Canvas, 122 x 169 (48 x 66¹/₂)
Prov.: Cardinal Mazarin*(?) (inventory of 1653);
Fesch collection; in England at the beginning of
the present century; acquired in 1936.
Cat.: Blunt 149; Thuillier 42; Wild R.57; Wright 51;
Oberhuber 62.
Exh.: Paris 1960, 26; Bologna 1962, 59; Rome-
Düsseldorf 1977–8, 20; Paris-New York-Chicago
1982, 87; Fort Worth, Texas 1988, 62.
Generally dated just before 1630. The exact
subject matter is still slightly unclear (see bibl. in
the exhibition catalogues cited *supra*).
See p. 45.

139   *The Rape of Europa*
Lost
Drawings: Several studies, including one in
Stockholm, National Museum (inv. no. NM 68/
1923).
Prov.: Painted in 1649 for M. Pucques*(?)
(correspondence).
Cat.: Blunt 153 (fragment; see note below);
Thuillier 165; Wild 153; Wright A.5.
Blunt published a fragment, corresponding to the
right-hand side of the work – canvas, 100 x 80
(39¹/₂ x 31¹/₂) – in a private collection in Cahors,
which seems to prove that the work was not left
unfinished. The iconography is complex,
intertwining the themes of Europa and Eurydice.

141   *The Empire of Flora*
Dresden, Staatliche Kunstsammlungen:
Gemäldegalerie
Canvas, 131 x 181 (51¹/₂ x 71¹/₄)
Prov.: Painted in 1631 for Fabrizio Valguarnera*;
collection of the Elector of Saxony from 1722.
Cat.: Blunt 155; Thuillier 67; Wild 32; Wright 62;
Oberhuber 85.
Exh.: Paris 1960, 20.
Bibl.: Spear 1965; Simon 1978; Worthen 1979.
See p. 63.

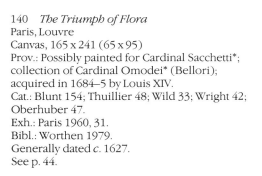

138   *Echo and Narcissus*
Paris, Louvre
Canvas, 74 x 100 (29 x 39¹/₂)
Prov.: Acquired before 1683 by Louis XIV.
Cat.: Blunt 151; Thuillier 49; Wild 19; Wright 53;
Oberhuber 71.
Exh.: Paris 1960, 22; Bologna 1962, 56; Rome-
Düsseldorf 1977–8, 16.
X-ray examination has revealed two previous
works, superimposed, beneath the visible picture
surface. Dated *c*. 1627 by Thuillier, this could be a
later work (*c*. 1630, according to Mahon and
Rosenberg).
See p. 62.

140   *The Triumph of Flora*
Paris, Louvre
Canvas, 165 x 241 (65 x 95)
Prov.: Possibly painted for Cardinal Sacchetti*;
collection of Cardinal Omodei* (Bellori);
acquired in 1684–5 by Louis XIV.
Cat.: Blunt 154; Thuillier 48; Wild 33; Wright 42;
Oberhuber 47.
Exh.: Paris 1960, 31.
Bibl.: Worthen 1979.
Generally dated *c*. 1627.
See p. 44.

142   *The Choice of Hercules*
Stourhead, Wiltshire, The National Trust
Canvas, 91 x 72 (35³/₄ x 28¹/₂)
Prov.: First recorded in England in 1747.
Cat.: Blunt 159; Thuillier B.35; Wright 116.
Exh.: Paris 1960, 49; Bologna 1962, 60.
This deceptive work is, according to Thuillier, a
copy or pastiche of a lost original, datable to
c. 1635–40.

143 Hercules and Deianira
Lost
Drawings: Windsor, Royal Library (inv. no. 11912);
Louvre, Department of Graphic Arts (inv. no.
32508), the latter engraved by Gérard Audran
(Wildenstein 158).
Prov.: Painted *c.* 1637 for Jacques Stella*
(Félibien); Chantelou*.
Cat.: Blunt L.63; Thuillier 103; Wild 86; Wright L.24.

145 The Nurture of Jupiter
Berlin, Dahlem Museum
Canvas, 97 x 133 (38¼ x 52½)
Prov.: In the collection of Frederick II of Prussia in
1786.
Cat.: Blunt 162; Thuillier 124; Wild 110; Wright
114.
Exh.: Paris 1960, 60.
Dates from just before Poussin's Paris sojourn
(1640–2).

147 Leda
Lost
Engraving: L. de Châtillon (Wildenstein 117).
Cat.: Thuillier 101.
Possibly *c.* 1636–8. A pastiche by the 'Master of
Hovingham' is extant (Worsley collection,
Hovingham Hall, Yorkshire), canvas 76 x 53
(30 x 21); cf. Blunt R.84, Thuillier R.75; Wild R.58a
and Wright A.10.

144 The Nurture of Jupiter
London, Dulwich Picture Gallery
Canvas, 95 x 118 (37½ x 46½)
Prov.: First mentioned 1757 in the collection of
Blondel de Gagny, Paris; Noël Desenfans; Sir
Francis Bourgeois; bequeathed by him to Dulwich
College, 1831.
Cat.: Blunt 161; Thuillier 120; Wild 58; Wright 89.
Exh.: Paris 1960, 48.
Datable to *c.* 1635–7. Accepted 'with reservations'
by Thuillier, who puts it a little later, *c.* 1639.
See p. 82.

146 The Nurture of Jupiter
Washington, D.C., National Gallery of Art
(Samuel H. Kress collection)
Canvas, 117 x 155 (46 x 61)
Prov.: Walpole collection; various English
collections; Kress collection, 1947; donated to the
museum in 1952.
Cat.: Blunt R.80; Thuillier R.71; Wild 94; Wright
A.31.
Exh.: Paris-New York-Chicago 1982, 92.
Rejected by Blunt and by Thuillier (who attributes
it to Charles-Alphonse Dufresnoy), but accepted
by Mahon and Rosenberg (who compares it
particularly to *Venus Presenting Arms to Aeneas* in
Rouen, No. 165). Datable to *c.* 1639.

148 Venus and Mars
Boston, Mass., Museum of Fine Arts
Canvas, 155 x 213.5 (61 x 84)
Prov.: In England in the eighteenth century;
Harcourt collection; acquired by the museum in
1940.
Cat.: Blunt 183; Thuillier 45; Wild R.17; Wright 44;
Oberhuber 80.
Exh.: Paris-New York-Chicago 1982, 86; Fort
Worth, Texas 1988, 80.
Slightly later than *The Death of Germanicus* of
1627 (No. 184), and certainly before 1630. A
drawing by Poussin with a similar composition
was engraved in 1635 by F. Chiari (Thuillier B.29).
See note to No. 163.

149   *The Hunt of Meleager and Atalanta*
Madrid, Prado
Canvas, 160 x 360 (63 x 141³/₄)
Prov.: Cassiano Dal Pozzo*(?) (inventory R. de Cotte, 1689); in the Spanish royal collection from 1701 (Poussin's name appeared for the first time in 1797).
Cat.: Blunt 163; Thuillier B.36; Wild 79; Wright A.19.
The large format and the composition would seem to indicate a hand other than Poussin's. In all probability the pendant of No. 156, *Dance in Honour of Priapus*, in São Paulo.

151   *Midas at the Source of the River Pactolus*
Ajaccio, Musée Fesch
Canvas, 50 x 66 (19³/₄ x 26)
Prov.: The painting referred to in 1631 as having been sold to Fabrizio Valguarnera* by Stefano Roccatagliata* (documented); Cardinal Fesch; entered the museum in 1839.
Cat.: Blunt 166; Thuillier 26; Wild 9; Wright 10; Oberhuber 34.
Exh.: Paris 1960, 16; Rome-Düsseldorf 1977–8, 12; Meaux 1988–9, 58.
Datable to *c.* 1626. See also the following entry.

153   *Midas Giving Thanks to Bacchus*
Munich, Alte Pinakothek
Canvas, 98 x 130 (37³/₄ x 51¹/₄)
Prov.: Possibly the painting cited 1631 à propos the Valguarnera* affair (documented); Schloss Nymphenburg, then in Munich in 1787.
Cat.: Blunt R.89; Thuillier 62; Wild 28; Wright 49; Oberhuber 7.
Exh.: Rome-Düsseldorf 1977–8, 18; Fort Worth, Texas 1988, 7.
Accepted by all the experts except Blunt, the work contains several clumsy touches – which leads Oberhuber to propose a date of 1624, which is extremely early (rather than 1629–30, which is the usually accepted date).
See p. 74.

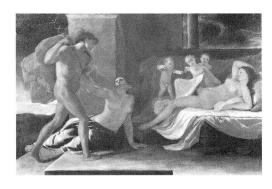

150   *Mercury, Herse and Aglauros*
Paris, Ecole Nationale Supérieure des Beaux-Arts
Canvas, 53 x 77 (20³/₄ x 30¹/₄)
Prov.: Edouard Gatteaux collection; damaged in a fire in 1871; bequeathed by Gatteaux to the Ecole des Beaux-Arts in 1881.
Cat.: Blunt 164; Thuillier B.13; Wild M.20; Wright A.26; Oberhuber 38.
Exh.: Rome-Düsseldorf 1977–8, 6; Paris 1988, p. 20, 133 (as by Claude Mellan); Meaux, 1988–9, 57.
In 1988, Thuillier cast aside his reservations about this work, which has recently been restored. In his opinion, it dates from the period immediately after Poussin's arrival in Rome, in other words 1624–5, which would explain certain inconsistencies (notably the treatment of the architecture).

152   *Midas Washing in the Pactolus*
New York, The Metropolitan Museum of Art
Canvas, 97.5 x 72.5 (38¹/₂ x 28¹/₂)
Prov.: Possibly in the collection of Cardinal Camillo Massimi* (inventory 1677); acquired by the museum in 1871.
Cat.: Blunt 165; Thuillier 35; Wild R.25; Wright 11; Oberhuber 51.
Exh.: Fort Worth, Texas 1988, 51.
A quite early work, certainly *c.* 1626–7, like the preceding entry. Another version – Oberhuber 52: canvas, 94 x 75 (37 x 29¹/₂) – is in the collection of Count Lothar zu Dohna, in New York.

154   *Marsyas and Olympus*
Private collection
Canvas, 102.5 x 89.5 (40¹/₄ x 35¹/₄)
Prov.: Fesch collection (sold in 1844); private collection, Paris; acquired in 1968 at auction (as 'School of Carracci') by the Louvre; returned to the vendors in 1988, after a long legal battle.
Cat.: Blunt L.49; Thuillier 34; Wild R.29; Wright 25; Oberhuber 15.
Bibl.: Rosenberg 1969.
Identified and published by Rosenberg, this is a very early work, *c.* 1625–6.

155 *Pan and Syrinx*
Dresden, Staatliche Kunstsammlungen:
Gemäldegalerie
Canvas, 106.5 x 82 (42 x 32½)
Prov.: Painted in 1637 for Nicolas-Guillaume de La
Fleur* (Félibien); acquired in Paris in 1742 by
Augustus III of Saxony.
Cat.: Blunt 171; Thuillier 104; Wild 75; Wright 97.
See p. 83.

157 *Venus and the Shepherds*
Dresden, Staatliche Kunstsammlungen:
Gemäldegalerie
Canvas, 71 x 96 (28 x 37¾)
Prov.: Acquired in Paris before 1722 by the Elector
of Saxony.
Cat.: Blunt 189: Thuillier B.12; Wild R.36; Wright
34; Oberhuber 12.
Exh.: Washington-New York-San Francisco,
1978–9, 531.
Accepted by Oberhuber, who dates the work to
1625, among the 'Titianesque' works of the early
Roman period. The attribution continues to be
challenged by several writers.

159 *Venus and Adonis*
Fort Worth, Texas, Kimbell Art Museum
Canvas, 98.5 x 134.6 (38¾ x 53)
Prov.: Cook collection, Richmond (on loan to the
Manchester City Art Gallery until 1983); acquired
by the museum in 1984.
Cat.: Blunt R.107; Thuillier 16; Wild R.42; Wright
35; Oberhuber 6.
Exh.: Fort Worth, Texas 1988, 6.
The best of the various versions known; datable to
c. 1624–5.
See p. 40.

156 *Dance in Honour of Priapus*
São Paulo, Museu de Arte
Canvas, 167 x 376 (65¾ x 148)
Prov.: Cassiano Dal Pozzo*(?) (inventory R. de
Cotte, 1689); Spanish royal collection from 1701;
sold at an unknown date and brought to England;
Beaumont collection, sold in 1896; Cook
collection; acquired by the museum in 1950.
Cat.: Blunt 176; Thuillier B.37; Wild 247; Wright
A.25.
In all probability the pendant of No. 149, though
rather later on grounds of style. The attribution
should be treated with caution.

158 *Venus Surprised by Satyrs*
Zurich, Kunsthaus
Canvas, 77 x 100 (30¼ x 39¼)
Prov.: the Earls of Yarborough, Brocklesby Park,
Lincolnshire; acquired in 1939.
Cat.: Blunt R.113; Thuillier B.14; Wild R.31; Wright
A.34; Oberhuber 16.
Exh.: Paris 1960, 34; Fort Worth, Texas 1988, 16.
Generally rejected (except by Oberhuber, who
dates it 1626). Even if this is a work by an imitator
of Poussin, this painting (and the variations of it in
other collections) gives an idea of Poussin's
'commercial' output at the beginning of his
Roman period.

160 *Venus and Adonis*
Providence, R.I., Museum of Art, Rhode Island
School of Design
Canvas, 75 x 99 (29½ x 39)
Prov.: In 1766 in the collection of Sir Joshua
Reynolds; several English collections; acquired in
1954.
Cat.: Blunt 185; Thuillier 29; Wild 6; Wright 21;
Oberhuber 37.
Original worn and over-painted, dated by
Thuillier to the early Roman years (c. 1626?).

161   *Venus and Adonis*
Caen, Musée des Beaux-Arts
Canvas, 57 x 126 (22^{1}/$_{2}$ x 49^{1}/$_{2}$)
Prov.: Collection of Louis XIV c. 1683; sent to Caen in 1803.
Cat.: Blunt 186; Thuillier 19; Wild 7; Wright 13; Oberhuber 33.
Exh.: Paris 1960, 25; Rome-Düsseldorf, 1977–8, 14.
Datable to c. 1627, possibly slightly earlier.

163 A and B *Venus and Mercury*
Canvas, cut into two pieces in the eighteenth century:
(A) London, Dulwich Picture Gallery (Venus and Mercury), 78 x 85 (30^{5}/$_{4}$ x 33^{1}/$_{2}$);
(B) Paris, Louvre (Concert of Cupids), 57 x 51 (22^{1}/$_{2}$ x 20).
Prov.: Lankrinck collection, sold in 1693; Van Meijer collection, sold in 1722; the Elector of Cologne, sold in 1764 (the division must have taken place at about this date); the Cupids fragment acquired by the Duc de Penthièvre in 1764, and confiscated in 1793, when it became part of the French national collections; the Venus and Mercury fragment passed from the J. B. P. Lebrun collection to Noël Desenfans, then to Sir Francis Bourgeois, by whom it was bequeathed to Dulwich College in 1811.

164   *Venus Presenting Arms to Aeneas*
Toronto, Art Gallery of Ontario
Canvas, 107 x 133 (42 x 52^{1}/$_{4}$)
Prov.: the Prince of Cellamare, Naples (inscription on the engraving by Aquila); the Duke of Lucca (collection sold in 1841); acquired by the gallery in 1948.
Cat.: Blunt 190; Thuillier 98; Wild 72; Wright 93.
Exh.: Paris 1960, 44.
The attribution is still doubtful. Close to Poussin's works of 1635–6.

162   *Venus and Cupid*
Lost
Engraving: Baudet (Rome, 1665)
Cat.: Blunt 187; Thuillier 122; Wild R.39; Wright L.29.
This work, whose history is unknown, may, according to Thuillier, have been executed c. 1638–40.

Cat.: Blunt 184; Thuillier 32; Wild R.18; Wright 12; Oberhuber 28.
Exh.: Paris 1960, 35–36; Dulwich 1986–7 ('dossier'); Fort Worth, Texas 1988, 28a (Dulwich fragment).
Generally thought to date from c. 1627 and believed by some to be the pendant of No. 148. A drawing by Poussin in the Louvre, an engraving by F. Chiari (1636) and an eighteenth-century copy (Lille, Musée des Beaux-Arts) made it possible to reconstitute the composition as a whole.

165   *Venus Presenting Arms to Aeneas*
Rouen, Musée des Beaux-Arts
Canvas, 105 x 142 (41^{1}/$_{4}$ x 56)
Prov.: Painted in 1639 for Jacques Stella* (Félibien); in several English collections in the eighteenth century; acquired by the museum in Paris in 1866.
Cat.: Blunt 191; Thuillier 119; Wild 90; Wright 112.
Exh.: Paris 1960, 59; Rouen 1961, 82.
See p. 86.

166 *Nymph on the Back of a Goat*
Leningrad, Hermitage Museum
Canvas, 72 x 56 (28¼ x 22)
Prov.: Possibly in the Crozat collection (acquired by Catherine the Great of Russia in 1771).
Cat.: Blunt 199; Thuillier 80; Wild 52; Wright 17.
Thuillier dates the work to *c.* 1633–5.

168 *Nymph and Satyr Drinking*
Dublin, National Gallery of Ireland
Canvas, 73 x 59 (28¾ x 23¼)
Prov.: The Dukes of Sutherland; Sir Hugh Lane; bequeathed by him to the gallery in 1918.
Cat.: Blunt 200 (copy); Thuillier 39; Wild R.24; Wright 19a; Oberhuber 43.
Exh.: Dublin 1985, 32; Fort Worth, Texas 1988, 43.
Like Nos. 169 and 170, this work can be dated *c.* 1626–7, a time when Poussin had to restrict himself to subjects which were easy to sell.

170 *Nympth and Satyr Drinking*
Moscow, Pushkin Museum
Canvas, 77 x 62 (30¼ x 24½)
Prov.: Crozat collection (inventory of 1755); acquired by Catherine the Great of Russia in 1771.
Cat.: Blunt 200; Thuillier 39b; Wild R.24; Wright 19c; Oberhuber 45.

167 *Nymph on the Back of a Satyr*
Canvas, 96.5 x 75.5 (38 x 29¾)
Kassel, Staatliche Gemäldegalerie
Prov.: From 1749 in the collection of Landgrave Wilhelm of Hesse.
Cat.: Blunt 198; Thuillier 38; Wild R.30; Wright 18; Oberhuber 79.
Dates from the latter half of the 1620s.

169 *Nymph and Satyr Drinking*
Madrid, Prado
Canvas, 74 x 60 (29 x 23½)
Prov.: Possibly acquired in 1724 by Philip V of Spain, as part of the Maratta collection.
Cat.: Blunt 200 (copy); Thuillier 39a; Wild R.24; Wright 19b; Oberhuber 44.
Exh.: Rome-Düsseldorf, 1977–8, 9; Fort Worth, Texas 1988, 44.

171 *Nymphs Bathing*
Lost
Engraving: E. Jeaurat (Andresen-Wildenstein 384)
Prov.: Painted in 1633–4 for Charles (I), Maréchal de Créquy* (Félibien); passed into the collection of Jacques Stella*, and then to his heirs.
Cat.: Blunt L.117; Thuillier 84; Wild 57; Wright A.18.
According to Wright, there is a canvas (ruined) – 110 x 81 (43¼ x 31¾) – in the collection of George Zarnecki in London, which could be a good early copy or even the original.

172   *Putto with a Cornucopia*
Rome, Pallavicini-Rospigliosi collection
Canvas (fragment), 54.8 x 51.8 (21¹/₂ x 20¹/₂)
Prov.: Mentioned in the 1713 inventory of the
Rospigliosi collection.
Cat.: Blunt 161 (copy); Thuillier 23; WIld R.32;
Wright A.28; Oberhuber 9.
According to Blunt, this is a copy of part of *The
Nurture of Jupiter* (No. 144). Thuillier, however,
considers it to be a fragment of a composition
from Poussin's very early years in Rome.

174   *Bacchanal of Putti*
Rome, Galleria Nazionale d'Arte Antica
(Palazzo Barberini).
Tempera on canvas, 56 x 76.5 (22 x 30)
Prov.: Cardinal Flavio Chigi (inventory of 1693);
Chigi collection; Incisa della Rocchetta collection;
acquired by the gallery in 1978.
Cat.: Blunt 192; Thuillier 27; Wild 39; Wright 47;
Oberhuber 56.
Exh.: Paris 1960, 5; Bologna 1962, 55; Rome-
Düsseldorf 1977–8, 3.
Possibly executed, like No. 175, before December
1626, when Cardinal Barberini* returned to
Rome. Poussin was then sharing lodgings with the
sculptor François Duquesnoy*, who specialized in
scenes with children.

176   *Cupids Playing*
Leningrad, Hermitage
Canvas, 95 x 72 (37¹/₄ x 28¹/₄)
Prov.: Crozat collection; acquired in 1771 by
Catherine the Great of Russia.
Cat.: Blunt 196; Thuillier 70; Wild R.59b; Wright
A.11.
Dated by Blunt and Thuillier *c.* 1630–3.

173   *Cupids and Dogs*
Leningrad, Hermitage Museum
Canvas, 68.5 x 51 (26³/₄ x 20)
Prov.: Possibly in the collection of Cardinal
Mazarin* (inventory of 1653); Crozat collection;
acquired in 1771 by Catherine the Great of Russia.
Cat.: Blunt 195; Thuillier B.33; Wild R.59a; Wright
A.12; Oberhuber 5.
Accepted by Blunt and Oberhuber (who dates it
1624), rejected by Thuillier, who attributes it to
Nicolas Chaperon – under whose name it
appeared in the Crozat inventory of 1740.

175   *Bacchanal of Putti*
Rome, Galleria Nazionale d'Arte Antica
(Palazzo Barberini)
Tempera on canvas 74.5 x 85.5 (29¹/₄ x 33³/₄)
Prov.: See previous entry.
Cat.: Blunt 193; Thuillier 28; Wild 38; Wright 38;
Oberhuber 57.
Exh.: Paris 1960, 6; Rome-Düsseldorf 1977–8, 4.
See note to No. 174.

177   *Five Cupids Playing*
Lisbon, Gulbenkian Foundation
Canvas, 52 x 39 (20¹/₂ x 15¹/₄)
Prov.: Possibly in the Nyert and Randon de Boisset
collections in the eighteenth century; collecton of
the Dukes of Westminster; acquired at auction in
London in 1924.
Cat.: Blunt R.109; Thuillier 86; Wild R.43; Wright
A.16.
Rejected by Blunt and Wild; accepted by Thuillier,
who dates the work *c.* 1633–5.

CLASSICAL SUBJECTS

HEROES,
ANCIENT HISTORY

179 *Achilles among the Daughters of Lycomedes*
Richmond, Va, Museum of Fine Arts
Canvas, 100.5 x 133.5 (39¹/₂ x 52¹/₂)
Prov.: No doubt the work painted for Charles (III),
Duc de Créquy* (receipt dated November 1656,
inventory of 1687); in several French collections,
and in English collections in the eighteenth
century; acquired by the museum in 1957.
Cat.: Blunt 127; Thuillier 199; Wild 191; Wright
A.27.
Exh.: Paris 1960, 111.
The composition was known to exist from an
anonymous engraving (Wildenstein 104), until the
reappearance of the painting, now in Richmond, a
work which Thuillier considers to be an early
copy, or rather 'an original which has undergone
considerable repainting'.

181 *Camillus and the Schoolmaster of Falerii*
Paris, Louvre
Canvas, 252 x 268 (99¹/₄ x 105¹/₂)
Prov.: Painted in 1637 for Louis Phélypeaulx de La
Vrillière* (Félibien); and hung in the gallery of
his town-house in Paris (the building owned
subsequently by the Comte de Toulouse and then
by the Duc de Penthièvre); confiscated in 1794,
after which it entered the French national
collections.
Cat.: Blunt 142; Thuillier 106; Wild 78; Wright 98.
Exh.: Paris 1960, 46; Paris 1988–9, 116.
See note to No. 180.
See p. 141.

178 *Achilles among the Daughters of Lycomedes*
Boston, Mass., Museum of Fine Arts
Canvas, 97 x 129.5 (38 x 51)
Prov.: Described by Bellori (1672); mentioned
from 1777 in several English collections; acquired
by the museum in 1946.
Cat.: Blunt 126; Thuillier 184; Wild 163; Wright
183.
Certainly dating from after 1650.
See p. 215.

180 *Camillus and the Schoolmaster of Falerii*
Pasadena, Cal., the Norton Simon Museum
Canvas, 100 x 137 (39¹/₄ x 54)
Prov.: Doubtless the work painted for M. Passart*
(Félibien); collection of the Princes of
Schaumburg-Lippe in the eighteenth century;
Prince Paul of Yugoslavia; Henry Levy; acquired by
the museum in 1980.
Cat.: Blunt 143; Thuillier 89; Wild 65; Wright 99.
Painted several years before the larger version for
La Vrillière (No. 181), which dates from 1637.
Blunt refused to recognize this work as the
version intended for Passart.

182 *Coriolanus*
Les Andelys, Musée Municipal
Canvas, 112 x 198.5 (44 x 78)
Prov.: In the collection of the Marquis d'Hauterive
at the end of the seventeenth century (Félibien);
in several French collections in the eighteenth
century; confiscated in 1794; sent to Evreux in
1802, then to Les Andelys in 1832.
Cat.: Blunt 147; Thuillier 183; Wild 152; Wright
139.
Exh.: Rouen 1961, 85; Rome-Düsseldorf 1977–8,
37; Dublin 1985, 36.
Dated by Mahon and Blunt to the mid- or
late-1640s, and by Thuillier 1650–5.
See p. 144.

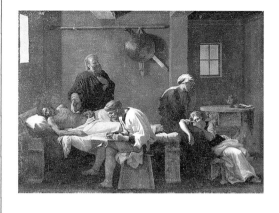

183 *The Testament of Eudamidas*
Copenhagen, Statens Museum for Kunst
Canvas, 110.5 x 138.5 (43¹/₂ x 54¹/₂)
Prov.: Painted for M. Passart* (Bellori); acquired
by the museum in 1931, from Count Moltke's
descendants.
Cat.: Blunt 152; Thuillier 187; Wild 122; Wright
177.
Exh.: Paris 1960, 97.
The Copenhagen picture, of uncertain
provenance, is very worn. There are known to be
many copies, and a 'preparatory sketch' in oils on
paper is cited in an English private collection
(Thuillier B.45). The date is controversial:
c. 1643–4 according to Mahon, between 1650 and
1655 according to Blunt and Thuillier, which
seems more likely.
See p. 140.

185 *Hannibal Crossing the Alps*
Cambridge, Mass., Fogg Art Museum
(on loan from Vermeer Associates)
Canvas, 100 x 133 (39¹/₄ x 52¹/₄)
Prov.: Sometimes identified as one of the two
'quadri d'Elefanti' cited in the Dal Pozzo*
collection in 1715; private collection, Paris;
Vermeer Associates.
Cat.: Blunt 157; Thuillier B.17; Wild 11; Wright 38;
Oberhuber 22.
Exh.: Rouen 1961, 94; Fort Worth, Texas 1988, 22.
Rejected by Thuillier, as being the work of an
imitator of Poussin, the painting was certainly by
one of Poussin's immediate circle, and dates from
c. 1626–7 (Blunt, Oberhuber).

187 *The Rape of the Sabine Women*
New York, The Metropolitan Museum of Art
Canvas, 154.5 x 210 (60³/₄ x 82³/₄)
Prov.: Charles (I), Maréchal de Créquy* (inventory
of 1638); Cardinal Richelieu*; then his niece, the
Duchesse d'Aiguillon; in various French, then
English, collections in the eighteenth century;
Cook collection, Richmond; acquired by the
museum in 1946.
Cat.: Blunt 180; Thuillier 88; Wild 62; Wright 84.
Exh.: Paris 1960, 51; Paris-New York-Chicago 1982,
90.
Bibl.: Arikha 1979; Boyer and Volf 1988 (p. 32,
no. cxxx).
The recent publication of the 1638 inventory has
made it possible to establish the date and original
owner of this work, painted June-July 1634, when
Maréchal de Créquy was ambassador in Rome.

184 *The Death of Germanicus*
Minneapolis, Minn., Institute of Arts
Canvas, 148 x 198 (58¹/₄ x 78)
Prov.: Painted between late 1626 and early 1628
for Cardinal Francesco Barberini* (Barberini
Archives); Barberini collection; Corsini collection;
acquired by the museum in 1958.
Cat.: Blunt 156; Thuillier 43; Wild 15; Wright 26;
Oberhuber 49.
Exh.: Paris 1973 ('dossier'); Rome-Düsseldorf,
1977–8, 13; Paris-New York-Chicago 1982, 85; Fort
Worth, Texas 1988, 49.
See p. 43.

186 *The Saving of the Young Pyrrhus*
Paris, Louvre
Canvas, 116 x 160 (45³/₄ x 63)
Prov.: Painted for Giovanni Maria Roscioli*
(payment of 1634); the Duc de Richelieu*;
acquired by Louis XIV in 1665.
Cat.: Blunt 178; Thuillier 94; Wild 47; Wright 85.
Exh.: Paris 1960, 54; Bologna 1962, 63; Rome-
Düsseldorf 1977–8, 24.
Bibl.; Barroero 1979.
The date of this work was brought forward by
three or four years following the discovery of the
account book belonging to Roscioli.

188 *The Rape of the Sabine Women*
Paris, Louvre
Canvas, 159 x 206 (62¹/₂ x 81)
Prov.: Painted for Cardinal Omodei* (Bellori);
acquired by Louis XIV in 1685.
Cat.: Blunt 179; Thuillier 114; Wild 61; Wright 101.
Exh.: Paris 1960, 41; Paris 1979 ('dossier').
Bibl.: Arikha 1979.
Considerably later than the New York version
(No. 187); datable to *c.* 1637–8.
See p. 194.

189   *The Continence of Scipio*
Moscow, Pushkin Museum
Canvas, 114.5 x 163.5 (45 x 64$^1/_2$)
Prov.: Painted for Giovanni Maria Roscioli*
(payment in 1640); Walpole collection; acquired
by Catherine the Great of Russia in 1779.
Cat.: Blunt 181; Thuillier 135; Wild 109; Wright
135.
Bibl.: Barroero, 1979.
Dated to between 1643 and 1649 by the experts,
until revised following the discovery of Roscioli's
account book. The work was executed shortly
before Poussin's departure for Paris at the end of
1640.
See p. 140.

191   *Queen Zenobia*
Leningrad, Hermitage
Canvas, 156 x 194 (61$^1/_2$ x 76$^1/_4$)
Prov.: Possibly in the Rospigliosi* collection
(inventory of 1713); entered the museum in 1931,
transferred from the Academy of Fine Arts.
Cat.: Blunt L.28; Thuillier 210; Wild 170 (sketch);
Wright A.13.
This painting, not developed beyond the stage of a
rough sketch, has been associated by Thuillier
with the artist's late works (*c*. 1657–60). Another
version of this composition was included in the
Dufourny sale (1819) as being by Dufresnoy. A
preparatory drawing is in the National Museum in
Stockholm (inv. no. NM 2451/1863).

190   *Theseus Finding his Father's Shield*
Chantilly, Musée Condé
Canvas, 98 x 134 (38$^1/_2$ x 52$^3/_4$)
Prov.: In the Knight and Higginson collections in
the nineteenth century; acquired in London in
1860 by the Duc d'Aumale.
Cat.: Blunt 182; Thuillier 77; Wild 60; Wright 73.
The Chantilly painting would appear to be of
better quality than any of the other known
versions – such as that in the Uffizi in Florence,
studied by Rosenberg (Rome-Düsseldorf
exhibition, 1977–8, 21). Poussin may have sought
Jean Lemaire's* collaboration as regards the
architecture. Probably executed about the same
time as *The Adoration of the Magi* (No. 59),
c. 1633.

192   *Rinaldo and Armida*
Moscow, Pushkin Museum
Canvas, 95 x 113 (37$^1/_2$ x 44$^1/_2$)
Prov.: Acquired in 1766 by Catherine the Great of
Russia; transferred from the Hermitage in
Leningrad in 1930.
Cat.: Blunt 203; Thuillier 10; Wild M.8; Wright 22;
Oberhuber 53.
Very early, according to Thuillier (*c*. 1624–5), but
generally thought to be later (1628 according to
Oberhuber, and the early 1630s according to
Blunt).

193   *Rinaldo and Armida*
London, Dulwich Picture Gallery
Canvas, 80 x 107 (31½ x 42)
Prov.: *c.* 1804 in England, in the Noël Desenfans
collection; Sir Francis Bourgeois; bequeathed by
him to Dulwich College in 1811.
Cat.: Blunt 202; Thuillier 24; Wild M.43; Wright 64;
Oberhuber 81.
Exh.: Paris 1960, 14; Edinburgh 1981, 8; Fort
Worth, Texas 1988, 81.
Generally dated to just before 1630, like the
Massacre of the Innocents in Chantilly (No. 64), to
which it relates, though Thuillier considers it to
be much earlier (*c.* 1625).
See p. 50.

195   *The Companions of Rinaldo*
New York, The Metropolitan Museum of Art
Canvas, 119 x 101 (46¾ x 39⅝)
Prov.: Cassiano Dal Pozzo*(?) (Robert de Cotte
inventory, 1689); Harrach collection in Austria;
Wrightsman collection, New York; acquired by the
museum in 1977.
Cat.: Blunt 205; Thuillier 74; Wild 71; Wright 78.
Exp.: Paris 1960, 32.
Dated *c.* 1631–3 by Thuillier, who believes this to
be a fragment of a larger canvas.

197   *Tancred and Erminia*
Birmingham, Barber Institute of Fine Arts
Canvas, 75 x 100 (29½ x 39¼)
Prov.: Purchased in Paris in 1717 by Sir James
Thornhill; various English collections; acquired by
the Barber Institute in 1938.
Cat.: Blunt 207; Thuillier 99; Wild 55; Wright 66.
Exh.: Paris 1960, 53; Edinburgh 1981, 14.
Datable to the mid-1630s.

194   *Rinaldo and Armida*
Lost
Engraving.: G. Chasteau (Wildenstein 164).
Prov.: Painted *c.* 1637 for Jacques Stella*
(Félibien).
Cat.: Blunt 204; Thuillier 102; Wild 77; Wright 90.
Known from several preparatory drawings (in the
Louvre and the Royal Library, Windsor) and from
early copies, the best of which – canvas, 122 x 151
(48 x 59½), formerly in Potsdam and now in the
Bodemuseum in Berlin – is sometimes regarded
as the original. A different composition on the
same theme is described by Bellori and
catalogued by Thuillier (97), who considers it to
be slightly earlier than the version painted for
Stella.

196   *Tancred and Erminia*
Leningrad, Hermitage Museum
Canvas, 98 x 147 (38½ x 57¾)
Prov.: Acquired in 1766 from Abel the painter, in
Paris, by Catherine the Great of Russia.
Cat.: Blunt 206; Thuillier 68; Wild (under entry
no. 55); Wright 65.
Exh.: Paris 1960, 42
Dated by Mahon and Thuillier to the very
beginning of the 1630s, but possibly earlier still
(the 'romantic' style is reminiscent of the second
half of the 1620s).
See p. 96.

ALLEGORICAL WORKS

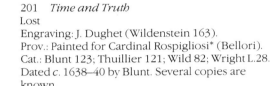

199 *Et in Arcadia Ego*
  (*The Arcadian Shepherds*)
Paris, Louvre,
Canvas, 85 x 121 (33½ x 47½)
Prov.: Doubtless painted for Cardinal Rospigliosi*
(Bellori); acquired by Louis XIV in 1685.
Cat.: Blunt 120; Thuillier 116; Wild 83; Wright 104.
Exh.: Paris 1960, 99.
Bibl.: Panofsky 1969.
Dates from slightly before 1640.
See p. 93.

201 *Time and Truth*
Lost
Engraving: J. Dughet (Wildenstein 163).
Prov.: Painted for Cardinal Rospigliosi* (Bellori).
Cat.: Blunt 123; Thuillier 121; Wild 82; Wright L.28.
Dated *c.* 1638–40 by Blunt. Several copies are
known.

198 *Et in Arcadia Ego*
  (*The Arcadian Shepherds*)
Chatsworth, Derbyshire, The Trustees of the
Chatsworth Settlement
Canvas, 101 x 82 (39¾ x 32½)
Prov.: Massimi* collection (Bellori); Loménie de
Brienne* (?); brought to England; recorded in the
collection of the Dukes of Devonshire from 1761.
Cat.: Blunt 119; Thuillier 55; Wild 13; Wright 54;
Oberhuber 50.
Exp.: Paris 1960, 19; Edinburgh 1981, 5; Fort
Worth, Texas 1988, 50.
Bibl.: Panofsky 1969.
Dates from the late 1620s.
See p. 92.

200 *The Dance to the Music of Time*
London, Wallace Collection
Canvas, 83 x 105 (32¾ x 41¼)
Prov.: Painted for Cardinal Rospigliosi* (Bellori);
Fesch collection, sold in 1845; the Marquess of
Hertford; Sir Richard Wallace.
Cat.: Blunt 121; Thuillier 123; Wild 95; Wright 115.
Bibl.: Blunt 1976.
Quite probably painted between 1638 and 1640.
See p. 94.

202 *Time and Truth Destroying Envy and
  Discord*
Paris, Louvre
Canvas, diameter 297 (117).
Prov.: Commissioned in 1641 by Cardinal
Richelieu* for the ceiling of the Grand Cabinet in
the Palais Cardinal, Paris (correspondence);
bequeathed to Louis XIII in 1642.
Cat.: Blunt 122; Thuillier 129; Wild 102; Wright
120.
Exh.: Paris 1960, 63; Rouen 1961, 83.
An oil sketch – on canvas, 50 x 38 (19¾ x 15) – with
numerous variations is in the Musée des Beaux-
Arts, Lille (Thuillier B.40); its attribution is still a
matter of dispute.
See p. 123.

203 *The Inspiration of the Poet*
Hanover, Niedersächsische Landesgalerie
Canvas, 94 x 69.5 (37 x 27½)
Prov.: In the collection of the Electors of Hanover from 1679.
Cat.: Blunt 125; Thuillier 56; Wild 14; Wright 55; Oberhuber 35.
Exh.: Paris 1960, 18; Paris 1989, 2.
Bibl.: See the following entry.
Dates from the latter part of the 1620s (1627 according to Oberhuber).

205 *The Triumph of Ovid*
Rome, Galleria Nazionale d'Arte Antica
(Palazzo Corsini)
Canvas, 148 x 176 (58¼ x 69¼)
Prov.: Chigi collection, Rome; entered the gallery in 1954.
Cat.: Blunt R.92; Thuiller B.5; Oberhuber 3.
Bibl.: Thuillier in *Colloque Poussin*, 1960, II, p. 266 (No. 9).
Thuillier believes this to be one of Poussin's earliest Roman paintings (1624), in honour of his patron, the poet Giambattista Marino*.

204 *The Inspiration of the Poet*
Paris, Louvre
Canvas 184 x 214 (72½ x 84¼)
Prov.: Cardinal Mazarin* (inventory of 1653); in the collection of the Marquis de Lassay in the eighteenth century; sold in England, 1772; Thomas Hope, then his descendants, until 1910; acquired by the museum in 1911.
Cat.: Blunt 124; Thuillier 61; Wild 18; Wright 56; Oberhuber 54.
Exh.: Paris 1960, 8; Paris 1989, 1 ('dossier').
Bibl.: Fumaroli 1989.
X-ray examination has revealed some important reworkings. Datable to *c*. 1630, or slightly later.
See p. 54.

206 *Spring*
(or *Adam and Eve in the Garden of Eden*)
Paris, Louvre
Canvas, 117 x 160 (46 x 63)
Prov.: Painted between 1660 and 1664 for the Duc de Richelieu* (Félibien); acquired in 1665 by Louis XIV.
Cat.: Blunt 3; Thuillier 211; Wild 204a; Wright 200.
Exh.: Paris 1960, 115.
Bibl.: Sauerländer 1956; Friedländer 1962.
See p. 238.

207   *Summer*
(or *Ruth and Boaz*)
Paris, Louvre
Canvas, 119 x 160 (46³/₄ x 63)
Prov.: As for No. 206.
Cat.: Blunt 4; Thuillier 212; Wild 204b; Wright 201.
Exh.: Paris 1960, 116, Bologna 1962, 86.
Bibl.: See No. 206.
See p. 239.

209   *Winter*
(or *The Flood*)
Paris, Louvre
Canvas, 118 x 160 (46¹/₂ x 63)
Prov.: As for No. 206.
Cat.: Blunt 6; Thuillier 214; Wild 204d; Wright 203.
Exh.: Paris 1960, 118.
Bibl.: See No. 206.
See p. 247.

208   *Autumn*
(or *The Promised Land*)
Paris, Louvre
Canvas, 117 x 160 (46 x 63)
Prov.: As for No. 206.
Cat.: Blunt 5; Thuillier 213; Wild 204c; Wright 202.
Exh.: Paris 1960, 117; Bologna 1962, 87.
Bibl.: See No. 206.
See p. 246.

210   *Landscape with Hagar and the Angel*
Rome, Private collection
Canvas 98 x 73 (38¹/₂ x 28³/₄)
Prov.: Altieri collection, Rome; Contessa Pasolini.
Cat.: Blunt 7; Thuillier 223; Wild 201; Wright 199.
Exh.: Rome-Düsseldorf, 1977–8, 47.
Bibl.: Chastel in *Colloque Poussin*, 1960, II, p. 239.
Possibly the right-hand side of a larger work, left unfinished and subsequently cut up. Published in 1960, this canvas is one of Poussin's very last works.

211   *St Rita of Cascia*
(also known as *The Virgin Protecting the City of Spoleto*)
London, Dulwich Picture Gallery
Panel, 48 x 37 (19 x 14¹/₂)
Prov.: In England in the Noël Desenfans collection *c.* 1800; Sir Francis Bourgeois; bequeathed by him to Dulwich College in 1811.
Cat.: Blunt 94; Thuillier 96; Wild R.28; Wright 92.
Exh.: Paris 1960, 43.
X-ray examination has revealed an earlier composition. According to Blunt, the town in the distance is Spoleto, of which Cardinal Francesco Barberini was Archbishop. The subject remains controversial, however. Dated between 1635 and 1638.
See p. 111.

212 *Landscape with Three Monks*
(also known as *Landscape with St Francis*)
Belgrade, Presidential Palace
Canvas, 117 x 193 (46 x 76)
Prov.: The Marquis d'Hauterive in the seventeenth
century (Félibien, Brienne); Prince Paul of
Yugoslavia.
Cat.: Blunt 100; Thuillier 172; Wild 165; Wright
159.
A little-known work, generally dated *c.* 1650, for
which the provenance is not fully documented. A
good early copy is in the Musée Ingres,
Montauban.

214 *Landscape with St Jerome*
Madrid, Prado
Canvas, 155 x 234 (61 x 92)
Prov.: Probably commissioned *c.* 1636–7 for Philip
IV of Spain (to hang in the Buen Retiro Palace in
Madrid).
Cat.: Blunt 103; Thuillier 95; Wild R.7; Wright 145.
Attributed to Gaspard Dughet by Wild.
See p. 110.

213 *Landscape with St John on Patmos*
Chicago, Ill., Art Institute of Chicago
Canvas, 102 x 133 (40 x 52¼)
Prov.: Painted for Giovanni Maria Roscioli*
(payment of 1640); Robit collection (sold, Paris, in
1801); then brought to England, then in the
Munich art trade; donated to the museum in 1930.
Cat.: Blunt 86; Thuillier 137; Wild 114; Wright 151.
Exh.: Paris 1960, 68; Rome-Düsseldorf 1977–8, 28;
Paris-New York-Chicago 1982, 91.
Bibl.: Barroero 1979.
Pendant of No. 215.
See p. 115.

215 *Landscape with St Matthew*
Berlin, Dahlem Museum
Canvas, 99 x 135 (39 x 53)
Prov.: Painted for Giovanni Maria Roscioli*
(payment of 1641); Barberini collection from 1671
to 1812; Colonna di Sciarra collection; acquired by
the museum in 1873.
Cat.: Blunt 87; Thuillier 136; Wild 115; Wright 150.
Exh.: Paris 1960, 66; Bologna 1962, 72; Rome-
Düsseldorf 1977–8, 27.
Bibl.: Barroero, 1979.
Pendant of No. 213. These two works are later than
was generally thought before the discovery of
Roscioli's account book.
See p. 114.

216 *Landscape with Diana and Orion*
New York, The Metropolitan Museum of Art
Canvas, 119 x 183 (47 x 72)
Prov.: Painted in 1658 for Passart* (Félibien);
known to have been in England by 1745; Lord
Methuen; acquired by the museum in 1924.
Cat.: Blunt 169; Thuillier 205; Wild 198; Wright
165.
Exh.: Paris 1960, 113; Paris-New York-Chicago
1982, 94.
Bibl.: Gombrich 1983.
See p. 229.

217   *Landscape with Hercules and Cacus*
Moscow, Pushkin Museum
Canvas, 156.5 x 202 (61½ x 79½)
Prov.: the Marquis de Conflans in the eighteenth century; acquired in 1772 by Catherine the Great of Russia; transferred from the Hermitage in Leningrad, 1930.
Cat.: Blunt 158; Thuillier 215; Wild 200; Wright 198.
Exh.: Paris 1960, 108.
Bibl.: Alpatov, 1965.
See p. 228.

219   *Landscape with Orpheus and Eurydice*
Paris, Louvre
Canvas, 120 x 200 (47¼ x 78¾)
Prov.: Acquired by Louis XIV in 1685.
Cat.: Blunt 170; Thuillier 173; Wild 174; Wright 161.
Exh.: Paris 1960, 93; Bologna 1962, 81.
Datable to between 1649 and 1651.
See p. 161.

221   *Landscape with Venus and Adonis*
Canvas, cut into two pieces.
A) Montpellier, Musée Fabre (Venus and Adonis) 75 x 113 (29½ x 44½)
B) Private collection, U.S.A (river-god, putti and dogs) 77 x 88 (30¼ x 34¾)
Prov.: Cassiano Dal Pozzo*, then his Boccapaduli heirs (inscription on the back of the painting); cut up at an unknown date; fragment A comes from the Fabre collection (bequeathed to Montpellier in 1825); fragment B comes from the Flandrin collection (acquired in a sale, London, in 1961).
Cat.: Blunt R.105 (fragment A); Thuillier B.9 and B.10; Wright 31; Oberhuber 20a and 20b. Exh.: Rome-Düsseldorf, 1977–8, 2 (fragment A); Fort Worth, Texas 1988, 20a and 20b (fragments A and B).

218   *Landscape with Juno and Argus*
Berlin, Staatliche Museen (Bodemuseum)
Canvas, 120 x 195 (47¼ x 76¾)
Prov.: Giustiniani* collection, Rome (inventory of 1638); acquired in 1812 with the Giustiniani collection by the Kaiser-Friedrich Museum, Berlin.
Cat.: Blunt 160; Thuillier 81; Wild R.5; Wright 91.
Dated by Blunt *c*. 1636–7, by Thuillier between 1633 and 1635.

220   *Landscape with Polyphemus*
Leningrad, Hermitage Museum
Canvas, 150 x 198 (59 x 78)
Prov.: Painted in 1649 for Pointel* (Félibien); the Marquis de Conflans in the eighteenth century; acquired in 1772 by Catherine the Great of Russia.
Cat.: Blunt 175; Thuillier 166; Wild 149; Wright 166.
Exh.: Paris 1960, 89.
See p. 159.

Bibl.: Whitfield 1979.
The work's attribution continues to be disputed (it could well be the work of a gifted imitator, close to both Poussin and Pietro Testa). The painting must date from before 1627. The scene is possibly Grottaferrata (cf. the inscription on the reverse of fragment A: AGRI PROPE CRYPTAM FERRATAM PROSPECTUS A NICO . . .).

222 *Landscape with Pyramus and Thisbe*
Frankfurt, Städelsches Kunstinstitut
Canvas, 192.5 x 273.5 (75³/₄ x 107³/₄)
Prov.: Painted in 1651 for Cassiano Dal Pozzo*
(correspondence); belonged to his heirs until
*c.*1740; brought to England in the middle of the
eighteenth century; acquired in 1931 from the
German art trade.
Cat.: Blunt 177; Thuillier 182; Wild 173; Wright
162.
Exh.: Frankfurt 1988, 1.
Bibl.: Marin 1981; Bätschmann 1987.
See p. 164.

224 *Landscape with Nymphs and Satyrs*
Liverpool, Walker Art Gallery
Canvas, 102.5 x 133.5 (40¹/₄ x 52¹/₂)
Prov.: Acquired in 1842 by Liverpool Royal
Institution; entered the gallery in 1949.
Cat.: Blunt R.119; Thuillier R.125; Wright 36;
Oberhuber 29.
Exh.: Rome-Düsseldorf, 1977–8, 5.
Generally rejected by the experts (apart from
Rosenberg and Oberhuber, who date it *c.* 1626–7).
This work is close to the previous entry.

223 *Amor Vincit Omnia*
(or *Landscape with Nymphs and Satyrs*)
Cleveland, Ohio, Museum of Art
Canvas, 97 x 127.5 (38¹/₄ x 50)
Prov.: Possibly in the Dal Pozzo* collection; in
several English collections during the nineteenth
century; bequeathed to the museum by J. H. Wade
in 1926.
Cat.: Blunt R.58; Thuillier R.124; Wright 37;
Oberhuber 13.
Exh.: Paris 1960, 33; Paris-New York-Chicago 1982,
84; Fort Worth, Texas 1988, 13.
Rejected by most writers, this work is sometimes
attributed to Pier Francesco Mola. Rosenberg and
Oberhuber still place it among Poussin's earliest
works, *c.* 1625.

225 *Landscape with Two Nymphs and a Snake
Attacking a Bird*
Chantilly, Musée Condé
Canvas, 118 x 179 (46¹/₂ x 70¹/₂)
Prov.: Possibly painted in 1659 for Charles Le
Brun* (Félibien); Radziwill collection; Reiset
collection; acquired in 1879 by the Duc d'Aumale.
Cat.: Blunt 208; Thuillier 208; Wild 141; Wright
197.

226 *Landscape with Diogenes*
Paris, Louvre
Canvas, 160 x 221 (63 x 87)
Prov.: Painted in 1648 for Lumagne* (Félibien);
the Duc de Richelieu*; acquired in 1665 by Louis
XIV.
Cat.: Blunt 150; Thuillier 160; Wild 139; Wright
156.
Exh.: Paris 1960, 82; Bologna 1962, 85; Rome-
Düsseldorf 1977–8, 32; Frankfurt 1988, P.8.
See p. 158.

227 *Landscape with Numa Pompilius and the Nymph Egeria*
Chantilly, Musée Condé
Canvas, 75 x 100 (29½ x 39¼)
Prov.: Possibly Dal Pozzo* collection; acquired in 1879 with the Reiset collection by the Duc d'Aumale.
Cat.: Blunt 168; Thuillier B.11; Wild R.56; Wright 33; Oberhuber 46.
The attribution is challenged by Thuillier and rejected by Wild. There are, however, clear links with Poussin's works of 1625–8.

229 *Landscape with the Gathering of the Ashes of Phocion*
Liverpool, Walker Art Gallery
Canvas, 116 x 176 (45¾ x 69¼)
Prov.: See No. 228; brought to England at an unknown date; in the collection of the Earls of Derby from 1782; Prescott, Knowsley Old Hall, Lancashire; acquired by the gallery in 1983.
Cat.: Blunt 174; Thuillier 156; Wild 176; Wright 153.
Exh.: Paris 1960, 81; Bologna 1962, 76.
Pendant of No. 228.
See p. 155

228 *Landscape with the Funeral of Phocion*
Cardiff, National Museum of Wales (on loan from the Earl of Plymouth)
Canvas, 114 x 175 (45 x 69)
Prov.: Painted in 1648 for Serisier* (Félibien); brought to England towards the middle of the eighteenth century; the Earl of Plymouth, Oakly Park, Shropshire.
Cat.: Blunt 173; Thuillier 155; Wild 175; Wright 152.
Exh.: Paris 1960, 80; Bologna 1962, 75.
Pendant of No. 229. A very good early copy in the Louvre was for long regarded as the original.
See p. 154.

230 *Landscape with a Man Washing his Feet*
London, National Gallery
Canvas, 74.5 x 100 (29¼ x 39½)
Prov.: Possibly in the Pointel* collection (inventory of 1660, No. 7); Sir George Beaumont; donated to the National Gallery in 1823.
Cat.: Blunt 211; Thuillier 159 (copy); Wild 144; Wright 158.
Generally regarded as the original, in spite of Thuillier's reservations. Datable to *c.* 1648, like the following entry.
See p. 151.

231 *Landscape with a Roman Road*
London, Dulwich Picture Gallery
Canvas, 78 x 99 (30³/₄ x 39)
Prov.: Painted in 1648 (Félibien); in 1685 in the collection of the Chevalier de Lorraine (Félibien); Noël Desenfans; Sir Francis Bourgeois; bequeathed by him to Dulwich College in 1811.
Cat.: Blunt 210; Thuillier 157 (copy); Wild 143; Wright 157.
Exh.: Paris 1960, 84.
Regarded by Blunt as the original, the Dulwich work – in a darkened and damaged state – is treated by Thuillier as a copy. The landscape has been painted over another composition which corresponds to the left-hand side of *Moses Trampling on Pharaoh's Crown* (No. 13) in the Louvre.
See p. 151.

233 *Landscape with a Man Drinking*
London, National Gallery
Canvas, 63 x 78 (24³/₄ x 30³/₄)
Prov.: Dal Pozzo* collection(?); reappeared in England in 1939; Sir George Leon collection; exhibited from 1945 on loan to the National Gallery; acquired in 1970.
Cat.: Blunt 213; Thuillier 133; Wild 113; Wright 148.
Exh.: Bologna 1962, 64.
Regarded as the pendant of No. 234; also close to No. 235. Correctly dated by Mahon before Poussin's journey to Paris, between 1637 and 1640.
See p. 110.

235 *Landscape with a Man Pursued by a Serpent* (also known as *The Effects of Terror*)
Montreal, Museum of Fine Arts
Canvas, 65 x 76 (25¹/₂ x 30)
Prov.: Possibly the work cited in 1739 by President de Brosses in the Dal Pozzo* collection; acquired in Paris *c.* 1920 by Duncan Grant; Anthony Blunt collection from 1964; acquired by the museum in 1975.
Bibl.: Blunt 1965.
Published by Blunt in 1965, and dated by him *c.* 1642–3, this work must pre-date the two paintings of Evangelists (Nos. 213 and 215) and probably dates from *c.* 1638–9, like Nos. 233, 234.

232 *Landscape with a Woman Washing her Feet*
Ottawa, National Gallery of Canada
Canvas, 114 x 175 (45 x 69)
Prov.: Painted in 1650 for Passart* (Félibien); reappeared in England at the end of the nineteenth century; acquired in 1944.
Cat.: Blunt 212; Thuillier 171; Wild 164; Wright 160.
Exh.: Paris 1960, 91.
There are other versions of this composition, of lesser quality (Chantilly, Rheims). The one in Ottawa is unanimously regarded as the original, but its subject remains a mystery.

234 *Landscape with Travellers at Rest*
London, National Gallery
Canvas, 63 x 78 (24³/₄ x 30³/₄)
Prov.: As for No. 233.
Cat.: Blunt 214; Thuillier 132; Wild 112; Wright 147.
Exh.: Bologna 1962, 65.
See previous entry.

236 *Landscape with a Man Killed by a Snake*
London, National Gallery
Canvas, 119 x 198.5 (47 x 78)
Prov.: Painted in 1648(?) for Pointel* (Félibien); brought to England at an unknown date; Strange collection, sold in 1773; acquired by the National Gallery in 1947.
Cat.: Blunt 209; Thuillier 159; Wild 140; Wright 155.
Exh.: Paris 1960, 83; Bologna 1962, 74.
Described by Fénelon in his *Deux Dialogues sur la peinture*, published in 1730. An early copy in the Musée Magnin in Dijon was for long regarded as the original.
See p. 152.

237 *Landscape with Three Men*
Madrid, Prado
Canvas, 120 x 187 (47¹/₄ x 73¹/₂)
Prov.: Possibly from the collection of Carlo
Maratta, acquired in 1722 by Philip IV of Spain;
listed in the Spanish royal collection in 1746.
Cat.: Blunt 216; Thuillier 180; Wild 142; Wright
154.
Exh.: Rome-Düsseldorf, 1977–8, 36.
Bibl.: Dempsey 1988, p. 1xiii, note 21.
Datable to *c.* 1650–1. The subject, in doubt until
recently, is, according to Dempsey, Diogenes
leaving Sparta for Athens.

239 *Landscape – a Calm*
Sudeley Castle, Gloucestershire, The Morrison
Trustees
Canvas, 97 x 131.5 (38¹/₄ x 51³/₄)
Prov.: See No. 238; in several English collections
during the eighteenth and nineteenth centuries;
Morrison collection from 1854.
Cat.: Wild 172b; Wright 164.
Exh.: Rome-Düsseldorf, 1977–8, 35.
Bibl.: Whitfield 1977.
The identification of this work and No. 238 as
pendants has been one of the most important
discoveries relating to Poussin in recent years.
See p. 162.

238 *Landscape – a Storm*
Rouen, Musée des Beaux-Arts
Canvas, 99 x 132 (39 x 52)
Prov.: Painted with its pendant (No. 239) in 1651
for Pointel* (Félibien); Bay collection, Lyons;
possibly in England at the end of the eighteenth
century; acquired in Rome in 1975.
Cat.: Blunt 217 (lost); Thuillier 181 (lost); Wild
172a; Wright 163.
Exh.: Rome-Düsseldorf 1977–8, 34.
Bibl.: Thuillier 1976.
See p. 163.

Biographical List
of Individuals Associated
with Poussin

AGUCCHI, Giovanni Battista

Born in Bologna in 1570, this prelate played an important part during the pontificate of Gregory XV (1621–3), under whom he was *Segretario dei brevi*. He was a close friend of Domenichino, and between 1607 and 1615 wrote a *Treatise on Painting* which circulated in manuscript form. He put forward the doctrine of classical idealism, which advocates a selective imitation of nature and urges the artist to express the universal while remaining close to reality. His ideas were put into practice most notably in landscape painting. They were taken up by Bellori in 1664 in his *Idea del pittore*.

ALEXANDER VII, Pope: see CHIGI, Fabio

ARPINO (Giuseppe Cesari, called the 'Cavaliere d'Arpino')

This painter, who was born in Arpino in 1568 and died in Rome in 1640, was without doubt the most fashionable painter in official Roman circles around 1600. His decorative style, influenced by late Mannerism, stood up to the innovations of the Carracci and Caravaggio. His art was beginning to go out of fashion by the time Poussin arrived in Rome, but Poussin's *Battle* pictures (cat. nos. 25 to 27) were inspired by decorative works by Cesari (1593) in the Conservatori Palace on the Capitol.

BAGLIONE, Giovanni

This painter (1573–1644) was born and died in Rome; he fell initially under the influence of Caravaggio, but later broke free. He was also an art historian and in 1642 brought out *Le Vite de' pittori, scultori et architetti, dal pontificato di Gregorio XIII nel 1572 in fino a' tempi di Papa Urbano ottavo nel 1642*, in which the young Poussin is mentioned.

BARBERINI, Antonio

Francesco's younger brother; he became a Cardinal in 1627 and was also a collector and passionately interested in natural history. Poussin is supposed to have painted pictures of birds for him (now lost). He was also a patron of both Sacchi and Maratta.

BARBERINI, Francesco

Born in Florence in 1587, he was the nephew of Pope Urban VIII (Maffeo Barberini). He became a Cardinal in 1623 and was sent on various diplomatic missions, including one to Paris in 1625. A great scholar and close friend of Cassiano Dal Pozzo and Marino, he was also a patron of artists such as Pietro da Cortona, Vouet and Le Valentin. He commissioned Poussin to paint *The Death of Germanicus* (cat. no. 184), which was delivered in 1628, and *The Capture of Jerusalem by Titus* (1638; cat. no. 33).

BARBERINI, Maffeo

Born in Florence in 1568, he was sent as a nuncio to Paris in 1604, became a Cardinal in 1617 and was elected Pope in 1623, taking the name Urban VIII. An enlightened francophile and a poet in his own right (his *Poemata* were published in 1631), he was the most notable of all patrons in Rome in the seventeenth century, commissioning work first from Caravaggio and Guido Reni, and then more particularly from Bernini and Pietro da Cortona. It was during his pontificate that Poussin painted *The Martyrdom of St Erasmus* (cat. no. 91) for St Peter's. Open to the most innovative trends, he was the chief promoter of the Roman Baroque style.

BELLORI, Giovanni Pietro

The leading Italian proponent of classical idealism was born and died in Rome (1613–96). An admirer of Raphael and the members of the Bolognese school, and a friend of both Duquesnoy and Poussin, he maintained that painting should improve on nature, and avoid the extremes of both naturalism and Mannerism. He wrote *L'Idea del pittore* (1664) and the *Vite de' pittori* (1672), which includes the first biography of Poussin.

BERNINI, Gian Lorenzo

Bernini was born in Naples in 1598 and died in Rome 1680, and dominated the whole *seicento* with his exceptional talent. He was a protégé of Urban VIII, and was the leading sculptor and architect of the first phase of the Baroque. Poussin was clearly influenced by his work *c.*1628–9, at the time when he painted *The Martyrdom of St Erasmus* (cat. no. 91) and *The Virgin Appearing to St James* (cat. no. 93). Thereafter their paths diverged, and *The Annunciation* (cat. no. 52) of 1657 perhaps constitutes a studied reply on Poussin's part to his *The Ecstasy of St Theresa*.

BORGHESE, Marcantonio

Borghese came from a family of great collectors, connected with the Aldobrandini, and commissioned three small pictures from Poussin in 1628, all of which are now lost: *St John the Baptist*, *St John the Evangelist* and *The Immaculate Conception*.

BOURDELOT, Pierre

Bourdelot was born at Sens in 1610 and died in Paris in 1684. He made a career as a doctor first in Rome, then in Paris as physician to Henri II of Condé. He acted as adviser to Christina of Sweden (1651), then to Mazarin (1653–9). Connected with the 'Libertine' group, and a friend of both Gabriel Naudé and Poussin, he wrote an *Histoire de la musique et de ses effets* (published posthumously in 1715).

BOUZONNET-STELLA, Antoine

Jacques Stella's nephew, born in Lyons in 1637 and like him a painter. He lived in Rome as part of Poussin's family circle from 1659 to 1664. After his return to France, he was elected to the Académie Royale de Peinture in 1666.

BOUZONNET-STELLA, Claudine

Jacques Stella's niece, born in Lyons in 1636; she engraved 125 plates after works by Poussin and her uncle. She and her brother Antoine inherited her uncle's collection.

BRIENNE, Louis-Henri de Loménie, Comte de

Born in Paris in 1635, Brienne had a turbulent life, starting out as a diplomat, being driven into exile, and even being interned for a time (from 1676 to 1695). He was extravagant, and a keen scholar and collector, and owned several paintings by Poussin, including *The Arcadian Shepherds: 'Et in Arcadia Ego'* (cat. no. 198) now at Chatsworth and the Woburn Abbey version of *Moses Trampling on Pharaoh's Crown* (cat. no. 12). He wrote a number of works which are still extant in manuscript form and contain a great many interesting observations about Poussin (*De Pinacotheca sua*, 1662; *Traité de la curiosité*, 1670–3; *Mémoires*, 1682–4; *Discours sur les ouvrages des plus excellents peintres anciens et modernes*).

CAMPANELLA, Tommaso

This Dominican monk, born in Calabria in 1568, put forward progressive religious, scientific and political ideas which offended the Inquisition. He was imprisoned in Naples in 1599, but was freed in 1626 thanks to Cassiano Dal Pozzo. In Paris, where he died in 1639, he was involved with the French 'Libertines'. His ideas were influenced by Stoicism and by Galileo, and were formulated primarily in his *Città del Sole*, published in Frankfurt in 1620. Poussin was clearly influenced by

Campanella in his last works (notably *The Birth of Bacchus* (cat. no. 122), the *Landscape with Diana and Orion* (cat. no. 216) and *Apollo and Daphne* (cat. no. 119).

CARAVAGGIO (Michelangelo Merisi)

A quotation from Félibien will suffice here. He reports that 'M. Pousin … could not abide Caravaggio, and said that he had come into the world to destroy painting.'

CARRACCI, Annibale

The famous Bolognese painter (1560–1609) produced the first real 'historical' landscape with *The Flight into Egypt* which he painted for the Aldobrandini, initiating a genre which Domenichino and Poussin were both to explore to good effect.

CASANATTA, Girolamo

This ecclesiastic, born in Naples in 1620, made a career at the court of Pope Innocent X, and owned Poussin's *The Triumph of David* (cat. no. 29).

CHAMPAIGNE, Philippe de

Champaigne, born in Brussels in 1602, was in Paris by 1621. He lived in the Collège de Laon with Poussin, to whom he gave one of his landscapes and with whom he worked on the decoration of the Palais du Luxembourg. He never went to Italy, however, and lived and worked in Paris until his death in 1674.

CHANTELOU, see FRÉART DE CHANTELOU

CHARMOIS, Martin de Lauzé, Sieur de

Charmois was a gentleman, born in 1605, who as a young man met Poussin and Stella in Rome. He was a painter and collector, and was a patron of the Académie Royale de Peinture from its institution in 1648. He owned *The Adoration of the Magi* (cat. no. 59).

CHIGI, Fabio

Born in Siena in 1599, he held various offices before being elected Pope in 1655 (taking the name Alexander VII). He was a patron of Bernini and Pietro da Cortona, and is chiefly famous for initiating huge restoration works in the city of Rome. He died in 1667.

CLAUDE LORRAIN (Claude Gellée)

Claude (1600–82) came to Rome when he was very young (some time between 1612 and 1620), and he worked under Agostino Tassi. He went on trips sketching the countryside around Rome with Poussin and Sandrart, and his landscape drawing is perhaps responsible for the taste which Poussin displayed for landscape in the late 1630s. The two painters remained close friends, although their individual styles developed along different lines.

COTTEBLANCHE, Monsieur de
Nothing is known about this collector, who owned the Woburn Abbey version of *Moses Trampling on Pharaoh's Crown* (cat. no. 12) after Brienne.

COURTOIS, Alexandre
Valet to Marie de Médicis and later keeper of the royal collections of paintings, Courtois was a print collector who is thought to have introduced the young Poussin to Italian Renaissance art when he first came to Paris.

CRÉQUY (or CRÉQUI), Charles I, Maréchal de
A duke and a Marshal of France, he was ambassador to the Holy See in 1633–4. While in Rome he collected a large number of pictures, recorded in the inventory of his effects carried out after his death in 1638. His collection included a great many Italian works, and several by Poussin: a version of *The Capture of Jerusalem by Titus*, now lost; another of *Woman Bathing* (cat. no. 171), also lost; and the New York version of *The Rape of the Sabine Women* (cat. no. 187).

CRÉQUY (or CRÉQUI), Charles III, Duc de
The grandson of the Marshal, he was also ambassador in Rome (in 1662–3 and 1664–5). There were at least three paintings by Poussin in his collection: *The Holy Family with the Infant St John the Baptist* now in Sarasota (cat. no. 40); *The Holy Family with St Elizabeth and St John the Baptist* (cat. no. 50), now jointly owned (Malibu and Pasadena); and *Achilles among the Daughters of Lycomedes* in Richmond (cat. no. 179).

DAL POZZO, Amadeo, Marchese di Voghera
Cassiano's cousin, who lived in Turin from 1579 to 1644. He probably com-

missioned Poussin to paint *St Margaret* (cat. no. 101), and *The Crossing of the Red Sea* (cat. no. 17) and its pendant *The Adoration of the Golden Calf* (cat. no. 21).

DAL POZZO, Carlo-Antonio
Cassiano's younger brother (1606–89) was also a member of the Barberini circle. He was passionately interested in natural history and is reputed to have commissioned Poussin to paint a set of pictures of birds for him.

DAL POZZO, Cassiano
Born in Turin in 1588 of an important Piedmontese family, Cassiano Dal Pozzo received a sound education in Bologna before settling in Rome *c.* 1612. He accompanied Cardinal Francesco Barberini on his diplomatic missions to France and Spain, and was a leading figure in Rome under Urban VIII. He had a passionate interest in history, archaeology and natural history, and conducted an enormous survey of the ancient world, the results of which were recorded and illustrated with drawings in the many volumes of the great *Museo Cartaceo*. He was a patron of artists such as Vouet, Pietro da Cortona and Pietro Testa, and played a very significant part in Poussin's early career in Rome. His collection included *Eliezer and Rebecca at the Well* (cat. no. 4), the *Virgin and Child* (cat. no. 34) and *Pietà* (cat. no. 80), *St John Baptizing the People* (cat. no. 68), *Christ in the Garden of Gethsemane* (cat. no. 77), *The Mystic Marriage of St Catherine* (cat. no. 127) and *Cephalus and Aurora* (cat. no. 135), as well as *Hannibal Crossing the Alps* (cat. no. 185), *The Companions of Rinaldo* (cat. no. 195) and a whole series of landscapes (cat. nos. 221, 222, 223, 227, 233, 234 and 235), of which the most important was the *Landscape with Pyramus and Thisbe* (222). On his death in 1657, Poussin painted *The Annunciation* (cat. no. 52) for his tomb.

DOMENICHINO (Domenico Zampieri)
This famous Bolognese painter (1581–1641) gave a more severe slant to the style developed by Annibale Carracci. His ideas were very similar to Aguchi's and he sought particularly to con-

jure up different *affetti*. Domenichino's fresco *The Scourging of St Andrew* (1608), his *Scenes from the Life of St Cecilia* (1614), and some of his large historical landscapes were among the paintings Poussin most admired in Rome *c.* 1630.

DUFRESNOY, Charles-Alphonse
Dufresnoy was a French painter and theoretician (1611–68) who spent many years in Rome (1633–53), along with Pierre Mignard. Some of his paintings owe a great deal to Poussin. *The Nurture of Jupiter* in Washington (cat. no. 174) has sometimes been attributed to him.

DUGHET, Gaspard (also called Gaspard Poussin)
Born in Rome in 1615, he was the son of Jacques Dughet, the French cook who took Poussin in and nursed him, and brother of Anne-Marie Dughet, who married Poussin in 1630. He lived with his sister and brother-in-law from 1631 to 1635, and was introduced to painting by Poussin. His taste for nature in the raw is manifest in his earliest landscapes, once attributed to a hypothetical 'Silver Birch Master'. He quickly became famous for this sort of landscape (witness the frescoes he painted in S. Martino al Monte in 1645), displaying a more 'romantic' attitude to his subject than Poussin. He died in 1675.

DUQUESNOY, François

Born in Brussels in 1594, Duquesnoy was in Rome by 1618, becoming one of the leading sculptors of the day. He shared lodgings for a time with Poussin, and the two artists studied antique art together. Like his brother Jérôme (1602–54), who was also a sculptor, he specialized in little figures of children, but his masterpiece is undoubtedly the statue of *St Susanna* (1633), with its very pure lines, which he produced for Sta Maria di Loreto.

EGGENBERG, Prince von

He was the Holy Roman Emperor's ambassador to Urban VIII in 1638, and owned *The Capture of Jerusalem by Titus* (cat. no. 33) now in Vienna.

ELLE, Ferdinand (the Elder)

Flemish and Calvinist by birth (he is said to have been born in Malines in 1580), Elle was working in Paris by 1609. He made his career there as a portrait-painter, and established an artistic dynasty. Poussin worked under him briefly as a young man. He is sometimes credited with a portrait of Poussin, now in Dresden (Staatliche Kunstsammlungen, Gemäldegalerie), painted *c.* 1641 and engraved by his grandson, Louis-Ferdinand, in 1698.

ERRARD, Charles

Born in 1606, Errard was one of the most famous painters of his day, but little or nothing of his output survives today. He was in Italy in 1627, where he studied the art of antiquity and acquired a great reputation as a draughtsman. He was appointed the first director of the Académie de France in Rome in 1666, in preference to Lebrun. Until recently some of his pictures were attributed to Poussin.

ÉTAMPES DE VALENÇAY, Henri d'

He was ambassador in Rome from 1649 to 1653, and owned *The Assumption of the Virgin* (cat. no. 87) now in the Louvre.

FÉLIBIEN, André, Sieur des Avaux

Félibien was born in Chartres in 1619, and received a good education. He went to Rome in 1647 as secretary to the French ambassador, the Marquis de Fontenay-Mareuil. He struck up a close friendship with Poussin. On his return to France, he was a protégé first of Fouquet, then of Colbert, and became Chronicler of the King's Buildings, then a member of the Académie des Inscriptions and of the Académie d'Architecture. His major work was the series of *Entretiens sur les vies et ouvrages des plus excellents peintres anciens et modernes* (1666–88), an entire volume of which he devoted to Poussin.

FERRARI, Giovanni Battista

Ferrari became a Jesuit in 1602, and taught Hebrew in Rome. He was passionately interested in botany, and in 1646 published his *Hesperides, sive de malorum aureorum cultura et usu libri IV*, a sumptuous folio illustrated with engravings by Cornelius Bloemaert after works by leading painters of the day, Poussin among them.

FOUCQUIÈRES, Jacques

Foucquières was a landscape painter, born in Antwerp between 1580 and 1590, who came to Paris in 1621 and had a career at court. He was commissioned to paint a series of views of French cities for the Grande Galerie of the Louvre, and fell foul of Poussin when he came to Paris in 1640–2, irritating him with his self-importance.

FOUQUET, Louis

The younger brother of Nicolas, he was a distinctly worldly-minded abbé, and was responsible for acquiring a great number of paintings and classical statues in Rome for the Surintendant, doubtless on the advice of Poussin, from whom he commissioned designs for a set of herms and a pair of vases for the gardens at Vaux-le-Vicomte.

FOUQUET, Nicolas

'The most splendid and remarkable man of his day,' Fouquet was appointed Surintendant des Finances in 1653, and amassed a great collection of art at Saint-Mandé and at Vaux-le-

Vicomte which was confiscated by Louis XIV in 1661. He bought *The Israelites Gathering Manna* (cat. no. 18) from Chantelou. His wife commissioned *The Holy Family with St Elizabeth and St John the Baptist in a Landscape* (cat. no. 43), now in the Louvre.

FRÉART DE CHAMBRAY, Roland

He was born in Le Mans in 1606, and, like his brother Paul, played an active part in implementing the new cultural policies of Richelieu and Sublet de Noyers. He wrote two theoretical works, *Parallèle de l'architecture antique avec la moderne* (1650) and *L'Idée de la perfection en peinture* (1662), in which he developed a purist theory of art based on Vitruvius, Palladio (whose writings he translated into French), Raphael and Poussin. He brought out a version of Leonardo da Vinci's *Treatise on Painting* in France in 1651.

FRÉART DE CHANTELOU, Jean

Like his two young brothers, Roland (see above) and Paul (see below), Jean was a member of the gentry from Le Mans and a cousin of Sublet de Noyers. He was an adviser to the king and a provincial commissioner of buildings. He owned the little *Baptism of Christ* (cat. no. 70) which Poussin painted in 1648.

FRÉART DE CHANTELOU, Paul (called Chantelou)

Born in Le Mans in 1609, Paul was the youngest of the three Fréart brothers. Like Roland, he took part in their cousin Sublet de Noyers's campaign to make Paris a 'second Rome'. After Sublet's fall from favour in 1643, he retired to the provinces for a while, before being appointed steward in ordinary to the king. Chantelou was charged with escorting Bernini around Paris on his visit there in 1665. He was Poussin's friend and patron and as well as including examples of classical art and copies after the great Italian painters of the Renaissance, his large collection featured a number of first-class works by Poussin which he himself commissioned: *The Israelites Gathering Manna* (cat. no. 18); *The Holy Family with St Elizabeth and St John the Baptist* (cat. no. 45) now in the Hermitage; the smaller of the two versions of *The Ecstasy of St Paul* (cat. no. 94); the second set of *Sacraments* (cat. nos. 109–15); *Hercules and Deianira* (cat. no. 143); and, last but not least, the *Self-Portrait* now in the Louvre (cat.

no. 2). His house was open to art-lovers and was something of a temple of classicism in Louis XIV's Paris. He died in 1694.
See also **MONTMORT, Madame de**

FRESNE, Monsieur de
The precise identity of this man, for whom Poussin painted a *Bacchanal before a Temple* (cat. no. 134), remains unknown. He may have been Léonard de Mousseau, Seigneur du Fresne (1610–80), who was assistant in charge of foreign affairs under Brienne.

FROMONT DE VENNE, Monsieur
This collector (who may perhaps be the Fromont mentioned by Conrart, who was in 1652, 'Secrétaire des Commandements' to the Duc d'Orléans, in his *Mémoires*) acquired two large pictures by Poussin: *The Holy Family with St Elizabeth and St John the Baptist* (cat. no. 48) now in Cambridge, Mass. and *The Death of Sapphira* (cat. no. 97).

GASSENDI, Pierre
Born in 1592, Gassendi was ordained a priest in 1615. He was a member to a greater or lesser extent of the 'Libertine' circles in which Poussin moved in Paris, and his interests were astronomy and philosophy. His theories attempt to reconcile Epicurean atomism with Christianity, and offer a critique of Aristotle and thus of Thomism.

GILLIER, Melchior de
Gillier was steward to Maréchal de Créquy, and adviser, then steward in ordinary to the king. He owned *Moses Striking the Rock* (cat. no. 19).

GIUSTINIANI, Marchese Vincenzo
Giustiniani (1564–1637) was born and died in Rome; he was a collector of eclectic tastes. He was a patron of Caravaggio and his followers, and then of Poussin, Claude Lorrain and François Perrier. His collection also included examples of Genoese and Venetian painting, and a unique body of classical art, engraved in 1640 and published under the title *Galleria Giustiniana*. He owned three paintings by Poussin: *The Massacre of the Innocents* (cat. no. 64), *The Assumption of the Virgin* (cat. no. 86) now in Washington, and the *Landscape with Juno and Argus* (cat. no. 218).

GUERCINO, IL (Giovanni Francesco Barbieri)
Born in 1591, died in 1666, early influences were the Carracci and the Bolognese school. He went to Rome in 1621, where he worked for Pope Gregory XV (on the decoration of the Casino Ludovisi). His painting was initially somewhat naturalistic and influenced by Caravaggio, but became much more austere in style. Poussin's first version of *The Arcadian Shepherds: 'Et in Arcadia Ego'* (cat. no. 198) is reminiscent of his treatment of the same subject (Rome, Galleria Nazionale d'Arte Antica).

HENNEQUIN DU FRESNE, Monsieur
He was master of the royal hunts and owned *The Madonna of the Steps* (cat. no. 42).

JABACH, Eberhardt (Evrard)
Born in Cologne in 1618, Jabach was a banker who settled in Paris *c.* 1640. There his business flourished thanks to the influence of Mazarin. Jabach amassed a large and wide-ranging collection – consisting not only of paintings (in 1649, for instance, he bought masterpieces assembled by Charles I of England), but also of drawings of every school – which was sold in 1671 to Louis XIV. He appears to have owned only one work by Poussin, *The Ecstasy of St Paul* (cat. no. 95) now in the Louvre, originally painted for Paul Scarron.

LAER, Pieter van (nicknamed Il Bamboccio)
Born in Haarlem in 1559, he lived in Rome from 1625 to 1639. A close friend of Swanevelt, Sandrart and Claude Lorrain, he was one of the leading northern painters and created a genre, for which he became famous. His lively scenes of low life, known as *bambocciata*, combined Dutch tradition with the style of Caravaggio, and were very popular.

LA FLEUR, Nicolas de (Nicolas Guillaume)
Born in Lorraine *c.* 1600, La Fleur was in Rome in 1626, and entered the Academy of St Luke along with Claude Lorrain and Poussin. He was a painter and engraver, and specialized in flowers, hence his nickname. Poussin painted *Pan and Syrinx* (cat. no. 155) for him. He settled in Paris in 1648 and died there in 1663.

LALLEMANT, Georges
Born in Nancy *c.* 1575, Lallemant settled in Paris in 1601. He ran the most influential studio in the French capital handling a wide range of work (producing altarpieces, mural decorations, drawings, engravings, and so on) in a heavily Mannerist style. Poussin, Champaigne and La Hyre were among the many young artists who passed through his studio. He died in 1636.

LANFRANCO, Giovanni
Lanfranco was born in Parma in 1582 and died in Rome in 1647. His painting provided a more sentimental, more readily appealing alternative to the 'grand manner' of classical idealism adopted by his great rival, Domenichino. His *Assumption of the Virgin* for the dome of S. Andrea della Valle in Rome (1625) heralded the advent of Baroque illusionism with its swirling figures and supernatural light.

LA VRILLIÈRE, Louis Phélypeaulx de

La Vrillière was Secretary of State from 1629 until his death in 1681, and had a magnificent town-house built in Paris, begun in 1635. The gallery was hung with a set of ten large history paintings (on themes drawn largely from Roman history) by the most famous Italian painters of the day: Guido Reni, Pietro da Cortona, Il Guercino, Maratta and Turchi. It was as part of this set that Poussin painted *Camillus and the Schoolmaster of Falerii* (cat. no. 181).

LEBRUN, Charles

Born in Paris in 1619, Lebrun accompanied Poussin to Rome when he returned there in 1642, and benefited from his advice, as is clear from paintings such as *Horatius Cocles* (Dulwich) and *Mucius Scaevola* (Mâcon). He returned to Paris in 1646 to begin his well-known and brilliant career there. He may have owned the *Landscape with two Nymphs and a Snake Attacking a Bird* (cat. no. 225), now in Chantilly.

LEMAIRE, Jean

Lemaire was in Rome by 1613, and got to know Poussin in 1624. He specialized in paintings of architecture with figures after the antique, and perhaps collaborated with Poussin on some occasions, e.g. on *Theseus Finding his Father's Shield* (cat. no. 190). In 1639 he returned to Paris where he acted as Poussin's principal associate in the project for decorating the Grande Galerie of the Louvre, which he continued to supervise for a while after Poussin's return to Rome in 1642. He died at Gaillon in 1659. His life and work are often confused with those of his younger brother, Pierre, who lived in Rome from 1632 until his death in 1688, and was also a close friend of Poussin.

LEMERCIER, Jacques

Lemercier (1585–1654) was an architect who worked mainly for Richelieu (on the Palais Cardinal and the church of the Sorbonne) and took over from Mansart at the church of the Val-de-Grâce in Paris in 1646. He and Poussin developed conflicting ideas about the decoration of the Grande Galerie of the Louvre.

LE NÔTRE, André

The famous garden designer (1613–1700) was also a collector; he owned three paintings by Poussin (*Moses Saved from the Water* (cat. no. 9), *St John Baptizing the People* (cat. no. 69), and *Christ and the Woman Taken in Adultery* (cat. no. 74), which he gave to Louis XIV in 1693.

LUMAGNE or LUMAGUE

A member of this family of bankers and industrialists from Lyons (possibly Marc-Antoine, who died in 1654) owned the *Landscape with Diogenes* (cat. no. 226).

MANCINI, Giulio

Born in 1558, Mancini was physician to Pope Urban VIII, he was also an art collector and critic. He combined a tradition of religious scholarship with that of the painter-connoisseur. In 1627 he listed Poussin as being one of the painters in the Barberini circle. His *Viaggio per Roma* and *Considerazioni sulla pittura* were not published in their entirety until this century.

MARINO, Giambattista (known in France as the Cavalier Marin)

This famous poet (1569–1625) was born and died in Naples. He had a tur-

bulent youth. He was in France in 1615 in the service of Marie de Médicis, and returned to Rome in 1623, after 'discovering' the young Poussin, from whom he commissioned a series of drawings on themes taken from Ovid (now in the Royal Library in Windsor). He devotes a great deal of attention to painting in his work (*La Galleria*, 1620; *L'Adone*, 1623). Poussin's *The Triumph of Ovid* (cat. no. 205) was perhaps a tribute by the artist to his first major patron.

MASSIMI, Camillo

This prelate (1620–77) was born and died in Rome. He was made a Cardinal in 1670, and assembled a library, a collection of classical art and a gallery of paintings which included works by Velázquez, Claude Lorrain and Maratta. He was a close friend of Poussin and owned *Moses Trampling on Pharaoh's Crown* (cat. no. 13), *Midas Washing in the Pactolus* (cat. no. 152), *The Arcadian Shepherds: 'Et in Arcadia Ego'* (cat. no. 198) and *Apollo and Daphne* (cat. no. 119), which Poussin presented to him, unfinished, shortly before he died. He also owned some Poussin drawings, the most notable being the *Self-Portrait* in red chalk now in the British Museum and the series of compositions for Marino.

MAUROY, Séraphin de

One of Sublet de Noyers's first assistants, he owned the smaller of the two versions of *The Assumption of the Virgin* (cat. no. 87) and possibly *The Adoration of the Shepherds* (cat. no. 58).

MAZARIN, Jules

Richelieu's political successor was brought up in Rome and became a keen collector. Paintings by French artists were something of a rarity in his collection, and of the few he owned three were by Poussin: *Diana and Endymion* (cat. no. 137), *The Inspiration of the Poet* (cat. no. 204) now in the Louvre, and *Cupids and Dogs* (cat. no. 173).

MELLAN, Claude
Born in Abbeville in 1598, this painter and engraver was a close friend of Simon Vouet, and was one of Poussin's first French friends in Rome.

MELLIN, Charles
Born in Nancy *c.* 1597, 'Carlo Lorenese' settled in Rome from 1622 and embarked on a career as a painter. In 1630 he was chosen to decorate a chapel in the church of S. Luigi dei Francesi in preference to Lanfranco and Poussin. He worked in Monte Cassino (1636–7) and Naples (1643–7). He died in Rome in 1649. For a long time Poussin tended to be credited with his paintings and drawings. Now the opposite seems to be true, with various early works credited to Poussin being attributed, more or less reliably, to Mellin.

MERCIER, Monsieur
This treasurer and merchant from Lyons owned *St Peter Healing a Sick Man* (cat. no. 96).

MIGNARD, Pierre
Born in Troyes in 1612, he went to Italy in 1635 and spent many years in Rome, until 1657. Although the French part of his career is well known, his early career in Rome remains something of a mystery. A number of recent discoveries seem to indicate that he was influenced by Poussin, notably the style of *The Death of Germanicus* (cat. no. 184) of 1627, when he first arrived in Rome, before turning to the Bolognese school.

MOLA, Pier Francesco
Born in 1612, this painter was in Rome by 1641. He was as adept at large-scale decoration as he was at easel-painting, and was one of the leading figures of the 'Neo-Venetian' movement. His landscape painting has similarities with Gaspard Dughet's and with Poussin's works of the 1630s.

MONCONYS, Balthasar de
Born in Lyons in 1611, Monconys was a great traveller and went to Rome in 1644. He visited Poussin and asked him to authenticate two pictures for him: a painting of *Narcissus* (perhaps the one now in the Louvre; cat. no. 138), and a

Bacchanal with Children. His *Journal* was published by his son in 1666.

MONTMORT, Madame de
She married Paul Fréart de Chantelou in 1656. Poussin painted *The Rest on the Flight into Egypt* (cat. no. 63) now in the Hermitage and *Christ and the Woman of Samaria* (cat. no. 72) for her.

NAUDÉ, Gabriel
Secretary to Cardinal de Bagni in Rome in 1631, and a close friend of Cassiano Dal Pozzo and Poussin, Naudé was a physician and bibliophile, and one of the leading figures in the 'Libertine' movement. He was Mazarin's librarian; summoned to the court of Sweden in 1652, he died the following year.

NICAISE, Claude
This abbé (1623–1701) was canon of the Sainte-Chapelle at Dijon. He spent several years in Rome, where he wrote a series of *Vies des artistes* (which were never published) and corresponded with Poussin, who wrote of him to Félibien: 'He deals with the art of painting like one who knows neither the theory nor the practice of it.' He wrote Poussin's epitaph.

OMODEI, Aluigi
Omodei (1608–85) was a Cardinal and chief commissioner of the papal militia. He owned two paintings by Poussin: *The Rape of the Sabine Women* (cat. no. 188) now in the Louvre and *The Triumph of Flora* (cat. no. 140).

PASSART, Michel
Passart went to Rome in 1643. He was a collector and art adviser to the Prince de Condé, and his highly eclectic tastes made him one of the most influential connoisseurs in Paris. He owned the smaller of the two versions of *Camillus and the Schoolmaster of Falerii* (cat. no. 180), *The Testament of Eudamidas* (cat. no. 183), the *Landscape with Diana and Orion* (cat no. 216), and the *Landscape with a Woman Washing her Feet* (cat. no. 232), as well as – according to Félibien – 'a very finished sketch of St Erasmus' (cf. cat. no. 90).

PASSERI, Giovanni Battista
This painter (1610–73) was a pupil of Domenichino; he wrote a sequel to Baglione's *Lives*, entitled *Vite de' pittori, scultori ed architetti che hanno lavorato in Roma, morti dal 1641 fino al 1673*, which was not published until 1772.

PATIN, Guy
Patin was a physician who was a friend of Naudé and involved with the 'Libertines', but a supporter of the Ancients rather than the Moderns. He taught at the Collège de France in 1654, and in his letters gave the most vivid account of the Fronde.

PERRIER, François
Born in 1590, he trained first in Lyons and then in Italy. He spent two periods in Rome: from 1625 to 1629 as part of Vouet's circle; and then from 1635 to 1645, when he engraved the most famous examples of classical art and came under the influence of Lanfranco and Pietro da Cortona. He was the pioneer of Roman Baroque in Paris from 1645 until his death in 1650. Although he was of the same generation as Poussin, their respective activities were in complete contrast.

PIETRE de CORTONE.

PIETRO DA CORTONA (Pietro Berrettini)
Pietro da Cortona (1596–1669) was to painting what Bernini was to sculpture and architecture; his career coincided with the rise of decorative Baroque. He was closely involved with the Barberini family and with Cassiano Dal Pozzo, and from 1621 began painting in a 'Neo-Venetian' style (as can be seen in *The Triumph of Bacchus* from the Capitol). The huge exuberant, swirling, illusionist ceiling painting *The Triumph of Divine Providence* in the Palazzo Barberini which he worked on from 1636 to 1639 was perhaps the culmination of his art. Poussin had by then already distanced himself from him.

POINTEL, Jean

This 'merchant and burgher of Paris' had associations with the industrial world of Lyons. His collection consisted largely of paintings by Poussin, acquired mostly between 1646 and 1651: the *Self-Portrait* now in Berlin (cat. no. 1); *Eliezer and Rebecca at the Well* (cat. no. 5); the version of *Moses Saved from the Water* now in the Louvre (cat. no. 10); *Moses Trampling on Pharaoh's Crown* now at Woburn Abbey (cat. no. 12); *The Judgment of Solomon* (cat. no. 31); *The Holy Family with the Infant St John the Baptist* (cat. no. 40) and *The Holy Family with St Anne, St Elizabeth and St John the Baptist* (cat. no. 49); *Lamentation over the Dead Christ* (cat. no. 83); and *Noli me tangere* (cat. no. 84). He also owned five landscapes: *Landscape with Polyphemus* (cat. no. 220); *Landscape with a Man Washing his Feet* (cat. no. 230); *Landscape with a Man Killed by a Snake* (cat. no. 236); and *Landscape – a Storm* and its pendant *Landscape – a Calm* (cat. nos. 238, 239). All of these works are listed in the inventory of his effects prepared after his death in 1660.

RENI, Guido

Poussin had far less regard for the almost morbid grace achieved by this famous Bolognese painter (1575–1642) than for the solidity which marked Domenichino's work. There are definite links, however, between Reni's marvellously constructed painting of *The Massacre of the Innocents* of 1611 and Poussin's version of the same subject now in Chantilly (cat. no. 64).

REYNON (or RAYNON), Monsieur

Raynon (or Reynon) was a manufacturer of silk and brocade from Lyons who probably died some time before 1660. He owned the version of *Moses Saved from the Water* (cat. no. 11) and *Christ Healing the Sick* (cat. no. 73).

POURBUS, Frans II (the Younger)

Pourbus, born in Antwerp in 1559, was a painter of portraits and religious subjects who had an international career. After spells in Brussels and Mantua, he was active in Paris in Marie de Médicis's day. According to Poussin himself, Pourbus's *The Last Supper* in the church of St Leu-St Gilles was among the works which had the greatest influence on him before he left for Rome.

PUCQUES, Monsieur

Poussin painted a version of *The Rape of Europa* (cat. no. 139), now lost, for this collector.

RICHELIEU, Armand Jean du Plessis, Cardinal de

The famous Cardinal and minister of Louis XIII had his château at Richelieu in Poitou decorated by Poussin with the *Triumphs* or *Bacchanals* (cat. nos. 128–31) and had him brought to Paris in 1640 to work on the Palais Cardinal, for which he painted *Moses*

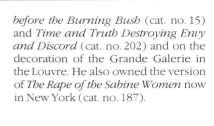

before the Burning Bush (cat. no. 15) and *Time and Truth Destroying Envy and Discord* (cat. no. 202) and on the decoration of the Grande Galerie in the Louvre. He also owned the version of *The Rape of the Sabine Women* now in New York (cat. no. 187).

RICHELIEU, Armand Jean de Vignerot du Plessis, Duc de

The Cardinal's nephew assembled in his Paris mansion a beautiful collection of paintings which included a series of works by Poussin: *Eliezer and Rebecca at the Well* originally painted for Pointel (cat. no. 5); the version of *Moses Saved from the Water* now in the Louvre (cat. no. 10); *Moses Trampling on Pharaoh's Crown* (cat. no. 12); *The Plague of Ashdod* (cat. no. 28); *Christ Healing the Sick* (cat. no. 73); *The Virgin Appearing to St James* (cat. no. 93); the Louvre version of *The Ecstasy of St Paul* (cat. no. 95); *Bacchanal with a Guitar Player: the Andrians* (cat. no. 132); *The Saving of the Young Pyrrhus* (cat. no. 186); *Landscape with Diogenes* (cat. no. 226); and, most importantly, the set of four *Seasons* (cat. nos. 206–9), which the aging Poussin was commissioned to paint in 1660, and which were delivered in 1664. A year later, this wonderful collection was sold to the king in order to pay off pressing debts. Before he died in 1715, Richelieu built up a second collection, dominated this time by Rubens.

RICHEOME, Louis

Richeome was a Jesuit who in 1601 published in Paris a work entitled *Tableaux sacrés des figures mystiques du très-auguste sacrifice et sacrament de l'Eucharistie*, illustrated with engravings by Léonard Gaultier and Charles de Mallery; this was one of the sources on which Poussin drew for his treatment of the seven *Sacraments*.

RICHER, Pierre

Richer was a brilliant physician who composed Latin poetry and was one of the group of 'Libertines' led by Naudé, with whom Poussin was involved in Paris in 1640–2.

ROCCATAGLIATA, Giovanni Stefano

This Roman picture dealer, who had associations with the Borghese family, is reputed to have sold Fabrizio Valguarnera a small painting of *Midas* by Poussin, together with a copy of his *Midas and Bacchus*. Poussin also painted the version of *The Holy Family* known as *The Roccatagliata Madonna* (cat. no. 37) for him.

ROSCIOLI, Giovanni Maria

Roscioli was in the service of Maffeo Barberini, finally becoming his secretary after he became Pope Urban VIII. Between 1634 and 1640 he bought four paintings from Poussin: *The Saving of the Young Pyrrhus* (cat. no. 186), *The Continence of Scipio* (cat. no. 189), and *Landscape with St John on Patmos* (cat. no. 212) and *Landscape with St Matthew* (cat. no. 214).

ROSPIGLIOSI, Giulio

Born in 1600, this learned ecclesiastic eventually became Pope (1667–9), taking the name Clement IX. He commissioned several paintings of allegorical and moral subjects from Poussin: the Louvre version of *Et in Arcadia Ego* (cat. no. 199), *The Dance to the Music of Time* (cat. no. 200). and *Time and Truth* (cat. no. 201). His collection also included a Holy Family, perhaps *The Holy Family with St Elizabeth and St John the Baptist* now in Chantilly (cat. no. 47), *The Rest on the Flight into Egypt* (cat. no. 60), and possibly *Queen Zenobia* (cat. no. 191). He also commissioned *The Vision of St Francesca Romana* (cat. no. 100).

SACCHETTI, Marcello

A Cardinal, poet and rich art-lover, Sacchetti was responsible for introducing Poussin to Cardinal Francesco Barberini when he arrived in Rome. It may have been Sacchetti who commissioned *The Triumph of Flora* (cat. no. 140).

SACCHI, Andrea

Sacchi (1599–1661) was the leading painter in the Barberini circle in Rome. His ceiling fresco of *Divine Wisdom* (1629–33) is a key work in terms of Roman painting, and its 'refined' style contrasts strongly with the exuberant Baroque of other artists such as Pietro da Cortona, with whom Sacchi was at odds in the great debate over the merits of drawing and colour. He seems to have been a friend of Duquesnoy and Poussin, who is thought to have worked in his studio after Domenchino left for Naples in 1631.

SANDRART, Joachim von

Born in Frankfurt in 1606, Sandrart was a great traveller who in 1629 went to Italy, where he remained until 1635, meeting all the important artists of the day. He became especially friendly with Claude Lorrain and Poussin, accompanying them on their sketching trips in the countryside around Rome. He returned to Germany in 1642. He was an eclectic painter, and composed

the first history of German art, entitled *Teutsche Academie der edlen Bau-, Bild- und Mahlereykünste* (1675–9), a valuable source of first-hand information.

SCARRON, Paul

The famous hunch-backed poet (1610–60) who established 'burlesque' as a genre in France (*Typhon*, 1644, and *Virgile travesti*, 1648–53). In 1645 he commissioned a painting from Poussin; after a great deal of procrastination, Poussin executed *The Ecstasy of St Paul* (cat. no. 95) for him.

SEGHERS, Daniel

Born in Antwerp in 1590, Seghers was a pupil of Jan Bruegel and became a Jesuit. He specialized in painting flowers, and ornamented the works of more famous artists with garlands of painted flowers. He is thought to have embellished Poussin's *Virgin and Child* (cat. no. 34) and *Pietà* (cat. no. 80) in this way during his stay in Rome between 1625 and 1628.

SERISIER (or CÉRISIERS), Jacques

A merchant from Lyons who had settled in Paris, Serisier was one of the principal collectors of Poussin's work. On visiting his house in 1665, Bernini admired a dozen paintings which included the *Self-Portrait* (cat. no. 1), *Esther before Ahasuerus* (cat. no. 32), a version of *The Virgin and Child* (possibly cat. no. 35), *The Holy Family with St Anne, St Elizabeth and St John the Baptist* (cat. no. 49) now in Dublin, *The Flight into Egypt* (cat. no. 61), as well as *Landscape with the Funeral of Phocion* and *Landscape with the Gathering of the Ashes of Phocion* (cat. nos. 228, 229).

STELLA, Jacques

A painter from Lyons, Stella was born in 1596. In 1619 he was in Florence, and in 1623 in Rome. There he became a close friend of Poussin. He returned to Paris in 1634, and was showered with favours by Richelieu. He was one of Poussin's rivals for the commission for the altarpiece in the Jesuit Noviciate in 1641. He corresponded with him and acted as his 'agent', maintaining contacts with collectors in Lyons. At the time of his death in 1657, Stella's personal collection included: *The Exposition of Moses* now in Oxford (cat. no. 8); the Leningrad version of *Moses Striking the Rock* (cat. no. 20); *The Crucifixion* (cat. no. 78); *St Peter Healing a Sick Man* (cat. no. 96); a version of *Apollo and Daphne* (cat. no. 118), now lost; *The Birth of Bacchus* (cat. no. 122); *Hercules and Deianira* (cat. no. 143); *Venus Presenting Arms to Aeneas* (cat. no. 165); *Nymphs Bathing* (cat. no. 171); and *Rinaldo and Armida* (cat. no. 194).
See also: **BOUZONNET-STELLA, Antoine and Claudine**

SUBLET DE NOYERS, François

Born in Le Mans in 1588, this protégé of Richelieu became Secrétary of State in 1636 and Surintendant des Bâtiments du Roi in 1638. With the support of his Fréart cousins, he carried out an ambitious cultural policy, which culminated in Poussin's return to Paris, 1640–2. He commissioned Poussin to paint *The Miracle of St Francis Xavier* (cat. no. 92) for the Jesuit Noviciate and employed him on all sorts of projects. He fell into disgrace on Richelieu's death, and died in 1645.

THOU, Jacques de

Thou was the son of the parliamentary president Jacques-Auguste de Thou, the famous historian, and was himself president of the Paris parliament in 1647 and ambassador to the States

General. He owned Poussin's painting of *The Crucifixion* (cat. no. 78).

URBAN VIII, Pope:
see BARBERINI, Maffeo

VALGUARNERA, Fabrizio
Valguarnera was a Sicilian adventurer, lover of paintings and trafficker who was involved in a diamond-stealing affair which led to a sensational trial in Rome in 1631, at which Poussin testified in person, along with a number of other painters. The thirty-seven pictures which he had in his possession included *The Plague of Ashdod* (cat. no. 28), together with the copy by Caroselli, *The Empire of Flora* (cat. no. 141), *Midas at the Source of the River Pactolus* (cat. no. 151), and *Midas and Bacchus* (possibly cat. no. 153).

VARIN, Quentin
Born in Beauvais *c.* 1570, Varin was an itinerant artist for the early part of his career. His visit to Les Andelys in 1611–12, during which he painted three pictures for the church of Notre Dame there, was to have a decisive effect on Poussin's career. Varin later settled in Paris and his style, which had initially been rather Mannerist in tendency, became more subdued as he came under the influence of the art of northern Italy. He died in 1634.

VOUET, Simon
Vouet was in Italy from 1614 to 1627, and was the leading figure among the French painters then in Rome. He was head of the Academy of St Luke, and in 1624 was commissioned to produce a work for St Peter's. His painting was at that stage influenced by Caravaggio, Valentin and Lanfranco. He was recalled to Paris by Louis XIII in 1627, and enjoyed a fine career there as a decorative painter until his death in 1649. His style was light and expansive, and influenced by Venetian art. He was one of Poussin's rivals for the commission for the altarpiece for the Jesuit Noviciate in 1641, and was critical of Poussin's work on the Grande Galerie of the Louvre. He is rumoured to have been at the heart of a conspiracy to discredit his rival. In reality Poussin brought a radically new style of painting to Paris which rapidly superseded Vouet's and influenced a number of the latter's pupils, such as Le Sueur and Lebrun.

VUIBERT, Rémy
Born in Troyes *c.* 1600, Vuibert was a pupil of Vouet in Rome. Poussin made him one of his chief assistants on the Louvre project. His work, which is known today mainly through engravings, is fundamentally 'classical' in style.

ZACCOLINI, Father Matteo
Zaccolini (1590–1630) was a member of the Theatine order and a friend of Domenichino; he was interested in optics and perspective and had access to the writings of Leonardo da Vinci. His own unpublished manuscripts have recently been rediscovered in Florence.

Selected Correspondence
and
Original Documents

I Poussin's Writings

CORRESPONDENCE

To Chantelou (Rome, 28 April 1639)

I will wait until, by the grace of God, I can be with you in person to express my obligation to you, if you think me worthy, not in words, but in deeds. For the moment I will not burden you with a long speech. I write simply to tell you that I have despatched your painting of *Manna* [cat. no. 18] by the Lyons courier, Bertholin. I have packed it carefully and expect that it will reach you in good condition. I have sent with it a smaller package for Monsieur de Bonnaire, which I have not had the opportunity of remitting to him until now. Please allow him to take it because it is rightfully his. When you have received your picture, I beg you, if you see fit, to embellish it with a little cornice. This will prevent objects around the painting jostling for attention, distracting the eye as it scans the picture, taking in its different parts and interfering with a clear perception of the whole.

It would be best if the said cornice were gilded a plain, dull gold because that will blend well with the colours and not conflict with them at all.

Furthermore, if you recall the first letter I wrote you regarding the different attitudes in which I promised to depict the figures, and if you look at the picture as a whole, I think you will have no difficulty in recognizing those people who are starving, those who are full of wonder or compassion, those displaying charity, those manifesting desperate need or ravenously eating, those consoling others, for you will find everything I have just described in the first seven figures starting from the left, the rest being in similar vein: read the story and the picture thoroughly to see if each detail is appropriate to the subject.

And, if after looking at it more than once, you feel satisfaction with it, please tell me, without dissembling in any way, so that I can rejoice at having been able to please you on the very first occasion I have had the honour of serving you. If not, I apologize in every way I can, and beg you to remember, as ever, that, though the spirit may be willing, the flesh is weak.

I have written to Monsieur Le Maire to tell him of the main circumstance which keeps me here this summer; and I beg you, Sir, with him, to make my excuses to Monsieur de Noyers. For this and all the courtesies you daily do me, I shall be eternally indebted to you ...

I will write to Monsieur Stella, who I believe to be in Lyons at present, to ask him to hold the picture for you, should anything unexpected happen. Before you show it, it would be a very good idea to decorate it a little. Very little of it should be above eye level, rather the opposite.

To Chantelou (Paris, 20 March 1642)

Seigneur Salomon Girard, my dear friend, who is leaving here for the Court, has offered to present you with my humble compliments and to deliver this letter into your hands. I am very grateful to you for honouring me with a letter and for telling me about all the beautiful things which you saw on your travels. I am quite sure that what you say is true and that this time you have derived more pleasure from beautiful works which previously you only saw in passing without reading

them properly. Things which partake of perfection should not be looked at in haste, but call for time, judgment and intelligence. The means employed in their appraisal must be the same as those used in their making. I am sure you will have found the young women you must have seen around Nîmes no less inspiring than the ravishing columns of the Maison Carrée – after all, the columns are just classical re-creations of their living beauty. Nothing so lightens our task, so it seems to me, as a sweet and pleasurable diversion from the demands of our work. I am never more stimulated to set to work with a will than when I have just seen some beautiful object. But alas! we are too far from the sun for there to be any question of finding anything delightful here. As long as I am not confronted by anything actually hideous, however, I can rely on what remains of my memories of real beauty to provide me, as it has for the frontispiece for the Horace, with some sort of an idea which will just about pass muster. I have entrusted it to Monsieur Chantelou your brother, so that Monsieur Mellan cannot say that I am responsible for holding up the completion of it now. As soon as Monsieur du Fresne has given me the subject of the frontispiece for the *Livre des Conciles*, I will get to work on it, having no greater desire in the world than to serve you. I should also have written to Monseigneur to thank him for the honour he paid me in writing to me about Charity, but I find myself too dull-witted and incapable of elegant turns of phrase for a person of his refinement. So as far as he is concerned, I will adopt the same strategy as the goslings which keep away from the Palus Meotides in order to avoid Mount Taurus and the fearsome eagles which live there. I beg you, Sir, to apologize to him on my behalf, and to assure him of my respect and my devotion.

To Sublet de Noyers (1642, undated; known through a transcription included by Félibien in his *Entretiens*, IV, pp. 279 ff.)

These comments [on the painting in the Jesuit Noviciate] would have had no effect on Poussin, had he not been aware that they reached the ears of Monsieur de Noyers, who took note and may perhaps have seen something in them. Poussin therefore wrote him a long letter which he began by saying "that he wished, as a certain philosopher had in the past, that it was possible to see what went on inside a man, because one would then be able not only to discover his vices and virtues, but also to ascertain the extent of his knowledge and whether or not he had good habits of mind; which would be a great advantage when dealing with learned people and make it easier to judge their merits; but nature has arranged matters differently, hence it is as difficult to assess people's intellectual and artistic abilities as it is to know whether they have a propensity towards good or bad moral conduct;

"that no amount of erudition or cleverness can oblige the rest of the world to believe implicitly what learned men say, a fact which has always been pretty well known as far as painters are concerned. Not only have earlier artists suffered, but recent ones too, like Annibale Carracci and Domenichino, whose merit remained unrecognized, as much through the

intrigues of their enemies as through ill-fortune, even though they had ample and demonstrable artistic talent and skill to prove it, while their rivals enjoyed during their own lifetimes a reputation and happiness which they really did not deserve;

"that he has suffered quite as much as the likes of the Carracci and Domenichino. And he is writing to Monsieur de Noyers to protest about his listening to the malicious talk of his enemies when he should in fact be protecting him, since it was he who gave them cause to slander him by ousting their works from where they were to make way for his.

"that those who had had a hand in what had been started in the Grande Galerie, and hoped to profit by it, who moreover hoped to own some picutres by him but found themselves thwarted by the ban placed on him, preventing him from working for individuals, are just as much his enemies with their constant railing against him. That he has nothing to fear from them, however, because by the grace of God he has acquired the kind of riches which cannot be taken away from him, but which allow him to go anywhere: the pain, nevertheless, of feeling so abused gave him sufficient grounds for wanting to show him why he believed his opinions were more solid than those of others, and for making him understand the impertinence of his detractors. But that the fear of burdening him with a tiresome discourse forces him to state in the briefest possible terms that those who turn him against the work started in the Grande Galerie are either ignorant or malicious. That anyone can see as much, and that he himself must realize that it was not by chance but with good reason that he avoided displaying the same faults as Le Mercier had done and creating the same unnatural effects so clearly evident in what he had started, in the unpleasant heaviness and unwieldiness of the work, for instance, the lowering of the vault which made it seem as if it were falling in, the extreme frigidity of the design, the melancholy, mean, unyielding feel of it all, the mingling – in a manner intolerable both to the senses and to reason – of contradictory and conflicting elements, the too broad next to the too slender, parts too large next to those that are too small, the too powerful next to the too weak, accompanied by a whole host of other unpleasant features.

"There was," he went on, "no variety; nothing could stand on its own; there was no linking together of elements, no continuity. The size of the frames bore no relation to how far away they were, with the result that they could not be seen easily because the frames were placed in the centre of the vault, and right above the heads of the spectators who would, as it were, have gone blind at the mere thought of looking at them. The whole method of dividing up the ceiling was unsatisfactory, the artchitect having tied himself down to certain consoles which run the entire length of the cornice, and which are unequal in number on the two sides, there being four on one side and five on the other: which meant either taking the whole design to pieces, or leaving it intact but with unacceptable faults."

Having pointed out these flaws and advanced the reasons he had for changing everything, he justified his management of the project and the scheme he produced by explaining how one should look at things in order to assess them properly.

"It is important to know," he said, "that there are two ways of looking at objects, one is simply to see them, the other is to consider them carefully. Simply seeing means nothing more than naturally taking in with the eye the form and appearance of the thing seen. Looking at an object and considering it carefully, however, means more that the eye's simple and natural taking in of a form, and involves making a special effort to understand a particular object fully: thus one can say that the simple seeing of an object is merely a natural process, while what I call the *prospect* is a function of reason, and depends on knowledge with which those who set about volunteering their judgment should be equipped."

"It should be noted," continued Poussin, "that the panelling of the gallery is twenty-one feet high with a distance of twenty-four feet between one window and the next. The width of the gallery, and therefore the distance from which we consider the expanse of panelling, is also twenty-four feet. The painting in the middle of the panelling is twelve feet wide by nine feet high, including the surround: the width of the gallery thus provides a perfect viewing distance, allowing the picture in the centre of the panelling to be taken in at a glance. Why then do people say that the paintings on the panelling are too small, when the whole gallery consists of parts, each of which has to be looked at in turn, one pier at a time? The intention is that one should take in at a glance, from the same point and distance, half the arch of each vault above the panelling, and it must be understood that everything I have set out in this vault should be considered as laid on to its surface. Nothing should break through this skin, figures should not be allowed to jut out beyond or be embedded deep into it. Instead everything on the surface should reinforce the form and structure of the vault.

"That if I had made the parts which are or are made to look as if they are attached to the vault, as well as the others which people say are too small, bigger than they are, I would have been making the same mistakes as were made before, and I would have appeared as ignorant as those who have worked and are still working today on a number of important projects, with results that clearly demonstrate that they do not know that it is against all order, as examples in nature itself prove, to reserve the largest and bulkiest elements for the highest places, and to make the weakest and most delicate parts support the heaviest and most powerful. It is through this gross ignorance that all buildings left to the management of people so lacking in skill and judgment appear to collapse, crumple and keel over under their own weight, instead of being lively, lissom and light, and seeming to carry themselves easily, as nature and reason teach us to make them.

"Who could fail to grasp the confusion that would have resulted if I had incorporated ornamental details in all the places my critics think I should have done; or to see that if those I did include had been bigger, then they would be visible from a wider angle and make too strong an impact, and so offend the eye, principally because the vault is lit throughout by an even and uniform light? Would not that part of the vault have seemed top-heavy and disconnected from the rest of the gallery, disrupting the decorative flow? If they had been the real objects I want them to appear to be, who would have been so foolish as to place the largest and heaviest of them in a position that could not possibly be sustained? But not everyone who goes about taking on large projects realizes that the illusion of a diminishing perspective is created by different means and for very particular reasons entails things being lifted upwards, along perpendicular lines, whose parallels meet at the centre of the earth."

In reply to those who thought the vault lacking in splendour, Poussin added: "that he had never been asked to produce the most magnificent scheme of decoration he could imagine; and that, if he had been, he would freely have voiced his opinion, and advised against a venture of such magnitude and one which was so difficult to execute well; firstly, because of the shortage of craftsmen in Paris competent to perform the task; secondly, because of the length of time it would take; and thirdly because of the excessive expense entailed, which he thought ill-justified on a gallery of such a vast extent which would never function as anything more than a thoroughfare, and which might one day be in as bad a state as it had been in when he first saw it, the disregard and appalling lack of love the people of our nation have for beautiful things being such that no sooner are they created than people cease to value them, and, on the contrary, often take pleasure in destroying them. That he thought therefore that he had served the King very well by producing a scheme which was more refined, more pleasing, more beautiful, better arranged, better distributed, more varied than the one previously started, and in less time, and at far less expense. But that if people wanted to listen to the different opinions and new ideas his enemies came up with every day, and if these were more pleasing than what he was trying to do, then, notwithstanding the good reasons which he gave for it, he could not stand in their way; on the contrary, he would willingly give up his place to any who might be deemed more capable. That at least he would have the joy of knowing that he was the cause of hitherto unknown and gifted people being discovered in France, who could beautify Paris with excellent works which would be a tribute to the nation."

He speaks next of his painting for the Jesuit Noviciate and says: "that those who maintain that the figure of Christ is more like a Thundering Jove than a God of mercy should realize that he is more than skilled enough to give his figures expressions congruent with what they represent; but that he cannot (and these were his very words, I remember), he cannot, I say, and could never imagine Christ in any context whatsoever as stiff-necked or as some molly-coddling parent, and that it was even difficult, being on earth among men, to visualize him at all."

He apologizes for his manner of expressing himself, and says "that he must be forgiven because he was used to living among people who understood him through his work, knowing how to write well not being his special skill."

Finally he ends his letter with a clear demonstration that he is well aware of his capabilities, without priding himself or seeking any kind of favour, but simply wishing as ever to bear witness to the truth, and to avoid sinking into flattery, which are too much opposites ever to be found together.'

To Chantelou (Rome, 24 November 1647)

I am writing in reply to your two last letters, of the 23rd of October and the 1st of this month. I have kept the promise I made you. That is to say, that I will not take up my paintbrushes for anyone but you until I have finished your *Seven Sacraments* [cat. nos. 109–15], and consequently, as soon as I had despatched *The Last Supper* – the sixth – I started work on the last, the one which you say you like least. I promise myself, however, that it will be no less successful than whichever of the six you like best.

I received payment for the last picture that I sent you from a clerk acting on Monsieur Gierico's behalf; you will be aware of this, moreover, from the bill of exchange which you will by now have received, and from the last letter I wrote to you, informing you that I had sent the aforementioned painting, which I am sure must have reached you by now. I have made up my mind to serve Monsieur de Lisle since you instruct me to, even though I had intended henceforth to do something for myself, without subjecting myself further to the whims of others, and particularly not of those who are only capable of seeing through someone else's eyes. The said nobleman must, however, be prepared to show patience – something which does not come easily to any Frenchman. I presented your compliments to Monsieur Dal Pozzo, who returned them with his customary courtesy. As regards what you say in your last letter, I can easily prove to you how utterly unfounded your suspicion is that I favour and love you less than I do other people. If I did, why would I have elected to work for you over the last five years rather than for the many people of worth and rank who have pressed me to paint something for them and have offered me their money to do so? Why is it that I have been content to work for so little, and that I have not even wanted to accept what you yourself have seen fit to offer me? Why is it that when, having sent you one picture in which there were only sixteen or eighteen figures, I could have made all the others the same or even reduced the number of figures in order to get to the end of a long and tiring labour sooner, I chose instead to enrich them with more figures, my sole concern being to gain your good will?

Why have I spent so much of my precious time running errands for you all over the place and in all weathers, if not to show how greatly I respect you? I will say no more about it – how can I when I have sworn to be your loyal servant? Believe me when I tell you that I have done for you what I would do for no other living soul, and when I say that I will always continue to serve you with all my heart. I am not a fickle person, given to switching my affections, when once I have committed myself.

If the picture of *Moses discovered in the Waters of the Nile* [cat. no. 10] in Monsieur Pointel's collection generates feelings of love in you, is that proof that I painted it with more love than I did the pictures I painted for you? Do you not see that it is the nature of the subject which is the cause of this, and your mood, and that the subjects which I undertake for you have to be represented in a different way? Therein lies all the skill of painting. Forgive me if I make so bold as to say that I think you have been precipitate in your assessment of my work. It is very difficult to be a good judge of this art if one does not have a profound experience of both the theory and practice of it. We should not let our judgment be guided by our desires alone, but by our reason too.

That is why I want to alert you to an important aspect of art which will enable you to see what has to be taken into account in the representation of different subjects in painting.

The fine old ancient Greeks, to whom we owe all the beautiful things in this world, devised a number of modes by means of which they achieved the most marvellous effects.

The term 'mode' properly speaking means a ratio or measure and form which we adopt when portraying a particular subject which we cannot exceed and which constrains us to display a certain moderateness and moderation in every aspect of the given work. This moderateness and moderation represent in effect, therefore, a certain determined and unfaltering manner or order which is brought to bear and through which the very essence of the thing is preserved.

The ancient Greek modes had their origin in a number of diverse elements brought together to form a whole. The variety of these elements gave rise to the notion of differentiating particular modes, by which was understood the distinctive intrinsic character, whatever it might be, which resulted when all the elements which made up the whole were assembled in particular proportions, and which gave the whole the power to induce different feelings in the minds of the viewers. This led the classical theorists to identify each mode with the effects which they saw it produce, and to define it accordingly. For this reason they called the Dorian mode steady, solemn and severe, and saw it as appropriate for serious, stern subjects full of wisdom. And, moving on from these to subjects by nature pleasant and joyful, they used the Phrygian when they wanted finer inflections and a higher pitch. Only these two were praised with Plato and Aristotle and met with their approval. All the others they deemed useless. The Phrygian they held to be vehement, violent, very severe, and of a kind to induce amazement in people.

I hope within a year to paint a subject in this Phrygian mode. Terrible war subjects are well suited to this mode.

The Lydian mode they believed was appropriate for the pitiful, because it has neither the restraint of the Lydian not the severity of the Phrygian.

The Hypolydian has a certain sweetness and softness about it which fills the mind of the viewer with bliss. It is suitable for religious subjects, glories and images of heaven. The ancient Greeks invented the Ionian mode for scenes of a joyous nature, using it to depict dances, bacchanals and merry-making.

The great poets have demonstrated enormous care and remarkable skill in making their lines reflect what is being said, and in adjusting the rhythm so that the words produce an appropriate sound when spoken. Virgil has observed these principles throughout his poem, adapting his verse to fit the three different sorts of speech which he distinguishes, and he is so skilful in giving each line the sound appropriate to its subject matter that in truth it seems he can make us see the things he describes, simply through the sound of the words he uses. In passages where he talks of love, for instance, we see that he has skilfully chosen words which are soft, agreeable and extremely pleasing to the ear; in contrast, where he sings of some feat of arms or describes a naval battle or a sea adventure, he has chosen hard, harsh, unpleasant sounding words designed to provoke a sense of terror in their hearing or uttering them. If I had painted a picture for you in this manner, you would undoubtedly have concluded that I did not love you.

If it did not mean that I would end up writing you a book rather than a letter, I would tell you about a number of other things which have to be considered in painting, so that you could see for yourself how greatly I strive to serve you well. For, although you are very well versed in all things, I fear that the mere company of the many stupid and ignorant people who surround you may taint your judgment.

To Chantelou (Rome, 25 November 1658)

The various infirmities with which I am afflicted, and which increase as I grow older, prevent me from writing to you more often than I do. I promised to explain the appurtenances in the background of the latest picture I have painted for you [cat. no. 63]. This is what you see.

A procession of priests, their shaven heads crowned with leaves, dressed in their peculiar fashion, carrying tambourines, flutes and trumpets, and sparrow hawks on poles. The ones shown passing under the portico are carrying the chest known as *Sero Apin*, which contained the relics and bones of their god Serapin, towards whose temple they are proceeding. As for the rest of it, the edifice which appears behind the woman dressed in yellow is quite simply a little building serving as a retreat for the bird Ibis, who is represented there, and the tower with the concave roof and great vase for collecting the dew, far from being mere products of my imagination, are both taken from the fine mosaic floor in the Temple of Fortuna at Palestrina, in which the natural and moral histories of both Egypt and Ethiopia are not only accurately but skilfully depicted. I have included all these things in this picture in order to give pleasure through innovation and variety and to show that the Virgin depicted here is in Egypt.

I have worked out a new composition for *The Fall of Saint Paul*, having had a new idea about it. I ask you to allow me time to finish this work, which I will find very tiring. I am not writing to Madame because of the difficulty I experience because of my shaky hand.

To Roland Fréart de Chambray (Rome, 1 March 1665)

One must in the end make an effort to rouse oneself after such a long silence. One must say one's piece while one's pulse still beats a little. I have had time to read and consider your book on the perfect *Idea of Painting*, which has provided sweet nourishment for my poor afflicted soul, and it gladdens me to think that you are the first person in France to open the eyes of those who hitherto saw only through other people's eyes and allowed themselves to be swayed by false commonly held opinions. You have now done the preparatory work of warming and softening up a topic which was hard and unwieldy, and made it possible in future for others to follow your example and make their own contribution, itself of value to painting.

Having considered the way Seigneur Franciscus Junius divides the different parts of this fine art, I have ventured to set down briefly here what I have learnt from it.

It is necessary first of all to know what this imitation is and to define it.

DEFINITION

With the use of line and colour painting is an imitation on a flat surface of all that is to be seen under the sun. Its purpose is to delight.

PRINCIPLES WHICH ANY MAN CAPABLE OF RATIONAL THOUGHT CAN LEARN

There can be no visual form without light.
There can be no visual form without a transparent medium.
There can be no visual form without a defined space.
There can be no visual form without colour.
There can be no visual form without distance.
There can be no visual form without an instrument.

What follows cannot be learnt, these are the painter's contributions.

But firstly as regards the subject matter:
It should be noble, and have no hint of the menial. So that the painter has scope to show his wit and ingenuity, it has to admit the finest form possible. The first thing to introduce is order, then ornament, decorum, beauty, grace, liveliness, costume, verisimilitude and judgment throughout. These elements come from the painter and constitute the aspect of art which cannot be learnt. It is the golden bough in Virgil which cannot be found or picked except by those who are led to it by fate. Each of these nine elements encompasses a number of beautiful things which deserve individual consideration at the hand of a fine scholar, but I beg you to look at this small sample and give me your frank opinion of it. I know that you are not only capable of snuffing out a light but you also know how to make it burn. I would say more, but nowadays my head gets overheated when I concentrate hard, and I feel ill. Moreover I am always ashamed to consider myself in the same bracket as men who are as far above me in worth and merit as the star of Saturn is above our heads. Indeed, your kind-heartedness makes you see in me a far greater person than I am.

To Abbé Nicaise (Rome, 26 July 1665)

I have received yours of 10 July. I find it difficult to reply to you because of the weakness of my shaky hand which will no longer do as I want it to. I need say no more to convince you that I am in no state to be able to satisfy M. de Chamilly's curiosity. I have abandoned my brushes for ever. I have nothing more to do now but die, this being the only cure for the ills which afflict me. May God will that it should be soon, because life weighs too heavily on me. You will show these lines to the aforementioned gentleman, whom I beg to forgive me for not writing to him. I hope he will allow me to present him with my most humble compliments, which I present to you too with all my heart.

TWELVE OBSERVATIONS ON PAINTING

ON THE EXAMPLE SET BY GOOD MASTERS

In addition to doctrine, there are the teachings regarding practice, where if precepts are not seen to be applied, they cannot be expected to leave their imprint, which should be the result of active study. In their absence the young man, follows long and winding paths which seldom lead to the journey's end, unless good examples of swifter methods and less complicated goals are to hand.

THE DEFINITION OF PAINTING AND OF ITS IMITATIONS

Painting is nothing more than an imitation of human actions, which are imitable in themselves; the rest are not imitable in themselves, but by chance, and not as principal parts, but as accessories, and in this way not only the actions of animals, but all natural things can be imitated.

HOW ART SURPASSES NATURE

Art is not something different from nature, nor can it go beyond its confines; since the light of doctrine, which is spread hither and thither owing to its natural properties and which reveals itself in different men, in different places and at different times, can be consolidated by art; this light is never to be found wholly or even largely in one individual.

HOW IMPOSSIBILITY EQUALS PERFECTION IN PAINTING AND IN POETRY

Taking Zeus as an example, Aristotle tries to show that it is permissible for the poet to say impossible things as long as they are better [than the possible], just as it is naturally impossible for any one woman to possess every quality of beauty, like Helen, who was most beautiful and consequently better than possible. . . .

ON THE LIMITS OF DRAWING AND COLOUR

Painting becomes elegant when its furthest limits and its simplest limits are united through the middle course of making their lines and colours converge neither too feebly not too harshly; and thus one can speak of the friendship or indeed the enmity of colours and their limits.

ON ACTION

There are two instruments by which the minds of listeners may be mastered: action and diction. The first is itself so valuable and efficacious that Demosthenes accorded it priority over rhetorical devices and Cicero called it the language of the body. Quintilian attributes such importance and vigour to it that he considers concepts trials and affections pointless without it, just as lines and colour are pointless without it.

ON SOME FORMS OF THE MAGNIFICENT MANNER

ON THE SUBJECT, CONCEPT, STRUCTURE AND STYLE

The magnificent manner consists of four things: subject, or topic, concept, structure and style. The first requirement, which is the basis for all the others, is that the subject or topic should be great, such as battles, heroic actions and divine matters. However, given the subject upon which the painter is engaged is great, he must first of all make every effort to avoid getting lost in minute detail, so as not to detract from the dignity of the story. He should describe the magnificent and great details with a bold brush and disregard anything that is vulgar and of little substance. Thus the painter should not only be skilled in formulating his subject matter, but wise enough to know it well and to choose something that lends itself naturally to embellishment and perfection. Those who choose vile topics take refuge in them on account of their own lack of ingenuity. Faint-heartedness is therefore to be despised, as is baseness of subject matter for which any amount of artifice is useless. As for the concept, it is simply part of the spirit, which concentrates on things, like the concept realized by Homer and Phidias of Olympian Zeus who could make the Universe tremble with a nod of his head. The drawing of things should be such that it expresses the concept of the things themselves. The structure, or composition of the parts, should not be studiously researched, and not sought after or contrived with effort but should be as natural as possible. Style is a particular method of painting and drawing, carried out in an individual way, born of the singular talent at work in its application and in the use of ideas. This style, and the manner and taste emanate from nature and from the mind.

ON THE IDEA OF BEAUTY

The idea of beauty only acquires substance once it has undergone as much preparation as possible. There are three elements to this preparation: order, measure and aspect or form. Order signifies the interval between the parts, measure is concerned with quantities and form consists of the lines and colours. Order and the interval between parts are not enough, even when all the constituent parts are in their natural places, without measure, which accords to each part the size appropriate to its bulk. This in turn must relate to space, in such a way that the lines are described gracefully with neighbouring areas of light and shade gently blended. From all these things it is plainly evident that beauty is well removed from the substance of the body, to which it never comes close unless it has been the subject of these incorporeal preparations. In conclusion, then, painting is none other than a perception of incorporeal things, and when it depicts bodies it merely represents the order and the measure in which these things are arranged, paying greater heed to the idea of beauty than to anything else. Hence some people have held that this alone is the sign of every good painter and, one might say, that this is his goal, and that painting is the lover of beauty and thus the queen of art.

ON NOVELTY

Novelty in painting does not primarily mean a subject never previously seen, rather a new and beautiful arrangement and expression whereby the old and the commonplace become singular and new. Thus the expressions and movements in Domenichino's *Last Communion of St Jerome* are quite different from those in Agostino Carracci's masterpiece.

ON HOW TO MAKE UP FOR THE SHORTCOMINGS IN A SUBJECT

If a painter wished to arouse a sense of marvel in people's minds and has no subject in hand capable of doing this, he should not introduce new things which are alien and have no proper place there, but use his skill to render his work marvellous through the excellence of his manner, so that it can be said: 'materiam superabat opus'.

ON THE FORM OF THINGS

The form of each thing is determined by its own use or purpose; some bring about laughter or terror, and their form is dependent on this.

ON THE ALLURE OF COLOUR

The colours in painting are akin to enticements to convince the eye, like the beauty of verses in poetry.

II Seventeenth-century Documents

Roland Fréart de Chambray: *Idée de la perfection de la peinture démonstrée par les principes de l'art* (Paris, 1662), pp. 121 ff.

[. . .] this Poussin is indeed a mighty eagle in his profession, or, to put it more clearly and without using metaphors, he is the most accomplished and perfect of all our modern painters. It is not difficult to convince scholars of this, men who study and judge matters in the manner of mathematicians, that is to say with precision, on the basis of pure demonstration, through analysis of the principles involved, and without allowing opinion or favour, which are the bane of truth, to intrude. Others, however, who have only a superficial knowledge, but yet have a very over-inflated view of their own judgment, will see this statement as a paradox, and in so doing render themselves incapable of ever being shown its truth. That is why I leave them to argue about it, and content myself with having established in this treatise the fundamental principles and the method by which it should be dissected, without involving myself any further in this dispute. I would only add by way of information that anyone who is curious enough to get to the stage of seeking decisive proof of Poussin's worth will find it amply demonstrated in his set of *Seven Sacraments* [cat. nos. 109–15], which are to be seen in Paris at the residence of Monsieur Chantelou, a steward in ordinary to the King, and a close friend of this illustrious Poussin. It is a series of seven uniform pictures, moderate in size, but of extraordinary diligence, in which this noble painter seems to have given us not only a perfect demonstration of the art in accordance with all the parts examined in this treatise, but also an illustration of the highest state of excellence which can be achieved, through his innovation and inventiveness, the nobility of his ideas on each subject, his scholarly and judicious observance of costume (in which he is almost unique), the force of his figures' expressions, and, in a word, all the same qualities discernible in the great geniuses of antiquity, among whom he would, I believe, have held one of the topmost places, since in all his works he demonstrates all the same parts of excellence which Pliny and the others pointed out in Apelles, Zeuxis, Timanthes and Protogenes, and the rest of that first class of painters.

Gian Lorenzo Bernini, in Paul Fréart de Chantelou's *Journal du voyage du Cavalier Bernin en France* (1665). Published by Ludovic Lalanne (Paris, 1885), pp. 64–7, 90.

[At Chantelou's] . . . He went [. . .] into the room where the *Seven Sacraments* [cat. nos. 109–15] hang. The only painting uncovered was *Confirmation*. He looked at it very intently and then said: 'He has imitated Raphael's colours in this picture; how much there is to say about it! What devotion! What silence! What beauty there is in that young girl!' His son and Mathie looked admiringly at the young priest, then at the woman dressed in yellow, and then at each of the figures in turn. Next I uncovered *Matrimony*, which he contemplated as he had the first, without saying anything, drawing back the curtain which obscured part of a figure behind a column [. . .] They praised its grandeur and majesty, and looked carefully at the whole; then, studying it in detail, they admired the nobility and attention manifest in the girls and women he had introduced into the scene, and among others, the one half-hidden by a column. Next they saw *Penance*, which they also looked at for a long time and admired. Meanwhile, I had *Extreme Unction* taken down and put close to the light so that Bernini might see it better. He stood for a while [looking at it], then got down on his knees in order to see it better, changing his glasses from time to time and demonstrating his astonishment without saying a word. In the end he got up and said that it had the same effect as a beautiful sermon to which one listens with rapt attention and after which one is left speechless, for one's innermost being has been moved.

I had *Baptism* brought to the window too, and I told Bernini that the scene was at dawn. He looked at it for a while sitting down, then got down on his knees again, changed position from time to time to see it better, looking not at one end, now at the other, and then he said: 'This one pleases me no less than the others'; he asked me if I had all seven. I told him I had. He did not tire of looking for an hour or more. Then, having got up, he said: 'You have filled me with self-disgust today by showing me [the work of] a man whose great talents make me realize that I know nothing.'

. . . He then saw the two remaining *Sacraments* and contemplated them with the same attention as he had the others [. . .]. *The Last Supper*, for its part, pleased him very much, and he pointed out the beauty of the different heads to Messrs. Paule and Mathie, running through them all one after the other, as well as the harmony and light in the picture. He took up first one, then another; and then he said: 'If I had to choose one of these pictures, I would find it very difficult', and he pointed to the painting by Raphael along with the others. 'I would not know which one to choose,' he said. 'I have always held Mr Poussin in high regard, and I remember that Guido Reni took issue with me over the way I spoke of his painting of *The Martyrdom of St Eramus* in St Peter's, because to his mind I had overstated its beauty to Urban VIII, and I said to him: "If I were a painter, that picture would mortify me greatly." He is a great genius and he has directed his attentions principally to the antique.'

(At Monsieur Cérisier's) . . . Next he saw the great landscape of *The Death of Phocion* [cat. no. 228], and thought it fine; of the other one, which shows the gathering of his ashes [cat. no. 229], he said, having contemplated it for a long while, 'Mr Poussin is a painter who works from up here', tapping his forehead. I told him that he painted with his mind, having always had weak hands.

André Félibien: *Entretiens sur les vies et les ouvrages des plus excellents peintres anciens et modernes* (Paris, 1666), preface.

Of the painters of considerable standing then in evidence in Rome, I should say here that the most famous were Lanfranco, Pietro da Cortona, and the renowned Mr Poussin, whom I leave to last, being the youngest of the three. I took great care to get to know them, and particularly Mr Poussin, with whom I struck up a very close friendship. His talent is universally recognized; and for my part, I do not think there has been another painter who has had such an exalted notion of painting or who has known better than him all that goes into making a perfect work of art. And although his knowledge still emerges powerfully from the pictures by him that we have, it was even more manifest in his conversation; and I am compelled to confess that it was from his conversation that I learned to appreciate what is finest in the works of the great masters, and even the rules which they followed in order to make them more perfect [. . .]

I will [thus] have the privlege of extolling a French painter – Mr Poussin – who has been the honour and glory of our nation, and who has, it can be said, snatched the art of painting from the arms, as it were, of both Greece and Italy, and brought it to France, which seems today to be the home of all the loftiest sciences and the finest arts. His paintings, both those which so greatly enhance the King's collection, and the many others scattered in different parts of Europe, will provide irreproachable evidence of the truth of the assertions I will make about this great man.

Antoine Le Blond de La Tour: *Lettre du Sieur Le Blond de La Tour à un de ses amis, contenamt quelques instructions touchant la peinture* (Bordeaux, 1669), pp. 38–41.

[. . .] I feel I have to tell him about the device perfected by Mr Poussin, who is almost unique in our time in being able to rival the beautiful inventions of the artists of antiquity with his own, which have earned him everlasting esteem among the learned. For by means of his invention it becomes possible to achieve one of the most difficult things in painting.

This wonderful, divine man devised an oblong board, let us call it, which he would cut to the shape he intended to give his subject, and in it he would make a number of holes into which he would then set pegs, designed to provide a firm and steady base for his model figures. Having placed the model figures in their proper and natural places, he would dress them in a manner appropriate to the figures he wanted to represent in his painting, shaping the draperies with the point of a tiny stick, as I have told you elsewhere, and fashioning their heads, feet, hands, and the rest of their bodies which he would leave bare, as one does in the case of angels, as well as the sections of landscape, the architectural elements and other pieces of the decor, using soft wax which he would shape with singular dexterity and ease: and having expressed his ideas in this way, he would take up a square box, or one longer than it was wide, depending on the shape of the board which provided the base for his picture, and carefully block up all the sides except the one which gave him access to the entire surface of the board supporting his little figures, positioning it in such a way that the edges of the box lined up with the edges of the board, enclosing and embracing, so to speak, this whole great machine.

Having prepared things in this way, he would then consider the layout of the place where his picture was to be placed. If it was a church, then he would look at the number of windows, and see which gave the most light in the spot intended for his picture, noting whether the light came from the front, the side or from above, or if it came from several angles, which was the strongest source. And by giving such careful thought to the matter, he could establish precisely how the light would fall on his picture when it was in position, and so always managed, by following the layout of the windows in the church, to make holes in all the right places in his box so as to give his composition the different degrees of full and half-light it needed. And finally he would make a small opening in the front of his box, so that he could look at the whole of his picture with regard to scale; and he made this opening so cleverly that no unwanted light could creep in, becaue he would block the hole with his eye, as he looked through it and with all his skill drew the picture he had created on a piece of paper, without omitting a single line or detail; having then sketched it out on the canvas, and painted and repainted it, he would at last put the finishing touches to his picture.

Gian Pietro Bellori: *Le Vite de' Pittori, Scultori et Architetti moderni* (Rome, 1672).

He led an extremely well-ordered life, for many are they who paint according to whim and who work for a time, full of ardour, but who then tire and cast aside their brushes for some long while. Poussin was in the habit of rising early in the morning and taking some exercise for an hour or two, sometimes walking through the City, more usually on the Monte della Trinità which is the Pincio hill, not far from his house, from which it is reached by way of a gentle slope, delicious with trees and fountains, whence the beautiful view of Rome and her pleasant hills unfolds, which together with its buildings is both scenic and theatrical. He lingered here with his friends, immersed in deep and learned conversations; returning home, he set about painting without a break, until midday. After a pause for refreshment, he continued painting for several hours; and thus he achieved more through continuous study than another artist would through practice. In the evening he again went out, and walking beneath the same hill, in the piazza, amid the crowd of foreigners who were wont to gather there. Here he was always surrounded by a retinue of intimate admirers; and those who, by dint of his reputation, desired to see him and to treat him as a friend found him here, admitting all good men to his circle. He listened readily to others, but then his observations were very serious, and attentively received: he would often talk about art, and with such expertise that not just painters but cultivated people in general came to hear him discourse on the supreme purpose of painting, not to educate [his listeners], but simply as ideas came to him. Having read widely and observed acutely, there was no subject about which he was ill-informed, and his words and ideas were so appropriate and well-ordered that they never gave the impression of being impromptu, rather the results of lengthy meditation. His unique talent was the reason for this, combined with the variety of his reading, in which history, fables and erudite tomes prevailed, but which also encompassed the other liberal arts and philosophy. His recollection of the Latin language, albeit imperfect, served him well, and his Italian was as good as if he had been a native of Italy. His reasoning was perspicacious, his ability to choose acute, his memory retentive: he thus possessed the most prized gifts of intelligence. The figures he drew in Leonardo's *Treatise on Painting*, printed with his drawings in Paris in 1651, are proof of his learning. He main-

tained that painting and sculpture were but one art, both dependent upon drawing and differing only in their excution, although the former was more artificial by dint of its feigning appearances. . . .

As regards the style of this craftsman, it can be said that he envisaged a study, such as he had begun in Paris during his youth, based on the antique and on Raphael, such as when he wanted to create his compositions: having thought up his inventions, he then made a rough sketch of what he had in mind; he then made small wax models, half a hand's breadth in height, of all the figures striking their attitudes, and then constructed the story or the fable in relief in order to study the natural effects of the light and the shadow of the bodies. He then made larger models, which he dressed, so as to make a separate study of their attire and the folds of material on the naked form, and for this purpose he used fine canvas, or wet cambric, with just a few pieces of cloth providing a variety of colours. Thus he gradually sketched nude life studies, and the drawings emanating from his imaginings were done with simple lines, using simple chiaroscuro watercolours, which nonetheless effectively conveyed movement and expression. He continually sought action in historical subjects and maintained that it was the painter himself who had the right to choose the subject matter and that he should avoid subjects that had no meaning; and this is certainly evident in his compositions. He read Greek and Latin histories and made notes, which he then used when the occasion arose. With regard to this, we have heard him condemn those who make up a story of six or indeed eight figures, or another set number, which a half figure more or less could ruin, and laugh about them. With his great knowledge of art, it was easy for him to see where others went astray and he was openly critical of their errors, unswayed by groundless opinions and firm in his own reasoning. . . .

He was a tall and well-proportioned man with an exceptional temperament; his complexion was quite olive and his black hair had mostly turned grey with age. His eyes were almost sky-blue, his nose sharp and his forehead wide, all of which gave his face a noble yet modest look. . . .

As regards his habits and his intellectual pursuits, apart from what has already been said, Poussin was very perceptive and very wise. He avoided Court life and the conversation of great men, though he was by no means at a loss when he met them, in fact his virtuous spirit rendered him superior to their worldly fortunes. . . .

He treated himself honestly; he did not wear fine clothes, but dressed soberly, and it suited him. Nor was he afraid when away from home to deal personally with his own affairs. There was nothing ostentatious about his home, and he treated all his friends alike, whatever their rank. One day Monsignor Camillo Massimi, now a very distinguished Cardinal, of whom Poussin was very fond and whose opinions he respected, visited his studio. They discoursed together until late at night, and when the time came for his guest to leave, Poussin accompanied him downstairs to his carriage, lantern in hand, causing his visitor to say 'How sorry I am that you have no servant', to which Poussin replied 'And I am even more sorry for your Illustrious self, because you have many.' He never discussed the price of his paintings either with this gentleman or with any other of his friends, but when he delivered their paintings he marked the back of the canvas, and payment in full was immediately sent round to his home. One day I was visiting some ruins with him in Rome, together with a foreigner who was very desirous of taking some rare antique back to his own country. Poussin said to him 'I

should like to give you the most beautiful antique you could possibly desire,' and, stretching out his hand, he picked out of the grass a handful of earth and pebbles, with tiny fragments of porphyry and marble turned almost to dust, saying 'Here, Sir, take this to your museum and tell them this is ancient Rome.' He had always planned to write a book about painting, making notes on various subjects or writing down his thoughts during the course of his readings and contemplations, with the intention of assembling them when he became too old to paint, for he was of the opinion that elderly painters should abandon their brushes once their spirits failed, as many of them have given us cause to think. . . .

Joachim von Sandrart: *L'Academia Todesca della Architectura, Scultura & Pittura: Oder Teutsche Academie der Edlen Bau-, Bild- und Mahlerey-Künste . . .*, (Nuremberg, 1675–9), Part 2, Book III, Chapter XXVI (Clause IV) and Chapter XIX (Clause CLXXXIV).

During [Poussin's] first time [in Rome] he kept in close touch with us foreigners, and indeed came frequently when he knew that the sculptor François Duquesnoy, Claude Lorrain and I were meeting, since it was our habit to communicate our plans to one another. Besides, he conversed well and always carried with him a little book in which he recorded everything essential, in both drawings and words. When he decided to start work on something, he would consider the subject carefully and then dash off two or three sketches outlining the composition. When a story was concerned, he positioned small naked figures, made of wax for the purpose, on a smooth board divided up into squares according to his scheme, and arranged them in suitable poses to portray the complete action of the story. He then placed on these the required garments made of wet paper or fine material, and sewed them on with threads that fixed them at the appropriate distance in relation to the horizon; after which he was able to paint his work on canvas with colours. But he would often use living models for the purpose, taking his time about it, since he often began work only to break soon afterwards and go for a walk, all the time, however, sunk in serious thought related to his task. He regulated his life in the admirable conviction that art was absolutely essential and central to him. At first his use of colour was in the style of Titian, but later immersed himself so deeply in Raphael's style that he abandoned Titian's palette and completely adopted that of Raphael (regardless of the fact that the former painted naked flesh much more nobly and strikingly). But he was highly regarded by the art-loving world and lived quietly at home with his wife, although without children, concerned only to immerse himself in his own thoughts. . . .

Another time, we – Poussin, Claude Lorrain and I – rode to Tivoli to paint or draw landscapes from life. . . .

André Félibien: *Entretiens sur les vies et les ouvrages des plus excellents peintres anciens et modernes*, third part, 5th and 6th Entretiens (Paris, 1679), pp. 58–61.

(Félibien and his interlocutor in the *Entretiens* are on the terrace at Saint-Cloud).

. . . All of a sudden the sky changed, and [. . .] clouds gathered from nowhere and covered it in an instant. A furious wind blew at the same time, whipping up the dust into whirls, and stirring up the atmosphere so much that is was almost impossible to distinguish either the sky or the earth. All one could see in this darkness was the white foam of the river wrestling to hold its own against the winds tossing it about. The tallest trees succumbed to the violence of the gusts, and bowed their heads right to the ground; while those which offered the most resistance could be heard splitting and splintering with a crack . . .

. . . It would be, [Pymandre] said to me, a wonderful thing for a painter to be able to see what we are seeing now. Do you not think it must have been on a similar clash that Mr Poussin based that painting which you showed me some while ago in which he portrays a storm like this one, which proves that he ranks as highly as ever Apelles did in the past, both men being so adept at depicting such subjects that each can be said as much as the other said to have imitated the inimitable.

[. . .] Sudden and momentary effects are not obvious material for painters; and when a painter does succeed [in capturing such an effect], the work which results is as much of a miracle in terms of his art [as the effect itself]. The cleverest do not often undertake such hazardous ventures. Those who have made it their business to produce good copies of Nature generally chose a few effects which do lend themselves to painting, and by representing only that part of these which seems the most beautiful and the most remarkable, managed to make people form a favourable opinion of the rest and imagine what is not actually visible. In Mr Poussin's pictures we find these kinds of effects which are astounding, not just for what they are, for what he has chosen to represent, but for the beauty with which they are expressed. Long before him, Titian had made a particular study of these, and with his paintings set an example which few painters have attempted to follow . . .

André Félibien: *Entretiens sur les vies et les ouvrages des plus excellents peintres anciens et modernes*, fourth part, 8th Entretien (Paris, 1685), pp. 250–5.

. . . I know too that he scarcely ever stooped to copy other pictures, and even when he saw something worthy of note among the classics, he would do no more than make quick sketches of it. But he would look long and hard at whatever he saw that was of exceptional beauty, firmly fixing the image in his mind, often commenting that a painter increased his skull by observing things rather than by wasting his energies on copying them.

This immensely sound and fine understanding which he displayed from his earliest years, coupled with the great passion he had for his art, meant that he was more than happy to devote himself to it wholeheartedly and that he never found greater enjoyment than when he was working. He regarded every day as a day to work and study, and every minute he spent painting or drawing was a recreation for him. He took every opportunity to study, wherever he happened to be. As he walked through the streets, he would watch everyone around him, and if he saw anything remarkable he would note it down in a book he always carried expressly for this purpose. He would avoid gatherings whenever possible and would steal away from his friends and go off on his own into the vineyards and remotest corners of Rome, where he was free to stop and look at any classical statue or pleasant views, and to observe the finest effects of nature. It was on these retreats and solitary walks that he would make quick sketches of things which he encountered and thought suitable either for landscapes – like terraces, trees, or particularly beautiful lighting effects – or for history pictures – like satisfying arrangements of figures combinations of clothes, or other details of decoration – sketches which he would later put to such good and judicious use.

He was not content simply to know the world through his senses, or to base his knowledge on the examples of the greatest masters: he strove particularly to discover the causes of the different sorts of beauty discernible in art, convinced as he was that a workman cannot achieve the perfection he seeks unless he knows the means by which he can do so and the traps he may fall into. For this reason, in addition to looking to the best books he could find to teach him what it was that constituted the good and the beautiful, what it was that caused ugliness, and in what way judgment should be exercized in the choice of subjects and in the execution of all the parts of a work, he also sought to make himself more competent in the practice as well as the theory of his art, by studying geometry, and particularly the science of optics, which is a vital instrument in painting, and helps set the senses straight, and prevent them, either from weakness or otherwise, from being deceived at times and taking illusions of form for solid truths. For this he turned to the writings of the Theatine, Father Matteo Zaccolini, of whom I have spoken to you. No painter has ever grasped the rules of perspective or understood the reasons for light and shade better then this priest. These writings are in the Barberini Library, and Poussin had a large part of them copied and studied them assiduously. Because some of his friends saw them in his hands, and because he talked so knowledgeably about [the science of] optics and made such felicitous use of it, people thought he had composed a treatise on light and shade. In fact, however, he never wrote anything on the subject; his own paintings, were sufficient evidence of all that he had learnt from Father Zaccolini, and indeed from the works of Alhazen and Vitellion. He also had a high regard for the writings of Albrecht Dürer and for Leone Battista Alberti's *Traité de la peinture*. He had learnt about anatomy while he was in Paris; but he studied it again and with even greater application when he was in Rome, as much through the writings and illustrations of Vesalius, as through the lessons he took with a learned surgeon who often performed dissections.

It was at the time when most of the young painters who were in Rome, attracted there by Guido Reni's great reputation, were flocking to copy his painting of *The Martyrdom of St Andrew* which is in S. Gregorio Magno. Poussin was almost alone in preferring to draw the painting by Domenichino in the same church; and so good was his exposition of its beauty that, swayed by his words and his example, the majority of other painters abandoned Guido Reni and copied the Domenichino instead.

For although Poussin looked primarily to the beautiful works of classical antiquity and to the works of Raphael, against which he measured all his own ideas, this did not prevent him from holding other masters in high esteem. He considered Domenichino to be the best of the Carracci school as a model for drawing and for powerful expressions. He also admired other artists for their fine brushwork, and it cannot be denied that in his early years he was more than a little influenced by Titian's use of colour. But it is notable that, as he perfected his skills, he became more and more insistent as regards the form and accuracy of drawing, which he rightly saw as the major aspect of painting, as have all the greatest painters who have, so to speak, abandoned all other aspects in its favour as soon as they have understood the essence of the excellence of their art.

André Félibien: *Entretiens sur les vies et les ouvrages des plus excellents peintres anciens et modernes*, fifth part, 9th and 10th Entretiens (Paris, 1688), pp. 3–5 and 193–6.

[. . .] when I compare the paintings of this excellent man with those of a number of painters of merit, I see that there is a great difference between painters who are merely good and those who are learned. I call a good painter one who displays order and a great deal of force, grace and clarity in the way he expresses himself in his works, and who, through skilful imitation of the reality he wants to depict, produces results which satisfy ordinary minds and are universally pleasing to the eye: but the only painter who seems to me to be worthy of being called learned is one who not only has all these beautiful qualities, but who also excites the admiration of the very finest minds through his works, because he ennobles even the most commonplace of subjects by the sublimity of his thought, and has in his imagination and his memory two inexhaustible springs from which he can draw all that he needs to render his paintings utterly perfect.

[On the subject of the way in which passions can be expressed through 'temperament']

The first sign, in my opinion, and the most general [indication] that nature gives us of this lies in the overall colour of a body [. . .], so that if the dominant colour in a person is a leaden and livid violet, which is the sign of a black bile, it indicates that a man is inclined to be angry and envious, and is liable to act in other bad ways which normally follow from this kind of temperament. That is why in his picture of *The Judgment of Solomon* [cat. no. 31] Poussin painted the wicked mother who so boldly and impudently claimed a child that was not hers in the way that he did. And because the real mother was honest and sincere, he painted her as a simple guileless woman, and gave her that slightly ruddy complexion which is the sign of natural goodness; for sanguine people are not as a rule capable of doing anything wicked . . .

. . . The colour of the face and the body does not depend solely on temperament and humour, but also on birth, education, country and occupation. Mariners, peasants, and people of that kind, who are continually exposed to the sun and to the ravages of the air, have tanned complexions; thus, if it is not possible by such means to indicate anything about people of this sort through their bodies and their complexion and colouring, the painter has to look for other appropriate ways of indicating the vices and virtues of those he wishes to represent. This is why we find that, in the picture about which we have already spoken, Poussin indicates the wickedness of the bad woman not only through the colour of her skin, but also through her thin and wizened appearance which comes from the bile that is dominant in bad people, and which is hot and burning, and dries bodies up and makes them thin; in contrast to those who have a slightly ruddy glow, whose skin is fresher and firmer.

Louis-Henri de Loménie, Comte de Brienne: *Discours sur les ouvrages des plus excellents peintres anciens et nouveaux, avec un traité de la peinture composé et imaginé par Mre. L. H. de L. C. de B. reclus*. Manuscript in the Bibliothèque Nationale, Paris, Anc. Saint-Germain 1696 (c. 1693–5).

He had none of the mistrustful nature of the Normans. He was candour itself. His was a great and noble soul and he was worthy not only of being a painter, a profession at which he excelled, but also of governing the nation, which he could have done if he had applied himself as diligently to politics and finance as his stars decreed he should to painting. He was a genius of the first order and destined from the first for the world of science and of art, his greatest love, and almost his only pleasure throughout his life, whether happy or unhappy. By that I mean, while he was unknown and when he became famous, poor and then comfortable: disparaged for a time through envy, and finally showered with glory and honours when he was no longer in a condition to enjoy them. Since he was endowed with a great deal of reason and a fine mind, a lively and strong imagination, a very accurate memory and very sound judgment, coupled with natural good sense of a kind which heaven does not bestow on all painters, he decided to devote himself to a profession about which there is nothing base other than the mean soubriquets which have been associated with the title and occupation of painter simply through the malice of other men. Since he had good eyesight and an excellent perception, and a tolerably good hand (for he has never seemed to me to be one of the most gifted in that direction), he made up his mind to become a painter. But he still lacked a sense of colour: and although his drawing was reasonably good, his painting could never be pleasing because of its lack of colour and harmony. Indeed his early works are very dry, and thin. He never excelled in colour as he did in the other aspects of painting, by which I mean drawing and composition, in which he surpassed not only all the painters of his day, but even, it is no exaggeration to say, Raphael. Van Dyck, who relied wholly on colour, is greatly inferior to him in terms of drawing. The same is true of Rubens and all the Flemish masters.

Roger de Piles: *Abrégé de la vie des peintres …* (Paris, 1699), pp. 470–81.

However great his genius was, he was not competent in every aspect of painting: for his love of the antique was so great that it dominated his mind and prevented him from considering his art from every side, I mean to say that he neglected colour, and it is easy, looking at his works in general, to see that he had no knowledge of this aspect painting, either as regards local colour or as regards chiaroscuro. It is for this reason that the majority of his paintings incline towards grey and seem to us lacking in force and effect. The pictures which he painted in his first manner are an exception to this, as are some painted in his second manner. But on closer study it will be discovered that what is good in terms of colour comes from his recollection of the paintings by Titian that he copied rather than from an understanding of the principles embodied by the Venetian painter. Finally, it seems that Poussin had little regard for colour, and in their accounts of his life both Félibien and Bellori openly acknowledge that it was something which he had not mastered and which he had in effect abandoned: which indicates clearly that he never mastered the theory of it. Indeed the colours which we see him use are only general tones instead of imitating the colours of nature, which he saw only rarely: I am talking about his figures, not his landscapes, where he seems to have been more careful to consult nature, the reason being obvious, that since no landscape is represented in classical sculpture, he was obliged to go and look at the real thing.

As for chiaroscuro, he had no notion of it, and if there is any evidence of it in any of his paintings it occurs entirely by chance, because if he had had any knowledge of this device which is one of the most essential in painting as much for establishing the angle of vision as for giving strength and truth to the entire composition of the picture, he would always have used it, he would have tried to find ways of grouping objects and light together to good effect instead of so dispersing them that the eye often does not know which way to look, but his main concern was to please the mind's eye, although it is a firmly established fact that painting can only instruct the mind by pleasing the eye, that is to say through a perfect imitation of reality, which is the essential goal of the painter.

Poussin's marked lack of affection for imitating nature, which is the fount of variety, caused him frequently and rather too obviously to repeat [human] features and expressions.

His talent expressed itself in a noble, forceful and severe fashion rather than a graceful one, and in his works we have a testimony to the fact that grace is not always to be found with beauty.

His manner is new and unique, he invented it, and it cannot be denied that in the parts of painting in which he was proficient, his style, as we have said, was heroic and grand: and that, all in all, Poussin was not only the cleverest painter of his nation, but he was on a par with the very greatest painters of Italy.

CHRONOLOGY OF POUSSIN'S LIFE

1594 (?June) Nicolas Poussin born, the son of Jean Poussin and his wife Marie (formerly Mme Delaisement), in the village of Villers, near Les Andelys, in Normandy.

1598 The peace treaty of Vervins signed.

1610 Henri IV assassinated. Marie de Médicie becomes regent.

1611–12 The painter Quentin Varin visits Les Andelys and is reputed to have encouraged Poussin to pursue a career in art.

1612–21 Poussin goes to Paris, where he works briefly under Elle and Lallemant, and studies engravings after paintings by Raphael and Giulio Romano, as well as the classical sculpture and Italian paintings in the royal collections. He travels in France and makes several abortive attempts to reach Rome, staying briefly in Florence.

1618 The Thirty Years' War begins.

1622 Poussin paints six pictures for the Jesuits in Paris, on the occasion of the Canonization of St Ignatius Loyola and St Francis Xavier. He meets Giambattista Marino (known as the Cavalier Marin), for whom he produces a series of drawings on subjects taken from Ovid.

1622–3 Poussin works on the decoration of the Palais du Luxembourg, alongside Philippe de Champaigne. He is commissioned to paint an altarpiece depicting *The Death of the Virgin* for Notre Dame in Paris. He leaves for Italy in the autumn of 1623.

1623 Cardinal Maffeo Barberini is elected Pope, taking the name Urban VIII.

1624 (March) Poussin arrives in Rome, after stopping off in Venice. Marino introduces him into papal circles, and to Cardinal Francesco Barberini in particular.

1624 Cardinal Richelieu enters the Conseil du Roi.

1625 Marino leaves for Naples, where he dies shortly afterwards. Cardinal Francesco Barberini departs for France. Poussin experiences financial difficulties. He makes a thorough study of art collections in Rome and of works by Domenichino.

1626 Poussin shares lodgings in the Strada Paolina with François Duquesnoy.

1627 Poussin is commissioned to paint *The Death of Germanicus* by Cardinal Francesco Barberini, who had returned to Rome.

1628–9 Poussin is commissioned to paint *The Martyrdom of St Erasmus* for St Peter's and *The Virgin Appearing to St James* for a church in Valenciennes.

1630 (1 September) Poussin marries Anne-Marie Dughet, the daughter of the French cook Jacques Dughet who earlier took Poussin in and nursed him during a serious illness. The commission for the decoration of a chapel in the church of S. Luigi dei Francesi is given to Charles Mellin. Domenichino leaves for Naples. Poussin studies in Andrea Sacchi's academy.

1631 Poussin becomes a member of the Academy of St Luke. He testifies at Fabrizio Valguarnera's trial, in the course of which two of his paintings are mentioned: *The Plague of Ashdod* and *The Empire of Flora*. Poussin is now living with his wife in the Via del Babuino, where they are joined by his brother-in-law Gaspard Dughet, who later becomes well known as a landscape painter.

1633   Poussin paints *The Adoration of the Magi* (exceptional in being signed and dated).

1635–6   Poussin finishes two of the *Triumphs* (or *Bacchanals*) for Cardinal Richelieu's château in Poitou.

1636   Corneille: Le Cid.

C. 1636   Poussin begins the set of seven *Sacraments* commissioned by his chief Roman patron, Cassiano Dal Pozzo. He completes the set in 1640.

1638–9   Poussin paints *The Israelites Gathering Manna* for Paul Fréart de Chantelou. He is approached by the new Surintendant des Bâtiments du Roi, Sublet de Noyers, but is reluctant to accede to his request to return to France (where Richelieu desires his services).

1640   Poussin leaves for France in November, arriving in Paris on 17 December. He is presented to Richelieu and to Louis XIII, who welcomes him with every consideration.

1640   Corneille: Horace.

1641   Poussin is appointed First Painter to the King. He is commissioned to paint *The Institution of the Eucharist* to hang in Saint-Germain-en-Laye, *Moses before the Burning Bush* and *Time and Truth Destroying Envy and Discord* for the Palais Cardinal, and *The Miracle of St Francis Xavier* for the Jesuit Noviciate. He produces the first drawings for the decoration of the Grande Galerie in the Louvre.

1642 (5 November)   Poussin returns to Rome, where spends the rest of his life.

1642 (4 December)   Richelieu dies.

1643 (14 May)   Louis XIII dies. Anne of Austria becomes regent. Sublet de Noyers disgraced.

1644   Urban VIII dies. Innocent X Pamphili elected Pope. The Barberini family disgraced.

1644   Poussin begins the second set of *Sacraments* for Chantelou (completed in 1648).

1646   Cardinals Francesco and Antonio Barberini flee to France.

1647   Masaniello leads a revolt in Naples. The Duc de Guise leads a military campaign in Campania.

1647   André Félibien, secretary to the French ambassador, arrives in Rome, where he becomes a close friend of Poussin.

1648   The Fronde begins in France. The peace treaty of Münster signed.

1648   Poussin produces the first of his large historical landscapes.

1649   The peace treaty of Rueil signed (bringing an end to the Fronde).

1649   Poussin paints *The Judgment of Solomon* and the first *Self-Portrait* for Pointel, and begins the second (for Chantelou), completed the following year, a Jubilee year.

1651   The Fronde breaks out again. Mazarin exiled.

1653   The Fronde comes to an end. Mazarin returns.

1655   Innocent X dies; he is succeeded by Alexander VII Chigi as Pope.

1655   Abbé Louis Fouquet, brother of the Surintendant Nicolas Fouquet, commissions Poussin to design a set of herms and a pair of vases for the gardens at Vaux-le-Vicomte.

1657   Poussin is elected head of the Academy of Luke, but declines the honour. He paints *The Annunciation* for the tomb of his former patron, Cassiano Dal Pozzo.

1658–60   Poussin paints his 'pantheist' landscapes: the *Landscape with Diana and Orion* and *The Birth of Bacchus*.

1659   The peace treaty of the Pyrénées signed.

1660   Poussin is now in poor health. He begins work, despite his shaky hand, on the four *Seasons*, a set of landscapes, for the Duc de Richelieu (despatched to Paris in 1664).

1664   Poussin gives *Apollo and Daphne*, unfinished, to Cardinal Massimi. Poussin's wife, Anne-Marie, dies on 16 October.

1665   Poussin is no longer able to work; he dies on 19 November, and is buried the following day in the church of S. Lorenzo in Lucina, Rome.

Select Bibliography

Only the most important works are listed, together with publications cited in the text, the Thematic Catalogue, biographies and original documents.

I EARLY SOURCES

BELLORI, Giovanni Pietro, *Le Vite de' pittori, scultori ed architetti moderni*, Rome, 1672 (new ed. by G. Previtali and E. Borea, Turin, 1976).

BOUSQUET, Jean, 'Chronologie du séjour romain de Poussin et de sa famille, d'après les archives romaines', in *Colloque Poussin* (cf. *infra*, section IV), 1960, II, pp. 1–10.

BRIENNE, Louis-Henri de Loménie, Comte de, *Discours sur les ouvrages des plus excellents peintres anciens et nouveaux, avec un traité de la peinture composé et imaginé par Mre. L. H. de L. C. de B. reclus*, ms., Paris, Bibliothèque Nationale, Anc. St Germain 16986. Extracts published by J. Thuillier, 'Corpus Pussinianum' in *Colloque Poussin* (cf. *infra*, section IV) 1960, II, pp. 210–24.)

CHANTELOU, Paul Fréart de, *Journal du voyage en France du Cavalier Bernin*, manuscript published by L. Lalanne in the *Gazette des Beaux-Arts*, 1877–84.

FÉLIBIEN, André, *Entretiens sur les vies et les ouvrages des plus excellents peintres anciens et modernes*, Paris, 1666–88 (5 vols.): section devoted to Poussin = 8th Entretien in Part 4 (1686).

LE BLOND DE LA TOUR, Antoine, *Lettre du Sieur Le Blond de La Tour à un de ses amis contenant quelques instructions touchant la peinture*, Bordeaux, 1669, cf. J. Thuillier, 'Corpus Pussinianum' in *Colloque Poussin* (cf. *infra*, section IV) 1960, II, pp. 145–7.

PASSERI, Giovanni Battista, *Vite de' Pittori, Scultori ed Architetti che hanno lavorato in Roma dal 1641 fino al 1673*, Rome, 1772 (critical edition by J. Hess, Vienna, 1934).

POUSSIN, Nicolas, *Correspondance de Nicolas Poussin*, edited by Charles Jouanny, Paris, 1911 (Archives de l'Art français, vol. V). Selected letters in A. Blunt, *Nicolas Poussin. Lettres et propos sur l'art*, Paris, 1989 (with contributions by J. Thuillier and Avigdor Arikha).

SANDRART, Joachim von, *Teutsche Academie der edlen Bau-, Bild- und Mahlerey-Künste*, Nuremberg, 1675–9.

THUILLIER, Jacques, 'Pour un Corpus Pussinianum', in *Colloque Poussin* (cf. *infra*, section IV), 1960, II, pp. 49–328.

II CATALOGUES RAISONNÉS

A PAINTINGS

BLUNT, Anthony, *The Paintings of Nicolas Poussin. A critical catalogue*, London, 1966.

GRAUTOFF, Otto, *Nicolas Poussin, sein Werk und sein Leben* (2 vols.), Munich, 1914.

MAGNE, Émile, *Nicolas Poussin, premier peintre du roi (1594–1665), suivi d'un catalogue raisonné*, Brussels–Paris, 1914.

OBERHUBER, Konrad, see section III – Exhibitions: Fort Worth, Texas 1988.

SMITH, John, *A Catalogue raisonné of the works of the most eminent Dutch, Flemish and French Painters* (8 vols., with a supplement), London, 1829–42).

THUILLIER, Jacques, *Tout l'œuvre peint de Poussin*, Paris, 1974 (new ed. forthcoming).

WILD, Doris, *Nicolas Poussin* (2 vols.), Freiburg, 1980.

WRIGHT, Christopher: *Poussin Paintings. A Catalogue Raisonné*, London, 1985.

B DRAWINGS

FRIEDLÄNDER, Walter and BLUNT, Anthony, *The Drawings of Nicolas Poussin* (5 vols.), London, 1939–74. Supplementary details published by Blunt in *Master Drawings*, XII (1974) and XVII (1979), and by Pierre Rosenberg, *ibid.*, XVIII (1980).

C ENGRAVINGS

ANDRESEN, Andreas, *Nicolas Poussin. Verzeichnis der nach seinen Gemälden gefertigten Kupferstiche*, Leipzig, 1863. French translation in *Gazette des Beaux-Arts*, July–August 1962, pp. 139–202.

WILDENSTEIN, Georges, *Poussin et ses graveurs au XVIIe siècle*, Paris, 1957. See also A. Blunt and M. Davies, 'Some Corrections and Additions to M. Wildenstein's *Graveurs de Poussin au XVII³ s.*', *Gazette des Beaux-Arts*, July–August 1962, pp. 205–22.

III EXHIBITIONS (listed alphabetically under place names)

BOLOGNA, 1962: *L'Ideale classico del Seicento in Italia e la pittura di paesaggio*, Palazzo dell'Archiginnasio, 1962 (introduction by Cesare Gnudi; commentaries on Poussin by D. Mahon).

DUBLIN, 1985: *Le Classicisme français. Masterpieces of Seventeenth Century Painting*, National Gallery of Ireland, 1985 (introduction by J. Thuillier, commentaries by S. Laveissière). Also shown in Budapest and Paris.

EDINBURGH, 1981: *Poussin. Sacraments and Bacchanals*, National Gallery of Scotland, 1981 (catalogue by H. Macandrew and H. Brigstocke).

EDINBURGH, 1990: *Cézanne and Poussin: the Classical Vision of Landscape*, National Gallery of Scotland, 1990 (catalogue by Richard Verdi).

FORT WORTH, TEXAS, 1988: *Poussin. The Early Years in Rome. The Origins of French Classicism*. The Kimbell Art Museum, 1988 (catalogue by Konrad Oberhuber).

FRANKFURT, 1988: *Nicolas Poussin, Claude Lorrain: Zu den Bildern im Städel*, Städelsches Kunstinstitut, 1988 (catalogue by M. Mack-Gerard, P. Waldeis and O. Bätschmann).

LONDON, 1986–7: *Nicolas Poussin: Venus and Mercury*, Dulwich Picture Gallery, 1986–7 (catalogue by R. Verdi *et al.*).

MEAUX, 1988–9: *De Nicolo dell'Abate à Nicolas Poussin: aux sources du Classicisme, 1550–1650*, Musée Bossuet, 1988–9 (commentaries on Poussin by J. Thuillier).

NEWCASTLE-UPON-TYNE, 1951–2: *Introduction to Poussin*, and *Nicolas Poussin. The Seven Sacraments*. Hatton Gallery, 1951–2 (catalogue by R. Holland).

PARIS, 1960: *Nicolas Poussin*, Louvre, 1960 (catalogue by A. Blunt and Charles Sterling).

PARIS, 1973–4: *La Mort de Germanicus*. Dossier of the Department of Paintings, no. 7, Louvre, 1973–4 (catalogue by P. Rosenburg and N. Butor).

PARIS, 1979: *L'Enlèvement des Sabines de Poussin*. Dossier of the Department of Paintings, no. 17, Louvre, 1979 (catalogue by A. Arikha). Also shown in Princeton, N.J., in 1980.

PARIS, 1988: *L'œil d'or de Claude Mellan*, Bibliothèque Nationale, 1988 (catalogue by M. Préaud).

PARIS, 1988–9: *Seicento: le siècle de Caravage dans les collections françaises*, Grand Palais, 1988–9 (preface by Y. Bonnefoy; commentary on Poussin by I. Auffret and A. Brejon de Lavergnée).

PARIS, 1989: *L'Inspiration du Poète de Poussin*. Dossier of the Department of Paintings, no. 26. Louvre, 1989 (catalogue by M. Fumaroli).

PARIS–NEW YORK–CHICAGO, 1982: *La peinture française de XVIIe s. dans les collections américaines / France in the Golden Age*, Paris, Grand Palais / New York, The Metropolitan Museum of Art / Chicago, Art Institute of Chicago, 1982 (preface by M. Fumaroli, catalogue by P. Rosenberg).

ROME–DÜSSELDORF, 1977–8: *Nicolas Poussin*, Rome, Villa Medici / Düsseldorf, Kunstmuseum (preface by A. Blunt and J. Thuillier, catalogue by P. Rosenberg).

ROUEN, 1961: *Nicolas Poussin et son temps*, Musée des Beaux-Arts, 1961 (preface by J. Thuillier, catalogue by P. Rosenberg).

WASHINGTON–NEW YORK–SAN FRANCISCO, 1978–9: *The Splendor of Dresden. Five Centuries of Art Collecting*, Washington, D.C., National Gallery / New York, The Metropolitan Museum of Art / San Francisco, Cal., Museum of Fine Arts.

IV PUBLICATIONS AND ARTICLES

ALPATOV, Michael, 'Poussin problems', *Art Bulletin*, XVII (1935), pp. 5ff.;

——, 'Poussins "Landschaft mit Herkules und Cacus" in Moskau' in *Walter Friedländer zum 90. Geburtstag*, Berlin, 1965, pp. 141ff.

ARIKHA, Avigdor, see section III above under Exhibitions: Paris, 1979;

——, 'Réflexion sur Poussin' in A. Blunt (ed.), *Nicolas Poussin. Lettres et propos sur l'art* (new ed.), Paris, 1989, pp. 203ff.

BADT, Kurt, *Die Kunst des Nicolas Poussin* (2 vols.), Cologne, 1969.

BARROERO, Liliana, 'Nuove acquisizioni per la cronologia di Poussin', *Bollettino d'Arte*, VI (1979–84), pp. 69ff.

BÄTSCHMANN, Oskar, *Dialektik der Malerei von Nicolas Poussin*, Munich, 1982;

——, *Nicolas Poussins Landschaft mit Pyramus und Thisbe. Das Liebesunglück und die Grenzen der Malerei*, Frankfurt, 1987.

BLUNT, Anthony, 'Poussin Studies' (I–XIV) in *Burlington Magazine* from 1947 to 1962;

——, 'Poussin and his Roman Patrons' in *Walter Friedländer zum 90. Geburtstag*, Berlin, 1965, pp. 58ff.;

——, *Nicolas Poussin* (2 vols.), Washington, D.C. and London, 1967 (includes the most extensive bibliography published up to 1967);

——, 'Poussin's "Dance to the Music of Time" revealed', *Burlington Magazine*, December 1976, pp. 844ff.;

——, *The Drawings of Poussin*, Hartford, Conn., 1979;

——, 'A newly discovered late work by Nicolas Poussin: "The Flight into Egypt"', *Burlington Magazine*, April 1982, pp. 208ff.

BONNEFOY, Yves, *Rome 1630. L'horizon du premier baroque*, Paris, 1970.

BOYER, Jeane-Claude and VOLF, Isabelle, 'Rome à Paris: les tableaux de maréchal de Créquy (1638)', *Revue de l'Art*, 79 (1988), pp. 22ff.

BREJON DE LAVERGNÉE, Arnauld, 'Tableaux inédits de Poussin et d'autres artistes français dans la collection Dal Pozzo: deux inventaires inédits', *Revue de l'Art*, 19 (1973), pp. 79ff.

Colloque Poussin, 1960: *Nicolas Poussin. Actes du colloque* (Paris, 19–21 September 1958), 2 vols., Paris, 1960 (published under the direction of André Chastel).

COSTELLO, Jane, 'The twelve pictures "ordered by Velasquez" and the trial of Valguarnera', *Journal of the Warburg and Courtauld Institutes*, XIIII (1950), pp. 237f.;

——, 'Poussin's drawings for Marino and the new classicism. I – Ovid's Metamorphoses', *Journal of the Warburg and Courtauld Institutes*, XVIII (1955), pp. 296ff.;

——, 'Poussin's Annunciation in London', *Essays in Honor of Walter Friedländer*, New York, 1965, pp. 16ff.;

——, *Nicolas Poussin: The Martyrdom of Saint Erasmus*, Ottawa, 1975.

CROPPER, Elizabeth, 'Poussin and Leonardo: Evidence from the Zaccolini manuscripts', *The Art Bulletin*, 62, No. 4 (December 1980), pp. 570ff.

DEMPSEY, Charles, 'The Greek Style and the Prehistory of Neo-Classicism' in exhibition catalogue, *Pietro Testa, 1612–1650, Prints and Drawings*, Philadelphia Museum of Art, 1988, pp. xxxvii ff.

DESJARDINS, Paul, *Poussin*, Paris, 1903.

FRIEDLÄNDER, Walter, *Nicolas Poussin. Die Entwicklung seiner Kunst*, Munich, 1914;

——, 'Poussin's Old Age', *Gazette des Beaux-Arts*, 1962, II, pp. 249 ff.;

——, *Nicolas Poussin*, Paris, 1965 and New York, 1966.

FUMAROLI, Marc, 'Muta Eloquentia: la représentation de l'éloquence dans l'œuvre de Nicolas Poussin', *Bulletin de la Société d'Histoire de l'Art français*, 1982 (1984), pp. 29ff.;

——, see section III above under Exhibitions: Paris, 1989.

GIDE, André, *Poussin*, Paris, 1945.

GNUDI, Cesare, see section III above – Exhibitions: Bologna, 1962. Preface reprinted in *L'Ideale classico. Saggi sulla tradizione classica nella pittura del Cinquecento e del Seicento*, Bologna, 1981, pp. 53ff.

GOMBRICH, Ernst, 'The Subject of Poussin's *Orion*', *Burlington Magazine*, February 1944, pp. 37–8, 41 (reprinted in E. Gombrich, *Symbolic Images. Studies in the Art of the Renaissance*, London and New York, 1972, pp. 119–22).

GRATE, Pontus, *Nationalmuseum Stockholm. French Painting I, Seventeenth Century*, Stockholm, 1988.

HASKELL, Francis, *Patrons and Painters. A Study in the Relations between Italian Art and Society in the Age of the Baroque*, London, 1963 (new ed., New York, 1971).

KAUFFMANN, Georg, *Poussin Studien*, Berlin, 1960.

LAVIN, Marylin Aronberg, *Seventeenth Century Barberini Documents and Inventories*, New York, 1976.

MAHON, Denis, 'Poussin's Early Development: an Alternative Hypothesis', *Burlington Magazine*, July 1960, pp. 288ff.;

——, 'Poussiniana', extract from *Gazette des Beaux-Arts*, July-August (with additions), 1962, pp. 1–138, Paris, 1962;

——, 'A Plea for Poussin as a Painter' in *Walter Friedländer zum 90. Geburtstag*, Berlin, 1965, pp. 113ff.;

——, 'The Dossier of a picture: Nicolas Poussin's "Rebecca al Pozzo"', *Apollo*, March 1965, pp. 196ff.

MÂLE, Émile, *L'art religieux de la fin du XVIᵉ s., du XVIIᵉ s. et du XVIIIᵉ s. Étude sur l'iconographie après le Concile de Trente*, Paris, 1932 (new ed., 1972).

MARIN, Louis, 'La description d'un tableau et le sublime en peinture. À propos d'un paysage de Poussin et de son sujet', *Communication*, 34 (1981), pp. 61ff.

PANOFSKY, Erwin, 'Apollo and Daphne in the Louvre', *Bulletin de la Société Poussin*, III, 1950, pp. 27ff.;

——, *A mythological painting by Poussin in the Nationalmuseum Stockholm*, Stockholm, 1960;

——, 'Et in Arcadia Ego . . .', in Raymond Klibansky and H. J. Paton (eds.), *Philosophy & History. Essays presented to Ernst Cassirer*, Oxford, 1936.

ROSENBERG, Pierre, 'Un nouveau Poussin au Louvre, *Olympos et Marsyas*', *Revue du Louvre*, 1969, pp. 87ff.

SANTUCCI, Paola, *Poussin. Tradizione Ermetica e Classicismo Gesuita*, Salerno, 1985.

SAUERLÄNDER, Willibald, 'Die Jahreszeiten: Ein Beitrag zur allegorischen Landschaft beim später Poussin', *Münchner Jahrbuch der bildenden Kunst*, 1956, pp. 169ff.

SIMON, Claude, *Orion aveugle*, Geneva, 1970.

SIMON, Robert B., 'Poussin, Marino and the Interpretation of Mythology', *The Art Bulletin*, 1978, pp. 56ff.

SPEAR, Richard E., 'The Literary Source of Poussin's Realm of Flora', *Burlington Magazine*, November 1965, pp. 563ff.

STANDRING, Timothy J., 'A lost Poussin work on copper: "The Agony in the Garden"', *Burlington Magazine*, September 1985, pp. 615ff.

THUILLIER, Jacques, *Nicolas Poussin*, Novara, 1969;

——, 'Poussin et le paysage tragique: L'Orage Pointel au Musée des Beaux-Arts de Rouen', *Revue du Louvre*, 1976, pp. 345ff.;

——, 'Propositions pour Charles Errard peintre', *Revue de l'Art*, 40–41 (1978), pp. 151ff.;

——, *Nicolas Poussin*, Paris, 1988.

THUILLIER, Jacques and MIGNOT, Claude, 'Collectionneur et peintre au XVIIᵉ siecle: Pointel et Poussin', *Revue de l'Art*, 39 (1978), pp. 39ff.

TZEUTSCHLER-LURIE, Anne, 'Poussin's Holy family on the steps in the Cleveland Museum of Art: new evidence from radiography', *Burlington Magazine*, November 1982, pp. 664ff.

VERDI, Richard, 'Poussin and the "Tricks of Fortune"', *Burlington Magazine*, November 1982, pp. 681ff.

WHITFIELD, Clovis, 'Nicolas Poussin's "Orage" et "Temps calme"', *Burlington Magazine*, January 1977, pp. 4ff.;

——, 'Poussin's Early Landscapes', *Burlington Magazine*, January 1979, pp. 10ff. (see also Anthony Blunt's reply, *ibid.*, August 1980, pp. 577ff.).

WILD, Doris, 'Charles Mellin ou Nicolas Poussin', extract from the *Gazette des Beaux-Arts* (October 1966–January 1967), Paris, 1967.

WINNER, Matthias, 'Poussins Selbstbildnis im Louvre', *Römisches Jahrbuch für Kunstgeschichte*, 1983, pp. 417ff.;

——, 'Poussins Selbstbildnis von 1649' in *Il se rendit en Italie*. *Mélanges offerts à André Chastel*, Paris–Rome, 1987, pp. 371ff.

WORTHEN, Thomas, 'Poussin's Paintings of Flora', *The Art Bulletin*, 1979, pp. 575ff.

Acknowledgments

The author wishes to express his warm thanks to Eric Hazan, who was in part responsible for the conception of this book, and to the staff of Hazan Éditions for their assistance in its presentation.

Thanks are also due to private owners and to representatives of museums and galleries for their help in providing photographs and information and for allowing works in their collections to be reproduced. The present owner of each work reproduced is stated in the caption and in the relevant entry in the Thematic Catalogue, pp. 252–96.

The following individuals have also provided invaluable assistance at various stages in the preparation of the book: Colin B. Bailey; Alain Faudemay; Jacques Poucart and the Service d'Étude et de Documentation des Peintures at the Louvre; Véronique Gérard-Powell; Jacques Mérot; Paul Micio; Patrick Violette; and Nathalie Voile.

This book, by its very nature, owes much to the scholarly publications and expert knowledge of other authorities, past and present, in particular the late Anthony Blunt, Pierre Rosenberg and Jacques Thuillier.

PICTURE CREDITS

Index

GENERAL INDEX

INDEX OF WORKS BY POUSSIN
listed by title of work
and by present location

GENERAL INDEX

INDEX OF WORKS BY POUSSIN

INDEX OF WORKS BY POUSSIN
listed by present location